The
Anti-Federalist
Writings of the
Melancton Smith
Circle

Melancton Smith

The
Anti-Federalist
Writings of the
Melancton Smith
Circle

EDITED AND WITH AN
INTRODUCTION BY
Michael P. Zuckert and Derek A. Webb

LIBERTY FUND | *Indianapolis*

Introduction, editorial additions, and index © 2009 by Liberty Fund, Inc.

The editors are grateful to The University of Chicago Press for
permission to draw from and adapt Herbert J. Storing's notes from
The Complete Anti-Federalist, © 1981 by The University of Chicago.

Frontispiece of Melancton Smith used by permission
of The New-York Historical Society.

Book design by Barbara E. Williams of BW&A Books, Inc., Durham, North Carolina

LIBRARY OF CONGRESS CATALOGING-IN-PUBLICATION DATA
The anti-federalist writings of the Melancton Smith circle
edited and with an introduction by Michael P. Zuckert and Derek A. Webb.
p.   cm.   Includes bibliographic references and index.
ISBN 978-0-86597-756-3 (hc: alk. paper)   ISBN 978-0-86597-757-0 (pbk.: alk. paper)
1. United States—Politics and government—1783–1789.   2. United States—
Politics and government—1783–1789—Sources.   3. Constitutional history—
United States.   4. Constitutional history—United States—Sources.
5. Smith, Melancton, 1744–1798—Political and social views.
I. Zuckert, Michael P., 1942–   II. Webb, Derek A.
320.473′049—dc22   JK155.A572 2009   2008043784

Liberty Fund, Inc.
8335 Allison Pointe Trail, Suite 300
Indianapolis, Indiana 46250-1684

In memory of Lance Banning

Contents

PART THREE: AFTER THE CONVENTION

Introduction

WHO IS Melancton Smith and whatever is the "Melancton Smith circle"? Why collect the various writings assembled in this volume? Even though Melancton Smith is no longer a household name (if he ever was), the first question is relatively easy to answer. Smith is best known as the leading spokesman for the Anti-Federalists at the New York ratifying convention in the summer of 1788. He is also known as the man who led one faction of the Anti-Federalists to accept ratification without prior conditions at the end of that convention, making New York the eleventh state to ratify the new Constitution. James M. Banner called Smith's change of position to make ratification possible in New York "arguably the nation's most weighty vote in favor of ratification of the Constitution of 1787."

Smith was born in 1744 on Long Island. He moved to Poughkeepsie at a young age and became caught up in the Revolution. Among other duties he served as one of three New York commissioners charged with dealing with Loyalists and other subversives during the Revolution. His commitment to republicanism was still visible later when he objected to the new Constitution as insufficiently republican. He not only helped the Republic by dealing with the Loyalists but also ended up helping himself: he had become wealthy from confiscated Loyalist estates by the end of the war. After the war he was one of those American jacks-of-all-trades who figure so prominently in the history of the early Republic. Land speculator, merchant, sheriff, lawyer, political activist—he plied all of these trades, and perhaps others, during the war and postwar years.

As part of the faction surrounding Governor Clinton in New York politics, he was elected under the Articles of Confederation to the Congress for the period 1785–87. His service in the Congress broadened his horizons and gave him something of a continental perspective, but it appears also to have reinforced his conviction that a "consolidated" (that is, a unitary) government for the whole of the United States would be quite unthinkable.

As one of the founders of the Anti-Federalist committee in New York, he was a leader of Anti-Federalist organizing efforts in New York State against the Constitution. He stood for election to the ratifying convention both in New York City, where he was resident at the time, and in upstate Dutchess County, where he had once lived and still owned property. He lost in Federalist New York City but won a seat in the upstate race.

His performance at the convention was quite remarkable, as the records of his speeches reprinted here will make evident. It was a battle of giants, as Smith on the Anti-Federalist side faced the great partisan champion of the Federalists, Alexander Hamilton. The exchanges between them rank among the finest examples of political debate in American history. They deserve to be far better known than they are.

When New Hampshire and Virginia ratified the Constitution in the summer of 1788, any serious possibility of New York rejecting it evaporated. With ten states accepting the Constitution, the new government was empowered to begin operation. Although Smith retained strong misgivings till the end (see p. 357, "Essays of a Federal Republican"), he also recognized that New York outside the Union would be untenable. Setting aside his desire for ratification conditional on amendments or a new convention, Smith worked hard to secure votes for the Constitution from his fellow Anti-Federalists.

In retrospect, Smith's action at the convention seems an act of great statesmanship. It proved also to be an act of self-sacrifice, to a degree, at least. The Clinton faction remained unreconciled to the Constitution, and Smith's political career suffered for his trouble. He never again achieved the level of political eminence of his ratifying-convention summer; he never held office, for example, in the new government of the Union. In the 1790s his political loyalties, not surprisingly, moved in the direction of the Jeffersonians and against his old nemesis at the convention, Alexander Hamilton. In the early years under the new Constitution, he became very actively involved in the antislavery movement as vice president of the New York Manumission Society. This political commitment has a significant bearing on the authorship issues we canvass herein. Smith died in 1798, still a relatively young man, a victim of the yellow fever epidemic of that year.

A nice career, a moderately distinguished life of achievement, yet not a career that could be expected to make him a household name. We claim that Smith is more worthy of note than his career as recounted would suggest. Smith left behind him one, perhaps even two, of the greatest political writings of the founding or of any era. The debate over the Constitution was hard-fought in many of the states—nowhere more so than in New York. The importance of securing ratification in that state and the strength of the opposition to the document there led to the production of what is by general consensus the finest political writing of the period: *The Federalist*, by Hamilton, James Madison, and John Jay. The Federalist Papers were conceived, written, and printed originally in New York and were particularly addressed to a New York audience.

The two best writings of the ratification debate on the Anti-Federalist side also appeared in New York. We refer to *Letters from the Federal Farmer*, which appeared in two batches of essays between October 1787 and January 1788, and *Brutus*, another series of essays, which appeared between October 1787 and April 1788. There is now, as there was then, general agreement that these were political writings of a very high caliber, but strangely nobody ever came forward to claim credit for having written them. Published anonymously, they have remained anonymous. There have, of course, been conjectures and attributions of authorship. Until recently most scholars thought that Richard Henry Lee of Virginia had written *Federal Farmer* and Robert Yates of New York, *Brutus*. As we will argue below, these attributions are no longer unquestioningly accepted; in fact, the weight of the evidence points strongly against them.

Instead of Lee and Yates, authorship of both sets of essays is increasingly being attributed to Smith. Serious scholars, whose work we endorse, have proposed Smith as the author of the *Federal Farmer*; others, equally serious and equally worthy of endorsement, have argued that Smith was *Brutus*. The problem is that the same man does not appear to be the author of both sets of essays. We thus write of a "Smith circle" of like-minded individuals.

– The Historical and Literary Cases –

A complete review of the evidence we and other scholars have compiled that links Smith to the two series in question and speaks against the heretofore most widely accepted attributions would far outstrip the space available to us here. We can only summarize that evidence as presented by others and assembled by us. In notes to the texts themselves we have attempted to supply further indications of the links among our three main texts—*Brutus*, *Federal Farmer*, and Smith's convention speeches and letters—by calling attention to some of the many suggestively similar passages, turns of phrase, and substantive ideas that appear in the different texts.

Melancton Smith as the Author of Letters
from the Federal Farmer

Case Against Lee as Federal Farmer

In 1974 and 1981 Gordon Wood and Herbert Storing raised doubts about the conventional attribution of *Letters from the Federal Farmer* to Richard Henry Lee.[1] From the last quarter of the nineteenth century until then, every historian who had dealt with the ratification debates, with one exception, had ascribed *Federal Farmer* to Lee.[2] The one exception had been William W. Crosskey, who stated in a note in the second volume of his *Politics and the Constitution* that "the letters from a *Federal Farmer*, usually attributed to Lee, were not written by him. (See discussion of this point in a later volume.)"[3] Unfortunately, Crosskey's death in 1968 prevented him from writing a third volume. That expression of doubt, however, was enough to stimulate Wood and Storing to reexamine the grounds for the attribution and to conclude with Crosskey that most of the evidence from Lee's life and writings points against Lee's authorship.

Lee, Wood noted, had never written an extended piece, confining himself exclusively to private correspondence, occasional newspaper essays, and reports and addresses of various committees of the Continental Congress.[4] The two sets of letters written by *Federal Farmer*, in contrast, totaled 181 pages and were produced in the relatively short time span of four months, beginning in early October 1787 and concluding in late January 1788. Such a prodigious output seems unlikely to have been the work of someone who tended to write less frequently.

Lee chose to express his dissatisfaction with the proposed Constitution in letters written to various figures such as George Mason, William Shippen Jr., Samuel Adams, and Governor Edmund Randolph of Virginia. One of these letters, written to Randolph on October 16, 1787, was published at Lee's request in various newspapers throughout Pennsylvania, New York,

---

1. Gordon Wood, "The Authorship of the *Letters from the Federal Farmer*," *William and Mary Quarterly* 31 (April 1974): 299–308; Herbert Storing, ed., *The Complete Anti-Federalist*, 7 vols. (Chicago: University of Chicago Press, 1981), II, 214–16.

2. Wood, 299.

3. William W. Crosskey, *Politics and the Constitution in the History of the United States*, 3 vols. (Chicago: University of Chicago Press, 1953), II, 1300.

4. Wood, 300.

and Connecticut.[5] More than any other document or speech he wrote or delivered, Lee's public letter to Randolph defined his objections to the Constitution for his contemporaries.

Wood and Storing observed that this letter contrasts in various important ways with *Letters from the Federal Farmer.* To begin with, the tone of the two varies considerably. While Lee's letter was quite emotionally charged, punctuated with phrases such as "highly and dangerously oligarchic" and "the silent, powerful, and ever-active conspiracy of those who govern," *Federal Farmer*'s letters were marked by "moderation, reasonableness, and tentativeness."[6] Furthermore, Lee's letter differs from the views expressed by *Federal Farmer* on several specific points. Storing observed that "the primary concern of *The Federal Farmer* is the question of consolidation and the destruction of the states, about which Lee's letter says nothing"; he regarded this difference as "most telling against the case for Lee's authorship."[7] Moreover, Lee suggested changes to the proposed constitution that *Federal Farmer* did not, such as the abolition of the vice presidency and protections against congressional regulation of southern commerce.[8] *Federal Farmer,* in contrast, rarely displayed any special concern for the South, on one occasion even denigrated southern planters as a "dissipated aristocracy,"[9] and drew nearly all of his local references from the northern states. Lee advocated a "privy council" of eleven individuals to be selected by the president, while *Federal Farmer* suggests an "executive council" of seven or nine members who would be elected by the people and Congress to serve as a check on presidential appointments and decision making.[10] Finally, while Lee said nothing about an executive veto, *Federal Farmer* proposed a council of revision that would be similar to the arrangement provided under the New York constitution in which the chief magistrate and the judges would veto legislation.[11]

5. *Pennsylvania Packet* (Philadelphia), December 20, 1787; *New York Journal,* December 22 and 24, 1787; *Pennsylvania Gazette* (Philadelphia), January 16, 1788; *Freeman's Journal* (Philadelphia), January 2, 1788; *Connecticut Courant* (Hartford), January 21, 1788; *American Museum,* II (1787) 553–58.

6. Wood, 301.

7. Storing, II, 215.

8. Wood, 302.

9. *Federal Farmer III,* October 10, 1787.

10. Wood, 302.

11. Ibid.

Wood and Storing further pointed out that the evidence on which the Lee attribution rested was relatively slight and questionable in the light of contemporaneous evidence. The attribution appears to have had its origin in a December 24, 1787, article in the *Connecticut Courant*. That article, written by the pseudonymous author "New England," singled out Lee as the author of *Letters from the Federal Farmer*. This piece was widely reprinted in Massachusetts and, according to Wood and Storing, appears to have been the ultimate source of the attribution.[12] Wood noted, however, that given Lee's unpopularity throughout Connecticut (on the grounds of a dispute with a Connecticut merchant named Silas Deane and mistaken rumors that he had an unfriendly relationship with George Washington), it was good Federalist politics to connect him with the Anti-Federalist literature circulating in New England.[13]

Moreover, those who were in a position to know did not generally cite Lee as the author. Edward Carrington, a colleague of Lee's in New York when Lee would have been writing *Federal Farmer*, sent a copy of the pamphlets to Thomas Jefferson but said that "the author was not known."[14] In February 1788, a writer in the *New York Journal* expressed admiration for *Federal Farmer* but declared "who he is I know not."[15] Timothy Pickering and Noah Webster, two individuals who had written extensive reviews of *Federal Farmer*, gave no indication that they knew the author.[16] Lee himself never acknowledged authorship, nor did his grandson and early biographer

12. The article was reprinted in at least seven newspapers. It was likely on the basis of this article that George Cabot of Massachusetts penciled in the words "Rd Henry Lee supposed" on his copy of the *Letters from the Federal Farmer*. This copy was obtained by the Boston Athenaeum, which then noted in its 1874 catalog that Lee was the author of *Federal Farmer*. In 1878 Joseph Sabin listed Lee as the author of both sets of letters by *Federal Farmer* in *A Dictionary of Books Relating to America from Its Discovery to the Present Time* and cited the Boston Athenaeum as his source. The historian Paul Leicester Ford (1865–1902) picked up this attribution in Sabin and included it in his 1888 *Pamphlets on the Constitution of the United States*. From there it was passed on to future historians.

13. Wood, 304.

14. Edward Carrington to Thomas Jefferson, June 9, 1788, in W. C. Ford, ed., "Federal Constitution in Virginia," Massachusetts Historical Society Proceedings, 2nd series, 17 (1903), 501.

15. *New York Journal*, February 14, 1788.

16. *American Magazine* 1 (1788): 422; Pickering to Charles Tillinghast, December 6, 1787.

suggest that he had written the essays.[17] Given the otherwise public nature of Lee's opposition to the Constitution, Wood and Storing argued that it would have been odd for Lee to have written the letters and yet never take credit for them. It must be said, however, that this objection to the Lee attribution could apply to any number of other possible candidates for authorship of *Federal Farmer*, including Smith.

Case for Smith as Federal Farmer

In 1987 and 1989 Robert Webking and Joseph Kent McGaughy took the investigation one step further.[18] Convinced by the arguments of Wood and Storing that Lee was unlikely to have written *Federal Farmer*, they sought a more likely candidate. Both concluded that the evidence points to Melancton Smith.

Webking drew this conclusion on the basis of a close comparison of *Letters from the Federal Farmer* and the speeches Smith delivered at the New York ratifying convention. He discovered "a remarkable degree of correspondence in general thrust as well as in particular points and concerns" and noted that the arguments each used against the Constitution were "so much alike in so many particulars, including fundamental issues and points raised by no other Anti-Federalists," that the possibility that the correspondence was a mere coincidence or a result of borrowing was slight.[19]

Webking noted four general areas in which *Federal Farmer* and Smith displayed such correspondence. First, and perhaps most important, both held a similar view of the theory and importance of representation. *Federal Farmer* counted as his one "important" objection to the proposed Constitution that "no substantial representation of the people is provided for in [the] government," and Smith devoted two of his four major speeches at the ratifying convention to the topic of representation.[20] Both embraced the view that representatives should mirror those they represent. *Federal*

17. Richard H. Lee, *Memoir of the Life of Richard Henry Lee* (Philadelphia, 1825), I, 240.

18. Robert H. Webking, "Melancton Smith and the *Letters from the Federal Farmer*," *William and Mary Quarterly* 44 (July 1987): 510–28; Joseph Kent McGaughy, "The Authorship of *The Letters from the Federal Farmer*, Revisited," *New York History*, April 1989, 153–70.

19. Webking, 512.

20. Webking, 513, 515; *Federal Farmer V*, October 13, 1787; Smith speeches, June 20 and 21, 1788.

Farmer thought that a representative branch should "possess abilities to discern the situation of the people and of public affairs, a disposition to sympathize with the people." Smith similarly argued that representatives "should be a true picture of the people."[21] Against this standard, both judged the House of Representatives to be woefully inadequate. The large congressional districts would have a ratio of representatives to citizens of one to thirty thousand, a number both found to be far too large. Such large districts would favor the "natural aristocrats," who would be better known and better organized than those from the middle classes. Both agreed this was problematic because the middle classes possessed virtues that made them naturally well suited to leadership in republican government. *Federal Farmer* described men from these classes as "nervous and firm in their opinions and habits"; Smith observed that such men were "more frugal, more restrained and temperate, and less ambitious than the aristocrats."[22] Both were concerned that if natural aristocrats were not elected, popular demagogues "destitute of principle" would be the other likely alternative.[23] Finally, both quoted the same passage from Cesare Beccaria, who observed that in all political societies "there is an effort to confer on one part the height of power and happiness, and to reduce the others to the extreme of weakness."[24]

Second, *Federal Farmer* and Smith proposed similar remedies for the problems regarding representation. Both acknowledged the difficulties in obtaining a more adequate representation in such a large country; their ideal of representation simply could not be fully realized.[25] Furthermore, even calculating such an ideal was an imperfect science and would not admit of "mathematical certainty."[26] Still, both observed that some general guidelines could be laid down. *Federal Farmer* said that while fifteen representatives would clearly be too few, fifteen hundred would be both unwieldy and

21. Webking, 514, 515; *Federal Farmer VII*, December 31, 1787; Smith speech, June 21, 1788.

22. Webking 514, 516; *Federal Farmer VII*, December 31, 1787.

23. Webking 513, 516; *Federal Farmer IX*, January 4, 1788; Smith speech, June 21, 1788.

24. Webking 516–17; *Federal Farmer VII*, December 31, 1787; Smith speech, June 21, 1788.

25. Webking, 518; *Federal Farmer IX*, January 4, 1788; Smith speech, June 23, 1788.

26. Webking, 518; *Federal Farmer VII*, December 31, 1787; Smith speech, June 21, 1788.

improper.[27] Smith offered a similar range, arguing that "ten is too small, and a thousand too large a number."[28] Indeed, both were willing to see the number of representatives doubled. *Federal Farmer* recommended that the number be doubled "at least" and that the ratio might be set at one to twelve thousand.[29] In an amendment he proposed at the convention, Smith concurred with the idea of doubling the representation and argued that the ratio should be one to twenty thousand.[30] Both were also sensitive to the possibility that the representative body might grow too large and un-wieldy for public debate. Accordingly, they propose that an upper limit be set when this happened and that the number of representatives be reappor-tioned according to each state's population.[31] They agreed that doubling the number of representatives would increase costs by about $20,000, but that amount could easily be compensated for by reducing the size of the state legislatures.[32] Finally, both insisted that members of the House of Representatives should be elected in districts by majority vote. Statewide elections governed by plurality voting, both argued, favored powerful and well-organized minorities at the expense of majorities.[33] *Federal Farmer* and Smith intended that these reform measures would start the government "on the right basis" with the right principles, helping to set the tone for how the government would operate for the next twenty-five to fifty years.[34]

Third, in addition to their concerns about representation, *Federal Farmer* and Smith agreed that the powers of the federal government should be lim-ited in two decisive ways. First, the federal government should continue to raise money through requisitions from the state governments and be per-mitted to levy internal taxes only when the states failed to meet their quota. Second, the states ought to be able to check the federal government's use of state militias. *Federal Farmer* proposed requiring "the express consent of the state legislature" before the federal government could use a state

27. Webking, 518; *Federal Farmer IX*, January 4, 1788.

28. Webking, 518; Smith speech, June 21, 1788.

29. Webking, 518, 519; *Federal Farmer IX*, January 4, 1788.

30. Webking, 519; Smith, in Jonathan Elliot, ed., *The Debates in the Several State Conventions on the Adoption of the Federal Constitution* (Philadelphia: Lippincott, 1863), II, 229–30.

31. Webking, 519; *Federal Farmer X*, January 7, 1788; Elliot, *Debates*, II, 229–30.

32. Webking, 520; *Federal Farmer IX*, January 4, 1788; Elliot, *Debates*, II, 244.

33. Webking, 520–21; *Federal Farmer XII*, January 12, 1788; Elliot, *Debates*, II, 246.

34. Webking, 519–20; *Federal Farmer X*, January 7, 1788; Elliot, *Debates*, II, 244.

militia; Smith proposed an amendment preventing militias from remaining in service outside the state "for more than six weeks without the consent of the state legislature." Both men made similar arguments when Federalists objected to such checks on federal power. While they agreed with the Federalists that the means of government should be proportionate to its ends, they disagreed with the Federalists' contention that the federal government possesses unlimited ends and therefore deserves unlimited means.

Fourth, Webking observed that *Federal Farmer* and Smith agreed on a range of smaller issues, which, he argued, "precisely because these additional matters are minor," carried significant weight. Both writers argued that the Senate would provide stability, that senators should be subject to recall, and that the Constitution should require rotation in office.[35] Both argued that the president should serve for seven years and be ineligible for reelection. They also suggested a popularly elected executive council to advise the president regarding appointments.[36] Both worried about the constitutional provision that granted Congress sole authority over the national capital, forts, magazines, arsenals, and dockyards.[37] Finally, both argued that monopolies ought to have been constitutionally prohibited; that Congress not be able to permit officials to receive presents, offices, or titles from foreign nations; and that federal officers be required to take an oath to support the state governments as well as the Constitution.[38]

While Webking built his argument strictly on the ground of textual comparison, McGaughy lent further support to the Smith thesis by providing additional biographical information that links Smith with *Federal Farmer*. Smith's extensive political and legal career in New York, which included positions such as county sheriff, state congressman, county and state judge, and delegate to the Continental Congress, would have put him in a good position to display the familiarity with New York law and politics that *Federal Farmer* demonstrated.[39] After the Constitution was reported by the Philadelphia convention, Smith quickly sided against it. He opposed it in

35. Webking, 523; *Federal Farmer XI*, January 10, 1788; Elliot, *Debates*, II, 309, 310, 312.

36. Webking, 523; *Federal Farmer XIII*, January 14, 1788; Elliot, *Debates*, II, 408.

37. Webking, 523; *Federal Farmer XVIII*, January 25, 1788; Elliot, *Debates*, II, 410.

38. Webking, 523; *Federal Farmer XVIII*, January 25, 1788; Elliot, *Debates*, II, 407, 409–10.

39. McGaughy, 161–62.

Congress, and along with General John Lamb and Marinus Willett formed the Federal Republican Society, a group dedicated to producing and disseminating literature against the Constitution.[40] Smith's performance at the New York ratifying convention, in which he spent the first half debating with Hamilton and the second half seeking a compromise between the Federalists and Anti-Federalists, demonstrated both the intellectual vitality and the moderation present in *Letters from the Federal Farmer*.[41] Hamilton himself at one point noted that Smith's argument at the convention regarding the natural aristocracy "reminds me of a description of the aristocracy I have seen in a late publication styled the *Federal Farmer*."[42] Finally, McGaughy pointed out that while Lee would have had no apparent reason to conceal his authorship of *Federal Farmer*, Smith did. After the Constitution was ratified, Smith returned to his work as a merchant and investor. One particular investment in a land deal set up by William Duer in 1791 and 1792 proved nearly disastrous for Smith. When the deal collapsed, Duer was sent to debtor's prison and Smith found himself $20,000 in debt. Smith was assisted financially by James Watson and Seth Johnson, both staunch Federalists, who loaned him the money to cover his debts and gave him a position as a land agent with the H&S Johnson Company.[43] If Smith had claimed credit for *Federal Farmer*, these and other financial dealings with Federalists might have been damaged.

Melancton Smith as the Author of Essays of Brutus

Case Against Yates as Brutus

There is growing consensus among scholars that Robert Yates, whom Paul Leicester Ford named as the author of the *Essays of Brutus*, was unlikely to have been their true author. Morton Borden suggested that Ford's attribution may have been incorrect since "Yates's other Antifederalist essays, under his well-known pen name 'Sydney' seem to be inferior in quality and style to the 'Brutus' essays."[44] Storing found Ford's attribution "somewhat questionable" given the fact that Ford himself had changed his mind on the

40. Ibid., 162.
41. Ibid., 162–63.
42. Ibid., 164.
43. Ibid., 166.
44. Morton Borden, *The Antifederalist Papers* (East Lansing: Michigan State University Press, 1965), 42.

matter and presented no evidence to support his attribution.[45] William Jeffrey cited Ford's lack of evidence as the primary reason for his doubts and went on to suggest that Melancton Smith may have been the real author.[46] Saul Cornell likewise disputed the Yates attribution but proposed Abraham Yates as the author.[47]

Five pieces of evidence from Yates's life cast further doubt on the Yates attribution. First, Yates lived his entire life in upstate New York (Albany), but the *Essays of Brutus* were published exclusively in a New York City newspaper. Indeed, Yates would have been resuming his work as an associate justice of the New York Supreme Court in Albany just as the first essays were being readied for publication in New York City. Furthermore, Yates could not have simply written and submitted the *Essays of Brutus* in large batches well in advance of their publication dates. Internal evidence within the *Essays of Brutus* indicates that the author of these essays frequently responded to points raised just weeks before by Hamilton and Madison in the Federalist Papers. To write regularly for a newspaper as far away from his residence as any in the entire state, to arrange for publication of his essays there just as he was resuming his work on the state supreme court in Albany, and to respond to points raised concurrently by Hamilton and Madison would have been at the very least highly difficult given the slowness with which mail and newspapers were transported at that time.[48]

Second, Yates appears to have lacked the specific kind of political moderation displayed by *Brutus*. Yates's actions from the time he was a delegate to the Constitutional Convention in Philadelphia in the summer of 1787 to the time he was a delegate to the New York ratifying convention in the summer of 1788 indicate an unremitting opposition to the Constitution that does not correspond well with *Brutus*'s more measured approach. Yates arrived in Philadelphia on May 25, 1787, for the convention and abruptly departed on July 10, 1787, convinced that his "forebodings"

45. Storing, II, 103.

46. William Jeffrey Jr., "The Letters of 'Brutus'—A Neglected Element in the Ratification Campaign of 1787–1788," *University of Cincinnati Law Review* 40 (1971): 644–46.

47. Saul Cornell, *The Other Founders: Anti-Federalism and the Dissenting Tradition in America, 1788–1828* (Chapel Hill: University of North Carolina Press, 1999), 312, 315, n6.

48. Jacob E. Cooke, *The Federalist* (Middletown, Conn.: Wesleyan University Press, 1961), 14.

about the proceedings had been "too much realized." Yates and fellow
Anti-Federalist delegate John Lansing wrote a formal letter to Governor
Clinton explaining that they left the convention early because a majority of
the delegates were firmly committed to plans "destructive to the political
happiness of the citizens of the United States."[49] Concluding that "no alteration was to be expected to conform it to our ideas of expediency and
safety," and judging that their further attendance would be "fruitless and
unavailing," the two chose to simply give "the principles of the constitution . . . [their] decided and unreserved dissent" and leave the convention.[50]
Yates maintained his strenuous opposition to the Constitution at the New
York ratifying convention, where he consistently opposed the efforts of
various moderate Anti-Federalists to compromise with the Federalists. His
opposition to the Constitution thus contrasts with *Brutus*'s more moderate
stance. Where *Brutus* hoped that his readers could be persuaded to come
to his view of the Constitution through "calm and dispassionate" reflection,
Yates quickly gave up any hope that he could persuade his fellow delegates
at the Philadelphia convention and concluded that his further participation
would be "fruitless and unavailing." Where *Brutus* expressed the hope that
the problems of the Constitution could be resolved through amendments
to the Constitution either before *or after* ratification,[51] Yates said that "no
alteration was to be expected to conform it to our ideas of expediency and
safety" and obstinately clung to the view that the Constitution could be
amended only *prior to* ratification.

Third, Yates seems to have lacked the specific intellectual and literary
capacities necessary to have written the essays. Whereas the author of *Brutus*
published sixteen 3,000-word essays at a biweekly and eventually a weekly
rate over a seven-month period, posing some of the most important criticisms made against the proposed Constitution, Yates had no publishing
experience prior to the ratification debate, was not considered a likely pam-
phleteer during the debate even by fellow Anti-Federalists in Albany, and
said practically nothing at the Constitutional Convention in Philadelphia
and the ratifying convention in New York.

Fourth, when Yates did put forward his thoughts on politics and the Con-

---

49. Linda G. De Pauw, *The Eleventh Pillar: New York State and the Federal Constitution* (Ithaca, N.Y.: Cornell University Press, 1966), 86.

50. Robert Yates and John Lansing, *Reasons of Dissent*, December 21, 1787, printed
in the *New York Journal*, January 14, 1788, in Storing, II, 16, 18.

51. *Brutus XV* (13).

stitution, his arguments contrasted substantively with the thought of *Bru-tus*. His joint letter with John Lansing to Governor George Clinton in 1787 is an example. First, Yates and Lansing argued that the Constitutional Convention had exceeded its express powers by proposing a new constitution instead of proposing amendments to the existing one.[52] This criticism was a common one among Anti-Federalist writers throughout the ratification debate and was one that James Madison responded to at length in *Federalist* 40.[53] But while this was a topic addressed by both sides, it is interesting to note that *Brutus*, despite having devoted nearly forty-five thousand words to criticism of the Constitution, never once raised this objection. Second, they argued that the consolidated government that the new Constitution proposed was impracticable. This illustrates an important point of contrast with *Brutus*. Yates judged the proposed Constitution to be, in itself, a proposal for consolidating the state governments into a national one.[54] *Brutus*, however, made painstaking and subtle efforts to establish the thesis that, though it did not itself propose a consolidation, the proposed Constitution contained the seeds of an eventual one. While Yates and *Brutus* were in agreement that a consolidation was undesirable, what Yates took as an obvious factual premise, *Brutus* regarded as a conclusion that needed to be established through argument, not assumption or assertion.[55]

Fifth, Yates's ownership of slaves makes his authorship of the essays of

52. Yates and Lansing, *Reasons of Dissent*, in Storing, II, 16–17, 2.3.3, 2.3.4–6.

53. Alexander Hamilton, John Jay, and James Madison, *The Federalist*, edited by George W. Carey and James McClellan (Indianapolis: Liberty Fund, 2001), no. 40, 199–206.

54. Yates and Lansing, in Storing, II, 16–17, 2.3.2–3, 2.3.7.

55. Yates identified the proposed Constitution as a consolidation in his notes on the debates from the Constitutional Convention as well. Recording the proposal of Governor Randolph for what would later come to be called the Virginia plan, Yates wrote the following: "He closed these remarks with a set of resolutions, fifteen in number, which he proposed to the convention for their adoption, and as leading principles whereon to form a new government—He candidly confessed that they were not intended for a federal government—he meant for a strong *consolidated* union, in which the idea of states should be nearly annihilated." (Max Farrand, ed., *The Records of the Federal Convention of 1787*, 4 vols. [New Haven: Yale University Press, 1966], I, 24.) No other records for that day in Philadelphia, including those taken by Madison, James McHenry, or William Patterson, suggest that Randolph himself used these terms to describe his proposal. It is probable, then, that Yates was putting his own interpretation of the proposal into Randolph's words.

Brutus more improbable.[56] Furthermore, no records exist of him arguing against the institution of slavery or joining a manumission society. *Brutus*'s third essay described the unjustness of slavery in the most unambiguous terms: "[I]n some of the states, a considerable part of the property of the inhabitants consists in a number of their fellow men, who are held in bondage, in defiance of every idea of benevolence, justice, and religion, and contrary to all the principles of liberty, which have been publickly avowed in the late glorious revolution."[57] Yates's ownership of slaves and lifelong reticence on the question of its morality make him an unlikely author of the deep moral objections to slavery that *Brutus* expressed in this and other passages.

The Case for Smith as Brutus

A more likely candidate for author of the *Essays of Brutus* is Melancton Smith; the facts of his life, his speeches at the New York ratifying convention, and his other writings and letters all support the probability. Smith's extensive legal and political career in New York City would have put him in a good position to write the particular *Essays of Brutus* that contained detailed references to New York's constitution and to have them published in the *New York Journal*. Smith's moderation, as demonstrated both in his overall character and in his various efforts at compromise at the New York ratifying convention, correspond well with *Brutus*'s moderation, which was characterized by a balanced, open-minded opposition to the proposed Constitution, an acknowledgment of the need for a stronger union, and a hope that amendments, secured either prior or subsequent to ratification, would be sufficient to address the Constitution's problems. Smith's abilities as a thinker, writer, and debater were recognized by his contemporaries, even by Federalists, who sought to prevent his election as a delegate to the ratifying convention. In the course of the debates in Poughkeepsie, Smith spoke nineteen times, voiced one-quarter of all the comments made throughout the summer, and emerged as the most outspoken and cerebral leader of the New York Anti-Federalists. One Federalist newspaper reportedly observed, "Mr. Smith, the Anti champion, adds the subtilty of Locke to the candour of Sidney." Finally, Smith's outspoken opposition to slavery,

56. M. E. Bradford, *A Worthy Company: Brief Lives of the Framers of the United States Constitution* (Marlborough, N.H.: Plymouth Rock Foundation, 1982), 53; Alfred Young, *The Democratic Republicans of New York: The Origins 1763–1797* (Chapel Hill: University of North Carolina Press, 1967), 253.

57. *Brutus III* (10).

as demonstrated by his opposition to the three-fifths clause at the ratifying convention, his membership on the committee that drafted the Northwest Ordinance of 1787 barring slavery from the territories, and his eleven-year membership and active participation in the New York Manumission Society, indicate that he was quite capable of denouncing slavery in the terms in which *Brutus* did.

Smith's speeches at the New York ratifying convention demonstrate a remarkable similarity both substantively and stylistically with the *Essays of Brutus*. Smith's argument against the three-fifths clause repeated nearly verbatim the argument *Brutus* made. On a host of what could be called "constitutional preliminaries" Smith and *Brutus* emerge as quite similar. Both acknowledged the ratification debate to represent a uniquely important moment in world history, believed the Articles of Confederation to be defective, supported a stronger union, and upheld liberty as the chief political value and ultimate standard for judging the wisdom of the proposed Constitution. Both also operated with four maxims for guiding constitution making: government must begin on the right principles, perfection in government is not to be expected, government effectiveness depends on the people's confidence in public officials, and auxiliary constitutional checks are needed to make up for what is lacking in the habits of citizen officials.

The speeches of Smith and the *Essays of Brutus* are also remarkably similar on a host of issues concerning representation. Both embraced the principle that people should make the laws by which they are governed and should view pure democracy as impractical. Both shared the theoretical ideal of representation as a mirror of the people, one that requires large numbers of representatives from all the classes in society to satisfy. Both judged the level of representation in the proposed Constitution to be inadequate on the grounds of size (citing authority as well as collective-action problems over such a large extent of territory), numbers (small numbers of representatives cannot know the people or resist the lure of corruption), and class (the natural aristocracy will dominate because of their conspicuous status, comfort with elevated offices, and ability to associate, thereby ensuring a government of oppression and demagoguery). Both suggested similar remedies for alleviating these inadequacies, encouraging in the House of Representatives a lower ratio of representatives to citizens and district and majority voting, and with regard to the Senate opposing perpetual reeligibility and calling for a system of rotation and recall.

Likewise, both Smith and *Brutus* argued for various limitations on the powers of the federal government because representation was inadequate. Both expressed concerns about the looseness of the necessary-and-proper clause. They made a similar response to the Federalist means-ends argument. Both expressed dissatisfaction with Hamilton's argument that the state governments could check the federal government through vigilance and, if necessary, violent resistance. Both argued that the federal government's power of borrowing and taxation should be significantly limited and that the state governments had to consent to national use of state militias.

Finally, beyond Smith's speeches at the ratifying convention, four documents written by Smith indicate a remarkable correspondence between his and *Brutus*'s views on the judiciary. The timing, urgency, and specific concerns Smith expressed in a letter to Abraham Yates on January 23, 1788, indicate an awareness of the failure of Anti-Federalists to discuss the judiciary adequately. The letter explained why *Brutus* might have made his abrupt transition into an extensive discussion of the judiciary and anticipated by just a week many of the central themes in his essays on the judiciary. Smith's opinion on *Rutgers v. Waddington* further reveals his capacity for intellectual leadership on the topic of the judiciary and emphasizes concerns about judicial review that would feature prominently in the writings of *Brutus*. Smith's draft of a circular letter highlights two concerns expressed directly by *Brutus:* the potential for expanding the Supreme Court's jurisdiction through legal fiction and the likelihood that the right to trial by jury would be threatened by the Supreme Court's extensive appellate jurisdiction. And, finally, Smith's private list of amendments to the Constitution included various rights of the accused and a provision against allowing states to be sued in federal court, all issues that were explicitly supported in the *Essays of Brutus*.

– The Statistical Evidence on Authorship –

As part of our research into the authorship of the essays, John Burrows, of the University of Newcastle, Newcastle, Australia, undertook a computerized analysis of the Anti-Federalist writings. We attach his essay as an appendix and summarize his findings here. The techniques deployed in computer-based statistical analyses do not allow for definitive judgments; rather they permit comparisons between texts that indicate the relative closeness of the texts compared. Thus, as a control measure Burrows divided each of the texts in his sample in half and concluded, not surprisingly but reassuringly, that the first half of *Brutus* is closer to the second half than to any other text, that the two Hamilton sections of *The Federalist* are closer to each other than to any other text, and so on. Since the techniques are powerful enough to work successfully in cases where we can check the results, we have some reason for confidence when they produce results for the texts whose authorship we are attempting to discover. Nonetheless, the method can tell us only the relative closeness of the texts in the sample; that is, which ones are most similar to the unknown texts.

Burrows worked with a very large sample of known writings by founding-era authors, including samples from all the suggested authors of *Brutus* and *Federal Farmer.* His essay explains both the sample he used and the tests he applied. These tests did not include punctuation analysis, since in eighteenth-century writings the printer's not uncommon practice of adding punctuation makes punctuation habits an unreliable indicator of authorship. Most significantly, he found that on a wide variety of different statistical tests Melancton Smith came up consistently as the most likely author of *both* the *Federal Farmer* and *Brutus.* More literary and impressionistic evidence leads us to hold back from the conclusion that the same individual wrote both of these major Anti-Federalist series; yet we recognize the force of Burrows's techniques, which can pick out deep similarities that elude the naked eye and may in fact be more revealing than the impressionistic kinds of evidence by which we have been swayed.

– THE IDEA OF A SMITH CIRCLE AND WHAT WE GAIN BY RECOGNIZING IT –

The assembled evidence has convinced us that Smith is indeed the author of at least one of the two sets of Anti-Federalist Papers. The evidence, both literary and statistical, says he could have been the author of *either* set—and therefore, it would seem, of both. That conclusion has a number of implications. The first of these, of course, is that Smith deserves recognition as the author of some of the best political analysis ever undertaken in America. The writings now attributed to him should be joined to other writings known to be by him or persuasively attributed to him. That is precisely what this volume does.

The second implication would seem to be that Smith wrote both sets of the best Anti-Federalist writings. We do not wholly reject that conclusion, but neither do we confidently endorse it. The thesis that he wrote both runs up against some stiff objections. The most obvious is implied by the commonsense questions: Why would Smith issue two series of papers, overlapping in time and topic, when one would do perfectly well? Why would he issue one set of papers early in the ratification debate period (*Federal Farmer I–V*), almost immediately begin a second series running on a very regular schedule for seven months or so (*Brutus*), and then in the midst of that series issue *Additional Letters of a Federal Farmer,* which appeared in some cases on the same day as a *Brutus* essay? (See Appendix 2 for the appearance dates of the two series.)

It seems to us that there are more serious reasons than these to doubt (although not necessarily to reject) the single-author thesis. Probably chief among them are stylistic differences between the two sets of essays. Lance Banning observed that "Brutus is more incisive, more direct, less oblique, more tightly organized, perhaps less eloquent on some points." Terminological differences exist also; for example, *Federal Farmer* regularly referred to the government to be instituted by the Constitution as a federal republic; *Brutus* did not use this phrase. *Brutus*, like Smith in his own voice, cited biblical references from time to time; *Federal Farmer* did not. *Federal Farmer* cited De Lolme, an authority on the British Constitution, fairly often; *Brutus* did not cite him at all. These are the sorts of differences that make us reluctant to attribute authorship of both sets of papers to one man.

We are thus in the odd situation of almost being led to deny an axiom of mathematics, for if Smith is plausibly the author of either *Brutus* or *Federal Farmer,* authorship of both should in principle be attributable to him. By the axiom that two things equal to a third are equal to each other, we should be able to conclude confidently that one person wrote both series. But we cannot. Another formulation paradoxically captures our sense of the situation: the two sets of essays are so substantively alike that they must have been written by one man, but so stylistically different that they cannot have been.

We are convinced that the idea of a Smith circle makes better sense of the evidence. That is, one of the sets was produced by another author or authors who were close to Smith; who discussed politics with him; and who shared an understanding, a mode of analysis, and a style of thinking. We are fairly certain that Smith wrote one of the collections, but not which one; we lean toward *Brutus*. We have some possible candidates for authorship of the other; many are individuals with whom Smith corresponded in the letters reprinted below, but none is compelling enough to rise even to the level of a hypothesis, and we see no point in engaging here in what can only be inconclusive sleuthing.

Our main pieces of evidence for positing a close connection between Smith and the other author are set forth in the discussion of the grounds for preferring Smith to Yates and Lee as author of both sets of papers. It would be worthwhile to leave the reader with a somewhat more general statement than the array of similarities that can be extracted from that earlier discussion. The Smith circle is marked by a number of shared doctrines or approaches to politics in addition to the myriad details we identify here and in the notes. First, they understood very well the novel federal system that Madison invented and the convention adopted. They knew it was intermediate between a unitary national government and a traditional federation. This recognition and a clear understanding of the character of the system distinguish these works from those of many other Anti-Federalists.

They accepted the basic Madisonian innovation: the direct connection as in a national system between the general government and the individual human citizens. They also accepted the corollary of this innovation: that the general government must have a proper executive and judiciary and that its legislature must have a proper, essentially population-based representation formula. These issues also distinguish them from many fellow Anti-Federalists. This acceptance of some of the main outlines of the new system no doubt accounts for the very similar moderation both *Brutus* and *Federal Farmer* (and Smith in his own name) displayed toward the new system, even while opposing it strongly.

Both saw that it was not a unitary or national government as it stood but were certain it would evolve into one. Both saw the potential for that evolution in the same features of the new Constitution, in particular, in the combination of uncontrolled and uncontrollable powers and insufficiently state-directed institutions. Both also saw that the system as designed would not be so terrible, but the system it would evolve into would not promote free and safe government.

Perhaps most significant, both *Brutus* and *Federal Farmer* (and also, emphatically, Smith) saw the system of representation in the legislature to be inadequate and grounded their analysis of that inadequacy in a political sociology/psychology that makes much of the distinction between the "natural aristocrats" and the "middling classes," or yeomanry. (It is striking that Burrows's computer analysis brings out the fact that of all the founding-era texts he analyzed only these three used the word "middling.") Both *Federal Farmer* and *Brutus* looked to an increase in representation designed to bring the "middling" classes into government in greater numbers as the necessary solution to the tendency of the system to become oligarchic and dangerous to liberty.

There are many other common elements to their analyses, but these pick out the central features that are the earmarks of "Smith circle" Anti-Federalism. Ironically, this analysis owes a great deal to John Adams's political science, to which Smith in particular was opposed. The Smith circle adopted much from Adams's sociology and psychology but strongly objected to Adams's efforts to move constitutional orders back toward British (that is, less purely republican) models.

The conviction under which the present collection has been assembled is not only that something like this "Smith circle" was at work in these essays but that systematically considering these statements as articulating a single political understanding is of great value. One reason Anti-Federal writings and political theory have suffered in comparison with Federalist theory and writings is that the Anti-Federalists did not produce a text of the heft, comprehension, analytic thoroughness, and topical coverage of *The Federalist*. The combination of *Brutus* and *Federal Farmer* comes closer to being a book of that character than anything else the Anti-Federalists wrote. *Brutus* suffers from the author's failure to analyze the projected institutions of the new government, with the exception of his marvelous treatment of the judiciary. This is a defect that *Federal Farmer* avoids; it *has* a treatment of the institutions where *Brutus* does not. It is of more than passing interest that *Federal Farmer*'s treatment of institutions is weak just where *Brutus*'s is strong—on the judiciary.

Federal Farmer suffers by comparison with *Brutus* in having a rather brief account of the powers of the new government, despite agreeing with *Brutus* that the defects in the way the Constitution treated governmental powers was one of the reasons why this novel federalism was likely to degenerate into an oppressive consolidation. In other words, although the two sets of papers overlap in topic and certainly in style of analysis and underlying theoretical orientation, they nonetheless complement each other: when put together, they are nearly as comprehensive and impressive as *The Federalist*. It is tempting to see each set of essays as written to fill in the points that the agenda of the other was omitting.

We have far more from *Brutus* and *Federal Farmer* than from Smith speaking in his own name. Had we more from Smith, the attribution issue would be much easier to settle. The relative paucity of Smith's contributions is largely an artifact of the way the New York ratifying convention did its work. Early in its meeting the decision was made to go through the proposed Constitution article by article, clause by clause. Smith produced wonderful analyses of the early parts of Article 1. But the news of ratification in Virginia and New Hampshire short-circuited the clause-by-clause debate. Thus we do not have speeches by Smith on the full range of topics that *Brutus* and *Federal Farmer* cover.

Nonetheless, Smith's speeches contribute significantly to an understanding and appreciation of arguments made by *Brutus* and *Federal Farmer*. On the theme of representation and the political sociology underlying the Smith circle analyses, Smith at the convention gave the best account, perhaps because of Hamilton's prodding. Although Smith's speeches endorsed the same analysis as the two written series, his presentation at the convention adds valuably to the other two sets of written statements.

In addition to the major writings we have discussed above, this collection includes all the extant political writings by Smith that we could find, including his writings before and after the constitutional ratification struggle. None are as important as the main items, but they help fill out Smith's views on the Constitution and relate in a variety of different ways to the main texts. Of these secondary writings, perhaps the most significant include the 1788 pamphlet entitled "An Address to the People of the State of New York," which Smith wrote under the pseudonym of "Plebian," and his 1784 memo on *Rutgers v. Waddington*, an early state court precedent for judicial review. This memo shows Smith fully in possession of the legal knowledge and voicing the sorts of concerns that make him a very possible author of the remarkable criticisms by *Brutus* of the institution of judicial review.

In the mirror of time, Smith and his circle stand up pretty well as political scientists. Not only do *Brutus*'s prognostications about judicial review ring very true, so does the general analysis that pinpointed the consolidationist tendencies of the new Constitution. Relatedly, so does the great concern that the revenue-raising powers of the general government would very likely limit the states' power to raise revenue and thus undermine the vitality of the states. We might say that Smith and his circle underestimated the possibilities of a free *extended* republic, for the more centralized system is certainly not the outright despotism they feared and prophesied; but only a short-sighted person would not concede that Smith's analysis of the threats to republicanism and liberty in the new system did in fact pick out features of the constitutional order that create cause for concern over the health and vitality of free republicanism in America.

Michael P. Zuckert
Derek A. Webb

A Note on the Texts

IN ORDER to enable readers to engage as readily as possible the entirety of an original text, we chose to adhere to the original style and spelling as found in the original sources. We have, however, silently corrected obvious typographical errors. In some cases, especially when working from hand-written materials, we have had to make a best guess about the text. We have marked such guesses with square brackets. We have added the paragraph numbers to some of the texts to facilitate cross-referencing.

The *Federal Farmer* and *Brutus* essays are drawn from Herbert Storing's *The Complete Anti-Federalist* and from the online source www.constitution .org. The bibliography included in this volume is a list of works we found invaluable to our editorial research.

Acknowledgments

LIKE MOST scholarly achievements this one is built on the earlier efforts of many persons, including the previous editors of the Anti-Federalist writings, especially Herbert Storing, the editor of *The Complete Anti-Federalist*, and his then-assistant, now an Anti-Federalist expert in his own right, Murray Dry. We are also grateful to Murray and a number of other first-rate Anti-Federalist scholars who attended a Liberty Fund conference on the chief writings collected in this volume. Their comments were particularly valuable in helping sort out the pros and cons of assembling this collection. We are especially indebted to Lance Banning, one of the participants in that conference, who sent us a very helpful summary of his thinking on the central authorship question we were exploring. Not long after that conference Lance fell ill and died. All who knew him as a friend and as a scholar feel, and will continue for a long time to feel, the loss. His qualities as a human being matched his widely acknowledged excellence as a scholar.

We would also like to acknowledge the aid of two collaborators on this project. Robert Floyd, at the time a graduate student in political science at Notre Dame and now an aspiring young lawyer, got the project off to a grand start with his diligent and faithful work. John Burrows, whose computer analysis of Anti-Federal writings is included as an appendix to this volume, was also of immense assistance. Not only did he bring his great skill and knowledge in computerized authorship studies to our project, but also he—an Australian—became so caught up in the project that his enthusiasm was contagious to us.

We also wish to thank Laura Goetz of Liberty Fund for her aid in preparing the manuscript. She has been ever helpful and supportive. Cheryl Reed of the Notre Dame clerical services office also gave us incomparable help in transcribing much of the material. She is so thoroughly reliable that she runs the risk of being taken for granted. Jeff Church lent indispensable aid in the final stages of the manuscript preparation. We are also grateful to the University of Chicago Press for permission to adapt the notes from Storing's *Complete Anti-Federalist*.

In the process of assembling the political writings of Melancton Smith we have accumulated debts to many librarians across the country. The reference librarians of Notre Dame's Hesburgh Library assisted in locating previously unpublished speeches, pamphlets, and essays by Smith among their considerable collection of early American newspapers. Dwight King of the Notre Dame Law Library devoted several of his afternoons to helping track down the legal writings of Smith and Robert Yates. The reference librarians of the University of Pennsylvania provided several crucial leads regarding secondary literature. The librarians of the New York State Library in Albany allowed one of us to spend two very pleasant days in their Manuscript and Special Collections Room, sifting through and copying nearly everything in their Melancton Smith Papers. Without those two days, this project would never have gotten off the ground.

We are particularly indebted to the following librarians for responding to multiple requests for items in their collections and for then granting permission to publish them in this volume: Lorraine Baratti (New-York Historical Society), Dan Brown (Beverly Historical Society), Rakashi Chand (Massachusetts Historical Society), Wayne Furman (New York Public Library), Thomas Knoles (American Antiquarian Society), Timothy Salls (New England Historic Genealogical Society), Kathi Stanley (New York State Library), and the librarians of the Manuscript Division of the Library of Congress.

Part One

BEFORE THE CONSTITUTIONAL CONVENTION

Essays

Pamphlet on *Rutgers v. Waddington*, 1784

To the PEOPLE of the State of New-York
Fellow Citizens,

It is the happiness of people who live in a free government, that they may upon every occasion, when they conceive their rights in danger, from whatever cause, meet, consult and deliberate upon the proper mode of relief, and address their fellow citizens; pointing out the dangers which they apprehend, and inviting them to concur in measures for their removal.

In the exercise of this privilege, a number of the free citizens of New-York did assemble, and having appointed us their committee, gave it in charge to us to address you on the subject of a late decision of the Mayor's court, in this city, on the law commonly called the trespass law, in a case brought to issue in that court between Rutgers and Waddington.

This action was founded on a law of this state, entitled, "An act for grant-

From the *New York Packet* and *American Advertiser,* November 4, 1784.

This essay was published on November 4, 1784, and distributed independently as a pamphlet. While nine individuals signed it, Smith was its lead author and is commonly assigned principal responsibility for it. The essay critiques the ruling by the Mayor's Court of New York in the case of *Rutgers v. Waddington*, brought by Elizabeth Rutgers under New York's Trespass Act of 1783. This act allowed patriots to sue Loyalists who had obtained and used their property during the British occupation of New York. In 1778 Rutgers, the owner of a brewery in New York City, fled the city upon the approach of the British. Her brewery was taken over by Joshua Waddington, an agent for two British merchants. After the war, Rutgers asked Waddington for back rent. While they bargained, a fire burned down the brewery. Rutgers responded by suing Waddington for eight thousand pounds. The case went to trial in the Mayor's Court in New York City, with Alexander Hamilton representing Waddington. Hamilton argued that the Trespass Act violated the law of nations and laws of war, which

3

ing more effectual relief in cases of certain trespasses," passed in March, 1783; by which it is declared, that it shall and may be lawful for any person or persons who are or were inhabitants of this state, and who by reason of the invasion of the enemy left his, her or their place or places of abode, &c. to bring an action of trespass against any person or persons who may have occupied, injured or destroyed, his, her or their estate, either real or personal within the power of the enemy. And that no defendant or defendants shall be admitted to plead in justification, any military order or command whatsoever for such occupancy.

The plaintiff charged the defendant for the use and occupancy of a certain brew-house and malt-house, in the city of New-York, the property of the plaintiff.

To this charge the defendant plead, that the premises in question were occupied part of the time under the British army, who took possession thereof by virtue of a permission from the commander in chief of said army, and the remainder of the time by virtue of license and permission granted by the said commander in chief to a certain person, under whom the defendant held; which licenses and permissions the said commander had authority to give by the law of nations.

The defendant further plead, that by the treaty of peace, all right, claim, &c. which either of the contracting parties, and the subjects and citizens of either of them might otherwise have to any compensation, &c. whatsoever, for or by reason of any injury or damage, whether to the public or individuals which either of the said contracting parties, and the subjects or citizens of either, might have done, or caused to be done to the other, in consequence of, or in any wise relating to the war between them, from the commencement to the determination thereof, were mutually and recipro-

---

permitted abandoned property to be used during wartime, and that the law of nations and war had come into New York law through English common law. Hamilton further argued that the court was therefore obliged to strike down the Trespass Law: "When Statutes contradict the essential policy and maxims of the common law the common law shall be preferred." The court ultimately sided with Hamilton, ruling that the Trespass Act must be interpreted from the standpoint of its consistency with the law of nations. Waddington was found liable for only the first two years he managed Rutgers' property. Rutgers was correspondingly awarded only a tenth of what she had sought. The Anti-Loyalist party, to which Smith belonged, was incensed by the decision and wrote this essay in response. (Richard Brookheiser, *Alexander Hamilton, American* [New York: Free Press, 1999], 58–59.)

cally, virtually and effectually relinquished, renounced and released to each other; and further [asserted] that the defendant was, from the time of his birth, and at all times since hath been, a British subject.

The plaintiff to the first plea of the defendant, namely, that the premises were held by virtue of authority and permission from the commander in chief of the British army, replied, that she ought not to be barred of her action by reason of that plea; because the law under which she brought her suit, did expressly declare, that no defendant or defendants should be admitted to plead any military order or command whatsoever for the occupancy.

As to the further plea of the defendant, namely, the treaty of peace, the plaintiff demurred, or denied its sufficiency in the law.

This cause, as above stated, was argued on the 29th of June past, before the Mayor's Court, and on the 27th of August judgment was given.

The two points which presented for the court's determination upon arising from the two pleas of the defendant were,

[1st] Whether permission and authority from the commander in chief of the British army, agreeably to the law of nations, was a sufficient justification to the defendant for the use and occupancy of the premises in question, notwithstanding the act of the Legislature declaring "that no defendant or defendants shall be admitted to plead in justification any military order or command whatsoever."

[2dly] Whether the treaty of peace includes in it such an indemnity as to justify the defendant for his use of the premises.

With respect to the first point, the judgment of the court was, that the plea of the defendant was good for so much of the time as he held the premises under the immediate authority of the British commander in chief; or in other words, notwithstanding the law declares that no defendant shall be allowed to plead in justification any military order or command whatsoever, yet the authority and permission of the British commander in chief shall be deemed a sufficient justification; because in the opinion of the court a liberal construction of the law of nations would make it so, and because the court could not believe that a repeal of, or an interference with the law of nations entered into the scheme of the Legislature.

The second plea, namely, the treaty of peace, the court declared insufficient.

From this state of the case it appears, that the Mayor's court have assumed and exercised a power to set aside an act of the state. That it has permitted the *vague and doubtful* custom of nations to be plead against, and to render abortive, a *clear and positive* statute; and military authority of the enemy to be plead against the express prohibition of our Legislature.

This proceeding, in the opinion of a great part of the citizens of this metropolis, and in our opinion, is an assumption of power in that court, which is inconsistent with the nature and genius of our government, and threatening to the liberties of the people.

We think the controversy, notwithstanding the immense learning and abilities which we are told have been displayed in it, lies within a narrow compass, and within the reach of every common understanding.

It is reducible to the two following questions, Does the plain and obvious meaning of the statute prohibit the pleading of any military orders, commands, permission and authority of the enemy in justification of any trespass for which a suit can be brought under it?

Can a court of judicature, consistently with our constitution and laws, adjudge contrary to the plain and obvious meaning of a statute?

If these questions are answered in the negative, authorities from Grotius, Puffendorff, Wolfius, Burlamaqui, Vattel, or any other Civilians, are no more to the purpose than so many opinions drawn from sages of the six Nations.

If they are answered in the affirmative, then there can be no disputing against the opinion of the court.

With regard to the meaning and intention of the Legislature, it may be inferred from the very enacting of the law; for in doing that they suppose that as laws before stood, actions could not lie in cases of this nature; to remedy this, they make it lawful for persons described in the act, to bring actions of trespass against, &c. and declare that no military authority whatsoever of the enemy shall be plead, or evidenced in justification of the trespass.

No point of controversy can arise on the case but must turn upon the propriety or impropriety of the law itself; not upon its construction. For the plain language of the law is this, that the military power of Great Britain, by taking possession of these estates, and giving authority, permission, order or commands to persons for occupying and improving them, should not excuse the occupier, from being considered as a trespasser, and thereby not liable to pay damages to the owner. We can hardly conceive it possible for the Legislature to have chosen words that would make the intention of their law more clear.

If what we have stated be not the true meaning of the law then we conceive that it has no meaning.

The time of passing the law, and the evident grounds of it, show the intention of the Legislature, and put it beyond a doubt that the spirit and literal construction of it are the same. To give a remedy to those citizens who had abandoned their estates on the approach of the enemy, and who had adhered to the fortunes of their country in all its vicissitudes; most of whom had suffered very great loss of personal property, and many of them reduced from affluence to penury and want. The real estates which they owned in the Southern district, it was well known, had been greatly injured; most of them irreparably so.

We were then at the close of the war. The Legislature had certain accounts that the preliminary articles of peace were signed. The time was considered as just at hand, when the exiles, the greater part of whom had expended all their loose property, were to be put in possession of their real estates, from which they had suffered voluntary banishment for more than seven years. The bad condition of their estates, and their incapacity to improve them, made the case, which the Legislature thought proper to afford relief in by the law.

It is well known that most of these estates were at that time held, or pretended to be held by virtue of authority from the British Commander in Chief. The law of nations was the same then as at this time, and the immutable principles of justice have not changed. Yet the wisdom and supreme authority of the state did declare that no military order or command of the enemy should be plead or given in evidence. The law being thus plain and explicit, it was never apprehended that its operation would be defeated by the plea of authority from the enemy.

Impressed with a belief of its compleat and entire operation, many of the persons themselves who held the estates of exiles under the British, abandoned the place with them to avoid paying the damages which would accrue from it.

The Gentlemen of the law, we are confident, almost universally considered it as expressed in plain and unequivocal language that could not be misunderstood or explained away. In short, no doubt was entertained of the meaning of the law until the case of *Rutgers* and *Waddington* was agitated, and then there was no way left for the Defendant to justify himself, but by inventing distinctions where there was no difference, and introducing matter which the law prohibited.

From what has been said, we think that no one can doubt of the meaning of the law. It remains to enquire, whether a court of judicature can consistently, with our constitution and laws, adjudging contrary to the plain and obvious meaning of a statute.

That the Mayor's Court have done so in this case, we think is manifest from the aforegoing remarks.

That there should be a power vested in courts of judicature, whereby they might controul the Supreme Legislative power we think is absurd in itself. Such power in courts would be destructive of liberty, and remove all security of property. The design of courts of justice in our government, from the very nature of their institution, is to declare laws, not to alter them.

Whenever they depart from this design of their institution, they confound legislative and judicial powers.

The laws govern where a government is free, and every citizen knows what remedy the laws give him, for every injury. But this cannot be the case, where courts, if they deem a law to be unreasonable, may set it aside.

Here, however plainly the law may be in his favour, he cannot be certain of redress, until he has the opinion of the court.

It may be *expressed generally*, and only say, that all persons in certain circumstances shall recover in certain cases. But it may not by name bar every objection that might possibly be argued against it, where interest and inclination hold invention upon the rack.

It may not particularly describe the man, say what country he is to spring from, or what his occupation is to be; and being thus *generally expressed*, it cannot be from the nature of things, but it will admit of some exceptions, and as it may admit of some exceptions, it must receive a *reasonable* and liberal interpretation from the court, *however arduous the task may be*. Now the reasoning of the court, and the reasoning of the legislature may lead them to very different conclusions, and as the court reason last upon the case, it is utterly impossible, for any man to guess when he brings a suit, however exactly it may apply to the law, until by a tedious and expensive process, he obtains the opinion of the court whether he shall recover or not.

It is not our intention to enter into a particular consideration of the evils which would result from the exercise of such a power in our courts; much less to consider all the arguments used to vindicate the decision in the case of *Rutgers* and *Waddington*. We are addressing an enlightened people, who are awake to every thing that may affect their dearly attained freedom; who know that the consequences which would flow from the establishment of such a power, would be of the most serious and pernicious kind; rendering abortive the first and great privilege of freemen, the privilege of making their own laws by their representatives. For if the power of abrogating or altering them may be assumed by our courts, and submitted to by the people, then, as far as liberty, and the security of property are concerned, they become as useless as other opinions which are not precedents, and from which judges may vary.

It is to be observed that the principal judges are in most cases appointed to act within the limits of a certain age, or during good behaviour. We do not wish to lessen their independency; for while they are content to move in their proper sphere, while they speak the plain and obvious meaning of the law, and do not presume to alter it, or explain it to mean any thing or nothing. While in the duties of their real province they cannot be too independent; nor ought they to be liable to a remove but for misbehaviour. But if they are to be invested with a power to over rule a plain law, though expressed in *general words*, as all general laws are and must be. When they may judge the law unreasonable, because not consonant to the law of nations, or to the opinions of ancient or modern civilians and philosophers, for whom they may have a greater veneration than for the solid statutes and supreme legislative power of the state. We say, if they are to assume and exercise such a power, the probable consequence of their independence will be, the most deplorable and wretched dependency of the people.

That the laws should be no longer absolute would be in itself a great evil; but a far more dreadful consequence arises; for that power is not lost in the controversy, but transferred to judges who are independent of the people.

These being our apprehensions, we have in compliance with the request of our fellow citizens, and from a conviction of its propriety, briefly stated to your [*sic*] our ideas on this important affair.

In a free government people should be informed of the conduct of their rulers and magistrates. It is a knowledge that is absolutely necessary to the preserving of their freedom.

Power presents so many charms to mankind, that there are very few indeed even of the best of men who have their avarice and ambition so perfectly under the correction of virtue and true wisdom, as not to feel an inclination to surmount the limits assigned them; especially, when the additional temptation of ignorance or inattention on the side of the people prompt to it.

A private and individual case would not justify the measures which we have taken. But we consider the decision in the case of *Rutgers* and *Wadding-ton* as an adjudication which may be drawn into precedent, and eventually affect every citizen of this state. It therefore merits the attention of us all.

To prevent this mischief, we do not advise our fellow citizens to measures which are unconstitutional; nor do we mean to use them ourselves. The mode of redress which our excellent constitution points out is, first, by an appeal to the supreme court, where this cause will be carried by writ of error. We feel a confidence from the characters of the gentlemen who preside in that court, that the law will have its operation restored in its plain and obvious meaning. But if we should be disappointed, the cause is of too much consequence to rest here. Its importance will grow with the difficulties and defeats it may meet with; for each of these will make a new discovery of the strength of its opponents; each defeat will create a new triumph over freedom, and give additional courage and importance to her adversaries, and all call upon us the more earnestly to support that cause, to defend that ground upon which the standard of liberty is erected, and which, if ever surrendered, we should be prepared to surrender with it every less and consequent privilege, whereby we might be allowed better terms, from despotism, than we should by discovering our wretchedness and imbecility in a contest which the first defeat will have rendered vain and hopeless.

The next mode pointed out by the constitution, is an appeal to the court of errors, one part of which the Senate constitute. Preparatory to such an event, we exhort you to be cautious in your future choice of members, that none be elected but those on whom, from long and certain experience you can rely, as men attached to the liberties of America, and firm friends to our laws and constitution. Men who will spurn at any proposition that has a tendency to curtail the privileges of the people, and who at the same time, that they protect us against judicial tyranny, have wisdom to see the propriety of supporting that necessary independency in courts of justice, both of the Legislature and people, without which the fear of dismission from office on the one hand, and of personal violence on the other, might steal into their decisions, and render them interested and corrupt.

Having confined ourselves to constitutional measures, and now solemnly declaring our disapprobation of all others, and having solely for our object, the support of our excellent constitution, and the absolute and entire operation of our laws, we feel a freedom in sounding the alarm to our fellow citizens.

If that independence and freedom which we have obtained at a risque which makes the acquisition little less than miraculous, was worth contending for against a powerful and enraged monarch, and at the expence of the best blood in America, surely its preservation is worth contending for against those among ourselves, who might impiously hope to build their greatness upon the ruins of that fabric which was so dearly established?

That the principle of decision in the case of *Rutgers* and *Waddington* is dangerous to the freedom of our government, and that a perseverance in that principle would leave our Legislature nothing but a name, and render their sessions nothing more than an expensive form of government, the preceding remarks must evidence.

Permit us, upon this occasion, earnestly to intreat you, to join us in a watchfulness against every attempt that may be used, either violently and suddenly, or gently and imperceptibly, to effect a revolution in the spirit and genius of our government; and should there be, amongst us, characters to whom the simplicity of it is offensive, let our attention and perseverance be such, as to preclude the hopes of a change. For even if our government was less excellent than it is, it would be better for us to be reconciled to a few inconveniences, than by a hasty and ill-judged revolution, to put to the hazard all that we now enjoy under the present.

Frequent changes or even alterations in government, where the people have so lately come to the exercise of one, may produce an instability in them that will be more disagreeable than trifling inconveniencies in the one already established.

Melancton Smith,	*Thomas Tucker,*
Peter Riker,	*Daniel Shaw,*
Jonathan Lawrence,	*Adam Gilchrist, jun.,*
Anthony Rutgers,	*John Wiley.*
Peter T. Curtenius,	

Letters

Letter to ?, 1767

December 2, 1767

Dear Sir,

If the Minds frequently conversing with an Object, in the greatest hurry of business, may be deemed a sufficient Argument of that Objects having a considerable place in their Affection, I have an unquestionable proof, that you maintain no inconsiderable place in mine, for notwithstanding the great bustle I have been making this Week, in order to be prepared for a Journey to New York, on which I expect to set out the day after tomorrow Morning. The Idea of your Person has not been absent from my Mind any long time together, especially since I received yours of the 24th Instant which has revived every pleasing Idea you have been the means of exciting in my Mind, as well as the hopes I have of enjoying many more pleasant Moments in your Company. You apologize for your superlative manner of writing in your last and say you are sorry it displeased me. I did not mean to condemn your use of Hyperboles, upon proper occasions, but thought my absence from the Society did not afford such a one. Though to tell the truth I was not in the least disgusted, as I suppose it was nothing more than the ebulitions (pardon the expression) of that (sometimes I don't know what to call it, but I mean nothing vicious), You and I both have our share

Reprinted courtesy of the New York State Library, Manuscripts and Special Collections. Melancton Smith Papers, 1786–1792, Letter to ?, December 2, 1767: MSS 10856.

Smith wrote this letter to an unidentified friend prior to embarking on an overland business trip to New York City. The "Society" to which he refers was the Dutchess County branch of the Sons of Liberty, a society organized for the purpose of advocating the rights of Englishmen prior to the Revolution. (Robin Brooks, "Melancton Smith: New York Anti-Federalist, 1744–1798," dissertation, 1964, 6.)

of. I go to the City by Land and intend if possible to return by the next meeting of the Society, but if not assure them my Zeal is not abated in the glorious cause of Liberty (if I ever had any) but rather augmented. I hope, nay I am sure every honest Man who has eyes to see, and a soul to perceive will ere long be heartily engaged in [the] same design.

I am Yours in truth,
Mel Smith

Letter to Henry Livingston,[1] 1771

Charlotte. February 2, 1771

My very good friend,

May the Smiles of a kind and indulgent Heaven, cheer you, while traveling through the gloomy vale of Life, till you arrive to the bright regions of a happy Eternity.

You say you are almost insane with the Madness of the Times in New York. Were it not that I firmly believed a God of infinite Wisdom and immaculate goodness presiding over human affairs, who is able and determined to so dispose of Things as finally, to bring about the greatest Good, I should be quite distracted with the shameless Conduct of Men in Power. I think we are bound to be very grateful to divine Providence, that the Majority of our House of Asses, have not understanding equal to the wickedness of their Hearts, for if this was the case, we should have awful Reason to fear, the province would soon be enslaved in egyptian Bondage.[2]

Reprinted courtesy of the New York State Library, Manuscripts and Special Collections. Melancton Smith Papers, 1786–1792, Letter to Henry Livingston Jr., February 2, 1771: MSS 7089.

1. Henry Livingston Jr., a member of the Poughkeepsie Livingstons, was a friend of Melancton Smith. From 1777 to 1789 he served as the clerk of Dutchess County. (Stephen L. Schechter, *The Reluctant Pillar: New York and the Adoption of the Federal Constitution* [Troy, N.Y.: Russell Sage College, 1985], 181.)

2. The "House of Asses" refers to the Provincial Assembly of New York, in which the Livingstons and the Delaneys competed for power. Smith supported the Livingston faction. (Brooks, 7.)

I am informed the Judge is turned over the Bar again—may Heaven grant a dissolution and open peoples eyes to a sense of their true Interest.[3]

How affairs will go in this County, should such an event take place, I am at a loss to determine. It is general opinion [that] Anthony Hoffman will be chosen for one, in the room of one of our sagacious Politicians, I cannot learn of any one else who will set up. I for my part can think of no one who will accept of it, that I like—

I am glad to hear you are engaged in an Amour, with a Young Lady of the same Name with one, who is dear to me—take a word of caution from your Friend, whose heart wishes you well.[4] Don't suffer your Passion to run away with your Reason, but endeavour to keep yourself capable of judging soberly of the qualifications of the Ladies, and when you have drawn up a rational Judgement, that she is possessed of such qualifications as will make you comfortable, if you feel a proper affection for her, and have reason to believe she has the same for you, my advice is to marry—for it is not good for Man to be alone. As to my amour, it would take a Volume to relate every particular.[5] It would afford subject matter for an excellent Tragi Comedy. I have some Thoughts of writing one on the subject. This much however I can inform you—Mr. Cooper and I have come to an open Rupture insomuch that he has forbid me to come to his house.[6] The young L[ady] and I continue upon Terms, and now and then meet—and it [is] not impossible but what we shall yet join, in matrimonial Bands, however, it is uncertain as all sublunary things are. I think I have learned the folly, of seeking Bliss below the skies.

I am to set out by [pleasure] of Providence, for a Journey to N. England— the day after tomorrow—expect much pleasure in exploring philosophical and theological subjects.

Heaven bless you—so prays your Friend,

Melancton Smith

3. Citing a law preventing judges from serving in the legislature, the Delaneys prevented Judge Robert R. Livingston of Clermont from taking his seat for Dutchess County. Smith hoped this controversy would lead to a new election. (Brooks, 7.)

4. Livingston at the time was writing love letters to his cousin Caty (Catherine) Livingston. Ten years later he would marry Sarah (Sally) Welles of Stamford, Connecticut. (Brooks, 25, n15.)

5. At the time Smith, a widower, was courting Margaret Mott. He had been married to Sarah Smith of New Jersey from 1766 until her death in 1770. (Brooks, 3, 5.)

6. Margaret's stepfather, Ezekiel Cooper, objected to the marriage. Over his objections, however, they would wed on March 17, 1772. (Brooks, 5.)

Part Two

THE RATIFICATION STRUGGLE

Pseudonymous Essays

Letters from the Federal Farmer

– I –

October 8th, 1787.

Dear Sir,

1. My letters to you last winter, on the subject of a well balanced national government for the United States, were the result of free enquiry;[1] when I passed from that subject to enquiries relative to our commerce, revenues, past administration, etc. I anticipated the anxieties I feel, on carefully examining the plan of government proposed by the convention. It appears to be a plan retaining some federal features; but to be the first important step, and to aim strongly to one consolidated government of the United States. It leaves the powers of government, and the representation of the people, so unnaturally divided between the general and state governments, that the operations of our system must be very uncertain. My uniform federal attachments, and the interest I have in the protection of property, and a steady execution of the laws, will convince you, that, if I am under any biass at all, it is in favor of any general system which shall promise those advantages. The instability of our laws increases my wishes for firm and steady government; but then, I can consent to no government, which, in my opinion, is not calculated equally to preserve the rights of all orders of men in the community. My object has been to join with those who have endeavoured to supply the defects in the forms of our govern-

From Herbert J. Storing, ed., *The Complete Anti-Federalist*, 7 vols. (Chicago: University of Chicago Press, 1981), II, 223–357.

1. The best efforts of scholars such as Herbert Storing have not been able to identify which letters *Federal Farmer* (hereafter abbreviated as *FF*) is referring to, nor who the addressee ("Republican") might be.

ments by a steady and proper administration of them. Though I have long apprehended that fraudulent debtors, and embarrassed men, on the one hand, and men, on the other, unfriendly to republican equality, would produce an uneasiness among the people, and prepare the way, not for cool and deliberate reforms in the governments, but for changes calculated to promote the interests of particular orders of men. Acquit me, sir, of any agency in the formation of the new system; I shall be satisfied with seeing, if it shall be adopted, a prudent administration. Indeed I am so much convinced of the truth of Pope's maxim, that "That which is best administered is best," that I am much inclined to subscribe to it from experience. I am not disposed to unreasonably contend about forms.[2] I know our situation is critical, and it behoves us to make the best of it. A federal government of some sort is necessary. We have suffered the present to languish; and whether the confederation was capable or not originally of answering any valuable purposes, it is now but of little importance. I will pass by the men, and states, who have been particularly instrumental in preparing the way for a change, and, perhaps, for governments not very favourable to the people at large. A constitution is now presented which we may reject, or which we may accept, with or without amendments; and to which point we ought to direct our exertions, is the question. To determine this question, with propriety, we must attentively examine the system itself, and the probable consequences of either step. This I shall endeavour to do, so far as I am able, with candor and fairness; and leave you to decide upon the propriety of my opinions, the weight of my reasons, and how far my conclusions are well drawn. Whatever may be the conduct of others, on the present occasion, I do not mean, hastily and positively to decide on the merits of the constitution proposed. I shall be open to conviction, and always disposed to adopt that which, all things considered, shall appear to me to be most for the happiness of the community. It must be granted, that if men hastily and blindly adopt a system of government, they will as hastily and as blindly be led to alter or abolish it; and changes must ensue, one after another, till the peaceable and better part of the community will grow weary with changes, tumults and disorders, and be disposed to accept any government, however despotic, that shall promise stability and firmness.

2. The first principal question that occurs, is, Whether, considering our situation, we ought to precipitate the adoption of the proposed constitution? If we remain cool and temperate, we are in no immediate danger of

2. Alexander Pope, *Essay on Man* (Sioux Falls, N.D.: NuVision, 2007), Epistle 3, lines 303–4.

any commotions; we are in a state of perfect peace, and in no danger of invasions; the state governments are in the full exercise of their powers; and our governments answer all present exigencies, except the regulation of trade, securing credit, in some cases, and providing for the interest, in some instances, of the public debts; and whether we adopt a change, three or nine months hence, can make but little odds with the private circumstances of individuals; their happiness and prosperity, after all, depend principally upon their own exertions. We are hardly recovered from a long and distressing war: The farmers, fishmen, &c. have not yet fully repaired the waste made by it. Industry and frugality are again assuming their proper station. Private debts are lessened, and public debts incurred by the war have been, by various ways, diminished; and the public lands have now become a productive source for diminishing them much more. I know uneasy men, who wish very much to precipitate, do not admit all these facts; but they are facts well known to all men who are thoroughly informed in the affairs of this country. It must, however, be admitted, that our federal system is defective, and that some of the state governments are not well administered; but, then, we impute to the defects in our governments many evils and embarrassments which are most clearly the result of the late war. We must allow men to conduct on the present occasion, as on all similar ones. They will urge a thousand pretences to answer their purposes on both sides. When we want a man to change his condition, we describe it as miserable, wretched, and despised; and draw a pleasing picture of that which we would have him assume. And when we wish the contrary, we reverse our descriptions. Whenever a clamor is raised, and idle men get to work, it is highly necessary to examine facts carefully, and without unreasonably suspecting men of falshood, to examine, and enquire attentively, under what impressions they act. It is too often the case in political concerns, that men state facts not as they are, but as they wish them to be; and almost every man, by calling to mind past scenes, will find this to be true.

3. Nothing but the passions of ambitious, impatient, or disorderly men, I conceive, will plunge us into commotions, if time should be taken fully to examine and consider the system proposed. Men who feel easy in their circumstances, and such as are not sanguine in their expectations relative to the consequences of the proposed change, will remain quiet under the existing governments. Many commercial and monied men, who are uneasy, not without just cause, ought to be respected; and, by no means, unreasonably disappointed in their expectations and hopes; but as to those who expect employments under the new constitution; as to those weak and ardent men

who always expect to be gainers by revolutions, and whose lot it generally is to get out of one difficulty into another, they are very little to be regarded: and as to those who designedly avail themselves of this weakness and ardor, they are to be despised. It is natural for men, who wish to hasten the adoption of a measure, to tell us, now is the crisis—now is the critical moment which must be seized, or all will be lost: and to shut the door against free enquiry, whenever conscious the thing presented has defects in it, which time and investigation will probably discover. This has been the custom of tyrants and their dependants in all ages. If it is true, what has been so often said, that the people of this country cannot change their condition for the worse, I presume it still behoves them to endeavour deliberately to change it for the better. The fickle and ardent, in any community, are the proper tools for establishing despotic government. But it is deliberate and thinking men, who must establish and secure governments on free principles. Before they decide on the plan proposed, they will enquire whether it will probably be a blessing or a curse to this people.

4. The present moment discovers a new face in our affairs. Our object has been all along, to reform our federal system, and to strengthen our governments—to establish peace, order and justice in the community—but a new object now presents. The plan of government now proposed is evidently calculated totally to change, in time, our condition as a people. Instead of being thirteen republics, under a federal head, it is clearly designed to make us one consolidated government. Of this, I think, I shall fully convince you, in my following letters on this subject. This consolidation of the states has been the object of several men in this country for some time past. Whether such a change can ever be effected in any manner; whether it can be effected without convulsions and civil wars; whether such a change will not totally destroy the liberties of this country—time only can determine.

5. To have a just idea of the government before us, and to shew that a consolidated one is the object in view, it is necessary not only to examine the plan, but also its history, and the politics of its particular friends.

6. The confederation was formed when great confidence was placed in the voluntary exertions of individuals, and of the respective states; and the framers of it, to guard against usurpation, so limited and checked the powers, that, in many respects, they are inadequate to the exigencies of the union. We find, therefore, members of congress urging alterations in the federal system almost as soon as it was adopted. It was early proposed to vest congress with powers to levy an impost, to regulate trade, etc. but such was known to be the caution of the states in parting with power, that

the vestment, even of these, was proposed to be under several checks and limitations. During the war, the general confusion, and the introduction of paper money, infused in the minds of people vague ideas respecting government and credit. We expected too much from the return of peace, and of course we have been disappointed. Our governments have been new and unsettled; and several legislatures, by making tender, suspension, and paper money laws, have given just cause of uneasiness to creditors. By these and other causes, several orders of men in the community have been prepared, by degrees, for a change of government; and this very abuse of power in the legislatures, which, in some cases, has been charged upon the democratic part of the community, has furnished aristocratical men with those very weapons, and those very means, with which, in great measure, they are rapidly effecting their favourite object. And should an oppressive government be the consequence of the proposed change, posterity may reproach not only a few overbearing unprincipled men, but those parties in the states which have misused their powers.

7. The conduct of several legislatures, touching paper money, and tender laws, has prepared many honest men for changes in government, which otherwise they would not have thought of—when by the evils, on the one hand, and by the secret instigations of artful men, on the other, the minds of men were become sufficiently uneasy, a bold step was taken, which is usually followed by a revolution, or a civil war. A general convention for mere commercial purposes was moved for—the authors of this measure saw that the people's attention was turned solely to the amendment of the federal system; and that, had the idea of a total change been started, probably no state would have appointed members to the convention. The idea of destroying, ultimately, the state government, and forming one consolidated system, could not have been admitted—a convention, therefore, merely for vesting in congress power to regulate trade was proposed. This was pleasing to the commercial towns; and the landed people had little or no concern about it. September, 1786, a few men from the middle states met at Annapolis, and hastily proposed a convention to be held in May, 1787, for the purpose, generally, of amending the confederation—this was done before the delegates of Massachusetts, and of the other states arrived—still not a word was said about destroying the old constitution, and making a new one—The states still unsuspecting, and not aware that they were passing the Rubicon, appointed members to the new convention, for the sole and express purpose of revising and amending the confederation—and, probably, not one man in ten thousand in the United States, till within these ten

or twelve days, had an idea that the old ship was to be destroyed, and he put to the alternative of embarking in the new ship presented, or of being left in danger of sinking—The States, I believe, universally supposed the convention would report alterations in the confederation, which would pass an examination in congress, and after being agreed to there, would be confirmed by all the legislatures, or be rejected. Virginia made a very respectable appointment, and placed at the head of it the first man in America:[3] In this appointment there was a mixture of political characters; but Pennsylvania appointed principally those men who are esteemed aristocratical. Here the favourite moment for changing the government was evidently discerned by a few men, who seized it with address. Ten other states appointed, and tho' they chose men principally connected with commerce and the judicial department yet they appointed many good republican characters—had they all attended we should now see, I am persuaded a better system presented. The non-attendance of eight or nine men, who were appointed members of the convention, I shall ever consider as a very unfortunate event to the United States.[4]—Had they attended, I am pretty clear, that the result of the convention would not have had that strong tendency to aristocracy now discernable in every part of the plan. There would not have been so great an accumulation of powers, especially as to the internal police of the country, in a few hands, as the constitution reported proposes to vest in them—the young visionary men, and the consolidating aristocracy, would have been more restrained than they have been. Eleven states met in the convention, and after four months close attention presented the new constitution, to be adopted or rejected by the people. The uneasy and fickle part of the community may be prepared to receive any form of government; but, I presume, the enlightened and substantial part will give any constitution presented for their adoption, a candid and thorough examination; and silence those designing or empty men, who weakly and rashly attempt to precipitate the adoption of a system of so much importance—We shall view the convention with proper respect—and, at the same time, that we reflect there were men of abilities and integrity in it, we must recollect how

    3. The reference is to George Washington.
    4. The author is thinking of such men as Abraham Clark of New Jersey; Richard Caswell and Willie Jones of North Carolina; and Patrick Henry, Thomas Nelson, and Richard Henry Lee of Virginia. All were critics of the Constitution and had been elected to the Constitutional Convention but had declined to serve or had failed to attend. (Storing, II, 350, n5.)

disproportionably the democratic and aristocratic parts of the community were represented—Perhaps the judicious friends and opposers of the new constitution will agree, that it is best to let it rest solely on its own merits, or be condemned for its own defects.

8. In the first place, I shall premise, that the plan proposed is a plan of accommodation—and that it is in this way only, and by giving up a part of our opinions, that we can ever expect to obtain a government founded in freedom and compact. This circumstance candid men will always keep in view, in the discussion of this subject.

9. The plan proposed appears to be partly federal, but principally however, calculated ultimately to make the states one consolidated government.

10. The first interesting question, therefore suggested, is, how far the states can be consolidated into one entire government on free principles. In considering this question extensive objects are to be taken into view, and important changes in the forms of government to be carefully attended to in all their consequences. The happiness of the people at large must be the great object with every honest statesman, and he will direct every movement to this point. If we are so situated as a people, as not to be able to enjoy equal happiness and advantages under one government, the consolidation of the states cannot be admitted.

11. There are three different forms of free government under which the United States may exist as one nation; and now is, perhaps, the time to determine to which we will direct our views. [1] Distinct republics connected under a federal head. In this case the respective state governments must be the principal guardians of the peoples rights, and exclusively regulate their internal police; in them must rest the balance of government. The congress of the states, or federal head, must consist of delegates amenable to, and removeable by the respective states: This congress must have general directing powers; powers to require men and monies of the states; to make treaties, peace and war; to direct the operations of armies, etc. Under this federal modification of government, the powers of congress would be rather advisory or recommendatory than coercive. [2] We may do away the several state governments, and form or consolidate all the states into one entire government, with one executive, one judiciary, and one legislature, consisting of senators and representatives collected from all parts of the union: In this case there would be a compleat consolidation of the states. [3] We may consolidate the states as to certain national objects, and leave them severally distinct independent republics, as to internal police generally. Let the general government consist of an executive, a judiciary, and

balanced legislature, and its powers extend exclusively to all foreign concerns, causes arising on the seas to commerce, imports, armies, navies, Indian affairs, peace and war, and to a few internal concerns of the community; to the coin, post-offices, weights and measures, a general plan for the militia, to naturalization, *and, perhaps to bankruptcies*,[5] leaving the internal police of the community, in other respects, exclusively to the state governments; as the administration of justice in all causes arising internally, the laying and collecting of internal taxes, and the forming of the militia according to a general plan prescribed. In this case there would be a compleat consolidation, *quoad* certain objects only.[6]

12. Touching the first, or federal plan, I do not think much can be said in its favor: The sovereignty of the nation, without coercive and efficient powers to collect the strength of it, cannot always be depended on to answer the purposes of government; and in a congress of representatives of sovereign states, there must necessarily be an unreasonable mixture of powers in the same hands.

13. As to the second, or compleat consolidating plan, it deserves to be carefully considered at this time, by every American: If it be impracticable, it is a fatal error to model our governments, directing our views ultimately to it.

14. The third plan, or partial consolidation, is, in my opinion, the only one that can secure the freedom and happiness of this people. I once had some general ideas that the second plan was practicable, but from long attention, and the proceedings of the convention, I am fully satisfied, that this third plan is the only one we can with safety and propriety proceed upon. Making this the standard to point out, with candor and fairness, the parts of the new constitution which appear to be improper, is my object. The convention appears to have proposed the partial consolidation evidently with a view to collect all powers ultimately, in the United States into one entire government; and from its views in this respect, and from the tenacity of the small states to have an equal vote in the senate,[7] probably originated the greatest defects in the proposed plan.

5. See *FF III*, where the author adds to the legitimate powers of the general government the regulation of trade between the states but omits to mention the militia and bankruptcy. On bankruptcy law, see *FF XVIII* (7), where he concludes that the power to pass bankruptcy laws should not be given to the federal government.

6. Cf. *Brutus I* (7) on the meaning of a federal system.

7. See *Brutus III* (11).

15. Independant of the opinions of many great authors, that a free elective government cannot be extended over large territories, a few reflections
must evince, that one government and general legislation alone, never can
extend equal benefits to all parts of the United States: Different laws, customs, and opinions exist in the different states, which by a uniform system
of laws would be unreasonably invaded. The United States contain about
a million of square miles, and in half a century will, probably, contain ten
millions of people; and from the center to the extremes is about 800 miles.

16. Before we do away the state governments, or adopt measures that
will tend to abolish them, and to consolidate the states into one entire government, several principles should be considered and facts ascertained:—
These, and my examination into the essential parts of the proposed plan, I
shall pursue in my next.

Your's &c.
The Federal Farmer.

– II –

October 9, 1787

Dear Sir,
1. The essential parts of a free and good government are a full and
equal representation of the people in the legislature, and the jury trial of
the vicinage in the administration of justice—a full and equal representation, is that which possesses the same interests, feelings, opinions, and
views the people themselves would were they all assembled—a fair representation, therefore, should be so regulated, that every order of men in
the community, according to the common course of elections, can have a
share in it—in order to allow professional men, merchants, traders, farmers, mechanics, etc. to bring a just proportion of their best informed men
respectively into the legislature, the representation must be considerably
numerous[8]—We have about 200 state senators in the United States, and
a less number than that of federal representatives cannot, clearly, be a full
representation of this people, in the affairs of internal taxation and police,
were there but one legislature for the whole union. The representation
cannot be equal, or the situation of the people proper for one government

8. Cf. *FF III* (2–3), *V* (1–2), *VI* (11–12), *VII–XII, XV* (8); *Brutus I* (14–16), *IV, V*;
"Address by a Plebeian to the People of the State of New York, 1788," paragraph 20,
in this volume.

only—if the extreme parts of the society cannot be represented as fully as the central—It is apparently impracticable that this should be the case in this extensive country—it would be impossible to collect a representation of the parts of the country five, six, and seven hundred miles from the seat of government.

2. Under one general government alone, there could be but one judiciary, one supreme and a proper number of inferior courts. I think it would be totally impracticable in this case to preserve a due administration of justice, and the real benefits of the jury trial of the vicinage,[9]—there are now supreme courts in each state in the union; and a great number of county and other courts subordinate to each supreme court—most of these supreme and inferior courts are itinerant, and hold their sessions in different parts every year of their respective states, counties and districts—with all these moving courts, our citizens, from the vast extent of the country must travel very considerable distances from home to find the place where justice is administered. I am not for bringing justice so near to individuals as to afford them any temptation to engage in law suits; though I think it one of the greatest benefits in a good government, that each citizen should find a court of justice within a reasonable distance, perhaps, within a day's travel of his home; so that, without great inconveniences and enormous expences, he may have the advantages of his witnesses and jury—it would be impracticable to derive these advantages from one judiciary—the one supreme court at most could only set in the centre of the union, and move once a year into the centre of the eastern and southern extremes of it—and, in this case, each citizen, on an average, would travel 150 or 200 miles to find this court—that, however, inferior courts might be properly placed in the different counties, and districts of the union, the appellate jurisdiction would be intolerable and expensive.

3. If it were possible to consolidate the states, and preserve the features of a free government, still it is evident that the middle states, the parts of the union, about the seat of government, would enjoy great advantages, while the remote states would experience the many inconveniences of remote provinces. Wealth, offices, and the benefits of government would collect in the centre: and the extreme states and their principal towns, become much less important.

4. There are other considerations which tend to prove that the idea of one consolidated whole, on free principles, is ill-founded—the laws of a free

9. See *FF IV* (11–13), *VI* (15), *XV* (8–12).

government rest on the confidence of the people, and operate gently—and never can extend their influence very far—if they are executed on free principles, about the centre, where the benefits of the government induce the people to support it voluntarily; yet they must be executed on the principles of fear and force in the extremes—This has been the case with every extensive republic of which we have any accurate account.[10]

5. There are certain unalienable and fundamental rights, which in forming the social compact, ought to be explicitly ascertained and fixed—a free and enlightened people, in forming this compact, will not resign all their rights to those who govern, and they will fix limits to their legislators and rulers, which will soon be plainly seen by those who are governed, as well as by those who govern: and the latter will know they cannot be passed unperceived by the former, and without giving a general alarm—These rights should be made the basis of every constitution:[11] and if a people be so situated, or have such different opinions that they cannot agree in ascertaining and fixing them, it is a very strong argument against their attempting to form one entire society, to live under one system of laws only.—I confess, I never thought the people of these states differed essentially in these respects; they having derived all these rights from one common source, the British systems; and having in the formation of their state constitutions, discovered that their ideas relative to these rights are very similar. However, it is now said that the states differ so essentially in these respects, and even in the important article of the trial by jury, that when assembled in convention, they can agree to no words by which to establish that trial, or by which to ascertain and establish many other of these rights, as fundamental articles in the social compact. If so, we proceed to consolidate the states on no solid basis whatever.[12]

6. But I do not pay much regard to the reasons given for not bottoming the new constitution on a better bill of rights. I still believe a complete federal bill of rights to be very practicable. Nevertheless I acknowledge the proceedings of the convention furnish my mind with many new and strong reasons, against a complete consolidation of the states. They tend to convince me, that it cannot be carried with propriety very far—that the convention have gone much farther in one respect than they found it practicable to go in another; that is, they propose to lodge in the general government very

10. Cf. *Brutus I.*
11. Cf. *Brutus II.*
12. See also *FF IV* (14), *XVI.* On kinds of rights, see *FF VI* (15–23).

extensive powers—*powers* nearly, if not altogether, complete and unlimited, over the purse and the sword. But, in its organization, they furnish the strongest proof that the proper limbs, or parts of a government, to support and execute those powers on proper principles (or in which they can be safely lodged) cannot be formed. These powers must be lodged somewhere in every society; but then they should be lodged where the strength and guardians of the people are collected. They can be wielded, or safely used, in a free country only by an able executive and judiciary, a respectable senate, and a secure, full, and equal representation of the people. I think the principles I have premised or brought into view, are well founded—I think they will not be denied by any fair reasoner. It is in connection with these, and other solid principles, we are to examine the constitution. It is not a few democratic phrases, or a few well formed features, that will prove its merits; or a few small omissions that will produce its rejection among men of sense; they will enquire what are the essential powers in a community, and what are nominal ones; where and how the essential powers shall be lodged to secure government, and to secure true liberty.[13]

7. In examining the proposed constitution carefully, we must clearly perceive an unnatural separation of these powers from the substantial representation of the people. The state governments will exist, with all their governors, senators, representatives, officers and expences; in these will be nineteen-twentieths of the representatives of the people; they will have a near connection, and their members an immediate intercourse with the people; and the probability is, that the state governments will possess the confidence of the people, and be considered generally as their immediate guardians.[14]

8. The general government will consist of a new species of executive, a small senate, and a very small house of representatives. As many citizens will be more than three hundred miles from the seat of this government as will be nearer to it, its judges and officers cannot be very numerous, without making our governments very expensive. Thus will stand the state and the general governments, should the constitution be adopted without any alterations in their organization; but as to powers, the general government will possess all essential ones, at least on paper, and those of the states a mere shadow of power. And therefore, unless the people shall make some great exertions to restore to the state governments their powers in mat-

13. Cf. *Brutus III.*
14. Cf. *Brutus III.*

ters of internal police; as the powers to lay and collect, exclusively, internal taxes, to govern the militia, and to hold the decisions of their own judicial courts upon their own laws final, the balance cannot possibly continue long; but the state governments must be annihilated, or continue to exist for no purpose.

9. It is however to be observed, that many of the essential powers given the national government are not exclusively given; and the general government may have prudence enough to forbear the exercise of those which may still be exercised by the respective states. But this cannot justify the impropriety of giving powers, the exercise of which prudent men will not attempt, and imprudent men will, or probably can, exercise only in a manner destructive of free government. The general government, organized as it is, may be adequate to many valuable objects, and be able to carry its laws into execution on proper principles in several cases; but I think its warmest friends will not contend, that it can carry all the powers proposed to be lodged in it into effect, without calling to its aid a military force, which must very soon destroy all elective governments in the country, produce anarchy, or establish despotism. Though we cannot have now a complete idea of what will be the operations of the proposed system, we may, allowing things to have their common course, have a very tolerable one. The powers lodged in the general government, if exercised by it, must intimately effect the internal police of the states, as well as external concerns; and there is no reason to expect the numerous state governments, and their connections, will be very friendly to the execution of federal laws in those internal affairs, which hitherto have been under their own immediate management. There is more reason to believe, that the general government, far removed from the people, and none of its members elected oftener than once in two years, will be forgot or neglected, and its laws in many cases disregarded, unless a multitude of officers and military force be continually kept in view, and employed to enforce the execution of the laws, and to make the government feared and respected. No position can be truer than this, that in this country either neglected laws, or a military execution of them, must lead to a revolution, and to the destruction of freedom. Neglected laws must first lead to anarchy and confusion; and a military execution of laws is only a shorter way to the same point—despotic government.

Your's, &c.
The Federal Farmer.

– III –

October 10th, 1787

Dear Sir,

1. The great object of a free people must be so to form their government
and laws, and so to administer them, as to create a confidence in, and respect for the laws; and thereby induce the sensible and virtuous part of the
community to declare in favor of the laws, and to support them without an
expensive military force.[15] I wish, though I confess I have not much hope,
that this may be the case with the laws of congress under the new constitution. I am fully convinced that we must organize the national government
on different principals, and make the parts of it more efficient, and secure
in it more effectually the different interests in the community; or else leave
in the state governments some powers proposed to be lodged in it—at least
till such an organization shall be found to be practicable. Not sanguine in
my expectations of a good federal administration, and satisfied, as I am,
of the impracticability of consolidating the states, and at the same time of
preserving the rights of the people at large, I believe we ought still to leave
some of those powers in the state governments, in which the people, in
fact, will still be represented—to define some other powers proposed to
be vested in the general government, more carefully, and to establish a few
principles to secure a proper exercise of the powers given it. It is not my
object to multiply objections, or to contend about inconsiderable powers or
amendments; I wish the system adopted with a few alterations; but those,
in my mind, are essential ones; if adopted without, every good citizen will
acquiesce though I shall consider the duration of our governments, and
the liberties of this people, very much dependant on the administration of
the general government. A wise and honest administration, may make the
people happy under any government; but necessity only can justify even
our leaving open avenues to the abuse of power, by wicked, unthinking, or
ambitious men. I will examine, first, the organization of the proposed government, in order to judge; 2d, with propriety, what powers are improperly,
at least prematurely lodged in it. I shall examine, 3d, the undefined powers;
and 4th, those powers, the exercise of which is not secured on safe and
proper ground.

2. First. As to the organization—the house of representatives, the democrative branch, as it is called, is to consist of 65 members: that is, about one

15. See also *FF II* (4), *V* (1), *VII* (1–5), *X* (1–12); *Brutus I.*

representative for fifty thousand inhabitants, to be chosen biennially—the federal legislature may increase this number to one for each thirty thousand inhabitants, abating fractional numbers in each state.—Thirty-three representatives will make a quorum for doing business, and a majority of those present determine the sense of the house.—I have no idea that the interests, feelings, and opinions of three or four millions of people, especially touching internal taxation, can be collected in such a house.—In the nature of things, nine times in ten, men of the elevated classes in the community only can be chosen—Connecticut, for instance, will have five representatives— not one man in a hundred of those who form the democrative branch in the state legislature, will, on a fair computation, be one of the five—The people of this country, in one sense, may all be democratic; but if we make the proper distinction between the few men of wealth and abilities, and consider them, as we ought, as the natural aristocracy of the country,[16] and the great body of the people, the middle and lower classes, as the democracy, this federal representative branch will have but very little democracy in it, even this small representation is not secured on proper principles.— The branches of the legislature are essential parts of the fundamental compact, and ought to be so fixed by the people, that the legislature cannot alter itself by modifying the elections of its own members. This, by a part of Art. 1. Sect. 4. the general legislature may do, it may evidently so regulate elections as to secure the choice of any particular description of men.—It may make the whole state one district—make the capital, or any places in the state, the place or places of election—it may declare that the five men (or whatever the number may be the state may chuse) who shall have the most votes shall be considered as chosen—In this case it is easy to perceive how the people who live scattered in the inland towns will bestow their votes on different men—and how a few men in a city, in any order or profession, may unite and place any five men they please highest among those that may be voted for—and all this may be done constitutionally, and by those silent operations, which are not immediately perceived by the people in general.—I know it is urged, that the general legislature will be disposed to regulate elections on fair and just principles:—This may be true—good men will generally govern well with almost any constitution: but why in laying the foundation of the social system, need we unnecessarily leave a door open to improper regulations?—This is a very general and unguarded clause, and many evils may flow from that part which authorises the con-

16. Also see *FF VI* (5); *Brutus III–IV.*

gress to regulate elections—Were it omitted, the regulations of elections would be solely in the respective states, where the people are substantially represented; and where the elections ought to be regulated, otherwise to secure a representation from all parts of the community, in making the constitution, we ought to provide for dividing each state into a proper number of districts, and for confining the electors in each district to the choice of some men, who shall have a permanent interest and residence in it; and also for this essential object, that the representative elected shall have a majority of the votes of those electors who shall attend and give their votes.[17]

3. In considering the practicability of having a full and equal representation of the people from all parts of the union, not only distances and different opinions, customs, and views, common in extensive tracts of country, are to be taken into view, but many differences peculiar to Eastern, Middle, and Southern states. These differences are not so perceivable among the members of congress, and men of general information in the states, as among the men who would properly form the democratic branch. The Eastern states are very democratic, and composed chiefly of moderate freeholders; they have but few rich men and no slaves; the Southern states are composed chiefly of rich planters and slaves; they have but few moderate freeholders, and the prevailing influence, in them, is generally a dissipated aristocracy: The Middle states partake partly of the Eastern, and partly of the Southern character.

4. Perhaps, nothing could be more disjointed, unweildly and incompetent to doing business with harmony and dispatch, than a federal house of representatives properly numerous for the great objects of taxation, et cetera collected from the several states; whether such men would ever act in concert; whether they would not worry along a few years, and then be the means of separating the parts of the union, is very problematical?—View this system in whatever form we can, propriety brings us still to this point, a federal government possessed of general and complete powers, as to those national objects which cannot well come under the cognizance of the internal laws of the respective states, and this federal government, accordingly, consisting of branches not very numerous.

5. The house of representatives is on the plan of consolidation, but the senate is intirely on the federal plan; and Delaware will have as much constitutional influence in the senate, as the largest state in the union: and in

17. Cf. *Brutus IV* (7).

this senate are lodged legislative, executive and judicial powers: Ten states in this union urge that they are small states, nine of which were present in the convention.—They were interested in collecting large powers into the hands of the senate, in which each state still will have its equal share of power. I suppose it was impracticable for the three large states, as they were called, to get the senate formed on any other principles: But this only proves, that we cannot form one general government on equal and just principles—and proves, that we ought not to lodge in it such extensive powers before we are convinced of the practicability of organizing it on just and equal principles.[18] The senate will consist of two members from each state, chosen by the state legislatures, every sixth year. The clause referred to, respecting the elections of representatives, empowers the general legislature to regulate the elections of senators also, "except as to the places of chusing senators."—There is, therefore, but little more security in the elections than in those of representatives: Fourteen senators make a quorum for business, and a majority of the senators present give the vote of the senate, except in giving judgment upon an impeachment, or in making treaties, or in expelling a member, when two-thirds of the senators present must agree—The members of the legislature are not excluded from being elected to any military offices, or any civil offices, except those created, or the emoluments of which shall be increased by themselves: two-thirds of the members present, of either house, may expel a member at pleasure. The senate is an independant branch of the legislature, a court for trying impeachments, and also a part of the executive, having a negative in the making of all treaties, and in appointing almost all officers.

6. The vice president is not a very important, if not an unnecessary part of the system—he may be a part of the senate at one period, and act as the supreme executive magistrate at another—The election of this officer, as well as of the president of the United States, seems to be properly secured; but when we examine the powers of the president, and the forms of the executive, we shall perceive that the general government, in this part, will have a strong tendency to aristocracy, or the government of the few. The executive is, in fact, the president and senate in all transactions of any importance; the president is connected with, or tied to the senate; he may always act with the senate, but never can effectually counteract its views: The president can appoint no officer, civil or military, who shall not be

18. Cf. *Brutus III* (11).

agreeable to the senate; and the presumption is, that the will of so important a body will not be very easily controuled, and that it will exercise its
powers with great address.

7. In the judicial department, powers ever kept distinct in well balanced
governments, are no less improperly blended in the hands of the same
men—in the judges of the supreme court is lodged, the law, the equity and
the fact.[19] It is not necessary to pursue the minute organical parts of the
general government proposed.—There were various interests in the convention, to be reconciled, especially of large and small states; of carrying
and non-carrying states; and of states more and states less democratic—vast
labour and attention were by the convention bestowed on the organization
of the parts of the constitution offered; still it is acknowledged there are
many things radically wrong in the essential parts of this constitution—but
it is said that these are the result of our situation: On a full examination of
the subject, I believe it; but what do the laborious inquiries and determinations of the convention prove? If they prove any thing, they prove that we
cannot consolidate the states on proper principles: The organization of the
government presented proves, that we cannot form a general government
in which all power can be safely lodged; and a little attention to the parts
of the one proposed will make it appear very evident, that all the powers
proposed to be lodged in it, will not be then well deposited, either for the
purposes of government, or the preservation of liberty. I will suppose no
abuse of powers in those cases, in which the abuse of it is not well guarded
against—I will suppose the words authorising the general government to
regulate the elections of its own members struck out of the plan, or free
district elections, in each state, amply secured.—That the small representation provided for shall be as fair and equal as it is capable of being made—I
will suppose the judicial department regulated on pure principles, by future
laws, as far as it can be by the constitution, and consistent with the situation
of the country—still there will be an unreasonable accumulation of powers
in the general government, if all be granted, enumerated in the plan proposed. The plan does not present a well balanced government.[20] The senatorial branch of the legislative and the executive are substantially united,
and the president, or the first executive magistrate, may aid the senatorial
interest when weakest, but never can effectually support the democratic,
however it may be oppressed;—the excellency, in my mind, of a well bal-

19. Cf. *Brutus XIII* (6–12).
20. Cf. *Brutus XVI* (12).

anced government is that it consists of distinct branches, each sufficiently strong and independant to keep its own station, and to aid either of the other branches which may occasionally want aid.[21]

8. The convention found that any but a small house of representatives would be expensive, and that it would be impracticable to assemble a large number of representatives. Not only the determination of the convention in this case, but the situation of the states, proves the impracticability of collecting, in any one point, a proper representation.

9. The formation of the senate, and the smallness of the house, being, therefore, the result of our situation, and the actual state of things, the evils which may attend the exercise of many powers in this national government may be considered as without a remedy.

10. All officers are impeachable before the senate only—before the men by whom they are appointed, or who are consenting to the appointment of these officers. No judgment of conviction, on an impeachment, can be given unless two thirds of the senators agree. Under these circumstances the right of impeachment, in the house, can be of but little importance; the house cannot expect often to convict the offender; and, therefore, probably, will but seldom or never exercise the right. In addition to the insecurity and inconveniences attending this organization beforementioned, it may be observed, that it is extremely difficult to secure the people against the fatal effects of corruption and influence. The power of making any law will be in the president, eight senators, and seventeen representatives, relative to the important objects enumerated in the constitution. Where there is a small representation a sufficient number to carry any measure, may, with ease, be influenced by bribes, offices and civilities; they may easily form private juntoes, and out door meetings, agree on measures, and carry them by silent votes.

11. Impressed, as I am, with a sense of the difficulties there are in the way of forming the parts of a federal government on proper principles, and seeing a government so unsubstantially organized, after so arduous an attempt has been made, I am led to believe, that powers ought to be given to it with great care and caution.

12. In the second place it is necessary, therefore, to examine the extent, and the probable operations of some of those extensive powers proposed to be vested in this government. These powers, legislative, executive, and judicial, respect internal as well as external objects. Those respecting external

21. Cf. *Brutus V* (1).

objects, as all foreign concerns, commerce, imposts, all causes arising on the seas, peace and war, and Indian affairs, can be lodged no where else, with any propriety, but in this government. Many powers that respect internal objects ought clearly to be lodged in it; as those to regulate trade between the states, weights and measures, the coin or current monies, post-offices, naturalization, etc. These powers may be exercised without essentially effecting the internal police of the respective states: But powers to lay and collect internal taxes, to form the militia, to make bankrupt laws, and to decide on appeals, questions arising on the internal laws of the respective states, are of a very serious nature, and carry with them almost all other powers. These taken in connection with the others, and powers to raise armies and build navies, proposed to be lodged in this government, appear to me to comprehend all the essential powers in the community, and those which will be left to the states will be of no great importance.

13. A power to lay and collect taxes at discretion, is, in itself, of very great importance. By means of taxes, the government may command the whole or any part of the subject's property. Taxes may be of various kinds; but there is a strong distinction between external and internal taxes.[22] External taxes are impost duties, which are laid on imported goods; they may usually be collected in a few seaport towns, and of a few individuals, though ultimately paid by the consumer; a few officers can collect them, and they can be carried no higher than trade will bear, or smuggling permit—that in the very nature of commerce, bounds are set to them. But internal taxes, as poll and land taxes, excises, duties on all written instruments, etc. may fix themselves on every person and species of property in the community; they may be carried to any lengths, and in proportion as they are extended, numerous officers must be employed to assess them, and to enforce the collection of them. In the United Netherlands the general government has compleat powers, as to external taxation; but as to internal taxes, it makes requisitions on the provinces. Internal taxation in this country is more important, as the country is so very extensive. As many assessors and collectors of federal taxes will be above three hundred miles from the seat of the federal government as will be less. Besides, to lay and collect internal taxes, in this extensive country, must require a great number of congressional ordinances, immediately operating upon the body of the people; these must continually interfere with the state laws, and thereby produce disorder and general dissatisfaction, till the one system of laws or the other, operating

22. Cf. *Brutus V* (13), *VII* (10).

upon the same subjects, shall be abolished. These ordinances alone, to say nothing of those respecting the militia, coin, commerce, federal judiciary, etc. etc. will probably soon defeat the operations of the state laws and governments.

14. Should the general government think it politic, as some administrations (if not all) probably will, to look for a support in a system of influence, the government will take every occasion to multiply laws, and officers to execute them, considering these as so many necessary props for its own support. Should this system of policy be adopted, taxes more productive than the impost duties will, probably, be wanted to support the government, and to discharge foreign demands, without leaving any thing for the domestic creditors. The internal sources of taxation then must be called into operation, and internal tax laws and federal assessors and collectors spread over this immense country. All these circumstances considered, is it wise, prudent, or safe, to vest the powers of laying and collecting internal taxes in the general government, while imperfectly organized and inadequate; and to trust to amending it hereafter, and making it adequate to this purpose? It is not only unsafe but absurd to lodge power in a government before it is fitted to receive it? [*sic*] It is confessed that this power and representation ought to go together. Why give the power first? Why give the power to the few, who, when possessed of it, may have address enough to prevent the increase of representation? Why not keep the power, and, when necessary, amend the constitution, and add to its other parts this power, and a proper increase of representation at the same time? Then men who may want the power will be under strong inducements to let in the people, by their representatives, into the government, to hold their due proportion of this power. If a proper representation be impracticable, then we shall see this power resting in the states, where it at present ought to be, and not inconsiderately given up.

15. When I recollect how lately congress, conventions, legislatures, and people contended in the cause of liberty, and carefully weighed the importance of taxation, I can scarcely believe we are serious in proposing to vest the powers of laying and collecting internal taxes in a government so imperfectly organized for such purposes. Should the United States be taxed by a house of representatives of two hundred members, which would be about fifteen members for Connecticut, twenty-five for Massachusetts, etc. still the middle and lower classes of people could have no great share, in fact, in taxation. I am aware it is said, that the representation proposed by the new constitution is sufficiently numerous; it may be for many purposes; but to

suppose that this branch is sufficiently numerous to guard the rights of the people in the administration of the government, in which the purse and sword is placed, seems to argue that we have forgot what the true meaning of representation is. I am sensible also, that it is said that congress will not attempt to lay and collect internal taxes; that it is necessary for them to have the power, though it cannot probably be exercised.—I admit that it is not probable that any prudent congress will attempt to lay and collect internal taxes, especially direct taxes: but this only proves, that the power would be improperly lodged in congress, and that it might be abused by imprudent and designing men.

16. I have heard several gentlemen, to get rid of objections to this part of the constitution, attempt to construe the powers relative to direct taxes, as those who object to it would have them; as to these, it is said, that congress will only have power to make requisitions, leaving it to the states to lay and collect them. I see but very little colour for this construction, and the attempt only proves that this part of the plan cannot be defended. By this plan there can be no doubt, but that the powers of congress will be complete as to all kinds of taxes whatever—Further, as to internal taxes, the state governments will have concurrent powers with the general government, and both may tax the same objects in the same year; and the objection that the general government may suspend a state tax, as a necessary measure for the promoting the collection of a federal tax, is not without foundation.[23]—As the states owe large debts, and have large demands upon them individually, there clearly would be a propriety in leaving in their possession exclusively, some of the internal sources of taxation, at least until the federal representation shall be properly encreased: The power in the general government to lay and collect internal taxes, will render its powers respecting armies, navies and the militia, the more exceptionable. By the constitution it is proposed that congress shall have power "to raise and support armies, but no appropriation of money to that use shall be for a longer term than two years; to provide and maintain a navy; to provide for calling forth the militia to execute the laws of the union, suppress insurrections, and repel invasions: to provide for organizing, arming, and disciplining the militia: reserving to the states the right to appoint the officers, and to train the militia according to the discipline prescribed by congress; congress will have unlimited power to raise armies, and to engage officers and men for any number of years; but a legislative act applying money for their support

23. Cf. *Brutus VI* (3–4).

can have operation for no longer term than two years, and if a subsequent congress do not within the two years renew the appropriation, or further appropriate monies for the use of the army, the army will be left to take care of itself." When an army shall once be raised for a number of years, it is not probable that it will find much difficulty in getting congress to pass laws for applying monies to its support. I see so many men in America fond of a standing army, and especially among those who probably will have a large share in administering the federal system; it is very evident to me, that we shall have a large standing army as soon as the monies to support them can be possibly found. An army is a very agreeable place of employment for the young gentlemen of many families. A power to raise armies must be lodged some where; still this will not justify the lodging this power in a bare majority of so few men without any checks; or in the government in which the great body of the people, in the nature of things, will be only nominally represented.[24] In the state governments the great body of the people, the yeomanry, etc. of the country, are represented: It is true they will chuse the members of congress, and may now and then chuse a man of their own way of thinking; but it is impossible for forty, or thirty thousand people in this country, one time in ten to find a man who can possess similar feelings, views, and interests with themselves: Powers to lay and collect taxes and to raise armies are of the greatest moment; for carrying them into effect, laws need not be frequently made, and the yeomanry, etc. of the country ought substantially to have a check upon the passing of these laws; this check ought to be placed in the legislatures, or at least, in the few men the common people of the country will, probably, have in congress, in the true sense of the word, "from among themselves." It is true, the yeomanry of the country possess the lands, the weight of property, possess arms, and are too strong a body of men to be openly offended—and, therefore, it is urged, they will take care of themselves, that men who shall govern will not dare pay any disrespect to their opinions. It is easily perceived, that if they have not their proper negative upon passing laws in congress, or on the passage of laws relative to taxes and armies, they may in twenty or thirty years be by means imperceptible to them, totally deprived of that boasted weight and strength: This may be done in a great measure by congress, if disposed to do it, by modelling the militia. Should one fifth, or one eighth part of the men capable of bearing arms, be made a select militia, as has been proposed, and those the young and ardent part of the community, possessed of

24. Cf. *Brutus X* (23).

but little or no property, and all the others put upon a plan that will render them of no importance, the former will answer all the purposes of an army, while the latter will be defenceless. The state must train the militia in such form and according to such systems and rules as congress shall prescribe: and the only actual influence the respective states will have respecting the militia will be in appointing the officers. I see no provision made for calling out the *posse comitatus* for executing the laws of the union, but provision is made for congress to call forth the militia for the execution of them—and the militia in general, or any select part of it, may be called out under military officers, instead of the sheriff to enforce an execution of federal laws, in the first instance and thereby introduce an entire military execution of the laws. I know that powers to raise taxes, to regulate the military strength of the community on some uniform plan, to provide for its defence and internal order, and for duly executing the laws, must be lodged somewhere; but still we ought not so to lodge them, as evidently to give one order of men in the community, undue advantages over others; or commit the many to the mercy, prudence, and moderation of the few. And so far as it may be necessary to lodge any of the peculiar powers in the general government, a more safe exercise of them ought to be secured, by requiring the consent of two-thirds or three-fourths of congress thereto—until the federal representation can be increased, so that the democratic members in congress may stand some tolerable chance of a reasonable negative, in behalf of the numerous, important, and democratic part of the community.

17. I am not sufficiently acquainted with the laws and internal policy of all the states to discern fully, how general bankrupt laws, made by the union, would effect them, or promote the public good. I believe the property of debtors, in the several states, is held responsible for their debts in modes and forms very different. If uniform bankrupt laws can be made without producing real and substantial inconveniences, I wish them to be made by congress.[25]

There are some powers proposed to be lodged in the general government in the judicial department, I think very unnecessarily, I mean powers respecting questions arising upon the internal laws of the respective states.[26] It is proper the federal judiciary should have powers co-extensive with the federal legislature—that is, the power of deciding finally on the laws of the union. By Art. 3. Sect. 2. the powers of the federal judiciary

25. On *FF*'s change of mind, see *XVIII* (8).
26. Also see *FF XV.*

are extended (among other things) to all cases between a state and citizens of another state—between citizens of different states—between a state or the citizens thereof, and foreign states, citizens or subjects. Actions in all these cases, except against a state government, are now brought and finally determined in the law courts of the states respectively; and as there are no words to exclude these courts of their jurisdiction in these cases, they will have concurrent jurisdiction with the inferior federal courts in them; and, therefore, if the new constitution be adopted without any amendment in this respect, all those numerous actions, now brought in the state courts between our citizens and foreigners, between citizens of different states, by state governments against foreigners, and by state governments against citizens of other states, may also be brought in the federal courts; and an appeal will lay in them from the state courts, or federal inferior courts, to the supreme judicial court of the union. In almost all these cases, either party may have the trial by jury in the state courts; excepting paper money and tender laws, which are wisely guarded against in the proposed constitution, justice may be obtained in these courts on reasonable terms; they must be more competent to proper decisions on the laws of their respective states, than the federal courts can possibly be. I do not, in any point of view, see the need of opening a new jurisdiction to these causes—of opening a new scene of expensive law suits—of suffering foreigners, and citizens of different states, to drag each other many hundred miles into the federal courts. It is true, those courts may be so organized by a wise and prudent legislature, as to make the obtaining of justice in them tolerably easy; they may in general be organized on the common law principles of the country: But this benefit is by no means secured by the constitution. The trial by jury is secured only in those few criminal cases, to which the federal laws will extend—as crimes committed on the seas, against the laws of nations, treason, and counterfeiting the federal securities and coin: But even in these cases, the jury trial of the vicinage is not secured—particularly in the large states, a citizen may be tried for a crime committed in the state, and yet tried in some states 500 miles from the place where it was committed; but the jury trial is not secured at all in civil causes. Though the convention have not established this trial, it is to be hoped that congress, in putting the new system into execution, will do it by a legislative act, in all cases in which it can be done with propriety. Whether the jury trial is not excluded from the supreme judicial court, is an important question. By Art. 3. Sect. 2. all cases affecting ambassadors, other public ministers, and consuls, and in those cases in which a state shall be party, the supreme court shall have jurisdiction. In all the other cases beforementioned, the supreme court shall have appellate jurisdiction, both as to *law and fact*, with such exception, and under such regulations, as the congress shall make. By court is understood a court consisting of judges; and the idea of a jury is excluded. This court, or the judges, are to have jurisdiction on appeals, in all the cases enumerated, as to law and fact; the judges are to decide the law and try the fact, and the trial of the fact being assigned to the judges by the constitution, a jury for trying the fact is excluded; however, under the exceptions and powers to make regulations, congress may, perhaps introduce the jury, to try the fact in most necessary cases.

18. There can be but one supreme court in which the final jurisdiction will centre in all federal causes—except in cases where appeals by law shall not be allowed: The judicial powers of the federal courts extends in law and equity to certain cases: and, therefore, the powers to determine on the law, in equity, and as to the fact, all will concentre in the supreme court:—These powers, which by this constitution are blended in the same hands, the same judges, are in Great-Britain deposited in different hands—to wit, the decision of the law in the law judges, the decision in equity in the chancellor, and the trial of the fact in the jury. It is a very dangerous thing to vest in the same judge power to decide on the law, and also general powers in equity; for if the law restrain him, he is only to step into his shoes of equity, and give what judgment his reason or opinion may dictate; we have no precedents in this country, as yet, to regulate the divisions in equity as in Great Britain; equity, therefore, in the supreme court for many years will be mere discretion. I confess in the constitution of this supreme court, as left by the constitution, I do not see a spark of freedom or a shadow of our own or the British common law.

19. This court is to have appellate jurisdiction in all the other cases before mentioned: Many sensible men suppose that cases before mentioned respect, as well the criminal cases as the civil ones, mentioned antecedently in the constitution, if so an appeal is allowed in criminal cases—contrary to the usual sense of law.[27] How far it may be proper to admit a foreigner or the citizen of another state to bring actions against state governments, which have failed in performing so many promises made during the war, is doubtful: How far it may be proper so to humble a state, as to oblige it to answer to an individual in a court of law, is worthy of consideration; the states are now subject to no such actions; and this new jurisdic-

27. Cf. *Brutus XIV* (6–8).

tion will subject the states, and many defendants to actions, and processes, which were not in the contemplation of the parties, when the contract was made; all engagements existing between citizens of different states, citizens and foreigners, states and foreigners; and states and citizens of other states were made the parties contemplating the remedies then existing on the laws of the states—and the new remedy proposed to be given in the federal courts, can be founded on no principle whatever.[28]

Your's &c.
The Federal Farmer.

– IV –

October 12th, 1787

Dear Sir,

1. It will not be possible to establish in the federal courts the jury trial of the vicinage so well as in the state courts.

2. Third. There appears to me to be not only a premature deposit of some important powers in the general government—but many of those deposited there are undefined, and may be used to good or bad purposes as honest or designing men shall prevail. By Art. 1. Sect. 2, representatives and direct taxes shall be apportioned among the several states, etc.—same art. sect. 8, the congress shall have powers to lay and collect taxes, duties, etc. for the common defence and general welfare, but all duties, imposts and excises, shall be uniform throughout the United States: By the first recited clause, direct taxes shall be apportioned on the states. This seems to favour the idea suggested by some sensible men and writers, that congress, as to direct taxes, will only have power to make requisitions, but the latter clause, power to lay and collect taxes, etc. seems clearly to favour the contrary opinion and, in my mind, the true one, that congress shall have power to tax immediately individuals, without the intervention of the state legislatures; in fact the first clause appears to me only to provide that each state shall pay a certain portion of the tax, and the latter to provide that congress shall have power to lay and collect taxes, that is to assess upon, and to collect of the individuals in the state, the state's quota; but these still I consider as undefined powers, because judicious men understand them differently.

3. It is doubtful whether the vice president is to have any qualifications;

28. Cf. *Brutus XIII* (3–4).

none are mentioned; but he may serve as president, and it may be inferred, he ought to be qualified therefore as the president; but the qualifications of the president are required only of the person to be elected president. By art. 2, sect. 2. "But the congress may by law vest the appointment of such inferior officers as they think proper in the president alone, in the courts of law, or in the heads of the departments": Who are inferior officers? May not a congress disposed to vest the appointment of all officers in the president, under this clause, vest the appointment of almost every officer in the president alone, and destroy the check mentioned in the first part of the clause, and lodged in the senate. It is true, this check is badly lodged, but then some check upon the first magistrate in appointing officers, ought it appears by the opinion of the convention, and by the general opinion, to be established in the constitution. By art. 3, sect. 2, the supreme court shall have appellate jurisdiction as to law and facts with such exceptions, etc. to what extent is it intended the exceptions shall be carried—Congress may carry them so far as to annihilate substantially the appellate jurisdiction, and the clause be rendered of very little importance.[29]

4. [4th] There are certain rights which we have always held sacred in the United States, and recognized in all our constitutions, and which, by the adoption of the new constitution in its present form, will be left unsecured. By article 6, the proposed constitution, and the laws of the United States, which shall be made in pursuance thereof; and all treaties made, or which shall be made under the authority of the United States, shall be the supreme law of the land; and the judges in every state shall be bound thereby; any thing in the constitution or laws of any state to the contrary notwithstanding.

5. It is to be observed that when the people shall adopt the proposed constitution it will be their last and supreme act; it will be adopted not by the people of New-Hampshire, Massachusetts, etc. but by the people of the United States; and wherever this constitution, or any part of it, shall be incompatible with the ancient customs, rights, the laws or the constitutions heretofore established in the United States, it will entirely abolish them and do them away: And not only this, but the laws of the United States which shall be made in pursuance of the federal constitution will be also supreme laws, and wherever they shall be incompatible with those customs, rights, laws or constitutions heretofore established, they will also entirely abolish them and do them away.

29. Cf. *Brutus XIV* (26).

6. By the article before recited, treaties also made under the authority of the United States, shall be the supreme law: It is not said that these treaties shall be made in pursuance of the constitution—nor are there any constitutional bounds set to those who shall make them: The president and two thirds of the senate will be empowered to make treaties indefinitely, and when these treaties shall be made, they will also abolish all laws and state constitutions incompatible with them. This power in the president and senate is absolute, and the judges will be bound to allow full force to whatever rule, article or thing the president and senate shall establish by treaty, whether it be practicable to set any bounds to those who make treaties, I am not able to say: if not, it proves that this power ought to be more safely lodged.

7. The federal constitution, the laws of congress made in pursuance of the constitution, and all treaties must have full force and effect in all parts of the United States; and all other laws, rights and constitutions which stand in their way must yield: It is proper the national laws should be supreme, and superior to state or district laws: but then the national laws ought to yield to unalienable or fundamental rights—and national laws, made by a few men, should extend only to a few national objects.[30] This will not be the case with the laws of congress: To have any proper idea of their extent, we must carefully examine the legislative, executive and judicial powers proposed to be lodged in the general government, and consider them in connection with a general clause in art. 1. sect. 8, in these words (after inumerating a number of powers) "To make all laws which shall be necessary and proper for carrying into execution the foregoing powers, and all other powers vested by this constitution in the government of the United States, or in any department or officer thereof."—The powers of this government as has been observed, extend to internal as well as external objects, and to those objects to which all others are subordinate; it is almost impossible to have a just conception of these powers, or of the extent and number of the laws which may be deemed necessary and proper to carry them into effect, till we shall come to exercise those powers and make the laws. In making laws to carry those powers into effect, it is to be expected, that a wise and prudent congress will pay respect to the opinions of a free people, and bottom their laws on those principles which have been considered as essential and fundamental in the British, and in our government. But a congress of a

30. Cf. *Brutus XIII* (1).

different character will not be bound by the constitution to pay respect to those principles.

8. It is said, that when the people make a constitution, and delegate powers that all powers not delegated by them to those who govern is [*sic*] reserved in the people; and that the people, in the present case, have reserved in themselves, and in their state governments, every right and power not expressly given by the federal constitution to those who shall administer the national government.[31] It is said on the other hand, that the people, when they make a constitution, yield all power not expressly reserved to themselves.[32] The truth is, in either case, it is mere matter of opinion and men usually take either side of the argument, as will best answer their purposes: But the general presumption being, that men who govern, will, in doubtful cases, construe laws and constitutions most favourably for encreasing their own powers; all wise and prudent people, in forming constitutions, have drawn the line, and carefully described the powers parted with and the powers reserved. By the state constitutions, certain rights have been reserved in the people; or rather, they have been recognized and established in such a manner, that state legislatures are bound to respect them, and to make no laws infringing upon them. The state legislatures are obliged to take notice of the bills of rights of their respective states. The bills of rights, and the state constitutions, are fundamental compacts only between those who govern, and the people of the same state.

9. In the year 1788 the people of the United States make a federal constitution, which is a fundamental compact between them and their federal rulers; these rulers, in the nature of things, cannot be bound to take notice of any other compact. It would be absurd for them, in making laws, to look over thirteen, fifteen, or twenty state constitutions, to see what rights are established as fundamental, and must not be infringed upon, in making laws in the society. It is true, they would be bound to do it if the people, in their federal compact, should refer to the state constitutions, recognize all parts not inconsistent with the federal constitution, and direct their federal rulers to take notice of them accordingly; but this is not the case, as the plan stands proposed at present; and it is absurd, to suppose so unnatural an idea is intended or implied. I think my opinion is not only founded in reason,

31. James Wilson most famously made this argument in opposing Anti-Federalist demands for a bill of rights. For another Anti-Federalist response, see *Brutus II* (6).

32. See also *FF XVI*.

but I think it is supported by the report of the convention itself. If there are a number of rights established by the state constitutions, and which will remain sacred, and the general government is bound to take notice of them—it must take notice of one as well as another; and if unnecessary to recognize or establish one by the federal constitution, it would be unnecessary to recognize or establish another by it.[33] If the federal constitution is to be construed so far in connection with the state constitutions, as to leave the trial by jury in civil causes, for instance, secured; on the same principles it would have left the trial by jury in criminal causes, the benefits of the writ of habeas corpus, etc. secured; they all stand on the same footing; they are the common rights of Americans, and have been recognized by the state constitutions: But the convention found it necessary to recognize or re-establish the benefits of that writ, and the jury trial in criminal cases. As to *expost facto* laws, the convention has done the same in one case, and gone further in another. It is part of the compact between the people of each state and their rulers, that no *expost facto* laws shall be made. But the convention, by Art. I Sect. 10 have put a sanction upon this part even of the state compacts. In fact, the 9th and 10th Sections in Art. I. in the proposed constitution, are no more nor less, than a partial bill of rights; they establish certain principles as part of the compact upon which the federal legislators and officers can never infringe. It is here wisely stipulated, that the federal legislature shall never pass a bill of attainder, or *expost facto* law; that no tax shall be laid on articles exported, etc. The establishing of one right implies the necessity of establishing another and similar one.

10. On the whole, the position appears to me to be undeniable, that this bill of rights ought to be carried farther, and some other principles established, as a part of this fundamental compact between the people of the United States and their federal rulers.

11. It is true, we are not disposed to differ much, at present, about religion; but when we are making a constitution, it is to be hoped, for ages and millions yet unborn, why not establish the free exercise of religion, as a part of the national compact. There are other essential rights, which we have justly understood to be the rights of freemen; as freedom from hasty and unreasonable search warrants, warrants not founded on oath, and not issued with due caution, for searching and seizing men's papers, property, and persons. The trials by jury in civil causes, it is said, vary so much in

33. Cf. *Brutus II* (13).

the several states, that no words could be found for the uniform establishment of it. If so, the federal legislation will not be able to establish it by any
general laws. I confess I am of opinion it may be established, but not in that
beneficial manner in which we may enjoy it, for the reasons beforementioned. When I speak of the jury trial of the vicinage, or the trial of the fact
in the neighbourhood,—I do not lay so much stress upon the circumstance
of our being tried by our neighbours: in this enlightened country men may
be probably impartially tried by those who do not live very near them: but
the trial of facts in the neighbourhood is of great importance in other respects. Nothing can be more essential than the cross examining witnesses,
and generally before the triers of the facts in question. The common people
can establish facts with much more ease with oral than written evidence;
when trials of facts are removed to a distance from the homes of the parties and witnesses, oral evidence becomes intolerably expensive, and the
parties must depend on written evidence, which to the common people is
expensive and almost useless; it must be frequently taken ex parte, and but
very seldom leads to the proper discovery of truth.[34]

   12. The trial by jury is very important in another point of view. It is essential in every free country, that common people should have a part and
share of influence, in the judicial as well as in the legislative department. To
hold open to them the offices of senators, judges, and offices to fill which an
expensive education is required, cannot answer any valuable purposes for
them; they are not in a situation to be brought forward and to fill those offices; these, and most other offices of any considerable importance, will be
occupied by the few. The few, the well born, etc. as Mr. Adams calls them, in
judicial decisions as well as in legislation, are generally disposed, and very
naturally too, to favour those of their own description.[35]

   13. The trial by jury in the judicial department, and the collection of the
people by their representatives in the legislature, are those fortunate inven-
tions which have procured for them, in this country, their true proportion
of influence, and the wisest and most fit means of protecting themselves
in the community. Their situation, as jurors and representatives, enables
them to acquire information and knowledge in the affairs and government
of the society; and to come forward, in turn, as the centinels and guardians
of each other. I am very sorry that even a few of our countrymen should
consider jurors and representatives in a different point of view, as ignorant

34. Cf. *Brutus II* (13).
35. John Adams, *Defence* I, preface (*Works*, IV, 290–91).

troublesome bodies, which ought not to have any share in the concerns of government.

14. I confess I do not see in what cases the congress can, with any pretence of right, make a law to suppress the freedom of the press; though I am not clear, that congress is restrained from laying any duties whatever on printing, and from laying duties particularly heavy on certain pieces printed, and perhaps congress may require large bonds for the payment of these duties. Should the printer say, the freedom of the press was secured by the constitution of the state in which he lived, congress might, and perhaps, with great propriety, answer, that the federal constitution is the only compact existing between them and the people; in this compact the people have named no others, and therefore congress, in exercising the powers assigned them, and in making laws to carry them into execution, are restrained by nothing beside the federal constitution, any more than a state legislature is restrained by a compact between the magistrates and people of a county, city, or town of which the people, in forming the state constitution, have taken no notice.

15. It is not my object to enumerate rights of inconsiderable importance; but there are others, no doubt, which ought to be established as a fundamental part of the national system.

16. It is worthy observation, that all treaties are made by foreign nations with a confederacy of thirteen states—that the western country is attached to thirteen states—thirteen states have jointly and severally engaged to pay the public debts.—Should a new government be formed of nine, ten, eleven, or twelve states, those treaties could not be considered as binding on the foreign nations who made them. However, I believe the probability to be, that if nine states adopt the constitution, the others will.

17. It may also be worthy our examination, how far the provision for amending this plan, when it shall be adopted, is of any importance. No measures can be taken towards amendments, unless two-thirds of the congress, or two-thirds of the legislatures of the several states shall agree.— While power is in the hands of the people, or democratic part of the community, more especially as at present, it is easy, according to the general course of human affairs, for the few influential men in the community, to obtain conventions, alterations in government, and to persuade the common people they may change for the better, and to get from them a part of the power: But when power is once transferred from the many to the few, all changes become extremely difficult; the government, in this case, being beneficial to the few, they will be exceedingly artful and adroit in prevent-

ing any measures which may lead to a change; and nothing will produce it, but great exertions and severe struggles on the part of the common people. Every man of reflection must see, that the change now proposed, is a transfer of power from the many to the few, and the probability is, the artful and ever active aristocracy, will prevent all peaceable measures for changes, unless when they shall discover some favourable moment to increase their own influence.[36] I am sensible, thousands of men in the United States, are disposed to adopt the proposed constitution, though they perceive it to be essentially defective, under an idea that amendments of it, may be obtained when necessary. This is a pernicious idea, it argues a servility of character totally unfit for the support of free government; it is very repugnant to that perpetual jealousy respecting liberty, so absolutely necessary in all free states, spoken of by Mr. Dickinson.[37]—However, if our countrymen are so soon changed, and the language of 1774, is become odious to them, it will be in vain to use the language of freedom, or to attempt to rouse them to free enquiries: But I shall never believe this is the case with them, whatever present appearances may be, till I shall have very strong evidence indeed of it.

Your's, &c.
The Federal Farmer.

– V –

October 13th, 1787

Dear Sir,

1. Thus I have examined the federal constitution as far as a few days leisure would permit. It opens to my mind a new scene; instead of seeing powers cautiously lodged in the hands of numerous legislators, and many magistrates, we see all important powers collecting in one centre, where a few men will possess them almost at discretion. And instead of checks in the formation of the government, to secure the rights of the people against the usurpations of those they appoint to govern, we are to understand the equal division of lands among our people, and the strong arm furnished them by nature and situation, are to secure them against those usurpations. If there

36. See also *FF VI* (5); "Address by a Plebeian to the People of the State of New York, 1788," paragraph 3, in this book.

37. *Empire and Nation: Letters from a Farmer in Pennsylvania*, XI (John Dickinson), *Letters from the* Federal Farmer (Richard Henry Lee), ed. Forrest McDonald (Indianapolis: Liberty Fund), 1999.

are advantages in the equal division of our lands, and the strong and manly habits of our people, we ought to establish governments calculated to give duration to them, and not governments which never can work naturally, till that equality of property, and those free and manly habits shall be destroyed; these evidently are not the natural basis of the proposed constitution. No man of reflection, and skilled in the science of government, can suppose these will move on harmoniously together for ages, or even for fifty years.[38] As to the little circumstances commented upon, by some writers, with applause—as the age of a representative, of the president, etc.—they have, in my mind, no weight in the general tendency of the system.

2. There are, however, in my opinion, many good things in the proposed system. It is founded on elective principles, and the deposits of powers in different hands, is essentially right. The guards against those evils we have experienced in some states in legislation are valuable indeed; but the value of every feature in this system is vastly lessened for the want of that one important feature in a free government, a representation of the people. Because we have sometimes abused democracy, I am not among those men who think a democratic branch a nuisance; which branch shall be sufficiently numerous, to admit some of the best informed men of each order in the community into the administration of government.

3. While the radical defects in the proposed system are not so soon discovered, some temptations to each state, and to many classes of men to adopt it, are very visible. It uses the democratic language of several of the state constitutions, particularly that of Massachusetts; the eastern states will receive advantages so far as the regulation of trade, by a bare majority, is committed to it: Connecticut and New-Jersey will receive their share of a general impost: The middle states will receive the advantages surrounding the seat of government: The southern states will receive protection, and have their negroes represented in the legislature, and large back countries will soon have a majority in it. This system promises a large field of employment to military gentlemen, and gentlemen of the law; and in case the government shall be executed without convulsions, it will afford security to creditors, to the clergy, salary-men and others depending on money payments. So far as the system promises justice and reasonable advantages, in these respects, it ought to be supported by all honest men: but whenever it promises unequal and improper advantages to any particular states, or orders of men, it ought to be opposed.

38. See also *FF VI* (5).

4. I have, in the course of these letters observed, that there are many good things in the proposed constitution, and I have endeavoured to point out many important defects in it. I have admitted that we want a federal system—that we have a system presented, which, with several alterations may be made a tolerable good one—I have admitted there is a well founded uneasiness among creditors and mercantile men. In this situation of things, you ask me what I think ought to be done? My opinion in this case is only the opinion of an individual, and so far only as it corresponds with the opinions of the honest and substantial part of the community, is it entitled to consideration. Though I am fully satisfied that the state conventions ought most seriously to direct their exertions to altering and amending the system proposed before they shall adopt it—yet I have not sufficiently examined the subject, or formed an opinion, how far it will be practicable for those conventions to carry their amendments. As to the idea, that it will be in vain for those conventions to attempt amendments, it cannot be admitted; it is impossible to say whether they can or not until the attempt shall be made; and when it shall be determined, by experience, that the conventions cannot agree in amendments, it will then be an important question before the people of the United States, whether they will adopt or not the system proposed in its present form. This subject of consolidating the states is new; and because forty or fifty men have agreed in a system, to suppose the good sense of this country, an enlightened nation, must adopt it without examination, and though in a state of profound peace, without endeavouring to amend those parts they perceive are defective, dangerous to freedom, and destructive of the valuable principles of republican government—is truly humiliating. It is true there may be danger in delay; but there is danger in adopting the system in its present form; and I see the danger in either case will arise principally from the conduct and views of two very unprincipled parties in the United States—two fires, between which the honest and substantial people have long found themselves situated. One party is composed of little insurgents, men in debt, who want no law, and who want a share of the property of others; these are called levellers, Shayites, etc.[39] The other party is composed of a few, but more dangerous men, with their servile dependents; these avariciously grasp at all power

39. The levelers, a group of radicals during the English civil war of the seventeenth century, were widely perceived to be enemies of private property. Shayites were followers of Daniel Shays, who led an abortive debtors' movement against foreclosures in 1786–87 in Massachusetts.

and property; you may discover in all the actions of these men, an evident dislike to free and equal government, and they will go systematically to work to change, essentially, the forms of government in this country; these are called aristocrats, M[onarch]ites, etc. etc. Between these two parties is the weight of the community; the men of middling property, men not in debt on the one hand, and men, on the other, content with republican governments, and not aiming at immense fortunes, offices, and power. In 1786, the little insurgents, the levellers, came forth, invaded the rights of others, and attempted to establish governments according to their wills. Their movements evidently gave encouragement to the other party, which, in 1787, has taken the political field, and with its fashionable dependants, and the tongue and the pen, is endeavouring to establish in great haste, a politer kind of government. These two parties, which will probably be opposed or united as it may suit their interests and views, are really insignificant, compared with the solid, free, and independent part of the community. It is not my intention to suggest, that either of these parties, and the real friends of the proposed constitution, are the same men. The fact is, these aristocrats support and hasten the adoption of the proposed constitution, merely because they think it is a stepping stone to their favorite object. I think I am well founded in this idea; I think the general politics of these men support it, as well as the common observation among them. That the proffered plan is the best that can be got at present, it will do for a few years, and lead to something better. The sensible and judicious part of the community will carefully weigh all these circumstances; they will view the late convention as a respectable assembly of men—America probably never will see an assembly of men of a like number, more respectable. But the members of the convention met without knowing the sentiments of one man in ten thousand in these states, respecting the new ground taken. Their doings are but the first attempts in the most important scene ever opened. Though each individual in the state conventions will not, probably, be so respectable as each individual in the federal convention, yet as the state conventions will probably consist of fifteen hundred or two thousand men of abilities, and versed in the science of government, collected from all parts of the community and from all orders of men, it must be acknowledged that the weight of respectability will be in them—In them will be collected the solid sense and the real political character of the country. Being revisers of the subject, they will possess peculiar advantages. To say that these conventions ought not to attempt, coolly and deliberately, the revision of the system, or that they cannot amend it, is very foolish or very assuming. If these conventions, after examining the system, adopt it, I shall be perfectly satisfied, and wish to see men make the administration of the government an equal blessing to all orders of men. I believe the great body of our people to be virtuous and friendly to good government, to the protection of liberty and property; and it is the duty of all good men, especially of those who are placed as centinels to guard their rights—it is their duty to examine into the prevailing politics of parties, and to disclose them—while they avoid exciting undue suspicions, to lay facts before the people, which will enable them to form a proper judgment. Men who wish the people of this country to determine for themselves, and deliberately to fit the government to their situation, must feel some degree of indignation at those attempts to hurry the adoption of a system, and to shut the door against examination. The very attempts create suspicions, that those who make them have secret views, or see some defects in the system, which, in the hurry of affairs, they expect will escape the eye of a free people.

5. What can be the views of those gentlemen in Pennsylvania, who precipitated decisions on this subject?[40] What can be the views of those gentlemen in Boston, who countenanced the Printers in shutting up the press against a fair and free investigation of this important system in the usual way?[41] The members of the convention have done their duty—why should some of them fly to their states—almost forget a propriety of behaviour, and precipitate measures for the adoption of a system of their own making? I confess candidly, when I consider these circumstances in connection with the unguarded parts of the system I have mentioned, I feel disposed to proceed with very great caution, and to pay more attention than usual to the conduct of particular characters. If the constitution presented be a good one, it will stand the test with a well informed people: all are agreed there shall be state conventions to examine it; and we must believe it will be adopted, unless we suppose it is a bad one, or that those conven-

40. The party controlling the legislature in Pennsylvania pushed for a very quick consideration of the Constitution. On December 7, 1787, Pennsylvania became the second state, after Delaware, to ratify it. Unlike in Delaware, however, ratification in Pennsylvania was far from unanimous, and Anti-Federalists were bitter because they felt the Constitution had too hastily been rammed down their throats.

41. Printers in Boston began to demand that writers on the Constitution leave their names with the printers. Thus, the anonymity and the relative freedom from private intimidation that typified political writing at the time were in danger of being compromised. See "Philadelphiensis" in Storing, III, 103–5.

tions will make false divisions respecting it. I admit improper measures are taken against the adoption of the system as well as for it—all who object to the plan proposed ought to point out the defects objected to, and to propose those amendments with which they can accept it, or to propose some other system of government, that the public mind may be known, and that we may be brought to agree in some system of government, to strengthen and execute the present, or to provide a substitute. I consider the field of enquiry just opened, and that we are to look to the state conventions for ultimate decisions on the subject before us; it is not to be presumed, that they will differ about small amendments, and lose a system when they shall have made it substantially good; but touching the essential amendments, it is to be presumed the several conventions will pursue the most rational measures to agree in and obtain them; and such defects as they shall discover and not remove, they will probably notice, keep them in view as the ground work of future amendments, and in the firm and manly language which every free people ought to use, will suggest to those who may hereafter administer the government, that it is their expectation, that the system will be so organized by legislative acts, and the government so administered, as to render those defects as little injurious as possible. Our countrymen are entitled to an honest and faithful government; to a government of laws and not of men; and also to one of their chusing—as a citizen of the country, I wish to see these objects secured, and licentious, assuming, and overbearing men restrained; if the constitution or social compact be vague and unguarded, then we depend wholly upon the prudence, wisdom and moderation of those who manage the affairs of government; or on what, probably, is equally uncertain and precarious, the success of the people oppressed by the abuse of government, in receiving it from the hands of those who abuse it, and placing it in the hands of those who will use it well.

6. In every point of view, therefore, in which I have been able, as yet, to contemplate this subject, I can discern but one rational mode of proceeding relative to it: and that is to examine it with freedom and candour, to have state conventions some months hence, which shall examine coolly every article, clause, and word in the system proposed, and to adopt it with such amendments as they shall think fit. How far the state conventions ought to pursue the mode prescribed by the federal convention of adopting or rejecting the plan in toto, I leave it to them to determine. Our examination of the subject hitherto has been rather of a general nature. The republican characters in the several states, who wish to make this plan more adequate to security of liberty and property, and to the duration of the principles of

a free government, will, no doubt, collect their opinions to certain points, and accurately define those alterations and amendments they wish; if it shall be found they essentially disagree in them, the conventions will then be able to determine whether to adopt the plan as it is, or what will be proper to be done.

7. Under these impressions, and keeping in view the improper and un-advisable lodgment of powers in the general government, organized as it at present is, touching internal taxes, armies and militia, the elections of its own members, causes between citizens of different states, etc. and the want of a more perfect bill of rights, etc. I drop the subject for the present, and when I shall have leisure to revise and correct my ideas respecting it, and to collect into points the opinions of those who wish to make the system more secure and safe, perhaps I may proceed to point out particularly for your consideration, the amendments which ought to be ingrafted into this system, not only in conformity to my own, but the deliberate opinions of others—you will with me perceive, that the objections to the plan proposed may, by a more leisure examination be set in a stronger point of view, espe-cially the important one, that there is no substantial representation of the people provided for in a government in which the most essential powers, even as to the internal police of the country, is proposed to be lodged.

8. I think the honest and substantial part of the community will wish to see this system altered, permanency and consistency given to the con-stitution we shall adopt; and therefore they will be anxious to apportion the powers to the features and organization of the government, and to see abuse in the exercise of power more effectually guarded against. It is sug-gested, that state officers, from interested motives will oppose the constitu-tion presented—I see no reason for this, their places in general will not be effected, but new openings to offices and places of profit must evidently be made by the adoption of the constitution in its present form.

Your's &c.
The Federal Farmer.

– VI –

December 25, 1787

Dear Sir,

1. My former letters to you, respecting the constitution proposed, were calculated merely to lead to a fuller investigation of the subject; having more extensively considered it, and the opinions of others relative to it,

I shall, in a few letters, more particularly endeavour to point out the defects, and propose amendments. I shall in this make only a few general and introductory observations, which, in the present state of the momentous question, may not be improper; and I leave you, in all cases, to decide by a careful examination of my works, upon the weight of my arguments, the propriety of my remarks, the uprightness of my intentions, and the extent of my candor—I presume I am writing to a man of candor and reflection, and not to an ardent, peevish, or impatient man.

2. When the constitution was first published, there appeared to prevail a misguided zeal to prevent a fair unbiassed examination of a subject of infinite importance to this people and their posterity—to the cause of liberty and the rights of mankind—and it was the duty of those who saw a restless ardor, or design, attempting to mislead the people by a parade of names and misrepresentations, to endeavour to prevent their having their intended effects. The only way to stop the passions of men in their career is, coolly to state facts, and deliberately to avow the truth—and to do this we are frequently forced into a painful view of men and measures.

3. Since I wrote to you in October, I have heard much said, and seen many pieces written, upon the subject in question; and on carefully examining them on both sides, I find much less reason for changing my sentiments, respecting the good and defective parts of the system proposed than I expected—The opposers, as well as the advocates of it, confirm me in my opinion, that this system affords, all circumstances considered, a better basis to build upon than the confederation. And as to the principal defects, as the smallness of the representation, the insecurity of elections, the undue mixture of powers in the senate, the insecurity of some essential rights, &c. the opposition appears, generally, to agree respecting them, and many of the ablest advocates virtually to admit them—Clear it is, the latter do not attempt manfully to defend these defective parts, but to cover them with a mysterious veil; they concede, they retract; they say we could do no better; and some of them, when a little out of temper, and hard pushed, use arguments that do more honor to their ingenuity, than to their candor and firmness.

4. Three states have now adopted the constitution without amendments;[42] these, and other circumstances, ought to have their weight in deciding the question, whether we will put the system into operation, adopt it, enumerate and recommend the necessary amendments, which afterwards, by

42. Delaware, Pennsylvania, and New Jersey.

three-fourths of the states, may be ingrafted into the system, or whether we will make the amendments prior to the adoption—I only undertake to shew amendments are essential and necessary—how far it is practicable to ingraft them into the plan, prior to the adoption, the state conventions must determine. Our situation is critical, and we have but our choice of evils—We may hazard much by adopting the constitution in its present form—we may hazard more by rejecting it wholly—we may hazard much by long contending about amendments prior to the adoption. The greatest political evils that can befall us, are discords and civil wars—the greatest blessings we can wish for, are peace, union, and industry, under a mild, free, and steady government. Amendments recommended will tend to guard and direct the administration—but there will be danger that the people, after the system shall be adopted, will become inattentive to amendments—Their attention is now awake—the discussion of the subject, which has already taken place, has had a happy effect—it has called forth the able advocates of liberty, and tends to renew, in the minds of the people, their true republican jealousy and vigilance, the strongest guard against the abuses of power; but the vigilance of the people is not sufficiently constant to be depended on— Fortunate it is for the body of a people, if they can continue attentive to their liberties, long enough to erect for them a temple, and constitutional barriers for their permanent security: when they are well fixed between the powers of the rulers and the rights of the people, they become visible boundaries, constantly seen by all, and any transgression of them is immediately discovered: they serve as centinels for the people at all times, and especially in those unavoidable intervals of inattention.

5. Some of the advocates, I believe, will agree to recommend *good* amendments; but some of them will only consent to recommend indefinite, specious, but unimportant ones; and this only with a view to keep the door open for obtaining in some favourable moment, their main object, a complete consolidation of the states, and a government much higher toned, less republican and free than the one proposed. If necessity, therefore, should ever oblige us to adopt the system, and recommend amendments, the true friends of a federal republic must see they are well defined, and well calculated, not only to prevent our system of government moving further from republican principles and equality, but to bring it back nearer to them— they must be constantly on their guard against the address, flattery, and manoeuvres of their adversaries.

6. The gentlemen who oppose the constitution, or contend for amendments in it, are frequently, and with much bitterness, charged with wan-

tonly attacking the men who framed it. The unjustness of this charge leads me to make one observation upon the conduct of parties, &c. Some of the advocates are only pretended federalists; in fact they wish for an abolition of the state governments. Some of them I believe to be honest federalists, who wish to preserve *substantially* the state governments united under an efficient federal head; and many of them are blind tools without any object. Some of the opposers also are only pretended federalists, who want no federal government, or one merely advisory. Some of them are the true federalists, their object, perhaps, more clearly seen, is the same with that of the honest federalists; and some of them, probably, have no distinct object. We might as well call the advocates and opposers tories and whigs, or any thing else, as federalists and anti-federalists. To be for or against the constitution, as it stands, is not much evidence of a federal disposition; if any names are applicable to the parties, on account of their general politics, they are those of republicans and anti-republicans. The opposers are generally men who support the rights of the body of the people, and are properly republicans. The advocates are generally men not very friendly to those rights, and properly anti-republicans.

7. Had the advocates left the constitution, as they ought to have done, to be adopted or rejected on account of its own merits or imperfections, I do not believe the gentlemen who framed it would ever have been even alluded to in the contest by the opposers. Instead of this, the ardent advocates begun by quoting names as incontestible authorities for the implicit adoption of the system, without any examination—treated all who opposed it as friends of anarchy; and with an indecent virulence addressed M——n G——y, L——e, and almost every man of weight they could find in the opposition by name.[43] If they had been candid men they would have applauded the moderation of the opposers for not retaliating in this pointed manner, when so fair an opportunity was given them; but the opposers generally saw that it was no time to heat the passions; but, at the same time, they saw there was something more than mere zeal in many of their adversaries; they saw them attempting to mislead the people, and to precipitate their divisions, by the sound of names, and forced to do it, the opposers, in general terms, alledged those names were not of sufficient authority to

---

43. The opposition writers referred to are George Mason and Richard Henry Lee of Virginia and Elbridge Gerry of Massachusetts. *Federal Farmer* is probably referring to the essays by "A Landholder" (Oliver Ellsworth). These essays contained personal attacks on Anti-Federalist leaders, in particular Lee. (Storing, II, 353, n52.)

justify the hasty adoption of the system contended for. The convention, as a body, was undoubtedly respectable; it was, generally, composed of members of the then and preceding Congresses: as a body of respectable men we ought to view it. To select individual names, is an invitation to personal attacks, and the advocates, for their own sake, ought to have known the abilities, politics, and situation of some of their favourite characters better, before they held them up to view in the manner they did, as men entitled to our implicit political belief: they ought to have known, whether all the men they so held up to view could, for their past conduct in public offices, be approved or not by the public records, and the honest part of the community. These ardent advocates seem now to be peevish and angry, because, by their own folly, they have led to an investigation of facts and of political characters, unfavourable to them, which they had not the discernment to foresee. They may well apprehend they have opened a door to some Junius,[44] or to some man, after his manner, with his polite addresses to men by name, to state serious facts, and unfold the truth; but these advocates may rest assured, that cool men in the opposition, best acquainted with the affairs of the country, will not, in the critical passage of a people from one constitution to another, pursue inquiries, which, in other circumstances, will be deserving of the highest praise. I will say nothing further about political characters, but examine the constitution; and as a necessary and previous measure to a particular examination, I shall state a few general positions and principles, which receive a general assent, and briefly notice the leading features of the confederation, and several state constitutions, to which, through the whole investigation, we must frequently have recourse, to aid the mind in its determinations.

8. We can put but little dependance on the partial and vague information transmitted to us respecting antient governments; our situation as a people is peculiar: our people in general have a high sense of freedom; they are high spirited, though capable of deliberate measures; they are intelligent, discerning, and well informed; and it is to their condition we must mould the constitution and laws. We have no royal or noble families, and all things concur in favour of a government entirely elective. We have tried our abilities as free men in a most arduous contest, and have succeeded; but we now find the main spring of our movements were the love of liberty, and a temporary ardor, and not any energetic principle in the federal system.

9. Our territories are far too extensive for a limited monarchy, in which

44. *The Letters of Junius;* see *FF VIII* (6). (Storing, II, 353, n53.)

the representatives must frequently assemble, and the laws operate mildly and systematically. The most elligible system is a federal republic, that is, a system in which national concerns may be transacted in the centre, and local affairs in state or district governments.

10. The powers of the union ought to be extended to commerce, the coin, and national objects; and a division of powers, and a deposit of them in different hands, is safest.

11. Good government is generally the result of experience and gradual improvements, and a punctual execution of the laws is essential to the preservation of life, liberty, and property. Taxes are always necessary, and the power to raise them can never be safely lodged without checks and limitation, but in a full and substantial representation of the body of the people; the quantity of power delegated ought to be compensated by the brevity of the time of holding it, in order to prevent the possessors increasing it. The supreme power is in the people, and rulers possess only that portion which is expressly given them; yet the wisest people have often declared this is the case on proper occasions, and have carefully formed stipulations to fix the extent, and limit the exercise of the power given.

12. The people by Magna Charta, &c. did not acquire powers, or receive privileges from the king, they only ascertained and fixed those they were entitled to as Englishmen; the title used by the king "we grant," was mere form. Representation, and the jury trial, are the best features of a free government ever as yet discovered, and the only means by which the body of the people can have their proper influence in the affairs of government.

13. In a federal system we must not only balance the parts of the same government, as that of the state, or that of the union; but we must find a balancing influence between the general and local governments—the latter is what men or writers have but very little or imperfectly considered.

14. A free and mild government is that in which no laws can be made without the formal and free consent of the people, or of their constitutional representatives; that is, of a substantial representative branch. Liberty, in its genuine sense, is security to enjoy the effects of our honest industry and labours, in a free and mild government, and personal security from all illegal restraints.

15. Of rights, some are natural and unalienable, of which even the people cannot deprive individuals: Some are constitutional or fundamental; these cannot be altered or abolished by the ordinary laws; but the people, by express acts, may alter or abolish them—These, such as the trial by jury, the benefits of the writ of habeas corpus, &c. individuals claim under the solemn

compacts of the people, as constitutions, or at least under laws so strengthened by long usuage as not to be repealable by the ordinary legislature—and some are common or mere legal rights, that is, such as individuals claim under laws which the ordinary legislature may alter or abolish at pleasure.

16. The confederation is a league of friendship among the states or sovereignties for the common defence and mutual welfare—Each state expressly retains its sovereignty, and all powers not expressly given to congress—All federal powers are lodged in a congress of delegates annually elected by the state legislatures, except in Connecticut and Rhode-Island, where they are chosen by the people—Each state has a vote in congress, pays its delegates, and may instruct or recall them; no delegate can hold any office of profit, or serve more than three years in any six years—Each state may be represented by not less than two, or more than seven delegates.

17. Congress (nine states agreeing) may make peace and war, treaties and alliances, grant letters of marque and reprisal, coin money, regulate the alloy and value of the coin, require men and monies of the states by fixed proportions, and appropriate monies, form armies and navies, emit bills of credit, and borrow monies.

18. Congress (seven states agreeing) may send and receive ambassadors, regulate captures, make rules for governing the army and navy, institute courts for the trial of piracies and felonies committed on the high seas, and for settling territorial disputes between the individual states, regulate weight and measures, post-offices, and Indian affairs.

19. No state, without the consent of congress, can send or receive embassies, make any agreement with any other state, or a foreign state, keep up any vessels of war or bodies of forces in time of peace, or engage in war, or lay any duties which may interfere with the treaties of congress— Each state must appoint regimental officers, and keep up a well regulated militia—Each state may prohibit the importation or exportation of any species of goods.

20. The free inhabitants of one state are intitled to the privileges and immunities of the free citizens of the other states—Credit in each state shall be given to the records and judicial proceedings in the others.

Canada, acceding, may be admitted, and any other colony may be admitted by the consent of nine states.

21. Alterations may be made by the agreement of congress, and confirmation of all the state legislatures.

22. The following, I think, will be allowed to be unalienable or fundamental rights in the United States:—

23. No man, demeaning himself peaceably, shall be molested on account of his religion or mode of worship—The people have a right to hold and enjoy their property according to known standing laws, and which cannot be taken from them without their consent, or the consent of their representatives; and whenever taken in the pressing urgencies of government, they are to receive a reasonable compensation for it—Individual security consists in having free recourse to the laws—The people are subject to no laws or taxes not assented to by their representatives constitutionally assembled—They are at all times intitled to the benefits of the writ of habeas corpus, the trial by jury in criminal and civil causes—They have a right, when charged, to a speedy trial in the vicinage; to be heard by themselves or counsel, not to be compelled to furnish evidence against themselves, to have witnesses face to face, and to confront their adversaries before the judge—No man is held to answer a crime charged upon him till it be substantially described to him; and he is subject to no unreasonable searches or seizures of his person, papers or effects—The people have a right to assemble in an orderly manner, and petition the government for a redress of wrongs—The freedom of the press ought not to be restrained—No emoluments, except for actual service—No hereditary honors, or orders of nobility, ought to be allowed—The military ought to be subordinate to the civil authority, and no soldier be quartered on the citizens without their consent—The militia ought always to be armed and disciplined, and the usual defence of the country—The supreme power is in the people, and power delegated ought to return to them at stated periods, and frequently—The legislative, executive, and judicial powers, ought always to be kept distinct—others perhaps might be added.

24. The organization of the state governments—Each state has a legislature, an executive, and a judicial branch—In general legislators are excluded from the important executive and judicial offices—Except in the Carolinas there is no constitutional distinction among Christian sects—The constitutions of New York, Delaware, and Virginia, exclude the clergy from offices civil and military—the other states do nearly the same in practice.

25. Each state has a democratic branch elected twice a-year in Rhode-Island and Connecticut, biennially in South Carolina, and annually in the other states—There are about 1500 representatives in all the states, or one to each 1700 inhabitants, reckoning five blacks for three whites—The states do not differ as to the age or moral characters of the electors or elected, nor materially as to their property.

26. Pennsylvania has lodged all her legislative powers in a single branch,

and Georgia has done the same; the other eleven states have each in their legislatures a second or senatorial branch. In forming this they have combined various principles, and aimed at several checks and balances. It is amazing to see how ingenuity has worked in the several states to fix a barrier against popular instability. In Massachusetts the senators are apportioned on districts according to the taxes they pay, nearly according to property. In Connecticut the freemen, in September, vote for twenty counsellers, and return the names of those voted for in the several towns; the legislature takes the twenty who have the most votes, and give them to the people, who, in April, chuse twelve of them, who, with the governor and deputy governor, form the senatorial branch. In Maryland the senators are chosen by two electors from each county; these electors are chosen by the freemen, and qualified as the members in the democratic branch are: In these two cases checks are aimed at in the mode of election. Several states have taken into view the periods of service, age, property, &c. In South-Carolina a senator is elected for two years, in Delaware three, and in New-York and Virginia four, in Maryland five, and in the other states for one. In New-York and Virginia one-fourth part go out yearly. In Virginia a senator must be twenty-five years old, in South Carolina thirty. In New-York the electors must each have a freehold worth 250 dollars, in North-Carolina a freehold of fifty acres of land; in the other states the electors of senators are qualified as electors of representatives are. In Massachusetts a senator must have a freehold in his own right worth 1000 dollars, or any estate worth 2000, in New-Jersey any estate worth 2666, in South Carolina worth 1300 dollars, in North-Carolina 300 acres of land in fee, &c. The numbers of senators in each state are from ten to thirty-one, about 160 in the eleven states, about one of 14000 inhabitants.

27. Two states, Massachusetts and New-York, have each introduced into their legislatures a third, but incomplete branch. In the former, the governor may negative any law not supported by two-thirds of the senators, and two-thirds of the representatives: in the latter, the governor, chancellor, and judges of the supreme court may do the same.

28. Each state has a single executive branch. In the five eastern states the people at large elect their governors; in the other states the legislatures elect them. In South Carolina the governor is elected once in two years; in New-York and Delaware once in three, and in the other states annually. The governor of New-York has no executive council, the other governors have. In several states the governor has a vote in the senatorial branch—the governors have similar powers in some instances, and quite dissimilar ones

in others. The number of executive counsellers in the states are from five to twelve. In the four eastern states, New-Jersey, Pennsylvania, and Georgia, they are of the men returned legislators by the people. In Pennsylvania the counsellers are chosen triennially, in Delaware every fourth year, in Virginia every three years, in South-Carolina biennially, and in the other states yearly.

29. Each state has a judicial branch; each common law courts, superior and inferior; some chancery and admiralty courts: The courts in general sit in different places, in order to accommodate the citizens. The trial by jury is had in all the common law courts, and in some of the admiralty courts. The democratic freemen principally form the juries; men destitute of property, of character, or under age, are excluded as in elections. Some of the judges are during good behaviour, and some appointed for a year, and some for years; and all are dependant on the legislatures for their salaries—Particulars respecting this department are too many to be noticed here.

The Federal Farmer.

– VII –

December 31, 1787

Dear Sir,

1. In viewing the various governments instituted by mankind, we see their whole force reducible to two principles—the important springs which alone move the machines, and give them their intended influence and con- troul, are force and persuasion: by the former men are compelled, by the latter they are drawn. We denominate a government despotic or free, as the one or other principle prevails in it. Perhaps it is not possible for a government to be so despotic, as not to operate persuasively on some of its subjects; nor is it, in the nature of things, I conceive, for a government to be so free, or so supported by voluntary consent, as never to want force to compel obedience to the laws. In despotic governments one man, or a few men, independant of the people, generally make the laws, command obedience, and inforce it by the sword: one-fourth part of the people are armed, and obliged to endure the fatigues of soldiers, to oppress the others and keep them subject to the laws. In free governments the people, or their representatives, make the laws; their execution is principally the effect of voluntary consent and aid; the people respect the magistrate, follow their private pursuits, and enjoy the fruits of their labour with very small deduc- tions for the public use. The body of the people must evidently prefer the

latter species of government; and it can be only those few, who may be well paid for the part they take in enforcing despotism, that can, for a moment, prefer the former. Our true object is to give full efficacy to one principle, to arm persuasion on every side, and to render force as little necessary as possible. Persuasion is never dangerous, not even in despotic governments; but military force, if often applied internally, can never fail to destroy the love and confidence, and break the spirits, of the people: and to render it totally impracticable and unnatural for him or them who govern, and yield to this force against the people, to hold their places by the people's elections.

2. I repeat my observation, that the plan proposed will have a doubtful operation between the two principles; and whether it will preponderate towards persuasion or force is uncertain.

3. Government must exist—If the persuasive principle be feeble, force is infallibly the next resort—The moment the laws of congress shall be disregarded they must languish, and the whole system be convulsed—that moment we must have recourse to this next resort, and all freedom vanish.

4. It being impracticable for the people to assemble to make laws, they must elect legislators, and assign men to the different departments of the government. In the representative branch we must expect chiefly to collect the confidence of the people, and in it to find almost entirely the force of persuasion. In forming this branch, therefore, several important considerations must be attended to. It must possess abilities to discern the situation of the people and of public affairs, a disposition to sympathize with the people, and a capacity and inclination to make laws congenial to their circumstances and condition: it must afford security against interested combinations, corruption and influence; it must possess the confidence, and have the voluntary support of the people.

5. I think these positions will not be controverted, nor the one I formerly advanced, that a fair and equal representation is that in which the interests, feelings, opinions and views of the people are collected, in such manner as they would be were the people all assembled.[45] Having made these general observations, I shall proceed to consider further my principal position, viz. that there is no substantial representation of the people provided for in a government, in which the most essential powers, even as to the internal police of the country, are proposed to be lodged; and to propose certain amendments as to the representative branch: 1st, That there ought to be

45. Cf. *FF II* (1), *III* (2–4).

an increase of the numbers of representatives: And, 2dly, That the elections of them ought to be better secured.

6. [1] The representation is unsubstantial and ought to be increased. In matters where there is much room for opinion, you will not expect me to establish my positions with mathematical certainty; you must only expect my observations to be candid, and such as are well founded in the mind of the writer. I am in a field where doctors disagree; and as to genuine representation, though no feature in government can be more important, perhaps, no one has been less understood, and no one that has received so imperfect a consideration by political writers. The ephori in Sparta,[46] and the tribunes in Rome,[47] were but the shadow; the representation in Great-Britain is unequal and insecure. In America we have done more in establishing this important branch on its true principles, than, perhaps, all the world besides: yet even here, I conceive, that very great improvements in representation may be made. In fixing this branch, the situation of the people must be surveyed, and the number of representatives and forms of election apportioned to that situation. When we find a numerous people settled in a fertile and extensive country, possessing equality, and few or none of them oppressed with riches or wants, it ought to be the anxious care of the constitution and laws, to arrest them from national depravity, and to preserve them in their happy condition.[48] A virtuous people make just laws, and good laws tend to preserve unchanged a virtuous people. A virtuous and happy people by laws uncongenial to their characters, may easily be gradually changed into servile and depraved creatures. Where the people, or their representatives, make the laws, it is probable they will generally be fitted to the national character and circumstances, unless the representation be partial, and the imperfect substitute of the people. However, the people may be electors, if the representation be so formed as to give one or more of the natural classes of men in the society an undue ascendency over the others, it is imperfect; the former will gradually become masters, and the latter slaves. It is the first of all among the political balances, to preserve in its proper station each of these classes. We talk of balances in the legislature, and

46. The ephori (or ephors) of Sparta: the elected representatives of the people in the constitution of Sparta.

47. The tribunes were the popularly elected representatives of the people in the constitution of the Roman republic. See *FF VIII* (6).

48. See *FF V* (1).

among the departments of government; we ought to carry them to the body of the people. Since I advanced the idea of balancing the several orders of men in a community, in forming a genuine representation, and [have] seen that idea considered as chemerical,[49] I have been sensibly struck with a sentence in the marquis Beccaria's treatise: this sentence was quoted by congress in 1774, and is as follows:—"In every society there is an effort continually tending to confer on one part the height of power and happiness, and to reduce the others to the extreme of weakness and misery; the intent of good laws is to oppose this effort, and to diffuse their influence universally and equally."[50] Add to this Montesquieu's opinion, that "in a free state every man, who is supposed to be a free agent, ought to be concerned in his own government: therefore, the legislative should reside in the whole body of the people, or their representatives."[51] It is extremely clear that these writers had in view the several orders of men in society, which we call aristocratical, democratical, merchantile, mechanic, &c. and perceived the efforts they are constantly, from interested and ambitious views, disposed to make to elevate themselves and oppress others. Each order must have a share in the business of legislation actually and efficiently. It is deceiving a people to tell them they are electors, and can chuse their legislators, if they cannot, in the nature of things, chuse men from among themselves, and genuinely like themselves. I wish you to take another idea along with you; we are not only to balance these natural efforts, but we are also to guard against accidental combinations; combinations founded in the connections

49. See *FF II* (1).

50. Cesare Bonesana Beccaria, *An Essay on Crimes and Punishments* (London, 1767), introduction; quoted in "Address to Inhabitants of Quebec, October 26, 1774" (written by R. H. Lee), *Journals of the Continental Congress*, I, 106. This edition of Beccaria's book, like the other early English translations, followed Beccaria's original (1764) organization of chapters. Beccaria later accepted an improved organization made in the 1766 translation into French by André Morellet. This is the preferable text, and it is the one used in most modern editions of Beccaria's work. However, the specific passage here, which was quoted by the Continental Congress and by several Anti-Federalists and which was the first sentence in the original introduction, was considerably altered in the revision, making the modern editions different in this crucial respect from those available to the American founding generation. (Storing, II, 266.)

51. Montesquieu, *The Spirit of the Laws* XI, trans. Thomas Nugent (New York: Hafner, 1949), chap. 6.

of offices and private interests, both evils which are increased in proportion as the number of men, among which the elected must be, are decreased. To set this matter in a proper point of view, we must form some general ideas and descriptions of the different classes of men, as they may be divided by occupations and politically: the first class is the aristocratical. There are three kinds of aristocracy spoken of in this country—the first is a constitutional one, which does not exist in the United States in our common acceptation of the word. Montesquieu, it is true, observes, that where a part of the persons in a society, for want of property, age, or moral character, are excluded any share in the government, the others, who alone are the constitutional electors and elected, form this aristocracy;[52] this according to him, exists in each of the United States, where a considerable number of persons, as all convicted of crimes, under age, or not possessed of certain property, are excluded any share in the government; the second is an aristocratic faction; a junto of unprincipled men, often distinguished for their wealth or abilities, who combine together and make their object their private interests and aggrandizement; the existence of this description is merely accidental, but particularly to be guarded against. The third is the natural aristocracy; this term we use to designate a respectable order of men, the line between whom and the natural democracy is in some degree arbitrary; we may place men on one side of this line, which others may place on the other, and in all disputes between the few and the many, a considerable number are wavering and uncertain themselves on which side they are, or ought to be. In my idea of our natural aristocracy in the United States, I include about four or five thousand men; and among these I reckon those who have been placed in the offices of governors, of members of Congress, and state senators generally, in the principal officers of Congress, of the army and militia, the superior judges, the most eminent professional men, &c. and men of large property[53]—the other persons and orders in the community form the natural democracy; this includes in general the yeomanry, the subordinate officers, civil and military, the fishermen, mechanics and traders, many of the merchants and professional men. It is easy to perceive that men of these two

52. *Spirit of the Laws* II, chap. 2.

53. Storing comments that "John Adams gave good and influential expression to the stock of ideas on the natural aristocracy upon which the Anti-Federalists drew. See his *Defence*, letter 25 (*Works*, IV, 396–98)." (Storing, II, 354, n64.) Also see *FF III* (2); *Brutus* (13).

classes, the aristocratical, and democratical, with views equally honest, have sentiments widely different, especially respecting public and private expences, salaries, taxes, &c. Men of the first class associate more extensively, have a high sense of honor, possess abilities, ambition, and general knowledge; men of the second class are not so much used to combining great objects; they possess less ambition, and a larger share of honesty: their dependence is principally on middling and small estates, industrious pursuits, and hard labour, while that of the former is principally on the emoluments of large estates, and of the chief offices of government. Not only the efforts of these two great parties are to be balanced, but other interests and parties also, which do not always oppress each other merely for want of power, and for fear of the consequences; though they, in fact, mutually depend on each other; yet such are their general views, that the merchants alone would never fail to make laws favourable to themselves and oppressive to the farmers, &c. the farmers alone would act on like principles; the former would tax the land, the latter the trade. The manufacturers are often disposed to contend for monopolies, buyers make every exertion to lower prices, and sellers to raise them; men who live by fees and salaries endeavour to raise them, and the part of the people who pay them, endeavour to lower them; the public creditors to augment the taxes, and the people at large to lessen them. Thus, in every period of society, and in all the transactions of men, we see parties verifying the observation made by the Marquis; and those classes which have not their centinels in the government, in proportion to what they have to gain or lose, must infallibly be ruined.

Efforts among parties are not merely confined to property; they contend for rank and distinctions; all their passions in turn are enlisted in political controversies—Men, elevated in society, are often disgusted with the changeableness of the democracy, and the latter are often agitated with the passions of jealousy and envy: the yeomanry possess a large share of property and strength, are nervous and firm in their opinions and habits—the mechanics of towns are ardent and changeable, honest and credulous, they are inconsiderable for numbers, weight and strength, not always sufficiently stable for the supporting free governments: the fishing interest partakes partly of the strength and stability of the landed, and partly of the changeableness of the mechanic interest. As to merchants and traders, they are our agents in almost all money transactions; give activity to government, and possess a considerable share of influence in it. It has been observed by an able writer, that frugal industrious merchants are generally advocates for

liberty. It is an observation, I believe, well founded, that the schools produce but few advocates for republican forms of government;[54] gentlemen
of the law, divinity, physic, &c. probably form about a fourth part of the
people; yet their political influence, perhaps, is equal to that of all the other
descriptions of men; if we may judge from the appointments to Congress,
the legal characters will often, in a small representation, be the majority;
but the more the representatives are encreased, the more of the farmers,
merchants, &c. will be found to be brought into the government.

7. These general observations will enable you to discern what I intend
by different classes, and the general scope of my ideas, when I contend
for uniting and balancing their interests, feelings, opinions, and views in
the legislature; we may not only so unite and balance these as to prevent
a change in the government by the gradual exaltation of one part to the
depression of others, but we may derive many other advantages from the
combination and full representation; a small representation can never be
well informed as to the circumstances of the people, the members of it
must be too far removed from the people, in general, to sympathize with
them, and too few to communicate with them: a representation must be
extremely imperfect where the representatives are not circumstanced to
make the proper communications to their constituents, and where the
constituents in turn cannot, with tolerable convenience, make known their
wants, circumstances, and opinions, to their representatives; where there is
but one representative to 30,000 or 40,000 inhabitants, it appears to me, he
can only mix, and be acquainted with a few respectable characters among
his constituents, even double the federal representation, and then there
must be a very great distance between the representatives and the people
in general represented. On the proposed plan, the state of Delaware, the
city of Philadelphia, the state of Rhode Island, the province of Maine, the
county of Suffolk in Massachusetts, will have one representative each; there
can be but little personal knowledge, or but few communications, between
him and the people at large of either of those districts. It has been observed,
that mixing only with the respectable men, he will get the best information
and ideas from them; he will also receive impressions favourable to their
purposes particularly. Many plausible shifts have been made to divert the

54. Storing found the thought expressed here a common one, but he could not
find the specific source of the observation about merchants. On the schools, see John
Adams, *Defence*, preface (*Works*, IV, 289). (Storing, II, 354, n65)

mind from dwelling on this defective representation, these I shall consider in another place.[55]

8. Could we get over all our difficulties respecting a balance of interests and party efforts, to raise some and oppress others, the want of sympathy, information and intercourse between the representatives and the people, an insuperable difficulty will still remain, I mean the constant liability of a small number of representatives to private combinations; the tyranny of the one, or the licentiousness of the multitude, are, in my mind, but small evils, compared with the factions of the few. It is a consideration well worth pursuing, how far this house of representatives will be liable to be formed into private juntos, how far influenced by expectations of appointments and offices, how far liable to be managed by the president and senate, and how far the people will have confidence in them. To obviate difficulties on this head, as well as objections to the representative branch, generally, several observations have been made—these I will now examine, and if they shall appear to be unfounded, the objections must stand unanswered.

9. That the people are the electors, must elect good men, and attend to the administration.

10. It is said that the members of Congress, at stated periods, must return home, and that they must be subject to the laws they may make, and to a share of the burdens they may impose.

11. That the people possess the strong arm to overawe their rulers, and the best checks in their national character against the abuses of power, that the supreme power will remain in them.

12. That the state governments will form a part of, and a balance in the system.

13. That Congress will have only a few national objects to attend to, and the state governments many and local ones.

14. That the new Congress will be more numerous than the present, and that any numerous body is unwieldy and mobbish.

15. That the states only are represented in the present Congress, and that the people will require a representation in the new one that in fifty or an hundred years the representation will be numerous.

16. That congress will have no temptation to do wrong; and that no system to enslave the people is practicable.

17. That as long as the people are free they will preserve free govern-

55. See *FF VIII–X*.

ments; and that when they shall become tired of freedom, arbitrary government must take place.

18. These observations I shall examine in the course of my letters; and, I think, not only shew that they are not well founded, but point out the fallacy of some of them; and shew that others do not very well comport with the dignified and manly sentiments of a free and enlightened people.

The Federal Farmer.

– VIII –

January 3, 1788

Dear Sir,

1. Before I proceed to examine the objections, I beg leave to add a valuable idea respecting representation, to be collected from De Lolme, and other able writers, which essentially tends to confirm my positions: They very justly impute the establishment of general and equal liberty in England to a balance of interests and powers among the different orders of men; aided by a series of fortunate events, that never before, and possibly never again will happen.[56]

2. Before the Norman conquest the people of England enjoyed much of this liberty. The first of the Norman kings, aided by foreign mercenaries and foreign attendants, obnoxious to the English, immediately laid arbitrary taxes, and established arbitrary courts, and severely oppressed all orders of people: The barons and people, who recollected their former liberties, were induced, by those oppressions, to unite their efforts in their common defence: Here it became necessary for the great men, instead of deceiving and depressing the people, to enlighten and court them; the royal power was too strongly fixed to be annihilated, and rational means were, therefore, directed to limiting it within proper bounds. In this long and arduous task, in this new species of contests, the barons and people succeeded, because they had been freemen, and knew the value of the object they were contending for; because they were the people of a small island—one people who found it practicable to meet and deliberate in one assembly, and act under one system of resolves, and who were not obliged to meet in different provincial assemblies, as is the case in large countries, as was the case in

---

56. J. L. De Lolme, *The Constitution of England*, 3rd ed. (London, 1781). (For a modern edition, see De Lolme, *The Constitution of England*, ed. David Lieberman [Indianapolis: Liberty Fund, 2007].) Cf. *FF IX* (17).

France, Spain, &c. where their determinations were inconsistent with each other, and where the king could play off one assembly against another.

3. It was in this united situation the people of England were for several centuries, enabled to combine their exertions, and by compacts, as Magna Charta, a bill of rights, &c. were able to limit, by degrees, the royal prerogatives, and establish their own liberties. The first combination was, probably, the accidental effect of pre-existing circumstances; but there was an admirable balance of interests in it, which has been the parent of English liberty, and excellent regulations enjoyed since that time. The executive power having been uniformly in the king, and he the visible head of the nation, it was chimerical for the greatest lord or most popular leader, consistent with the state of the government, and opinion of the people, to seriously think of becoming the king's rival, or to aim at even a share of the executive power; the greatest subject's prospect was only in acquiring a respectable influence in the house of commons, house of lords, or in the ministry; circumstances at once made it the interests of the leaders of the people to stand by them. Far otherwise was it with the ephori in Sparta, and tribunes in Rome. The leaders in England have led the people to freedom, in almost all other countries to servitude. The people in England have made use of deliberate exertions, their safest and most efficient weapons. In other countries they have often acted like mobs, and been enslaved by their enemies, or by their own leaders. In England, the people have been led uniformly, and systematically by their representatives to secure their rights by compact, and to abolish innovations upon the government: they successively obtained Magna Charta, the powers of taxation, the power to propose laws, the habeas corpus act, bill of rights, &c. they, in short, secured general and equal liberty, security to their persons and property; and, as an everlasting security and bulwark of their liberties, they fixed the democratic branch in the legislature, and jury trial in the execution of the laws, the freedom of the press, etc.

4. In Rome, and most other countries, the reverse of all this is true. In Greece, Rome, and wherever the civil law has been adopted, torture has been admitted. In Rome the people were subject to arbitrary confiscations, and even their lives would be arbitrarily disposed of by consuls, tribunes, dictators, masters, &c. half of the inhabitants were slaves, and the other half never knew what equal liberty was; yet in England the people have had king, lords, and commons; in Rome they had consuls, senators and tribunes: why then was the government of England so mild and favorable to the body of the people, and that of Rome an ambitious and oppressive aristocracy?

Why in England have the revolutions always ended in stipulations in favour of general liberty, equal laws, and the common rights of the people and in most other countries in favour only of a few influential men? The reasons, in my mind, are obvious: In England the people have been substantially represented in many respects; in the other countries it has not been so. Perhaps a small degree of attention to a few simple facts will illustrate this.—In England, from the oppressions of the Norman kings to the revolution in 1688, during which period of two or three hundred years, the English liberties were ascertained and established, the aristocratic part of that nation was substantially represented by a very large number of nobles, possessing similar interests and feelings with those they represented. The body of the people, about four or five millions, then mostly a frugal landed people, were represented by about five hundred representatives, taken not from the order of men which formed the aristocracy, but from the body of the people, and possessed of the same interests and feelings. De Lolme, speaking of the British representation, expressly founds all his reasons on this union; this similitude of interests, feelings, views and circumstances. He observes, the English have preserved their liberties, because they and their leaders or representatives have been strictly united in interests, and in contending for general liberty.[57] Here we see a genuine balance founded in the actual state of things. The whole community, probably, not more than two-fifths more numerous than we now are, were represented by seven or eight hundred men; the barons stipulated with the common people, and the king with the whole. Had the legal distinction between lords and commons been broken down, and the people of that island been called upon to elect forty-five senators, and one hundred and twenty representatives, about the proportion we propose to establish, their whole legislature evidently would have been of the natural aristocracy, and the body of the people would not have had scarcely a single sincere advocate; their interests would have been neglected, general and equal liberty forgot, and the balance lost; contests and conciliations, as in most other countries, would have been merely among the few, and as it might have been necessary to serve their purposes, the people at large would have been flattered or threatened, and probably not a single stipulation made in their favour.

5. In Rome the people were miserable, though they had three orders, the consuls, senators and tribunes, and approved the laws, and all for want of a genuine representation. The people were too numerous to assemble,

57. De Lolme, *Constitution of England*, II, chap. 6.

and do any thing properly themselves; the voice of a few, the dupes of artifice, was called the voice of the people. It is difficult for the people to defend themselves against the arts and intrigues of the great, but by selecting a suitable number of men fixed to their interests to represent them, and to oppose ministers and senators. And the people's all depends on the number of the men selected, and the manner of doing it. To be convinced of this, we need only attend to the reason of the case, the conduct of the British commons, and of the Roman tribunes: equal liberty prevails in England, because there was a representation of the people, in fact and reality, to establish it; equal liberty never prevailed in Rome, because there was but the shadow of a representation. There were consuls in Rome annually elected to execute the laws; several hundred senators represented the great families; the body of the people annually chose tribunes from among themselves to defend them and to secure their rights; I think the number of tribunes annually chosen never exceeded ten. This representation, perhaps, was not proportionally so numerous as the representation proposed in the new plan; but the difference will not appear to be so great, when it shall be recollected, that these tribunes were chosen annually; that the great patrician families were not admitted to these offices of tribunes, and that the people of Italy who elected the tribunes were a long while, if not always, a small people compared with the people of the United States. What was the consequence of this triffling representation? The people of Rome always elected for their tribunes men conspicuous for their riches, military commands, professional popularity, &c. great commoners, between whom and the noble families there was only the shadowy difference of legal distinction. Among all the tribunes the people chose for several centuries, they had scarcely five real friends to their interests. These tribunes lived, felt and saw, not like the people, but like the great patrician families, like senators and great officers of state, to get into which it was evident, by their conduct, was their sole object. These tribunes often talked about the rights and prerogatives of the people, and that was all; for they never even attempted to establish equal liberty: so far from establishing the rights of the people, they suffered the senate, to the exclusion of the people, to engross the powers of taxation; those excellent and almost only real weapons of defence even the people of England possess. The tribunes obtained that the people should be eligible to some of the great offices of state, and marry, if they pleased, into the noble families; these were advantages in their nature, confined to a few elevated commoners, and of triffling importance to the people at large. Nearly the same observations may be made as to the ephori of Sparta.

6. We may amuse ourselves with names; but the fact is, men will be governed by the motives and temptations that surround their situation. Political evils to be guarded against are in the human character, and not in the name of patrician or plebian. Had the people of Italy, in the early period of the republic, selected yearly, or biennially, four or five hundred of their best informed men, emphatically from among themselves, these representatives would have formed an honest respectable assembly, capable of combining in them the views and exertions of the people, and their respectability would have procured them honest and able leaders, and we should have seen equal liberty established. True liberty stands in need of a fostering hand; from the days of Adam she has found but one temple to dwell in securely; she has laid the foundation of one, perhaps her last, in America; whether this is to be compleated and have duration, is yet a question. Equal liberty never yet found many advocates among the great: it is a disagreeable truth, that power perverts mens views in a greater degree, than public employments inform their understandings—they become hardened in certain maxims, and more lost to fellow feelings. Men may always be too cautious to commit alarming and glaring iniquities: but they, as well as systems, are liable to be corrupted by slow degrees. Junius well observes, we are not only to guard against what men will do, but even against what they may do.[58] Men in high public offices are in stations where they gradually lose sight of the people, and do not often think of attending to them, except when necessary to answer private purposes.

7. The body of the people must have this true representative security placed some where in the nation; and in the United States, or in any extended empire, I am fully persuaded can be placed no where, but in the forms of a federal republic, where we can divide and place it in several state or district legislatures, giving the people in these the means of opposing heavy internal taxes and oppressive measures in the proper stages. A great empire contains the amities and animosities of a world within itself. We are not like the people of England, one people compactly settled on a small island, with a great city filled with frugal merchants, serving as a common centre of liberty and union: we are dispersed, and it is impracticable for any but the few to assemble in one place: the few must be watched, checked, and often resisted—tyranny has ever shewn a predilection to be in close amity with them, or the one man. Drive it from kings and it flies to sena-

58. *The Letters of Junius I*, letter 18. (Storing, II, 384, n69.)

tors, to dicemvirs, to dictators, to tribunes, to popular leaders, to military chiefs, &c.

8. De Lolme well observes, that in societies, laws which were to be equal to all are soon warped to the private interests of the administrators, and made to defend the usurpations of a few.[59] The English, who had tasted the sweets of equal laws, were aware of this, and though they restored their king, they carefully delegated to parliament the advocates of freedom.

9. I have often lately heard it observed, that it will do very well for a people to make a constitution, and ordain, that at stated periods they will chuse, in a certain manner, a first magistrate, a given number of senators and representatives, and let them have all power to do as they please. This doctrine, however it may do for a small republic, as Connecticut, for instance, where the people may chuse so many senators and representatives to assemble in the legislature, in an eminent degree, the interests, the views, feelings, and genuine sentiments of the people themselves, can never be admitted in an extensive country; and when this power is lodged in the hands of a few, not to limit the few, is but one step short of giving absolute power to one man—in a numerous representation the abuse of power is a common injury, and has no temptation—among the few, the abuse of power may often operate to the private emolument of those who abuse it.

The Federal Farmer.

– IX –

January 4, 1788

Dear Sir,

1. The advocates of the constitution say we must trust to the administration, and elect good men for representatives. I admit, that in forming the social compact, we can fix only general principles, and, of necessity, must trust something to the wisdom and integrity of the administration. But the question is, do we not trust too much, and to men also placed in the vortex of temptation, to lay hold of proffered advantages for themselves and their connections, and to oppress the body of the people.

2. It is one thing to authorise a well organized legislature to make laws, under the restraints of a well guarded constitution, and another to assemble a few men, and to tell them to do what they please. I am not the more shaken in my principles, or disposed to despair of the cause of liberty, because some

59. De Lolme, *Constitution of England*, II, chap. 5.

of our able men have adopted the yielding language of non-resistance, and writers dare insult the people with the signatures of Caesar, Mark Antony, and of other tyrants; because I see even moderate and amiable men, forced to let go of monarchy in 1775, still in love with it, to use the simile of our countrymen, when the political pot boils, the skum will often get uppermost and make its appearance. I believe the people of America, when they shall fully understand any political subject brought before them, will talk in a very different stile, and use the manly language of freedom.

3. But "the people must elect good men":—Examine the system, Is it practicable for them to elect fit and proper representatives where the number is so small? "But the people may chuse whom they please."[60] This is an observation, I believe, made without due attention to facts and the state of the community. To explain my meaning, I will consider the descriptions of men commonly presented to the people as candidates for the offices of representatives—we may rank them in three classes: 1. The men who form the natural aristocracy, as before defined. 2. Popular demagogues: these men also are often politically elevated, so as to be seen by the people through the extent of large districts; they often have some abilities, without principle, and rise into notice by their noise and arts. 3. The substantial and respectable part of the democracy: they are a numerous and valuable set of men, who discern and judge well, but from being generally silent in public assemblies are often overlooked: they are the most substantial and best informed men in the several towns, who occasionally fill the middle grades of offices, &c. who hold not a splendid, but a respectable rank in private concerns: these men are extensively diffused through all the counties, towns, and small districts in the union; even they, and their immediate connections, are raised above the majority of the people, and as representatives are only brought to a level with a more numerous part of the community, the middle orders, and a degree nearer the mass of the people. Hence it is that the best practical representation, even in a small state, must be several degrees more aristocratical than the body of the people. A representation so formed as to admit but few or none of the third class, is, in my opinion, not deserving of the name—even in armies, courts-martial are so formed as to admit subaltern officers into them. The true idea is, so to open and enlarge the representation as to let in a due proportion of the third class with those of the first. Now, my opinion is, that the representation proposed is so small as that ordinarily very few or none of them can be elected; and, therefore,

60. See *Federalist* 35.

after all the parade of words and forms the government must possess the soul of aristocracy, or something worse, the spirit of popular leaders.[61]

4. I observed in a former letter, that the state of Delaware, of Rhode-Island, the Province of Maine, and each of the great counties in Massachusetts &c. would have one member, and rather more than one when the representatives shall be increased to one for each 30,000 inhabitants. In some districts the people are more dispersed and unequal than in others: In Delaware they are compact, in the Province of Main dispersed; how can the elections in either of those districts be regulated so as that a man of the third class can be elected?—Exactly the same principles and motives, the same uncontroulable circumstances, must govern the elections as in the choice of the governors. Call upon the people of either of those districts to chuse a governor, and it will, probably, never happen that they will not bestow a major part, or the greatest number, of their votes on some very conspicuous or very popular character. A man that is known among a few thousands of people, may be quite unknown among thirty or forty thousand. On the whole, it appears to me to be almost a self-evident position, that when we call on thirty or forty thousand inhabitants to unite in giving their votes for one man, it will be uniformly impracticable for them to unite in any men, except those few who have become eminent for their civil or military rank, or their popular legal abilities: it will be found totally impracticable for men in the private walks of life, except in the profession of the law, to become conspicuous enough to attract the notice of so many electors and have their suffrages.

5. But if I am right, it is asked why so many respectable men advocate the adoption of the proposed system. Several reasons may be given—many of our gentlemen are attached to the principles of monarchy and aristocracy; they have an aversion to democratic republics. The body of the people have acquired large powers and substantial influence by the revolution. In the unsettled state of things, their numerous representatives, in some instances, misused their powers and have induced many good men suddenly to adopt ideas unfavourable to such republics, and which ideas they will discard on reflection. Without scrutinizing into the particulars of the proposed system, we immediately perceive that its general tendency is to collect the powers of government, now in the body of the people in reality, and to place them in the higher orders and fewer hands; no wonder then that all those of and about these orders are attached to it; they feel there

61. See Smith speech at New York Ratifying Convention, June 21, 1788 (15–18).

is something in this system advantageous to them. On the other hand, the body of the people evidently feel there is something wrong and disadvantageous to them; both descriptions perceive there is something tending to bestow on the former the height of power and happiness, and to reduce the latter to weakness, insignificance, and misery. The people evidently feel all this though they want expressions to convey their ideas. Further, even the respectable part of the democracy, have never yet been able to distinguish clearly where the fallacy lies; they find there are defects in the confederation; they see a system presented, they think something must be done; and, while their minds are in suspence, the zealous advocates force a reluctant consent. Nothing can be a stronger evidence of the nature of this system, than the general sense of the several orders in the community respecting its tendency: the parts taken generally by them proves my position, that notwithstanding the parade of words and forms, the government must possess the soul of aristocracy.

6. Congress, heretofore, have asked for moderate additional powers, the cry was give them—be federal: but the proper distinction between the cases that produce this disposition, and the system proposed, has not been fairly made and seen in all its consequences. We have seen some of our state representations too numerous and without examining a medium we run into the opposite extreme. It is true, the proper number of federal representatives, is matter of opinion in some degree: but there are extremes which we immediately perceive, and others, which we clearly discover on examination. We should readily pronounce a representative branch of 15 members small in a federal government, having complete powers as to taxes, military matters, commerce, the coin, &c &c. On the other hand, we should readily pronounce a federal representation as numerous as those of the several states, consisting of about 1500 representatives, unwieldy and totally improper. It is asked, has not the wisdom of the convention found the medium? perhaps not: The convention was divided on this point of numbers: at least some of its ablest members urged, that instead of 65 representatives there ought to be 130 in the first instance: They fixed one representative for each 40,000 inhabitants, and at the close of the work, the president suggested, that the representation appeared to be too small and without debate, it was put at, not exceeding one for each 30,000. I mention these facts to shew, that the convention went on no fixed data. In this extensive country it is difficult to get a representation sufficiently numerous: Necessity, I believe, will oblige us to sacrifice in some degree the true genuine principles of representation. But this sacrifice ought to

be as little as possible: How far we ought to increase the representation I will not pretend to say; but that we ought to increase it very considerably, is clear—to double it at least, making full allowances for the state representations: and this we may evidently do, and approach accordingly towards safety and perfection, without encountering any inconveniences. It is with great difficulty the people can unite these different interests and views even tolerably, in the state senators, who are more than twice as numerous as the federal representatives, as proposed by the convention; even these senators are considered as so far removed from the people, that they are not allowed immediately to hold their purse strings.

7. The principle objections made to the increase of the representation are, the expence and difficulty in getting the members to attend. The first cannot be important; the last, if founded, is against any federal government. As to the expence, I presume, the house of representatives will not be in sessions more than four months in the year. We find by experience, that about two-thirds of the members of representative assemblies usually attend; therefore, of the representation proposed by the convention, about forty five members probably will attend, doubling their number, about 90 will probably attend: their pay, in one case, at four dollars a day each (which is putting it high enough) will amount to, yearly, 21,600 dollars; in the other case, 43,200 dollars: difference 21,600 dollars;—reduce the state representatives from 1500 down to 1000, and thereby save the attendance of two-thirds of the 500, say three months in a year at one dollar and a quarter a day each: 37,125 dollars. Thus we may leave the state representations sufficient large, and yet save enough by the reduction nearly to support exceeding well the whole federal representation I propose. Surely we never can be so unwise as to sacrifice, essentially, the all-important principles of representation for so small a sum as 21,600 dollars a year for the United States; a single company of soldiers would cost this sum. It is a fact that can easily be shewn, that we expend three times this sum every year upon useless inferior offices and very triffling concerns. It is also a fact which can be shewn, that the United States in the late war suffered more by a faction in the federal government, than the pay of the federal representation will amount to for twenty years.

8. As to the attendance—Can we be so unwise as to establish an unsafe and inadequate representative branch, and give it as a reason, that we believe only a few members will be induced to attend; we ought certainly to establish an adequate representative branch, and adopt measures to induce an attendance; I believe that a due proportion of 130 or 140 members may

be induced to attend: there are various reasons for the non-attendance of the members of the present congress; it is to be presumed that these will not exist under the new system.

9. To compensate for the want of a genuine representation in a government, where the purse and sword, and all important powers, are proposed to be lodged, a variety of unimportant things are enumerated by the advocates of it.

10. In the second place, it is said the members of congress must return home, and share in the burdens they may impose; and, therefore, private motives will induce them to make mild laws, to support liberty, and ease the burdens of the people: this brings us to a mere question of interest under this head. I think these observations will appear, on examination, altogether fallacious; because this individual interest, which may coincide with the rights and interests of the people, will be far more than balanced by opposite motives and opposite interests. If, on a fair calculation, a man will gain more by measures oppressive to others than he will lose by them, he is interested in their adoption. It is true, that those who govern, generally, by increasing the public burdens increase their own share of them; but by this increase they may, and often do, increase their salaries, fees, and emoluments, in a ten-fold proportion, by increasing salaries, forming armies and navies, and by making offices—If it shall appear the members of congress will have these temptations before them, the argument is on my side—they will view the account, and be induced continually to make efforts advantageous to themselves and connections, and oppressive to others.

11. We must examine facts—Congress, in its present form, have but few offices to dispose of worth the attention of the members, or of men of the aristocracy; yet, from 1774 to this time, we find a large proportion of those offices assigned to those who were or had been members of congress, and though the states chuse annually sixty or seventy members, many of them have been provided for: but few men are known to congress in this extensive country, and, probably, but few will be to the president and senate, except those who have or shall appear as members of congress, or those whom the members may bring forward. The states may now chuse yearly ninety-one members of congress; under the new constitution they will have it in their power to chuse exactly the same number, perhaps afterwards, one hundred and fifteen, but these must be chosen once in two and six years; so that, in the course of ten years together, not more than two-thirds so many members of congress will be elected and brought into view, as there now are under the confederation in the same term of time: but at least there will

be five, if not ten times, as many offices and places worthy the attention of
the members, under the new constitution, as there are under the confederation: therefore, we may fairly presume, that a very great proportion of
the members of congress, especially the influential ones, instead of return-
ing to private life, will be provided for with lucrative offices, in the civil or
military department, and not only the members, but many of their sons,
friends, and connection. These offices will be in the constitutional disposition of the president and senate, and, corruption out of the question, what
kind of security can we expect in a representation, so many of the members
of which may rationally feel themselves candidates for these offices?—
let common sense decide. It is true, that members chosen to offices must
leave their seats in congress, and to some few offices they cannot be elected
till the time shall be expired for which they were elected members; but
this scarcely will effect the biass arising from the hopes and expectations
of office.[62]

12. It is not only in this point of view, the members of congress, by their
efforts, may make themselves and friends powerful and happy, while the
people may be oppressed: but there is another way in which they may soon
warp laws, which ought to be equal, to their own advantages, by those imperceptible means, and on those doubtful principles which may not alarm.
No society can do without taxes; they are the efficient means of safety and
defence, and they too have often been the weapons by which the blessings of
society have been destroyed. Congress will have power to lay taxes at pleasure for the general welfare; and if they mis-judge of the general welfare,
and lay unnecessary oppressive taxes, the constitution will provide, as I shall
hereafter shew, no remedy for the people or states—the people must bear
them, or have recourse, not to any constitutional checks or remedies, but to
that resistence which is the last resort, and founded in self-defence.[63]

13. It is well stipulated, that all duties, imposts, and excises shall be equal;
and that direct taxes shall be apportioned on the several states by a fixed
rule, but nothing further. Here commences a dangerous power in matters
of taxation, lodged without any regard to the balance of interests of the
different orders of men, and without any regard to the internal policy of the
states. Congress having assigned to any state its quota, say to New-Jersey,
80,000 dollars in a given tax, congress will be entirely at liberty to apportion that sum on the counties and towns, polls, lands, houses, labour, &c.

62. *FF VII* (7).
63. See also *FF X* (2–3).

and appoint the assessors and collectors in that state in what manner they please; there will be nothing to prevent a system of tax laws being made, unduly to ease some descriptions of men and burden others: though such a system may be unjust and injudicious, though we may complain, the answer will be, congress have the power delegated by the people, and, probably, congress has done what it thought best.

14. By the confederation taxes must be quotaed on the several states by fixed rules, as before mentioned: but then each state's quota is apportioned on the several numbers and classes of citizens in the state, by the state legislature, assessed and collected by state laws. Great pains have been taken to confound the two cases, which are as distinct as light and darkness; this I shall endeavour to illustrate, when I come to the amendment respecting internal taxes. I shall only observe, at present, that in the state legislatures the body of the people will be genuinely represented, and in congress not; that the right of resisting oppressive measures is inherent in the people, and that a constitutional barrier should be so formed, that their genuine representatives may stop an oppressive ruinous measure in its early progress, before it shall come to maturity, and the evils of it become in a degree fixed.

15. It has lately been often observed, that the power or body of men intrusted with the national defence and tranquility, must necessarily possess the purse unlimitedly, that the purse and sword must go together[64]—this is new doctrine in a free country, and by no means tenable. In the British government the king is particularly intrusted with the national honor and defence, but the commons solely hold the purse. I think I have amply shewn that the representation in congress will be totally inadequate in matters of taxation, &c. and, therefore, that the ultimate controul over the purse must be lodged elsewhere.

16. We are not to expect even honest men rigidly to adhere to the line of strict impartiality, where the interest of themselves or friends is particularly concerned; if we do expect it, we shall deceive ourselves, and make a wrong estimate of human nature.

17. But it is asked how shall we remedy the evil, so as to complete and perpetuate the temple of equal laws and equal liberty? Perhaps we never can do it. Possibly we never may be able to do it in this immense country, under any one system of laws however modified; nevertheless, at present, I think the experiment worth a making. I feel an aversion to the disunion of the states, and to separate confederacies; the states have fought and bled

64. See *Federalist* 23, 26, 28, 31.

in a common cause, and great dangers too may attend these confederacies. I think the system proposed capable of very considerable degrees of perfection, if we pursue first principles. I do not think that De Lolme, or any writer I have seen, has sufficiently pursued the proper inquiries and efficient means for making representation and balances in government more perfect; it is our task to do this in America. Our object is equal liberty, and equal laws diffusing their influence among all orders of men; to obtain this we must guard against the biass of interest and passions, against interested combinations, secret or open; we must aim at a balance of efforts and strength.

18. Clear it is, by increasing the representation we lessen the prospects of each member of congress being provided for in public offices; we proportionably lessen official influence and strengthen his prospects of becoming a private citizen, subject to the common burdens, without the compensation of the emoluments of office. By increasing the representation we make it more difficult to corrupt and influence the members; we diffuse them more extensively among the body of the people, perfect the balance, multiply information, strengthen the confidence of the people, and consequently support the laws on equal and free principles. There are two other ways, I think, of obtaining in some degree the security we want; the one is, by excluding more extensively the members from being appointed to offices; the other is, by limiting some of their powers; but these two I shall examine hereafter.

The Federal Farmer.

– X –

January 7, 1788

Dear Sir,

1. It is said that our people have a high sense of freedom, possess power, property, and the strong arm; meaning, I presume, that the body of the people can take care of themselves, and awe their rulers; and, therefore, particular provision in the constitution for their security may not be essential. When I come to examine these observations, they appear to me too triffling and loose to deserve a serious answer.

2. To palliate for the smallness of the representation, it is observed, that the state governments in which the people are fully represented, necessarily form a part of the system. This idea ought to be fully examined. We ought to enquire if the convention have made the proper use of these es-

sential parts; the state governments then we are told will stand between the arbitrary exercise of power and the people: true they may, but armless and helpless, perhaps, with the privilege of making a noise when hurt—this is no more than individuals may do. Does the constitution provide a single check for a single measure, by which the state governments can constitutionally and regularly check the arbitrary measures of congress?[65] Congress may raise immediately fifty thousand men, and twenty millions of dollars in taxes, build a navy, model the militia, &c. and all this constitutionally. Congress may arm on every point, and the state governments can do no more than an individual, by petition to congress, suggest their measures are alarming and not right.

3. I conceive the position to be undeniable, that the federal government will be principally in the hands of the natural aristocracy, and the state governments principally in the hands of the democracy, the representatives of the body of the people. These representatives in Great-Britain hold the purse, and have a negative upon all laws. We must yield to circumstances, and depart something from this plan, and strike out a new medium, so as to give efficacy to the whole system, supply the wants of the union, and leave the several states, or the people assembled in the state legislatures, the means of defence.

4. It has been often mentioned, that the objects of congress will be few and national, and require a small representation; that the objects of each state will be many and local, and require a numerous representation.[66] This circumstance has not the weight of a feather in my mind. It is certainly unadvisable to lodge in 65 representatives, and 26 senators, unlimited power to establish systems of taxation, armies, navies, model the militia, and to do every thing that may essentially tend soon to change, totally, the affairs of the community; and to assemble 1500 state representatives, and 160 senators, to make fence laws, and laws to regulate the descent and conveyance of property, the administration of justice between man and man, to appoint militia officers, &c.

5. It is not merely the quantity of information I contend for. Two taxing powers may be inconvenient; but the point is, congress, like the senate of Rome, will have taxing powers, and the people no check—when the power is abused, the people may complain and grow angry, so may the state governments; they may remonstrate and counteract, by passing laws to prohibit

65. See *FF XVII* (7); *Federalist* 16; *Brutus X* (21).
66. See *Federalist* 55.

the collection of congressional taxes; but these will be acts of the people, acts of sovereign power, the dernier resort unknown to the constitution; acts operating in terrorum, acts of resistence, and not the exercise of any constitutional power to stop or check a measure before matured: a check properly is the stopping, by one branch in the same legislature, a measure proposed by the other in it. In fact the constitution provides for the states no check, properly speaking, upon the measures of congress—Congress can immediately enlist soldiers, and apply to the pockets of the people.

6. These few considerations bring us to the very strong distinction between the plan that operates on federal principles, and the plan that operates on consolidated principles. A plan may be federal or not as to its organization; each state may retain its vote or not; the sovereignty of the state may be represented, or the people of it. A plan may be federal or not as to its operations—federal when it requires men and monies of the states, and the states as such make the laws for raising the men and monies—Not federal, when it leaves the states governments out of the question, and operates immediately upon the persons and property of the citizens. The first is the case with the confederation, the second with the new plan: in the first the state governments may be a check, in the last none at all. This distinction I shall pursue further hereafter, under the head before mentioned, of amendments as to internal taxes.[67] And here I shall pursue a species of checks which writers have not often noticed.

7. To excuse the smallness of the representation, it is said the new congress will be more numerous than the old one. This is not true; and for the facts I refer you to my letter of the 4th instant, to the plan and confederation; besides there is no kind of similitude between the two plans. The confederation is a mere league of the states, and congress is formed with the particular checks, and possess the united powers, enumerated in my letter of the 25th ult. The new plan is totally a different thing: a national government to many purposes administered, by men chosen for two, four, and six years, not recallable, and among whom there will be no rotation; operating immediately in all money and military matters, &c. on the persons and property of the citizens—I think, therefore, that no part of the confederation ought to be adduced for supporting or injuring the new constitution. It is also said that the constitution gives no more power to congress than the confederation, respecting money and military matters; that congress, under the confederation, may require men and monies to any amount, and

67. See *FF XVII* (1–2), *I* (9–13), *X* (2); *Brutus I* (14).

the states are bound to comply. This is generally true; but, I think, I shall in a subsequent letter satisfactorily prove, that the states have well founded checks for securing their liberties.[68]

8. I admit the force of the observation, that all the federal powers, by the confederation, are lodged in a single assembly; however, I think much more may be said in defence of the leading principles of the confederation. I do not object to the qualifications of the electors of representatives, and I fully agree that the people ought to elect one branch.

9. Further, it may be observed, that the present congress is principally an executive body, which ought not to be numerous; that the house of representatives will be a mere legislative branch, and being the democratic one, ought to be numerous. It is one of the greatest advantages of a government of different branches, that each branch may be conveniently made conformable to the nature of the business assigned it, and all be made conformable to the condition of the several orders of the people. After all the possible checks and limitations we can devise, the powers of the union must be very extensive; the sovereignty of the nation cannot produce the object in view, the defence and tranquility of the whole, without such powers, executive and judicial. I dislike the present congress, a single assembly, because it is impossible to fit it to receive those powers: the executive and judicial powers, in the nature of things, ought to be lodged in a few hands, the legislature in many hands; therefore, want of safety, and unavoidable hasty measures, out of the question, they never can all be lodged in one assembly properly—it, in its very formation, must imply a contradiction.

10. In objection to increasing the representation, it has also been observed, that it is difficult to assemble a hundred men or more without making them tumultuous and a mere mob,[69] reason and experience do not support this observation. The most respectable assemblies we have any knowledge of and the wisest, have been those, each of which consisted of several hundred members; as the senate of Rome, of Carthage, of Venice, the British Parliament, &c. &c. I think I may without hazarding much, affirm, that our more numerous state assemblies and conventions have universally discovered more wisdom, and as much order, as the less numerous ones: There must be also a very great difference between the characters of two or three hundred men assembled from a single state, and the characters of the number or half the number assembled from all the united states.

68. *FF XVII.*
69. *Federalist* 55.

11. It is added, that on the proposed plan the house of representatives in fifty or a hundred years, will consist of several hundred members:[70] The plan will begin with sixty-five, and we have no certainty that the number ever will be encreased, for this plain reason—that all that combination of interests and influence which has produced this plan, and supported so far, will constantly oppose the increase of the representation, knowing that thereby the government will become more free and democratic: But admitting, after a few years, there will be a member for each 30,000 inhabitants, the observation is trifling, the government is in a considerable measure to take its tone from its early movements, and by means of a small representation it may in half of 50 or 100 years, get moved from its basis, or at least so far as to be incapable of ever being recovered. We ought, therefore, on every principle now to fix the government on proper principles, and fit to our present condition—when the representation shall become too numerous, alter it; or we may now make provision, that when the representation shall be increased to a given number, that then there shall be one for each given number of inhabitants, &c.

12. Another observation is, that congress will have no temptations to do wrong—the men that make it must be very uninformed, or suppose they are talking to children. In the first place, the members will be governed by all those motives which govern the conduct of men, and have before them all the allurements of offices and temptations, to establish unequal burdens, before described. In the second place, they and their friends, probably, will find it for their interests to keep up large armies, navies, salaries, &c. and in laying adequate taxes. In the third place, we have no good grounds to presume, from reason or experience, that it will be agreeable to their characters or views, that the body of the people should continue to have power effectually to interfere in the affairs of government. But it is confidently added, that congress will not have it in their power to oppress or enslave the people, that the people will not bear it. It is not supposed that congress will act the tyrant immediately, and in the face of day light. It is not supposed congress will adopt important measures, without plausible pretences, especially those which may tend to alarm or produce opposition. We are to consider the natural progress of things: that men unfriendly to republican equality will go systematically to work, gradually to exclude the body of the people from any share in the government, first of the substance, and then of the forms. The men who will have these views will not be without their

70. See *Federalist* 58.

agents and supporters. When we reflect, that a few years ago we established democratic republics, and fixed the state governments as the barriers between congress and the pockets of the people; what great progress has been made in less than seven years to break down those barriers, and essentially to change the principles of our governments, even by the armless few: is it chimerical to suppose that in fifteen or twenty years to come, that much more can be performed, especially after the adoption of the constitution, when the few will be so much better armed with power and influence, to continue the struggle? probably, they will be wise enough never to alarm, but gradually prepare the minds of the people for one specious change after another, till the final object shall be obtained. Say the advocates, these are only possibilities—they are probabilities, a wise people ought to guard against; and the address made use of to keep the evils out of sight, and the means to prevent them, confirm my opinion.

13. But to obviate all objections to the proposed plan in the last resort: it is said our people will be free, so long as they possess the habits of freemen, and when they lose them, they must receive some other forms of government. To this I shall only observe, that this is very humiliating language, and can, I trust, never suit a manly people, who have contended nobly for liberty, and declared to the world they will be free.

14. I have dwelt much longer than I expected upon the increasing the representation, the democratic interest in the federal system; but I hope the importance of the subject will justify my dwelling upon it. I have pursued it in a manner new, and I have found it necessary to be somewhat prolix, to illustrate the point I had in view. My idea has ever been, when the democratic branch is weak and small, the body of the people have no defence, and every thing to fear; if they expect to find genuine political friends in kings and nobles, in great and powerful men, they deceive themselves. On the other hand, fix a genuine democratic branch in the government, solely to hold the purse, and with the power of impeachment, and to propose and negative laws, cautiously limit the king and nobles, or the executive and the senate, as the case may be, and the people, I conceive, have but little to fear, and their liberties will be always secure.

15. I think we are now arrived to a new aera in the affairs of men, when the true principles of government will be more fully unfolded than heretofore, and a new world, as it were, grow up in America. In contemplating representation, the next thing is the security of elections. Before I proceed to this, I beg leave to observe, that the pay of the representatives of the people is essentially connected with their interests.

16. Congress may put the pay of the members unreasonably high, or so low as that none but the rich and opulent can attend; there are very strong reasons for supposing the latter, probably, will be the case, and a part of the same policy, which uniformly and constantly exerts itself to transfer power from the many to the few. Should the pay be well fixed, and made alterable by congress, with the consent of a majority of the state legislatures, perhaps, all the evils to be feared on this head might, in the best practicable manner, be guarded against, and proper security introduced. It is said the state legislatures fix their own pay—the answer is, that congress is not, nor can it ever be well formed on those equal principles the state legislatures are. I shall not dwell on this point, but conclude this letter with one general observation, that the checks I contend for in the system proposed, do not, in the least, any of them tend to lessen the energy of it; but giving grounds for the confidence of the people, greatly to increase its real energy, by insuring their constant and hearty support.

The Federal Farmer.

– XI –

January 10, 1788

Dear Sir,

1. I shall now add a few observations respecting the organization of the senate, the manner of appointing it, and its powers.

2. The senate is an assembly of 26 members, two from each state, though the senators are apportioned on the federal plan, they will vote individually; they represent the states, as bodies politic, sovereign to certain purposes; the states being sovereign and independent, are all considered equal, each with the other in the senate. In this we are governed solely by the ideal equalities of sovereignties; the federal and state governments forming one whole, and the state governments an essential part, which ought always to be kept distinctly in view, and preserved: I feel more disposed, on reflection, to acquiesce in making them the basis of the senate, and thereby to make it the interest and duty of the senators to preserve distinct, and to perpetuate the respective sovereignties they shall represent.[71]

3. As to the appointments of senators, I have already observed, that they must be appointed by the legislatures, by concurrent acts, and each branch

---

71. See *FF III* (5); *Brutus III* (11), *XV* (13).

have an equal share of power, as I do not see any probability of amendments, if advisable, in these points, I shall not dwell upon them.

4. The senate, as a legislative branch, is not large, but as an executive branch quite too numerous. It is not to be presumed that we can form a genuine senatorial branch in the United States, a real representation of the aristocracy and balance in the legislature, any more than we can form a genuine representation of the people. Could we separate the aristocratical and democratical interests; compose the senate of the former, and the house of assembly of the latter, they are too unequal in the United States to produce a balance. Form them on pure principles, and leave each to be supported by its real weight and connections, the senate would be feeble, and the house powerful:—I say, on pure principles; because I make a distinction between a senate that derives its weight and influence from a pure source, its numbers and wisdom, its extensive property, its extensive and permanent connections; and a senate composed of a few men, possessing small property, small and unstable connections, that derives its weight and influence from a corrupt or pernicious source; that is, merely from the power given it by the constitution and laws, to dispose of the public offices, and the annexed emoluments, and by those means to interest officers, and the hungry expectants of offices, in support of its measures. I wish the proposed senate may not partake too much of the latter description.

5. To produce a balance and checks, the constitution proposes two branches in the legislature; but they are so formed, that the members of both must generally be the same kind of men—men having similar interests and views, feelings and connections—men of the same grade in society, and who associate on all occasions (probably, if there be any difference, the senators will be the most democratic). Senators and representatives thus circumstanced, as men, though convened in two rooms, to make laws, must be governed generally by the same motives and views, and therefore pursue the same system of politics; the partitions between the two branches will be merely those of the building in which they sit: there will not be found in them any of those genuine balances and checks, among the real different interests, and efforts of the several classes of men in the community we aim at; nor can any such balances and checks be formed in the present condition of the United States in any considerable degree of perfection: but to give them the greatest degree of perfection practicable, we ought to make the senate respectable as to numbers, the qualifications of the electors and of the elected; to increase the numbers of the representatives, and so to

model the elections of them, as always to draw a majority of them substantially from the body of the people. Though I conclude the senators and representatives will not form in the legislature those balances and checks which correspond with the actual state of the people; yet I approve of two branches, because we may notwithstanding derive several advantages from them. The senate, from the mode of its appointment, will probably be influenced to support the state governments, and, from its periods of service will produce stability in legislation, while frequent elections may take place in the other branch. There is generally a degree of competition between two assemblies even composed of the same kind of men; and by this, and by means of every law's passing a revision in the second branch, caution, coolness, and deliberation are produced in the business of making laws. By means of a democratic branch we may particularly secure personal liberty; and by means of a senatorial branch we may particularly protect property. By the division, the house becomes the proper body to impeach all officers for misconduct in office, and the senate the proper court to try them; and in a country where limited powers must be lodged in the first magistrate, the senate, perhaps, may be the most proper body to be found to have a negative upon him in making treaties, and in managing foreign affairs.

6. Though I agree the federal senate, in the form proposed, may be useful to many purposes, and that it is not very necessary to alter the organization, modes of appointment, and powers of it in several respects; yet, without alterations in others, I sincerely believe it will, in a very few years, become the source of the greatest evils. Some of these alterations, I conceive, to be absolutely necessary, and some of them at least advisable.

7. [1] By the confederation the members of congress are chosen annually. By art. 1. sect. 2. of the constitution, the senators shall be chosen for six years. As the period of service must be, in a considerable degree, matter of opinion on this head, I shall only make a few observations, to explain why I think it more advisable to limit it to three or four years.[72]

8. The people of this country have not been accustomed to so long appointments in their state governments, they have generally adopted annual elections. The members of the present congress are chosen yearly, who, from the nature and multiplicity of their business, ought to be chosen for longer periods than the federal senators—Men six years in office absolutely contract callous habits, and cease, in too great a degree, to feel their dependance, and for the condition of their constituents. Senators continued in of-

72. Cf. *Brutus XVI* (5).

fices three or four years, will be in them longer than any popular erroneous opinions will probably continue to actuate their electors—men appointed for three or four years, will generally be long enough in office to give stability, and amply to acquire political information. By a change of legislators, as often as circumstances will permit, political knowledge is diffused more extensively among the people, and the attention of the electors and elected more constantly kept alive; circumstances of infinite importance in a free country. Other reasons might be added, but my subject is too extensive to admit of my dwelling upon less material points.

9. [2] When the confederation was formed, it was considered essentially necessary that the members of congress should at any time be recalled by their respective states, when the states should see fit, and others be sent in their room. I do not think it less necessary that this principle should be extended to the members of congress under the new constitution, and especially to the senators.[73] I have had occasion several times to observe, that let us form a federal constitution as extensively, and on the best principles in our power, we must, after all, trust a vast deal to a few men, who, far removed from their constituents, will administer the federal government; there is but little danger these men will feel too great a degree of dependance: the necessary and important object to be attended to, is to make them feel dependant enough. Men elected for several years, several hundred miles distant from their states, possessed of very extensive powers, and the means of paying themselves, will not, probably, be oppressed with a sense of dependance and responsibility.

10. The senators will represent sovereignties, which generally have, and always ought to retain, the power of recalling their agents; the principle of responsibility is strongly felt in men who are liable to be recalled and censured for their misconduct; and, if we may judge from experience, the latter will not abuse the power of recalling their members; to possess it, will, at least be a valuable check. It is in the nature of all delegated power, that the constituents should retain the right to judge concerning the conduct of their representatives; they must exercise the power, and their decision itself, their approving or disapproving that conduct implies a right, a power to continue in office, or to remove from it. But whenever the substitute acts under a constitution, then it becomes necessary that the power of recalling him be expressed. The reasons for lodging a power to recall are stronger, as they respect the senate, than as they respect the representatives; the latter

73. Cf. *Brutus XVI* (6).

will be more frequently elected, and changed of course, and being chosen by the people at large, it would be more difficult for the people than for the legislatures to take the necessary measures for recalling: but even the people, if the powers will be more beneficial to them than injurious, ought to possess it. The people are not apt to wrong a man who is steady and true to their interests; they may for a while be misled by party representations, and leave a good man out of office unheard; but every recall supposes a deliberate decision, and a fair hearing; and no man who believes his conduct proper, and the result of honest views, will be the less useful in his public character, on account of the examination his actions may be liable to; and a man conscious of the contrary conduct, ought clearly to be restrained by the apprehensions of a trial. I repeat it, it is interested combinations and factions we are particularly to guard against in the federal government, and all the rational means that can be put into the hands of the people to prevent them, ought to be provided and furnished for them. Where there is a power to recall, trusty centinels among the people, or in the state legislatures, will have a fair opportunity to become useful. If the members in congress from the states join in such combinations, or favour them, or pursue a pernicious line of conduct, the most attentive among the people, or in the state legislatures, may formally charge them before their constituents: the very apprehensions of such constitutional charges may prevent many of the evils mentioned, and the recalling the members of a single state, a single senator, or representative, may often prevent many more; nor do I, at present, discover any danger in such proceedings, as every man who shall move for a recall will put his reputation at stake, to shew he has reasonable grounds for his motion; and it is not probable such motions will be made unless there be good apparent grounds for succeeding; nor can the charge or motion be any thing more than the attack of an individual or individuals, unless a majority of the constituents shall see cause to go into the enquiry. Further, the circumstance of such a power being lodged in the constituents, will tend continually to keep up their watchfulness, as well as the attention and dependance of the federal senators and representatives.

11. [3] By the confederation it is provided, that no delegate shall serve more than three years in any term of six years, and thus, by the forms of the government, a rotation of members is produced: a like principle has been adopted in some of the state governments, and also in some antient and modern republics. Whether this exclusion of a man for a given period, after he shall have served a given time, ought to be ingrafted into a constitution or not, is a question, the proper decision materially depends upon the

leading features of the government: some governments are so formed as to produce a sufficient fluctuation and change of members of course, in the ordinary course of elections, proper numbers of new members are, from time to time, brought into the legislature, and a proportionate number of old ones go out, mix, and become diffused among the people. This is the case with all numerous representative legislatures, the members of which are frequently elected, and constantly within the view of their constituents. This is the case with our state governments, and in them a constitutional rotation is unimportant. But in a government consisting of but a few members, elected for long periods, and far removed from the observation of the people, but few changes in the ordinary course of elections take place among the members; they become in some measure a fixed body, and often inattentive to the public good, callous, selfish, and the fountain of corruption. To prevent these evils, and to force a principle of pure animation into the federal government, which will be formed much in this last manner mentioned, and to produce attention, activity, and a diffusion of knowledge in the community, we ought to establish among others the principle of rotation.[74] Even good men in office, in time, imperceptibly lose sight of the people, and gradually fall into measures prejudicial to them. It is only a rotation among the members of the federal legislature I shall contend for: judges and officers at the heads of the judicial and executive departments, are in a very different situation, their offices and duties require the information and studies of many years for performing them in a manner advantageous to the people. These judges and officers must apply their whole time to the detail business of their offices, and depend on them for their support: then they always act under masters or superiors, and may be removed from office for misconduct; they pursue a certain round of executive business: their offices must be in all societies confined to a few men, because but few can become qualified to fill them: and were they, by annual appointments, open to the people at large, they are offices of such a nature as to be of no service to them; they must leave these offices in the possession of the few individuals qualified to fill them, or have them badly filled. In the judicial and executive departments also, the body of the people possess a large share of power and influence, as jurors and subordinate officers, among whom there are many and frequent rotations. But in every free country the legislatures are all on a level, and legislation becomes partial whenever, in practice, it rests for any considerable time in a few hands. It is the true

74. Cf. *Brutus XVI* (6–7); Smith speech, June 25, 1788 (1).

republican principle to diffuse the power of making the laws among the people, and so to modify the forms of the government as to draw in turn the well informed of every class into the legislature.

12. To determine the propriety or impropriety of this rotation, we must take the inconveniencies as well as the advantages attending it into view: on the one hand, by this rotation, we may sometimes exclude good men from being elected. On the other hand, we guard against those pernicious connections, which usually grow up among men left to continue long periods in office, we increase the number of those who make the laws and return to their constituents; and thereby spread information, and preserve a spirit of activity and investigation among the people: hence a balance of interests and exertions are preserved, and the ruinous measures of factions rendered more impracticable. I would not urge the principle of rotation, if I believed the consequence would be an uninformed federal legislature; but I have no apprehension of this in this enlightened country. The members of congress, at any one time, must be but very few, compared with the respectable well informed men in the United States; and I have no idea there will be any want of such men for members of congress, though by a principle of rotation the constitution should exclude from being elected for two years those federal legislators, who may have served the four years immediately preceding, or any four years in the six preceding years. If we may judge from experience and fair calculations, this principle will never operate to exclude at any one period a fifteenth part, even of those men who have been members of congress. Though no man can sit in congress, by the confederation, more than three years in any term of six years, yet not more than three, four, or five men in any one state, have been made ineligible at any one period; and if a good man happen to be excluded by this rotation, it is only for a short time. All things considered, the inconveniencies of the principle must be very inconsiderable compared with the many advantages of it. It will generally be expedient for a man who has served four years in congress to return home, mix with the people, and reside some time with them: this will tend to reinstate him in the interests, feelings, and views similar to theirs, and thereby confirm in him the essential qualifications of a legislator. Even in point of information, it may be observed, the useful information of legislators is not acquired merely in studies in offices, and in meeting to make laws from day to day; they must learn the actual situation of the people, by being among them, and when they have made laws, return home, and observe how they operate. Thus occasionally to be among the people, is not only necessary to prevent or banish the callous habits and

self interested views of office in legislators, but to afford them necessary information, and to render them useful: another valuable end is answered by it, sympathy, and the means of communication between them and their constituents, is substantially promoted; so that on every principle legislators, at certain periods, ought to live among their constituents.

13. Some men of science are undoubtedly necessary in every legislature; but the knowledge, generally, necessary for men who make laws, is a knowledge of the common concerns, and particular circumstances of the people. In a republican government seats in the legislature are highly honorable; I believe but few do, and surely none ought to consider them as places of profit and permanent support. Were the people always properly attentive, they would, at proper periods, call their law makers home, by sending others in their room: but this is not often the case, and therefore, in making constitutions, when the people are attentive, they ought cautiously to provide for those benefits, those advantageous changes in the administration of their affairs, which they are often apt to be inattentive to in practice. On the whole, to guard against the evils, and to secure the advantages I have mentioned, with the greatest degree of certainty, we ought clearly, in my opinion, to increase the federal representation, to secure elections on proper principles, to establish a right to recall members, and a rotation among them.

14. [4] By the art. 2. sect. 2. treaties must be made with the advice and consent of the senate, and two-thirds of those present must concur: also, with consent of the senate, almost all federal officers, civil and military, must be appointed. As to treaties I have my doubts; but as to the appointments of officers, I think we may clearly shew the senate to be a very improper body indeed to have any thing to do with them.[75] I am not perfectly satisfied, that the senate, a branch of the legislature, and court for trying impeachments, ought to have a controuling power in making all treaties; yet, I confess, I do not discern how a restraint upon the president in this important business, can be better or more safely lodged: a power to make and conclude all treaties is too important to be vested in him alone, or in him and an executive council, only sufficiently numerous for other purposes, and the house of representatives is too numerous to be concerned in treaties of peace and of alliance. This power is now lodged in congress, to be exercised by the consent of nine states. The federal senate, like the delegations in the present congress, will represent the states, and the consent of two-thirds

75. Cf. *Brutus XVI* (13).

of that senate will bear some similitude to the consent of nine states. It is probable the United States will not make more than one treaty, on an average, in two or three years, and this power may always be exercised with great deliberation: perhaps the senate is sufficiently numerous to be trusted with this power, sufficiently small to proceed with secrecy, and sufficiently permanent to exercise this power with proper consistency and due deliberation. To lodge this power in a less respectable and less numerous body might not be safe; we must place great confidence in the hands that hold it, and we deceive ourselves if we give it under an idea, that we can impeach, to any valuable purpose, the man or men who may abuse it.

15. On a fair construction of the constitution, I think the legislature has a proper controul over the president and senate in settling commercial treaties. By art. 1. sect. 2. the legislature will have power to regulate commerce with foreign nations, &c. By art. 2. sect. 2. the president, with the advice and consent of two-thirds of the senate, may make treaties. These clauses must be considered together, and we ought never to make one part of the same instrument contradict another, if it can be avoided by any reasonable construction. By the first recited clause, the legislature has the power, that is, as I understand it, the sole power to regulate commerce with foreign nations, or to make all the rules and regulations respecting trade and commerce between our citizens and foreigners: by the second recited clause, the president and senate have power generally to make treaties.—There are several kinds of treaties—as treaties of commerce, of peace, of alliance, &c. I think the words to "make treaties," may be consistently construed, and yet so as it shall be left to the legislature to confirm commercial treaties; they are in their nature and operation very distinct from treaties of peace and of alliance; the latter generally require secrecy, it is but very seldom they interfere with the laws and internal police of the country; to make them is properly the exercise of executive powers, and the constitution authorises the president and senate to make treaties, and gives the legislature no power, directly or indirectly, respecting these treaties of peace and alliance. As to treaties of commerce, they do not generally require secrecy, they almost always involve in them legislative powers, interfere with the laws and internal police of the country, and operate immediately on persons and property, especially in the commercial towns: (they have in Great-Britain usually been confirmed by parliament); they consist of rules and regulations respecting commerce; and to regulate commerce, or to make regulations respecting commerce, the federal legislature, by the constitution, has the power. I do not see that any commercial regulations can be made in trea-

ties, that will not infringe upon this power in the legislature: therefore, I infer, that the true construction is, that the president and senate shall make treaties; but all commercial treaties shall be subject to be confirmed by the legislature. This construction will render the clauses consistent, and make the powers of the president and senate, respecting treaties, much less exceptionable.

The Federal Farmer.

– XII –

January 12, 1788

Dear Sir,

1. On carefully examining the parts of the proposed system, respecting the elections of senators, and especially of the representatives, they appear to me to be both ambiguous and very defective. I shall endeavour to pursue a course of reasoning, which shall fairly lead to establishing the impartiality and security of elections, and then to point out an amendment in this respect.

2. It is well observed by Montesquieu, that in republican governments, the forms of elections are fundamental; and that it is an essential part of the social compact, to ascertain by whom, to whom, when, and in what manner suffrages are to be given.[76]

3. Wherever we find the regulation of elections have not been carefully fixed by the constitution, or the principles of them, we constantly see the legislatures new modifying its own form, and changing the spirit of the government to answer partial purposes.

4. By the proposed plan it is fixed, that the qualifications of the electors of the federal representatives shall be the same as those of the electors of state representatives; though these vary some in the several states the electors are fixed and designated.

5. The qualifications of the representatives are also fixed and designated, and no person under 25 years of age, not an inhabitant of the state, and not having been seven years a citizen of the United States, can be elected; the clear inference is, that all persons 25 years of age, and upwards, inhabitants of the state, and having been, at any period or periods, seven years citizens of the United States, may be elected representatives. They have a right to be elected by the constitution, and the electors have a right to chuse them.

76. *Spirit of the Laws* II, chap. 2.

This is fixing the federal representation, as to the elected, on a very broad basis: it can be no objection to the elected, that they are Christians, Pagans, Mahometans, or Jews; that they are of any colour, rich or poor, convict or not: Hence many men may be elected, who cannot be electors. Gentlemen who have commented so largely upon the wisdom of the constitution, for excluding from being elected young men under a certain age, would have done well to have recollected, that it positively makes pagans, convicts, &c. eligible. The people make the constitution; they exclude a few persons, by certain descriptions, from being elected, and all not thus excluded are clearly admitted. Now a man 25 years old, an inhabitant of the state, and having been a citizen of the states seven years, though afterwards convicted, may be elected, because not within any of the excluding clauses; the same of a beggar, an absentee, &c.

6. The right of the electors, and eligibility of the elected being fixed by the people, they cannot be narrowed by the state legislatures, or congress: it is established, that a man being (among other qualifications) an inhabitant of the state, shall be eligible. Now it would be narrowing the right of the people to confine them in their choice to a man, an inhabitant of a particular county or district in the state. Hence it follows, that neither the state legislatures or congress can establish district elections; that is, divide the state into districts, and confine the electors of each district to the choice of a man resident in it. If the electors could be thus limited in one respect, they might in another be confined to chuse a man of a particular religion, of certain property, &c. and thereby half of the persons made eligible by the constitution be excluded. All laws, therefore, for regulating elections must be made on the broad basis of the constitution.

7. Next, we may observe, that representatives are to be chosen by the people of the state. What is a choice by the people of the state? If each given district in it choose one, will that be a choice within the meaning of the constitution? Must the choice be by plurality of votes, or a majority? In connection with these questions, we must take the 4th sect. art. 1, where it is said the state legislatures shall prescribe the times, places, and manner of holding elections; but congress may make or alter such regulations.[77] By this clause, I suppose, the electors of different towns and districts in the state may be assembled in different places, to give their votes; but when so assembled, by another clause they cannot, by congress or the state legislatures, be restrained from giving their votes for any man an inhabitant

77. Cf. *Brutus IV* (8–9).

of the state, and qualified as to age, and having been a citizen the time required. But I see nothing in the constitution by which to decide, whether the choice shall be by a plurality or a majority of votes: this, in my mind, is by far the most important question in the business of elections. When we say a representative shall be chosen by the people, it seems to imply that he shall be chosen by a majority of them; but states which use the same phraseology in this respect, practice both ways. I believe a majority of the states, chuse by pluralities, and, I think it probable, that the federal house of representatives will decide that a choice of its members by pluralities is constitutional. A man who has the most votes is chosen in Great-Britain. It is this, among other things, that gives every man fair play in the game of influence and corruption. I believe that not much stress was laid upon the objection that congress may assemble the electors at some out of the way place. However, the advocates seem to think they obtain a victory of no small glory and importance, when they can shew, with some degree of colour, that the evil is rather a possibility than a probability.

8. When I observed that the elections were not secured on proper principles,[78] I had an idea of far more probable and extensive evils, secret mischiefs, and not so glaring transgressions, the exclusions of proper district elections, and of the choice by a majority.

9. It is easy to perceive that there is an essential difference between elections by pluralities and by majorities, between choosing a man in a small or limited district, and choosing a number of men promiscuously by the people of a large state; and while we are almost secure of judicious unbiassed elections by majorities in such districts, we have no security against deceptions, influence and corruption in states or large districts in electing by pluralities. When a choice is made by a plurality of votes, it is often made by a very small part of the electors, who attend and give their votes, when by a majority, never by so few as one half of them. The partialities and improprieties attending the former mode may be illustrated by a case that lately happened in one of the middle states.—Several representatives were to be chosen by a large number of inhabitants compactly settled, among whom there were four or five thousand voters. Previous to the time of election a number of lists of candidates were published, to divide and distract the voters in general—about half a dozen men of some influence, who had a favourite list to carry, met several times, fixed their list, and agreed to hand it about among all who could probably be induced to adopt it, and to

78. *FF II* (1).

circulate the other lists among their opponents, to divide them. The poll was opened, and several hundred electors, suspecting nothing, attended and put in their votes; the list of the half dozen was carried, and men were found to be chosen, some of whom were very disagreeable to a large majority of the electors: though several hundred electors voted, men on that list were chosen who had only 45, 43, 44, &c. votes each; they had a plurality, that is, more than any other persons: the votes generally were scattered, and those who made even a feeble combination succeeded in placing highest upon the list several very unthought of and very unpopular men. This evil never could have happened in a town where all the voters meet in one place, and consider no man as elected unless he have a majority, or more than half of all the votes; clear it is, that the men on whom thus but a small part of the votes are bestowed, cannot possess the confidence of the people, or have any considerable degree of influence over them.

10. But as partial, as liable to secret influence, and corruption as the choice by pluralities may be, I think, we cannot avoid it, without essentially increasing the federal representation, and adopting the principles of district elections. There is but one case in which the choice by the majority is practicable, and that is, where districts are formed of such moderate extent that the electors in each can conveniently meet in one place, and at one time, and proceed to the choice of a representative; when, if no man have a majority, or more than half of all the votes the first time, the voters may examine the characters of those brought forward, accommodate, and proceed to repeat their votes till some one shall have that majority. This, I believe, cannot be a case under the constitution proposed in its present form. To explain my ideas, take Massachusetts, for instance, she is entitled to eight representatives, she has 370,000 inhabitants, about 46,000 to one representative; if the elections be so held that the electors throughout the state meet in their several towns or places, and each elector puts in his vote for eight representatives, the votes of the electors will ninety-nine times in a hundred, be so scattered that on collecting the votes from the several towns or places, no men will be found, each of whom have a majority of the votes, and therefore the election will not be made. On the other hand, there may be such a combination of votes, that in thus attempting to chuse eight representatives, the electors may chuse even fifteen. Suppose 10,000 voters to attend and give their votes, each voter will give eight votes, one for each of eight representatives; in the whole 80,000 votes will be given—eight men, each having 5001 votes, in the whole 40,008 will have each a majority, and be chosen—39,092 votes will be bestowed on other men, and if they

all be bestowed on seven men, they may have each a considerable majority, and also be chosen. This indeed is a very rare combination: but the bestowing all the votes pretty equally upon nine, ten, or eleven men, and chusing them all, is an event too probable not to be guarded against.

11. If Massachusetts be divided into eight districts, each having about 46,000 inhabitants, and each district directed to chuse one representative, it will be found totally impracticable for the electors of it to meet in one place; and, when they meet in several towns and places in the district, they will vote for different men, and nineteen times in twenty, so scatter their votes, that no one man will have a majority of the whole and be chosen: we must, therefore, take the man who has the most votes, whether he has three quarters, one quarter, or one tenth part of the whole; the inconveniencies of scattering votes will be increased, as men not of the district, as well as those that are in it, may be voted for.

12. I might add many other observations to evince the superiority and solid advantages of proper district elections, and a choice by a majority, and to prove, that many evils attend the contrary practice: these evils we must encounter as the constitution now stands.

13. I see no way to fix elections on a proper footing, and to render tolerably equal and secure the federal representation, but by increasing the representation, so as to have one representative for each district, in which the electors may conveniently meet in one place, and at one time, and chuse by a majority.[79] Perhaps this might be effected pretty generally, by fixing one representative for each twelve thousand inhabitants; dividing, or fixing the principles for dividing the states into proper districts; and directing the electors of each district to the choice, by a majority, of some men having a permanent interest and residence in it. I speak of a representation tolerably equal, &c. because I am still of opinion, that it is impracticable in this extensive country to have a federal representation sufficiently democratic, or substantially drawn from the body of the people: the principles just mentioned may be the best practical ones we can expect to establish. By thus increasing the representation, we not only make it more democratical and secure, strengthen the confidence of the people in it, and thereby render it more nervous and energetic; but it will also enable the people essentially to change, for the better, the principles and forms of elections. To provide for the people's wandering throughout the state for a representative, may

79. Cf. *Brutus IV* (9).

sometimes enable them to elect a more brilliant or an abler man, than by confining them to districts, but generally this latitude will be used to pernicious purposes, especially connected with the choice by plurality; when a man in the remote part of the state, perhaps, obnoxious at home, but ambitious and intriguing, may be chosen to represent the people in another part of the state far distant, and by a small part of them, or by a faction, or by a combination of some particular description of men among them. This has been long the case in Great-Britain, it is the case in several of the states, nor do I think that such pernicious practices will be merely possible in our federal concerns, but highly probable. By establishing district elections, we exclude none of the best men from being elected; and we fix what, in my mind, is of far more importance than brilliant talents, I mean a sameness, as to residence and interests, between the representative and his constituents; and by the election by a majority, he is sure to be the man, the choice of more than half of them.

14. Though it is impossible to put elections on a proper footing as the constitution stands, yet I think regulations respecting them may be introduced of considerable service: it is not only, therefore, important to enquire how they may be made, but also what body has the controuling power over them. An intelligent, free and unbiassed choice of representatives by the people is of the last importance: we must then carefully guard against all combinations, secret arts, and influence to the contrary. Various expedients have been adopted in different countries and states to effect genuine elections; as the constitution now stands, I confess, I do not discover any better than those adopted in Connecticut, in the choice of counsellers, before mentioned.[80]

15. The federal representatives are to be chosen every second year (an odd mode of expression). In all the states, except South-Carolina, the people, the same electors, meet twice in that time to elect state representatives. For instance, let the electors in Massachusetts, when they meet to chuse state representatives, put in their votes for eight federal representatives, the number that state may chuse (merely for distinction sake, we may call these the votes of nomination), and return a list of the men voted for, in the several towns and places, to the legislature, or some proper body; let this list be immediately examined and published, and some proper number, say 15 or 20, who shall have the most votes upon the list, be sent out to the people; and when the electors shall meet the next year to chuse state

80. *FF VI* (26).

representatives, let them put in their votes for the eight federal representatives, confining their votes to the proper number so sent out; and let the eight highest of those thus voted for in the two votes (which we may call, by way of distinction, votes of election), be the federal representatives: thus a choice may be made by the people, once in two years, without much trouble and expence, and, I believe, with some degree of security. As soon as the votes of nomination shall be collected and made known, the people will know who are voted for, and who are candidates for their votes the succeeding year; the electors will have near a year to enquire into their characters and politics, and also into any undue means, if any were taken, to bring any of them forward; and such as they find to be the best men, and agreeable to the people, they may vote for in giving the votes of election. By these means the men chosen will ultimately always have a majority, or near a majority, of the votes of the electors, who shall attend and give their votes. The mode itself will lead to the discovery of truth and of political characters, and to prevent private combinations, by rendering them in a great measure of no effect. As the choice is to be made by the people, all combinations and checks must be confined to their votes. No supplying the want of a majority by the legislatures, as in Massachusetts in the choice of senators, &c. can be admitted: the people generally judge right when informed, and, in giving their votes the second time, they may always correct their former errors.

16. I think we are all sufficiently acquainted with the progress of elections to see, that the regulations, as to times, places, and the manner merely of holding elections, may, under the constitution, easily be made useful or injurious. It is important then to enquire, who has the power to make regulations, and who ought to have it. By the constitution, the state legislatures shall prescribe the times, places, and manner of holding elections, but congress may make or alter such regulations. Power in congress merely to alter those regulations, made by the states, could answer no valuable purposes; the states might make, and congress alter them *ad infinitum:* and when the state should cease to make, or should annihilate its regulations, congress would have nothing to alter. But the states shall make regulations, and congress may make such regulations as the clause stands: the true construction is, that when congress shall see fit to regulate the times, places, and manner of holding elections, congress may do it, and state regulations, on this head, must cease; for if state regulations could exist, after congress should make a system of regulations, there would, or might, be two incompatible systems of regulations relative to the same subject.

17. It has been often urged, that congress ought to have power to make these regulations, otherwise the state legislatures, by neglecting to make provision for elections, or by making improper regulations, may destroy the general government. It is very improbable that any state legislature will adopt measures to destroy the representation of its own constituents in congress, especially when the state must, represented in congress or not, pay its proportion of the expence of keeping up the government, and even of the representatives of the other states, and be subject to their laws. Should the state legislatures be disposed to be negligent, or to combine to break up congress, they have a very simple way to do it, as the constitution now stands—they have only to neglect to chuse senators, or to appoint the electors of the president, and vice-president: there is no remedy provided against these last evils: nor is it to be presumed, that if a sufficient number of state legislatures to break up congress, should, by neglect or otherwise, attempt to do it, that the people, who yearly elect those legislatures, would elect under the regulations of congress. These and many other reasons must evince, that it was not merely to prevent an annihilation of the federal government that congress has power to regulate elections.[81]

18. It has been urged also, that the state legislatures chuse the federal senators, one branch, and may injure the people, who chuse the other, by improper regulations; that therefore congress, in which the people will immediately have one, the representative branch, ought to have power to interfere in behalf of the people, and rectify such improper regulations. The advocates have said much about the opponents dwelling upon possibilities; but to suppose the people will find it necessary to appeal to congress to restrain the oppressions of the state legislatures, is supposing a possibility indeed. Can any man in his senses suppose that the state legislatures, which are so numerous as almost to be the people themselves, all branches of them depending yearly, for the most part, on the elections of the people, will abuse them in regulating federal elections, and make it proper to transfer the power to congress, a body, one branch of which is chosen once in six years by these very legislatures, and the other biennially, and not half so numerous as even the senatorial branches in those legislatures?

19. Senators are to be chosen by the state legislatures, where there are two branches the appointment must be, I presume, by a concurrent resolution, in passing which, as in passing all other legislative acts, each branch will have a negative; this will give the senatorial branch just as much weight

81. Cf. *Brutus IV* (9).

in the appointment as the democratic: the two branches form a legislature only when acting separately, and therefore, whenever the members of the two branches meet, mix and vote individually in one room, for making an election, it is expressly so directed by the constitutions. If the constitution, by fixing the choice to be made by the legislatures, has given each branch an equal vote, as I think it has, it cannot be altered by any regulations.

20. On the whole, I think, all general principles respecting electors ought to be carefully established by the constitution, as the qualifications of the electors and of elected: the number of the representatives, and the inhabitants of each given district, called on to chuse a man from among themselves by a majority of votes; leaving it to the legislature only so to regulate, from time to time, the extent of the districts so as to keep the representatives proportionate to the number of inhabitants in the several parts of the country; and so far as regulations as to elections cannot be fixed by the constitution, they ought to be left to the state legislatures, they coming far nearest to the people themselves; at most, congress ought to have power to regulate elections only where a state shall neglect to make them.

The Federal Farmer.

– XIII –

January 14, 1788

Dear Sir,

1. In this letter I shall further examine two clauses in the proposed constitution respecting appointments to office.—By art. 2. sect. 2. the president shall nominate, and by and with the advice and consent of the senate, shall appoint ambassadors, other public ministers and consuls, judges of the supreme court, and all other officers of the United States, whose appointments, &c. By art. 1, sect. 6. No senator or representative shall, during the term for which he was elected, be appointed to any civil office under the authority of the United States, which shall have been created, or the emoluments whereof shall have been increased during such time.

2. Thus the president must nominate, and the senate concur in the appointment of all federal officers, civil and military, and the senators and representatives are made ineligible only to the few civil offices abovementioned. To preserve the federal government pure and uncorrupt, peculiar precautions relative to appointments to office will be found highly necessary from the very forms and character of the government itself. The honours and emoluments of public offices are the objects in all communities, that

ambitious and necessitous men never lose sight of. The honest, the modest, and the industrious part of the community content themselves, generally, with their private concerns; they do not solicit those offices which are the perpetual source of cabals, intrigues, and contests among men of the former description, men embarrassed, intriguing, and destitute of modesty. Even in the most happy country and virtuous government, corrupt influence in appointments cannot always be avoided; perhaps we may boast of our share of virtue as a people, and if we are only sufficiently aware of the influence, biasses, and prejudices, common to the affairs of men, we may go far towards guarding against the effects of them.

3. We all agree, that a large standing army has a strong tendency to depress and inslave the people; it is equally true that a large body of selfish, unfeeling, unprincipled civil officers has a like, or a more pernicious tendency to the same point. Military, and especially civil establishments, are the necessary appendages of society; they are deductions from productive labour, and substantial wealth, in proportion to the number of men employed in them; they are oppressive where unnecessarily extended and supported by men unfriendly to the people; they are injurious when too small, and supported by men too timid and dependant. It is of the last importance to decide well upon the necessary number of offices, to fill them with proper characters, and to establish efficiently the means of punctually punishing those officers who may do wrong.

4. To discern the nature and extent of this power of appointments,[82] we need only to consider the vast number of officers necessary to execute a national system in this extensive country, the prodigious biasses the hopes and expectations of offices have on their conduct, and the influence public officers have among the people—these necessary officers, as judges, state's attornies, clerks, sheriffs, &c. in the federal supreme and inferior courts, admirals and generals, and subordinate officers in the army and navy, ministers, consuls, &c. sent to foreign countries; officers in the federal city, in the revenue, post-office departments, &c. &c. must, probably, amount to several thousands, without taking into view the very inferior ones. There can be no doubt but that the most active men in politics, in and out of congress, will be the foremost candidates for the best of these offices; the man or men who shall have the disposal of them, beyond dispute, will have by far the greatest share of active influence in the government; but appointments

82. Cf. *Brutus I* (20).

must be made, and who shall make them? what modes of appointments will be attended with the fewest inconveniencies? is the question. The senators and representatives are the law makers, create all offices, and whenever they see fit, they impeach and try officers for misconduct; they ought to be in session but part of the year, and as legislators, they must be too numerous to make appointments, perhaps, a few very important ones excepted. In contemplating the necessary officers of the union, there appear to be six different modes in which, in whole or in part, the appointments may be made, 1. By the legislature; 2. by the president and senate—3. by the president and an executive council—4. by the president alone—5. by the heads of the departments—and 6. by the state governments—Among all these, in my opinion, there may be an advantageous distribution of the power of appointments. In considering the legislators, in relation to the subject before us, two interesting questions particularly arise—1. Whether they ought to be eligible to any offices whatever during the period for which they shall be elected to serve, and even for some time afterwards—and 2. How far they ought to participate in the power of appointments. As to the first, it is true that legislators in foreign countries, or in our state governments, are not generally made ineligible to office: there are good reasons for it; in many countries the people have gone on without ever examining the principles of government. There have been but few countries in which the legislators have been a particular set of men periodically chosen: but the principal reason is, that which operates in the several states, viz. the legislators are so frequently chosen, and so numerous, compared with the number of offices for which they can reasonably consider themselves as candidates, that the chance of any individual member's being chosen, is too small to raise his hopes or expectations, or to have any considerable influence upon his conduct. Among the state legislators, one man in twenty may be appointed in some committee business, &c. for a month or two; but on a fair computation, not one man in a hundred sent to the state legislatures is appointed to any permanent office of profit: directly the reverse of this will evidently be found true in the federal administration. Throughout the United States, about four federal senators, and thirty-three representatives, averaging the elections, will be chosen in a year; these few men may rationally consider themselves as the fairest candidates for a very great number of lucrative offices, which must become vacant in the year, and pretty clearly a majority of the federal legislators, if not excluded, will be mere expectants for public offices. I need not adduce further arguments to establish a position so clear; I need only call to your recollection my observations in a former letter, wherein I endeavoured to shew the fallacy of the argument, that the members must return home and mix with the people.[83] It is said, that men are governed by interested motives, and will not attend as legislators, unless they can, in common with others, be eligible to offices of honor and profit. This will undoubtedly be the case with some men, but I presume only with such men as never ought to be chosen legislators in a free country; an opposite principle will influence good men; virtuous patriots, and generous minds, will esteem it a higher honor to be selected as the guardians of a free people; they will be satisfied with a reasonable compensation for their time and service; nor will they wish to be within the vortex of influence. The valuable effects of this principle of making legislators ineligible to offices for a given time, has never yet been sufficiently attended to or considered: I am assured, that it was established by the convention after long debate, and afterwards, on an unfortunate change of a few members, altered.[84] Could the federal legislators be excluded in the manner proposed, I think it would be an important point gained; as to themselves, they would be left to act much more from motives consistent with the public good.

5. In considering the principle of rotation I had occasion to distinguish the condition of a legislator from that of mere official man[85]—We acquire certain habits, feelings, and opinions, as men and citizens—others, and very different ones, from a long continuance in office: It is, therefore, a valuable observation in many bills of rights, that rulers ought frequently to return and mix with the people. A legislature, in a free country, must be numerous; it is in some degree a periodical assemblage of the people, frequently formed—the principal officers in the executive and judicial departments, must have more permanency in office. Hence it may be inferred, that the legislature will remain longer uncorrupted and virtuous; longer congenial to the people, than the officers of those departments. If it is not, therefore, in our power to preserve republican principles, for a series of ages, in all the departments of government, we may a long while preserve them in a well formed legislature. To this end we ought to take every precaution to pre-

83. See *FF IX* (10–14).

84. In its early deliberations the convention accepted the provision of the Virginia resolution for ineligibility. The decisive shift toward the milder prohibition that found its way into the Constitution came on September 3. See Farrand, II, 489–92. (Storing, II, 355, n100.)

85. See *FF XI* (5).

vent legislators becoming mere office-men; chuse them frequently, make them recallable, establish rotation among them, make them ineligible to offices, and give them as small a share as possible in the disposal of them. Add to this, a legislature, in the nature of things, is not formed for the detail business of appointing officers; there is also generally an impropriety in the same men's making offices and filling them, and a still greater impropriety in their impeaching and trying the officers they appoint. For these, and other reasons, I conclude, the legislature is not a proper body for the appointment of officers in general. But having gone through with the different modes of appointment, I shall endeavour to shew what share in the distribution of the power of appointments the legislature must, from necessity, rather than from propriety, take. 2. Officers may be appointed by the president and senate—this mode, for general purposes, is clearly not defensible. All the reasoning touching the legislature will apply to the senate; the senate is a branch of the legislature, which ought to be kept pure and unbiassed; it has a part in trying officers for misconduct, and in creating offices, it is too numerous for a council of appointment, or to feel any degree of responsibility: if it has an advantage of the legislature, in being the least numerous, it has a disadvantage in being more unsafe: add to this, the senate is to have a share in the important branch of power respecting treaties. Further, this sexennial senate of 26 members, representing 13 sovereign states, will not, in practice, be found to be a body to advise, but to order and dictate in fact; and the president will be a mere *primus inter pares.* The consequence will be, that the senate, with these efficient means of influence, will not only dictate, probably, to the president, but manage the house, as the constitution now stands; and under appearances of a balanced system, in reality, govern alone. There may also, by this undue connection, be particular periods when a very popular president may have a very improper influence upon the senate and upon the legislature. A council of appointment must very probably sit all, or near all, the year—the senate will be too important and too expensive a body for this. By giving the senate, directly or indirectly, an undue influence over the representatives, and the improper means of fettering, embarrassing, or controuling the president or executive, we give the government, in the very out set, a fatal and pernicious tendency to that middle undesirable point—aristocracy. When we, as a circumstance not well to be avoided, admit the senate to a share of power in making treaties, and in managing foreign concerns, we certainly progress full far enough towards this most undesirable point in government. For with this power, also, I believe, we must join that of appointing ambassa-

dors, other foreign ministers, and consuls, being powers necessarily connected.—In every point of view, in which I can contemplate this subject, it
appears extremely clear to me, that the senate ought not generally to be a
council of appointment.[86] The legislature, after the people, is the great
fountain of power, and ought to be kept as pure and uncorrupt as possible,
from the hankerings, biasses, and contagion of offices—then the streams
issuing from it, will be less tainted with those evils. It is not merely the
number of impeachments, that are to be expected to make public officers
honest and attentive in their business. A general opinion must pervade the
community, that the house, the body to impeach them for misconduct, is
disinterested, and ever watchful for the public good; and that the judges
who shall try impeachments, will not feel a shadow of biass. Under such
circumstances, men will not dare transgress, who, not deterred by such
accusers and judges, would repeatedly misbehave. We have already suffered
many and extensive evils, owing to the defects of the confederation, in not
providing against the misconduct of public officers. When we expect the
law to be punctually executed, not one man in ten thousand will disobey it:
it is the probable chance of escaping punishment that induces men to transgress. It is one important mean to make the government just and honest,
rigidly and constantly to hold, before the eyes of those who execute it,
punishment, and dismission from office, for misconduct. These are principles no candid man, who has just ideas of the essential features of a free
government, will controvert. They are, to be sure, at this period, called visionary, speculative and anti-governmental—but in the true stile of court-
iers, selfish politicians, and flatterers of despotism—discerning republican
men of both parties see their value. They are said to be of no value, by
empty boasting advocates for the constitution, who, by their weakness and
conduct, in fact, injure its cause much more than most of its opponents.
From their high sounding promises, men are led to expect a defence of it,
and to have their doubts removed. When a number of long pieces appear,
they, instead of the defence, &c. they expected, see nothing but a parade of
names—volumes written without ever coming to the point—cases quoted
between which and ours there is not the least similitude—and partial extracts made from histories and governments, merely to serve a purpose.
Some of them, like the true admirers of royal and senatorial robes, would
fain prove, that nations who have thought like freemen and philosophers
about government, and endeavoured to be free, have often been the most

86. Cf. *Brutus XVI* (13).

miserable: if a single riot, in the course of five hundred years happened in a free country, if a salary, or the interest of a public or private debt was not paid at the moment, they seem to lay more stress upon these triffles (for triffles they are in a free and happy country) than upon the oppressions of despotic government for ages together. (As to the lengthy writer in New-York you mention,[87] I have attentively examined his pieces; he appears to be a candid good-hearted man, to have a good stile, and some plausible ideas; but when we carefully examine his pieces, to see where the strength of them lies; when the mind endeavours to fix on those material parts, which ought to be the essence of all voluminous productions, we do not find them: the writer appears constantly to move on a smooth surface, the part of his work, like the parts of a cob-house, are all equally strong and all equally weak, and all like those works of the boys, without an object; his pieces appear to have but little relation to the great question, whether the constitution is fitted to the condition and character of this people or not.) But to return—3. Officers may be appointed by the president and an executive council—when we have assigned to the legislature the appointment of a few important officers—to the president and senate the appointment of those concerned in managing foreign affairs—to the state governments the appointment of militia officers, and authorise the legislature, by legislative acts, to assign to the president alone, to the heads of the departments, and courts of law respectively, the appointment of many inferior officers; we shall then want to lodge some where a residuum of power, a power to appoint all other necessary officers, as established by law. The fittest receptacle for this residuary power is clearly, in my opinion, the first executive magistrate, advised and directed by an executive council of seven or nine members, periodically chosen from such proportional districts as the union may for the purpose be divided into. The people may give their votes for twice the number of counsellers wanted, and the federal legislature take twice the number also from the highest candidates, and from among them chuse the seven or nine, or number wanted. Such a council may be rationally formed for the business of appointments; whereas the senate, created for other purposes, never can be—Such councils form a feature in some of the best executives in the union—they appear to be essential to every first magistrate, who may frequently want advice.

6. To authorise the president to appoint his own council would be un-

87. Presumably Publius. Thirty-eight numbers of *The Federalist* had appeared by the date of this letter. (Storing, II, 356, n102.)

safe: to give the sole appointment of it to the legislature, would confer an undue and unnecessary influence upon that branch. Such a council for a year would be less expensive than the senate for four months. The president may nominate, and the counsellers always be made responsible for their advice and opinions, by recording and signing whatever they advise to be done. They and the president, to many purposes, will properly form an independent executive branch; have an influence unmixed with the legislative, which the executive never can have while connected with a powerful branch of the legislature. And yet the influence arising from the power of appointments be less dangerous, because in less dangerous hands—hands properly adequate to possess it. Whereas the senate, from its character and situation, will add a dangerous weight to the power itself, and be far less capable of responsibility, than the council proposed. There is another advantage; the residuum of power, as to appointments, which the president and council need possess, is less than that the president and senate must have. And as such a council would render the sessions of the senate unnecessary many months in the year, the expences of the government would not be increased, if they would not be lessened by the institution of such a council. I think I need not dwell upon this article, as the fitness of this mode of appointment will perhaps amply appear by the evident unfitness of the others.

7. [5] Officers may be appointed by the president alone. It has been almost universally found, when a man has been authorized to exercise power alone, he has never done it alone; but, generally, aided his determinations by, and rested on the advice and opinions of others. And it often happens when advice is wanted, the worst men, the most interested creatures, the worst advice is at hand, obtrude themselves, and misdirect the mind of him who would be informed and advised. It is very seldom we see a single executive depend on accidental advice and assistance; but each single executive has, almost always, formed to itself a regular council, to be assembled and consulted on important occasions; this proves that a select council, of some kind, is, by experience, generally found necessary and useful. But in a free country, the exercise of any considerable branch of power ought to be under some checks and controuls. As to this point, I think the constitution stands well, the legislature may, when it shall deem it expedient, from time to time, authorise the president alone to appoint particular inferior officers, and when necessary to take back the power. His power, therefore, in this respect, may always be increased or decreased by the legislature,

as experience, the best instructor, shall direct: always keeping him, by the constitution, within certain bounds.

The Federal Farmer.

– XIV –

January 17, 1788

Dear Sir,

    1. To continue the subject of appointments:—Officers, in the fifth place, may be appointed by the heads of departments or courts of law. Art. 2. sect. 2. respecting appointments, goes on—"But congress may by law vest the appointment of such inferior officers as they think proper in the president alone, in the courts of law, or in the heads of departments." The probability is, as the constitution now stands, that the senate, a branch of the legislature, will be tenacious of the power of appointment, and much too sparingly part with a share of it to the courts of law, and heads of departments. Here again the impropriety appears of the senate's having, generally, a share in the appointment of officers. We may fairly presume, that the judges, and principal officers in the departments, will be able well informed men in their respective branches of business; that they will, from experience, be best informed as to proper persons to fill inferior offices in them; that they will feel themselves responsible for the execution of their several branches of business, and for the conduct of the officers they may appoint therein.—From these, and other considerations, I think we may infer, that impartial and judicious appointments of subordinate officers will, generally, be made by the courts of law, and the heads of departments. This power of distributing appointments, as circumstances may require, into several hands, in a well formed disinterested legislature, might be of essential service, not only in promoting beneficial appointments, but, also, in preserving the balance in government: a feeble executive may be strengthened and supported by placing in its hands more numerous appointments; an executive too influential may be reduced within proper bounds, by placing many of the inferior appointments in the courts of law, and heads of departments; nor is there much danger that the executive will be wantonly weakened or strengthened by the legislature, by thus shifting the appointments of inferior officers, since all must be done by legislative acts, which cannot be passed without the consent of the executive, or the consent of two-thirds of both branches—a good legislature will use this power to

preserve the balance and perpetuate the government. Here again we are brought to our ultimatum:—is the legislature so constructed as to deserve our confidence?

2. [6] Officers may be appointed by the state governments. By art. 1. sect. 8. the respective states are authorised exclusively to appoint the militia-officers. This not only lodges the appointments in proper places, but it also tends to distribute and lodge in different executive hands the powers of appointing to offices, so dangerous when collected into the hands of one or a few men.

3. It is a good general rule, that the legislative, executive, and judicial powers, ought to be kept distinct; but this, like other general rules, has its exceptions; and without these exceptions we cannot form a good government, and properly balance its parts:[88] and we can determine only from reason, experience, and a critical inspection of the parts of the government, how far it is proper to intermix those powers. Appointments, I believe, in all mixed governments, have been assigned to different hands—some are made by the executive, some by the legislature, some by the judges and some by the people. It has been thought adviseable by the wisest nations, that the legislature should so far exercise executive and judicial powers as to appoint some officers, judge of the elections of its members, and impeach and try officers for misconduct—that the executive should have a partial share in legislation—that judges should appoint some subordinate officers, and regulate so far as to establish rules for their own proceedings. Where the members of the government, as the house, the senate, the executive, and judiciary, are strong and complete, each in itself, the balance is naturally produced, each party may take the powers congenial to it, and we have less need to be anxious about checks, and the subdivision of powers.

4. If after making the deductions, already alluded to, from the general power to appoint federal officers the residuum shall be thought to be too large and unsafe, and to place an undue influence in the hands of the president and council, a further deduction may be made, with many advantages, and, perhaps, with but a few inconveniencies; and that is, by giving the appointment of a few great officers to the legislature—as of the commissioners of the treasury—of the comptroller, treasurer, master coiner, and some of the principal officers in the money department—of the sheriffs or marshalls of the United States—of states attornies, secretary of the home department, and secretary at war, perhaps, of the judges of the supreme

88. Cf. *Brutus XVI* (12).

court— of major-generals and admirals. The appointments of these officers, who may be at the heads of the great departments of business, in carrying into execution the national system, involve in them a variety of considerations; they will not often occur, and the power to make them ought to remain in safe hands. Officers of the above description are appointed by the legislatures in some of the states, and in some not. We may, I believe, presume that the federal legislature will possess sufficient knowledge and discernment to make judicious appointments: however, as these appointments by the legislature tend to increase a mixture of power, to lessen the advantages of impeachments and responsibility, I would by no means contend for them any further than it may be necessary for reducing the power of the executive within the bounds of safety. To determine with propriety how extensive power the executive ought to possess relative to appointments, we must also examine the forms of it, and its other powers; and these forms and other powers I shall now proceed briefly to examine.

5. By art. 2. sect. 1. the executive power shall be vested in a president elected for four years, by electors to be appointed from time to time, in such manner as the state legislatures shall direct—the electors to be equal in numbers to the federal senators and representatives: but congress may determine the time of chusing electors, and the day on which they shall give their votes; and if no president be chosen by the electors, by a majority of votes, the states, as states in congress, shall elect one of the five highest on the list for president. It is to be observed, that in chusing the president, the principle of electing by a majority of votes is adopted; in chusing the vice-president, that of electing by a plurality. Viewing the principles and checks established in the election of the president, and especially considering the several states may guard the appointment of the electors as they shall judge best, I confess there appears to be a judicious combination of principles and precautions. Were the electors more numerous than they will be, in case the representation be not increased, I think, the system would be improved; not that I consider the democratic character so important in the choice of the electors as in the choice of representatives: be the electors more or less democratic, the president will be one of the very few of the most elevated characters. But there is danger, that a majority of a small number of electors may be corrupted and influenced, after appointed electors, and before they give their votes, especially if a considerable space of time elapse between the appointment and voting. I have already considered the advisory council in the executive branch: there are two things further in the organization of the executive, to which I would particularly draw your attention; the first,

which is a single executive, I confess, I approve; the second, by which any person from period to period may be re-elected president, I think very exceptionable.

6. Each state in the union has uniformly shewn its preference for a single executive, and generally directed the first executive magistrate to act in certain cases by the advice of an executive council. Reason, and the experience of enlightened nations, seem justly to assign the business of making laws to numerous assemblies; and the execution of them, principally, to the direction and care of one man. Independent of practice, a single man seems to be peculiarly well circumstanced to superintend the execution of laws with discernment and decision, with promptitude and uniformity: the people usually point out a first man—he is to be seen in civilized as well as uncivilized nations—in republics as well as in other governments. In every large collection of people there must be a visible point serving as a common centre in the government, towards which to draw their eyes and attachments. The constitution must fix a man, or a congress of men, superior in the opinion of the people to the most popular men in the different parts of the community, else the people will be apt to divide and follow their respective leaders. Aspiring men, armies and navies, have not often been kept in tolerable order by the decrees of a senate or an executive council. The advocates for lodging the executive power in the hands of a number of equals, as an executive council, say, that much wisdom may be collected in such a council, and that it will be safe; but they agree, that it cannot be so prompt and responsible as a single man—they admit that such a council will generally consist of the aristocracy, and not stand so indifferent between it and the people as a first magistrate. But the principal objection made to a single man is, that when possessed of power he will be constantly struggling for more, disturbing the government, and encroaching on the rights of others. It must be admitted, that men, from the monarch down to the porter, are constantly aiming at power and importance; and this propensity must be as constantly guarded against in the forms of the government. Adequate powers must be delegated to those who govern, and our security must be in limiting, defining, and guarding the exercise of them, so that those given shall not be abused, or made use of for openly or secretly seizing more. Why do we believe this abuse of power peculiar to a first magistrate? Is it because in the wars and contests of men, one man has often established his power over the rest? Or are men naturally fond of accumulating powers in the hands of one man? I do not see any similitude between the cases of those tyrants, who have sprung up in the midst of wars and tumults, and

the cases of limited executives in established governments; nor shall we, on a careful examination, discover much likeness between the executives in Sweden, Denmark, Holland, &c. which have, from time to time, increased their powers, and become more absolute, and the executives, whose powers are well ascertained and defined, and which remain, by the constitution, only for a short and limited period in the hands of any one man or family. A single man, or family, can long and effectually direct its exertions to one point. There may be many favourable opportunities in the course of a man's life to seize on additional powers, and many more where powers are hereditary; and there are many circumstances favourable to usurpations, where the powers of the man or family are undefined, and such as often may be unduly extended before the people discover it. If we examine history attentively, we shall find that such exertions, such opportunities, and such circumstances as these have attended all the executives which have usurped upon the rights of the people, and which appear originally to have been, in some degree, limited. Admitting that moderate and even well defined powers, long in the hands of the same man or family, will, probably, be unreasonably increased, it will not follow that even extensive powers placed in the hands of a man only for a few years will be abused. The Roman consuls and Carthagenian suffetes possessed extensive powers while in office; but being annually appointed, they but seldom, if ever, abused them. The Roman dictators often possessed absolute power while in office; but usually being elected for short periods of time, no one of them for ages usurped upon the rights of the people. The kings of France, Spain, Sweden, Denmark, &c. have become absolute merely from the encroachments and abuse of power made by the nobles. As to kings, and limited monarchs, generally, history furnishes many more instances in which their powers have been abridged or annihilated by the nobles or people, or both, than in which they have been increased or made absolute; and in almost all the latter cases, we find the people were inattentive and fickle, and evidently were not born to be free. I am the more particular respecting this subject, because I have heard many mistaken observations relative to it. Men of property, and even men who hold powers for themselves and posterity, have too much to lose, wantonly to hazard a shock of the political system; the game must be large, and the chance of winning great, to induce them to risque what they have, for the uncertain prospect of gaining more. Our executive may be altogether elective, and possess no power, but as the substitute of the people, and that well limited, and only for a limited time. The great object is, in a republican government, to guard effectually against perpetuating any portion of power, great or small, in the same man or family; this perpetuation of power is totally uncongenial to the true spirit of republican governments: on the one hand the first executive magistrate ought to remain in office so long as to avoid instability in the execution of the laws; on the other, not so long as to enable him to take any measures to establish himself. The convention, it seems, first agreed that the president should be chosen for seven years, and never after to be eligible. Whether seven years is a period too long or not, is rather matter of opinion; but clear it is, that this mode is infinitely preferable to the one finally adopted. When a man shall get the chair, who may be re-elected, from time to time, for life, his greatest object will be to keep it; to gain friends and votes, at any rate; to associate some favourite son with himself, to take the office after him: whenever he shall have any prospect of continuing the office in himself and family, he will spare no artifice, no address, and no exertions, to increase the powers and importance of it; the servile supporters of his wishes will be placed in all offices, and tools constantly employed to aid his views and sound his praise. A man so situated will have no permanent interest in the government to lose, by contests and convulsions in the state, but always much to gain, and frequently the seducing and flattering hope of succeeding. If we reason at all on the subject, we must irresistably conclude, that this will be the case with nine-tenths of the presidents; we may have, for the first president, and, perhaps, one in a century or two afterwards (if the government should withstand the attacks of others) a great and good man, governed by superior motives; but these are not events to be calculated upon in the present state of human nature.

7. A man chosen to this important office for a limited period, and always afterwards rendered, by the constitution, ineligible, will be governed by very different considerations: he can have no rational hopes or expectations of retaining his office after the expiration of a known limited time, or of continuing the office in his family, as by the constitution there must be a constant transfer of it from one man to another, and consequently from one family to another. No man will wish to be a mere cypher at the head of the government: the great object of each president then will be, to render his government a glorious period in the annals of his country. When a man constitutionally retires from office, he retires without pain; he is sensible he retires because the laws direct it, and not from the success of his rivals, nor with that public disapprobation which being left out, when eligible, implies. It is said, that a man knowing that at a given period he must quit his office, will unjustly attempt to take from the public, and lay in store the

means of support and splendour in his retirement; there can, I think, be but very little in this observation. The same constitution that makes a man eligible for a given period only, ought to make no man eligible till he arrive to the age of forty or forty-five years: if he be a man of fortune, he will retire with dignity to his estate; if not, he may, like the Roman consuls, and other eminent characters in republics, find an honorable support and employment in some respectable office. A man who must, at all events, thus leave his office, will have but few or no temptations to fill its dependant offices with his tools, or any particular set of men; whereas the man constantly looking forward to his future elections, and, perhaps, to the aggrandizement of his family, will have every inducement before him to fill all places with his own props and dependants. As to public monies, the president need handle none of them, and he may always rigidly be made [to] account for every shilling he shall receive.

8. On the whole, it would be, in my opinion, almost as well to create a limited monarchy at once, and give some family permanent power and interest in the community, and let it have something valuable to itself to lose in convulsions in the state, and in attempts of usurpation, as to make a first magistrate eligible for life, and to create hopes and expectations in him and his family, of obtaining what they have not. In the latter case, we actually tempt them to disturb the state, to foment struggles and contests, by laying before them the flattering prospect of gaining much in them without risking any thing.

9. The constitution provides only that the president shall hold his office during the term of four years; that, at most, only implies, that one shall be chosen every fourth year; it also provides, that in case of the removal, death, resignation, or inability, both of the president and vice-president, congress may declare what officer shall act as president; and that such officers shall act accordingly, until the disability be removed, *or a president shall be elected:* it also provides that congress may determine the time of chusing electors, and the day on which they shall give their votes. Considering these clauses together, I submit this question—whether in case of a vacancy in the office of president, by the removal, death, resignation, or inability of the president and vice-president, and congress should declare, that a certain officer, as secretary for foreign affairs, for instance, shall act as president, and suffer such officer to continue several years, or even for his life, to act as president, by omitting to appoint the time for chusing electors of another president, it would be any breach of the constitution? This appears to me to be an intended provision for supplying the office of president, not only for any

remaining portion of the four years, but in cases of emergency, until another president shall be elected; and that at a period beyond the expiration of the four years: we do not know that it is impossible; we do not know that it is improbable, in case a popular officer should thus be declared the acting president, but that he might continue for life, and without any violent act, but merely by neglects and delays on the part of congress.

10. I shall conclude my observations on the organization of the legislature and executive, with making some remarks, rather as a matter of amusement, on the branch, or partial negative, in the legislation:—The third branch in the legislature may answer three valuable purposes, to impede in their passage hasty and intemperate laws, occasionally to assist the senate or people, and to prevent the legislature from encroaching upon the executive or judiciary. In Great Britain the king has a complete negative upon all laws, but he very seldom exercises it. This may be well lodged in him, who possesses strength to support it, and whose family has independent and hereditary interests and powers, rights and prerogatives, in the government, to defend: but in a country where the first executive officer is elective, and has no rights, but in common with the people, a partial negative in legislation, as in Massachusetts and New-York, is, in my opinion, clearly best: in the former state, as before observed, it is lodged in the governor alone; in the latter, in the governor, chancellor, and judges of the supreme court—the new constitution lodges it in the president. This is simply a branch of legislative power, and has in itself no relation to executive or judicial powers. The question is, in what hands ought it to be lodged, to answer the three purposes mentioned the most advantageously? The prevailing opinion seems to be in favour of vesting it in the hands of the first executive magistrate. I will not say this opinion is ill founded. The negative, in one case, is intended to prevent hasty laws, not supported and revised by two-thirds of each of the two branches; in the second, it is to aid the weaker branch; and in the third, to defend the executive and judiciary. To answer these ends, there ought, therefore, to be collected in the hands which hold this negative, firmness, wisdom, and strength; the very object of the negative is occasional opposition to the two branches. By lodging it in the executive magistrate, we give him a share in making the laws, which he must execute; by associating the judges with him, as in New York, we give them a share in making the laws, upon which they must decide as judicial magistrates; this may be a reason for excluding the judges: however, the negative in New-York is certainly well calculated to answer its great purposes: the governor and judges united must possess more firmness and strength, more wisdom and information,

than either alone, and also more of the confidence of the people; and as to the balance among the departments, why should the executive alone hold the scales, and the judicial be left defenceless? I think the negative in New-York is found best in practice; we see it there frequently and wisely put upon the measures of the two branches; whereas in Massachusetts it is hardly ever exercised, and the governor, I believe, has often permitted laws to pass to which he had substantial objections, but did not make them; he, however, it is to be observed, is annually elected.

The Federal Farmer.

– XV –

January 18, 1788

Dear Sir,

1. Before I proceed to examine particularly the powers vested, or which ought to be, vested in each branch of the proposed government, I shall briefly examine the organization of the remaining branch, the judicial, referring the particular examining of its powers to some future letters.[89]

2. In forming this branch, our objects are—a fair and open, a wise and impartial interpretation of the laws—a prompt and impartial administration of justice, between the public and individuals, and between man and man. I believe, there is no feature in a free government more difficult to be well formed than this, especially in an extensive country, where the courts must be numerous, or the citizens travel to obtain justice.

3. The confederation impowers congress to institute judicial courts in four cases. 1. For settling disputes between individual states. 2. For determining, finally, appeals in all cases of captures. 3. For the trial of piracies and felonies committed on the high seas: And, 4. For the administration of martial law in the army and navy.[90] The state courts in all other cases possess the judicial powers, in all questions arising on the laws of nations, of the union, and of the states individually—nor does congress appear to have any controul over state courts, judges or officers. The business of the judicial department is, properly speaking, judicial in part, in part executive, done by judges and juries, by certain recording and executive officers, as clerks, sheriffs, &c. they are all properly limbs, or parts, of the judicial

89. He does treat some of the judicial powers in this letter, but he returns to them in *FF XVIII.*

90. Articles of Confederation, Art. 9.

courts, and have it in charge, faithfully to decide upon, and execute the laws, in judicial cases, between the public and individuals, between man and man. The recording and executive officers, in this department, may well enough be formed by legislative acts, from time to time: but the offices, the situation, the powers and duties of judges and juries, are too important, as they respect the political system, as well as the administration of justice, not to be fixed on general principles by the constitution. It is true, the laws are made by the legislature; but the judges and juries, in their interpretations, and in directing the execution of them, have a very extensive influence for preserving or destroying liberty, and for changing the nature of the government. It is an observation of an approved writer, that judicial power is of such a nature, that when we have ascertained and fixed its limits, with all the caution and precision we can, it will yet be formidable, somewhat arbitrary and despotic—that is, after all our cares, we must leave a vast deal to the discretion and interpretation—to the wisdom, integrity, and politics of the judges[91]—These men, such is the state even of the best laws, may do wrong, perhaps, in a thousand cases, sometimes with, and sometimes without design, yet it may be impracticable to convict them of misconduct. These considerations shew, how cautious a free people ought to be in forming this, as well as the other branches of their government, especially when connected with other considerations equally deserving of notice and attention. When the legislature makes a bad law, or the first executive magistrates usurp upon the rights of the people, they discover the evil much sooner, than the abuses of power in the judicial department; the proceedings of which are far more intricate, complex, and out of their immediate view. A bad law immediately excites a general alarm; a bad judicial determination, though not less pernicious in its consequences, is immediately felt, probably, by a single individual only, and noticed only by his neighbours, and a few spectators in the court. In this country, we have been always jealous of the legislature, and especially the executive; but not always of the judiciary: but very few men attentively consider the essential parts of it, and its proceedings, as they tend to support or to destroy free government: only a few professional men are in a situation properly to do this; and it is often alledged, that instances have not frequently occurred, in which they have been found very alert watchmen in the cause of liberty, or in the cause of democratic republics. Add to these considerations, that particular circumstances exist at this time to increase our inattention to limiting properly the

91. See De Lolme, *The Constitution of England*, I, chap. 12, end.

judicial powers, we may fairly conclude, we are more in danger of sowing
the seeds of arbitrary government in this department than in any other. In
the unsettled state of things in this country, for several years past, it has
been thought, that our popular legislatures have, sometimes, departed from
the line of strict justice, while the law courts have shewn a disposition more
punctually to keep to it. We are not sufficiently attentive to the circumstances, that the measures of popular legislatures naturally settle down in
time, and gradually approach a mild and just medium; while the rigid systems of the law courts naturally become more severe and arbitrary, if not
carefully tempered and guarded by the constitution, and by laws, from time
to time. It is true, much has been written and said about some of these
courts lately, in some of the states; but all has been about their fees, &c. and
but very little to the purposes, as to their influence upon the freedom of the
government. By art. 3. sect. 1. the judicial power of the United States shall
be vested in one supreme court, and in such inferior courts, as congress
may, from time to time, ordain and establish—the judges of them to hold
their offices during good behaviour, and to receive, at stated times, a compensation for their services, which shall not be diminished during their
continuance in office; but which, I conceive, may be increased. By the same
art. sect. 2. the supreme court shall have original jurisdiction, "in all cases
affecting ambassadors, and other public ministers, and consuls, and those
in which a state shall be a party, and appellate jurisdiction, *both as to law and
fact*, in all other federal causes, with such exceptions, and under such regulations, as the congress shall make." By the same section, the judicial power
shall extend in law and equity to all the federal cases therein enumerated.
By the same section the jury trial, in criminal causes, except in cases of
impeachment, is established; but not in civil causes, and the whole state
may be considered as the vicinage in cases of crimes. These clauses present
to view the constitutional features of the federal judiciary: this has been
called a monster by some of the opponents, and some, even of the able advocates, have confessed they do not comprehend it. For myself, I confess, I
see some good things in it, and some very extraordinary ones. "There shall
be one supreme court." There ought in every government to be one court,
in which all great questions in law shall finally meet and be determined: in
Great-Britain, this is the house of lords, aided by all the superior judges; in
Massachusetts, it is, at present, the supreme judicial court, consisting of five
judges; in New-York, by the constitution, it is a court consisting of the
president of the senate, the senators, chancellor and judges of the supreme
court; and in the United States the federal supreme court, or this court in

the last resort, may, by the legislature, be made to consist of three, five, fifty, or any other number of judges. The inferior federal courts are left by the constitution to be instituted and regulated altogether as the legislature shall judge best; and it is well provided, that the judges shall hold their offices during good behaviour. I shall not object to the line drawn between the original and appellate jurisdiction of the supreme court; though should we for safety, &c. be obliged to form a numerous supreme court, and place in it a considerable number of respectable characters, it will be found inconvenient for such a court, originally, to try all the causes affecting ambassadors, consuls, &c.[92] Appeals may be carried up to the supreme court, under such regulations as congress shall make. Thus far the legislature does not appear to be limited to improper [proper?] rules or principles in instituting judicial courts: indeed the legislature will have full power to form and arrange judicial courts in the federal cases enumerated, at pleasure, with these eight exceptions only. 1. There can be but one supreme federal judicial court. 2. This must have jurisdiction as to law and fact in the appellate causes. 3. Original jurisdiction, when foreign ministers and the states are concerned. 4. The judges of the judicial courts must continue in office during good behaviour—and, 5. Their salaries cannot be diminished while in office. 6. There must be a jury trial in criminal causes. 7. The trial of crimes must be in the state where committed—and, 8. There must be two witnesses to convict of treason.

4. In all other respects Congress may organize the judicial department according to their discretion; the importance of this power, among others proposed by the legislature (perhaps necessarily) I shall consider hereafter. Though there must, by the constitution, be but one judicial court, in which all the rays of judicial powers as to law, equity, and fact, in the cases enumerated must meet; yet this may be made by the legislature, a special court, consisting of any number of respectable characters or officers, the federal legislators excepted, to superintend the judicial department, to try the few causes in which foreign ministers and the states may be concerned, and to correct errors, as to law and fact, in certain important causes on appeals. Next below this judicial head, there may be several courts, such as are usually called superior courts, as a court of chancery, a court of criminal jurisdiction, a court of civil jurisdiction, a court of admiralty jurisdiction, a court of exchequer, &c. giving an appeal from these respectively to the supreme judicial court. These superior courts may be considered as so

92. Cf. *Brutus XIV* (1).

many points to which appeals may be brought up, from the various inferior courts, in the several branches of judicial causes. In all these superior and inferior courts, the trial by jury may be established in all cases, and the law and equity properly separated. In this organization, only a few very important causes, probably, would be carried up to the supreme court.—The superior courts would, finally, settle almost all causes. This organization, so far as it would respect questions of law, inferior, superior, and a special supreme court, would resemble that of New-York in a considerable degree, and those of several other states. This, I imagine, we must adopt, or else the Massachusetts plan; that is, a number of inferior courts, and one superior or supreme court, consisting of three, or five, or seven judges, in which one supreme court all the business shall be immediately collected from the inferior ones. The decision of the inferior courts, on either plan, probably will not much be relied on; and on the latter plan, there must be a prodigious accumulation of powers and business in all cases touching law, equity and facts, and all kinds of causes in a few hands, for whose errors of ignorance or design, there will be no possible remedy. As the legislature may adopt either of these, or any other plan, I shall not dwell longer on this subject.

5. In examining the federal judiciary, there appears to be some things very extraordinary and very peculiar. The judges or their friends may seize every opportunity to raise the judges salaries; but by the constitution they cannot be diminished. I am sensible how important it is that judges shall always have adequate and certain support; I am against their depending upon annual or periodical grants, because these may be withheld, or rendered too small by the dissent or narrowness of any one branch of the legislature; but there is a material distinction between periodical grants, and salaries held under permanent and standing laws: the former at stated periods cease, and must be renewed by the consent of all and every part of the legislature; the latter continue of course, and never will cease or be lowered, unless all parts of the legislature agree to do it. A man has as permanent an interest in his salary fixed by a standing law, so long as he may remain in office, as in any property he may possess; for the laws regulating the tenure of all property, are always liable to be altered by the legislature. The same judge may frequently be in office thirty or forty years; there may often be times, as in cases of war, or very high prices, when his salary may reasonably be increased one half or more; in a few years money may become scarce again, and prices fall, and his salary, with equal reason and propriety be decreased and lowered: not to suffer this to be done by consent of all the branches of the legislature, is, I believe, quite a novelty

in the affairs of government. It is true, by a very forced and unnatural construction, the constitution of Massachusetts, by the governor and minority in the legislature, was made to speak this kind of language. Another circumstance ought to be considered; the mines which have been discovered are gradually exhausted, and the precious metals are continually wasting: hence the probability is, that money, the nominal representative of property, will gradually grow scarcer hereafter, and afford just reasons for gradually lowering salaries. The value of money depends altogether upon the quantity of it in circulation, which may be also decreased, as well as encreased, from a great variety of causes.

6. The supreme court, in cases of appeals, shall have jurisdiction both as to law and fact: that is, in all civil causes carried up to the supreme court by appeals, the court, or judges, shall try the fact and decide the law. Here an essential principle of the civil law is established, and the most noble and important principle of the common law exploded. To dwell a few minutes on this material point: the supreme court shall have jurisdiction both as to law and fact. What is meant by court? Is the jury included in the term, or is it not? I conceive it is not included: and so the members of convention, I am very sure, understand it. Court, or curia, was a term well understood long before juries existed; the people, and the best writers, in countries where there are no juries, uniformly use the word court, and can only mean by it the judge or judges who determine causes: also, in countries where there are juries we express ourselves in the same manner; we speak of the court of probate, court of chancery, justices court, alderman's court, &c. in which there is no jury. In our supreme courts, common pleas, &c. in which there are jury trials, we uniformly speak of the court and jury, and consider them as distinct. Were it necessary I might cite a multitude of cases from law books to confirm, beyond controversy, this position, that the jury is not included, or a part of the court.

7. But the supreme court is to have jurisdiction as to law and fact, under such regulations as congress shall make. I confess it is impossible to say how far congress may, with propriety, extend their regulations in this respect. I conceive, however, they cannot by any reasonable construction go so far as to admit the jury, on true common law principles, to try the fact, and give a general verdict. I have repeatedly examined this article: I think the meaning of it is, that the judges in all final questions, as to property and damages, shall have complete jurisdiction, to consider the whole cause, to examine the facts, and on a general view of them, and on principles of equity, as well as law, to give judgment.

8. As the trial by jury is provided for in criminal causes, I shall confine my observations to civil causes[93]—and in these, I hold it is the established right of the jury by the common law, and the fundamental laws of this country, to give a general verdict in all cases when they chuse to do it, to decide both as to law and fact, whenever blended together in the issue put to them. Their right to determine as to facts will not be disputed, and their right to give a general verdict has never been disputed, except by a few judges and lawyers, governed by despotic principles. Coke, Hale, Holt, Blackstone, De Lolme,[94] and almost every other legal or political writer, who has written on the subject, has uniformly asserted this essential and important right of the jury. Juries in Great-Britain and America have universally practised accordingly. Even Mansfield,[95] with all his wishes about him, dare not directly avow the contrary. What fully confirms this point is, that there is no instance to be found, where a jury was ever punished for finding a general verdict, when a special one might, with propriety, have been found. The jury trial, especially politically considered, is by far the most important feature in the judicial department in a free country, and the right in question is far the most valuable part, and the last that ought to be yielded, of this trial. Juries are constantly and frequently drawn from the body of the people, and freemen of the country; and by holding the jury's right to return a general verdict in all cases sacred, we secure to the people at large, their just and rightful controul in the judicial department. If the conduct of judges shall be severe and arbitrary, and tend to subvert the laws, and change the forms of government, the jury may check them, by deciding against their opinions and determinations, in similar cases. It is true, the freemen of a country are not always minutely skilled in the laws, but they have common sense in its purity, which seldom or never errs in making and applying laws to the condition of the people, or in determining judicial causes, when

93. Cf. *Brutus XIV* (13).

94. Sir Edward Coke (1552–1634) was one of the great judges and commentators on the English common law. His four-volume *Institutes* was the leading text on the law until Blackstone's *Commentaries*. Sir Matthew Hale (1609–1676) served as Lord Chief Justice of England from 1671 to 1676 and wrote *The History of the Common Law of England* (1713). Sir John Holt (1642–1710) was Lord Chief Justice of England from 1689 to 1710. Henry Bracton (ca. 1210–1268) was a justice of what came to be known as the "King's Bench" during the periods 1247–50 and 1253–57. He wrote a well-known early treatise on the law, *De legibus et consuetudinibus Angliae*.

95. William Murray, Lord Mansfield (1705–1793), became Chief Justice of the King's Bench in 1756 and served until 1788.

stated to them by the parties. The body of the people, principally, bear the burdens of the community; they of right ought to have a controul in its important concerns, both in making and executing the laws, otherwise they may, in a short time, be ruined. Nor is it merely this controul alone we are to attend to: the jury trial brings with it an open and public discussion of all causes, and excludes secret and arbitrary proceedings. This, and the democratic branch in the legislature, as was formerly observed, are the means by which the people are let into the knowledge of public affairs—are enabled to stand as the guardians of each others rights, and to restrain, by regular and legal measures, those who otherwise might infringe upon them. I am not unsupported in my opinion of the value of the trial by jury; not only British and American writers, but De Lolme, and the most approved foreign writers, hold it to be the most valuable part of the British constitution, and indisputably the best mode of trial ever invented.

9. It was merely by the intrigues of the popish clergy, and of the Norman lawyers, that this mode of trial was not used in maritime, ecclesiastical, and military courts, and the civil law proceedings were introduced; and, I believe, it is more from custom and prejudice, than for any substantial reasons, that we do not in all the states establish the jury in our maritime as well as other courts.

10. In the civil law process the trial by jury is unknown; the consequence is, that a few judges and dependant officers, possess all the power in the judicial department. Instead of the open fair proceedings of the common law, where witnesses are examined in open court, and may be cross examined by the parties concerned—where council is allowed, &c. we see in the civil law process judges alone, who always, long previous to the trial, are known and often corrupted by ministerial influence, or by parties. Judges once influenced, soon become inclined to yield to temptations, and to decree for him who will pay the most for their partiality. It is, therefore, we find in the Roman, and almost all governments, where judges alone possess the judicial powers and try all cases, that bribery has prevailed. This, as well as the forms of the courts, naturally lead to secret and arbitrary proceedings—to taking evidence secretly—exparte, &c. to perplexing the cause—and to hasty decisions:—but, as to jurors, it is quite impracticable to bribe or influence them by any corrupt means; not only because they are untaught in such affairs, and possess the honest characters of the common freemen of a country; but because it is not, generally, known till the hour the cause comes on for trial, what persons are to form the jury.

11. But it is said, that no words could be found by which the states could agree to establish the jury-trial in civil causes. I can hardly believe men to

be serious, who make observations to this effect. The states have all derived judicial proceedings principally from one source, the British system; from the same common source the American lawyers have almost universally drawn their legal information. All the states have agreed to establish the trial by jury, in civil as well as in criminal causes. The several states, in congress, found no difficulty in establishing it in the Western Territory, in the ordinance passed in July 1787.[96] We find, that the several states in congress, in establishing government in that territory, agreed, that the inhabitants of it, should always be entitled to the benefit of the trial by jury. Thus, in a few words, the jury trial is established in its full extent; and the convention with as much ease, have established the jury trial in criminal cases. In making a constitution, we are substantially to fix principles.—If in one state, damages on default are assessed by a jury, and in another by the judges—if in one state jurors are drawn out of a box, and in another not—if there be other trifling variations, they can be of no importance in the great question. Further, when we examine the particular practices of the states, in little matters in judicial proceedings, I believe we shall find they differ near as much in criminal processes as in civil ones. Another thing worthy of notice in this place—the convention have used the word equity, and agreed to establish a chancery jurisdiction; about the meaning and extent of which, we all know, the several states disagree much more than about jury trials—in adopting the latter, they have very generally pursued the British plan; but as to the former, we see the states have varied, as their fears and opinions dictated.

12. By the common law, in Great Britain and America, there is no appeal from the verdict of the jury, as to facts, to any judges whatever—the jurisdiction of the jury is complete and final in this; and only errors in law are carried up to the house of lords, the special supreme court in Great Britain; or to the special supreme courts in Connecticut, New-York, New-Jersey, &c. Thus the juries are left masters as to facts: but, by the proposed constitution, directly the opposite principle is established. An appeal will lay in all appellate causes from the verdict of the jury, even as to mere facts, to the judges of the supreme court. Thus, in effect, we establish the civil law in this point; for if the jurisdiction of the jury be not final, as to facts, it is of little or no importance.

13. By art. 3. sect. 2. "the judicial power shall extend to all cases in law and equity, arising under this constitution, the laws of the United States," &c. What is here meant by equity? what is equity in a case arising under the constitution? possibly the clause might have the same meaning, were

96. The Northwest Ordinance of 1787, Art. 2.

the words "in law and equity," omitted. Cases in law must differ widely from cases in law and equity. At first view, by thus joining the word equity with the word law, if we mean any thing, we seem to mean to give the judge a discretionary power.[97] The word equity, in Great Britain, has in time acquired a precise meaning—chancery proceedings there are now reduced to system—but this is not the case in the United States. In New-England, the judicial courts have no powers in cases in equity, except those dealt out to them by the legislature, in certain limited portions, by legislative acts. In New-York, Maryland, Virginia, and South-Carolina, powers to decide, in cases of equity, are vested in judges distinct from those who decide in matters of law: and the states generally seem to have carefully avoided giving unlimitedly, to the same judges, powers to decide in cases in law and equity. Perhaps, the clause would have the same meaning were the words, "this constitution," omitted: there is in it either a careless complex misuse of words, in themselves of extensive signification, or there is some meaning not easy to be comprehended. Suppose a case arising under the constitution—suppose the question judicially moved, whether, by the constitution, congress can suppress a state tax laid on polls, lands, or as an excise duty, which may be supposed to interfere with a federal tax. By the letter of the constitution, congress will appear to have no power to do it: but then the judges may decide the question on principles of equity as well as law. Now, omitting the words, "in law and equity," they may decide according to the spirit and true meaning of the constitution, as collected from what must appear to have been the intentions of the people when they made it. Therefore, it would seem, that if these words mean any thing, they must have a further meaning: yet I will not suppose it intended to lodge an arbitrary power or discretion in the judges, to decide as their conscience, their opinions, their caprice, or their politics might dictate. Without dwelling on this obscure clause, I will leave it to the examination of others.

The Federal Farmer.

– XVI –

January 20, 1788

Dear Sir,

1. Having gone through with the organization of the government, I shall now proceed to examine more particularly those clauses which re-

97. Cf. *Brutus XI* (16–24).

spect its powers. I shall begin with those articles and stipulations which are necessary for accurately ascertaining the extent of powers, and what is given, and for guarding, limiting, and restraining them in their exercise.[98] We often find, these articles and stipulations placed in bills of rights; but they may as well be incorporated in the body of the constitution, as selected and placed by themselves. The constitution, or whole social compact, is but one instrument, no more or less, than a certain number of articles or stipulations agreed to by the people, whether it consists of articles, sections, chapters, bills of rights, or parts of any other denomination, cannot be material. Many needless observations, and idle distinctions, in my opinion, have been made respecting a bill of rights. On the one hand, it seems to be considered as a necessary distinct limb of the constitution, and as containing a certain number of very valuable articles, which are applicable to all societies: and, on the other, as useless, especially in a federal government, possessing only enumerated power—nay, dangerous, as individual rights are numerous, and not easy to be enumerated in a bill of rights, and from articles, or stipulations, securing some of them, it may be inferred, that others not mentioned are surrendered. There appears to me to be general indefinite propositions without much meaning—and the man who first advanced those of the latter description, in the present case, signed the federal constitution, which directly contradicts him.[99] The supreme power is undoubtedly in the people, and it is a principle well established in my mind, that they reserve all powers not expressly delegated by them to those who govern; this is as true in forming a state as in forming a federal government. There is no possible distinction but this founded merely in the different modes of proceeding which take place in some cases. In forming a state constitution, under which to manage not only the great but the little concerns of a community: the powers to be possessed by the government are often too numerous to be enumerated; the people to adopt the shortest way often give general powers, indeed all powers, to the government, in some general words, and then, by a particular enumeration, take back, or rather say they however reserve certain rights as sacred, and which no laws shall be made to violate: hence the idea that all powers are given which are not reserved: but in forming a federal constitution, which *ex vi termine*, supposes state governments existing, and which is only to manage a few great national concerns, we often find it easier to enumerate particularly

---

98. See *FF II* (5–6).
99. James Wilson, "Address to the Citizens of Philadelphia"; cf. *Brutus II* (13).

the powers to be delegated to the federal head, than to enumerate particularly the individual rights to be reserved; and the principle will operate in its full force, when we carefully adhere to it. When we particularly enumerate the powers given, we ought either carefully to enumerate the rights reserved, or be totally silent about them; we must either particularly enumerate both, or else suppose the particular enumeration of the powers given adequately draws the line between them and the rights reserved, particularly to enumerate the former and not the latter, I think most advisable: however, as men appear generally to have their doubts about these silent reservations, we might advantageously enumerate the powers given, and then in general words, according to the mode adopted in the 2d art. of the confederation, declare all powers, rights and privileges, are reserved, which are not explicitly and expressly given up. People, and very wisely too, like to be express and explicit about their essential rights, and not to be forced to claim them on the precarious and unascertained tenure of inferences and general principles, knowing that in any controversy between them and their rulers, concerning those rights, disputes may be endless, and nothing certain:—But admitting, on the general principle, that all rights are reserved of course, which are not expressly surrendered, the people could with sufficient certainty assert their rights on all occasions, and establish them with ease, still there are infinite advantages in particularly enumerating many of the most essential rights reserved in all cases; and as to the less important ones, we may declare in general terms, that all not expressly surrendered are reserved. We do not by declarations change the nature of things, or create new truths, but we give existence, or at least establish in the minds of the people truths and principles which they might never otherwise have thought of, or soon forgot. If a nation means its systems, religious or political, shall have duration, it ought to recognize the leading principles of them in the front page of every family book. What is the usefulness of a truth in theory, unless it exists constantly in the minds of the people, and has their assent:—we discern certain rights, as the freedom of the press, and the trial by jury, &c. which the people of England and of America of course believe to be sacred, and essential to their political happiness, and this belief in them is the result of ideas at first suggested to them by a few able men, and of subsequent experience; while the people of some other countries hear these rights mentioned with the utmost indifference; they think the privilege of existing at the will of a despot much preferable to them. Why this difference amongst beings every way formed alike? The reason of the difference is obvious—it is the effect of education, a series of notions impressed upon the minds of the people by examples, precepts and declarations. When the people of England got together, at the time they formed Magna Charta, they did not consider it sufficient, that they were indisputably entitled to certain natural and unalienable rights, not depending on silent titles, they, by a declaratory act, expressly recognized them, and explicitly declared to all the world, that they were entitled to enjoy those rights; they made an instrument in writing, and enumerated those they then thought essential, or in danger, and this wise men saw was not sufficient; and therefore, that the people might not forget these rights, and gradually become prepared for arbitrary government, their discerning and honest leaders caused this instrument to be confirmed near forty times, and to be read twice a year in public places, not that it would lose its validity without such confirmations, but to fix the contents of it in the minds of the people, as they successively come upon the stage.—Men, in some countries do not remain free, merely because they are entitled to natural and unalienable rights; men in all countries are entitled to them, not because their ancestors once got together and enumerated them on paper, but because, by repeated negociations and declarations, all parties are brought to realize them, and of course to believe them to be sacred. Were it necessary, I might shew the wisdom of our past conduct, as a people in not merely comforting ourselves that we were entitled to freedom, but in constantly keeping in view, in addresses, bills of rights, in news-papers, &c. the particular principles on which our freedom must always depend.

2. It is not merely in this point of view, that I urge the engrafting in the constitution additional declaratory articles. The distinction, in itself just, that all powers not given are reserved, is in effect destroyed by this very constitution, as I shall particularly demonstrate—and even independent of this, the people, by adopting the constitution, give many general undefined powers to congress, in the constitutional exercise of which, the rights in question may be effected. Gentlemen who oppose a federal bill of rights, or further declaratory articles, seem to view the subject in a very narrow imperfect manner. These have for their objects, not only the enumeration of the rights reserved, but principally to explain the general powers delegated in certain material points, and to restrain those who exercise them by fixed known boundaries. Many explanations and restrictions necessary and useful, would be much less so, were the people at large all well and fully acquainted with the principles and affairs of government. There appears to be in the constitution, a studied brevity, and it may also be probable, that several explanatory articles were omitted from a circumstance very

common. What we have long and early understood ourselves in the common concerns of the community, we are apt to suppose is understood by others, and need not be expressed; and it is not unnatural or uncommon for the ablest men most frequently to make this mistake. To make declaratory articles unnecessary in an instrument of government, two circumstances must exist; the rights reserved must be indisputably so, and in their nature defined; the powers delegated to the government, must be precisely defined by the words that convey them, and clearly be of such extent and nature as that, by no reasonable construction, they can be made to invade the rights and prerogatives intended to be left in the people.

3. The first point urged, is, that all power is reserved not expressly given, that particular enumerated powers only are given, that all others are not given, but reserved, and that it is needless to attempt to restrain congress in the exercise of powers they possess not.[100] This reasoning is logical, but of very little importance in the common affairs of men; but the constitution does not appear to respect it even in any view. To prove this, I might cite several clauses in it. I shall only remark on two or three. By article 1, section 9, "No title of nobility shall be granted by congress." Was this clause omitted, what power would congress have to make titles of nobility? in what part of the constitution would they find it? The answer must be, that congress would have no such power—that the people, by adopting the constitution, will not part with it. Why then by a negative clause, restrain congress from doing what it would have no power to do? This clause, then, must have no meaning, or imply, that were it omitted, congress would have the power in question, either upon the principle that some general words in the constitution may be so construed as to give it, or on the principle that congress possess the powers not expressly reserved. But this clause was in the confederation, and is said to be introduced into the constitution from very great caution. Even a cautionary provision implies a doubt, at least, that it is necessary; and if so in this case, clearly it is also alike necessary in all similar ones. The fact appears to be, that the people in forming the confederation, and the convention, in this instance, acted, naturally, they did not leave the point to be settled by general principles and logical inferences; but they settle the point in a few words, and all who read them at once understand them.

4. The trial by jury in criminal as well as in civil causes, has long been considered as one of our fundamental rights, and has been repeatedly rec-

100. Cf. *Brutus II* (6).

ognized and confirmed by most of the state conventions. But the constitution expressly establishes this trial in criminal, and wholly omits it in civil causes. The jury trial in criminal causes, and the benefit of the writ of habeas corpus, are already as effectually established as any of the fundamental or essential rights of the people in the United States. This being the case, why in adopting a federal constitution do we now establish these, and omit all others, or all others, at least with a few exceptions, such as again agreeing there shall be no ex post facto laws, no titles of nobility, &c. We must consider this constitution, when adopted, as the supreme act of the people, and in construing it hereafter, we and our posterity must strictly adhere to the letter and spirit of it, and in no instance depart from them: in construing the federal constitution, it will be not only impracticable, but improper to refer to the state constitutions. They are entirely distinct instruments and inferior acts: besides, by the people's now establishing certain fundamental rights, it is strongly implied, that they are of opinion, that they would not otherwise be secured as a part of the federal system, or be regarded in the federal administration as fundamental. Further, these same rights, being established by the state constitutions, and secured to the people, our recognizing them now, implies, that the people thought them insecure by the state establishments, and extinguished or put afloat by the new arrangement of the social system, unless re-established.—Further, the people, thus establishing some few rights, and remaining totally silent about others similarly circumstanced, the implication indubitably is, that they mean to relinquish the latter, or at least feel indifferent about them. Rights, therefore, inferred from general principles of reason, being precarious and hardly ascertainable in the common affairs of society, and the people, in forming a federal constitution, explicitly shewing they conceive these rights to be thus circumstanced, and accordingly proceed to enumerate and establish some of them, the conclusion will be, that they have established all which they esteem valuable and sacred. On every principle, then, the people especially having began, ought to go through enumerating, and establish particularly all the rights of individuals, which can by any possibility come in question in making and executing federal laws. I have already observed upon the excellency and importance of the jury trial in civil as well as in criminal causes, instead of establishing it in criminal causes only; we ought to establish it generally;—instead of the clause of forty or fifty words relative to this subject, why not use the language that has always been used in this country, and say, "the people of the United States shall always be entitled to the trial by jury." This would shew the people still hold the right sacred, and enjoin it upon congress substantially to preserve the jury trial in all cases, according to the usage and custom of the country. I have observed before, that it is *the jury trial* we want; the little different appendages and modifications tacked to it in the different states, are no more than a drop in the ocean: the jury trial is a solid uniform feature in a free government; it is the substance we would save, not the little articles of form.

5. Security against expost facto laws, the trial by jury, and the benefits of the writ of habeas corpus, are but a part of those inestimable rights the people of the United States are entitled to, even in judicial proceedings, by the course of the common law.[101] These may be secured in general words, as in New-York, the Western Territory, &c. by declaring the people of the United States shall always be entitled to judicial proceedings according to the course of the common law, as used and established in the said states. Perhaps it would be better to enumerate the particular essential rights the people are entitled to in these proceedings, as has been done in many of the states, and as has been done in England. In this case, the people may proceed to declare, that no man shall be held to answer to any offence, till the same be fully described to him; nor to furnish evidence against himself: that, except in the government of the army and navy, no person shall be tried for any offence, whereby he may incur loss of life, or an infamous punishment, until he be first indicted by a grand jury: that every person shall have a right to produce all proofs that may be favourable to him, and to meet the witnesses against him face to face: that every person shall be entitled to obtain right and justice freely and without delay; that all persons shall have a right to be secure from all unreasonable searches and seizures of their persons, houses, papers, or possessions; and that all warrants shall be deemed contrary to this right, if the foundation of them be not previously supported by oath, and there be not in them a special designation of persons or objects of search, arrest, or seizure: and that no person shall be exiled or molested in his person or effects, otherwise than by the judgment of his peers, or according to the law of the land. A celebrated writer observes upon this last article, that in itself it may be said to comprehend the whole end of political society.[102] These rights are not necessarily reserved, they are established, or enjoyed but in few countries: they are stipulated rights, almost peculiar to British and American laws. In the execution of those laws, individuals, by long custom, by magna charta, bills of rights

101. Cf. *Brutus II* (7–8).
102. Blackstone, *Commentaries on the Laws of England*, III, 379.

&c. have become entitled to them. A man, at first, by act of parliament, became entitled to the benefits of the writ of habeas corpus—men are entitled to these rights and benefits in the judicial proceedings of our state courts generally: but it will by no means follow, that they will be entitled to them in the federal courts, and have a right to assert them, unless secured and established by the constitution or federal laws. We certainly, in federal processes, might as well claim the benefits of the writ of habeas corpus, as to claim trial by a jury—the right to have council—to have witnesses face to face—to be secure against unreasonable search warrants, &c. was the constitution silent as to the whole of them:—but the establishment of the former, will evince that we could not claim them without it; and the omission of the latter, implies they are relinquished, or deemed of no importance. These are rights and benefits individuals acquire by compact; they must claim them under compacts, or immemorial usage—it is doubtful, at least, whether they can be claimed under immemorial usage in this country; and it is, therefore, we generally claim them under compacts, as charters and constitutions.

6. The people by adopting the federal constitution, give congress general powers to institute a distinct and new judiciary, new courts, and to regulate all proceedings in them, under the eight limitations mentioned in a former letter; and the further one, that the benefits of the habeas corpus act shall be enjoyed by individuals. Thus general powers being given to institute courts, and regulate their proceedings, with no provision for securing the rights principally in question, may not congress so exercise those powers, and constitutionally too, as to destroy those rights? Clearly, in my opinion, they are not in any degree secured. But, admitting the case is only doubtful, would it not be prudent and wise to secure them and remove all doubts, since all agree the people ought to enjoy these valuable rights, a very few men excepted, who seem to be rather of opinion that there is little or nothing in them? Were it necessary I might add many observations to shew their value and political importance.

7. The constitution will give congress general powers to raise and support armies. General powers carry with them incidental ones, and the means necessary to the end. In the exercise of these powers, is there any provision in the constitution to prevent the quartering of soldiers on the inhabitants? you will answer, there is not. This may sometimes be deemed a necessary measure in the support of armies; on what principle can the people claim the right to be exempt from this burden? they will urge, perhaps, the practice of the country, and the provisions made in some of

the state constitutions—they will be answered, that their claim thus to be exempt, is not founded in nature, but only in custom and opinion, or at best, in stipulations in some of the state constitutions, which are local, and inferior in their operation, and can have no controul over the general government—that they had adopted a federal constitution—had noticed several rights, but had been totally silent about this exemption—that they had given general powers relative to the subject, which, in their operation, regularly destroyed the claim. Though it is not to be presumed, that we are in any immediate danger from this quarter, yet it is fit and proper to establish, beyond dispute, those rights which are particularly valuable to individuals, and essential to the permanency and duration of free government. An excellent writer observes, that the English, always in possession of their freedom, are frequently unmindful of the value of it:[103] we, at this period, do not seem to be so well off, having, in some instances abused ours; many of us are quite disposed to barter it away for what we call energy, coercion, and some other terms we use as vaguely as that of liberty—There is often as great a rage for change and novelty in politics, as in amusements and fashions.

8. All parties apparently agree, that the freedom of the press is a fundamental right, and ought not to be restrained by any taxes, duties, or in any manner whatever. Why should not the people, in adopting a federal constitution, declare this, even if there are only doubts about it. But, say the advocates, all powers not given are reserved:—true; but the great question is, are not powers given, in the exercise of which this right may be destroyed?[104] The people's or the printers claim to a free press, is founded on the fundamental laws, that is, compacts, and state constitutions, made by the people. The people, who can annihilate or alter those constitutions, can annihilate or limit this right. This may be done by giving general powers, as well as by using particular words. No right claimed under a state constitution, will avail against a law of the union, made in pursuance of the federal constitution: therefore the question is, what laws will congress have a right to make by the constitution of the union, and particularly touching the press? By art. 1. sect. 8. congress will have power to lay and collect taxes, duties, imposts and excise. By this congress will clearly have power to lay and collect all kind of taxes whatever—taxes on houses, lands,

103. Storing (II, 356, n121) could not find the precise reference, but he believes that the context suggests De Lolme, *Constitution of England*, perhaps II, chap. 21.
104. Cf. *Brutus II* (14).

polls, industry, merchandize, &c.—taxes on deeds, bonds, and all written instruments—on writs, pleas, and all judicial proceedings, on licences, naval officers papers, &c. on newspapers, advertisements, &c. and to require bonds of the naval officers, clerks, printers, &c. to account for the taxes that may become due on papers that go through their hands. Printing, like all other business, must cease when taxed beyond its profits; and it appears to me, that a power to tax the press at discretion, is a power to destroy or restrain the freedom of it. There may be other powers given, in the exercise of which this freedom may be effected; and certainly it is of too much importance to be left thus liable to be taxed, and constantly to constructions and inferences. A free press is the channel of communication as to mercantile and public affairs; by means of it the people in large countries ascertain each others sentiments; are enabled to unite, and become formidable to those rulers who adopt improper measures. Newspapers may sometimes be the vehicles of abuse, and of many things not true; but these are but small inconveniencies, in my mind, among many advantages. A celebrated writer, I have several times quoted, speaking in high terms of the English liberties, says, "lastly the key stone was put to the arch, by the final establishment of the freedom of the press."[105] I shall not dwell longer upon the fundamental rights, to some of which I have attended in this letter, for the same reasons that these I have mentioned, ought to be expressly secured, lest in the exercise of general powers given they may be invaded: it is pretty clear, that some other of less importance, or less in danger, might with propriety also be secured.

9. I shall now proceed to examine briefly the powers proposed to be vested in the several branches of the government, and especially the mode of laying and collecting internal taxes.

The Federal Farmer.

– XVII –

January 23, 1788

Dear Sir,

1. I believe the people of the United States are full in the opinion, that a free and mild government can be preserved in their extensive territories, only under the substantial forms of a federal republic. As several of the ablest advocates for the system proposed, have acknowledged this (and I

---

105. De Lolme, *Constitution of England,* I, chap. 3.

hope the confessions they have published will be preserved and remembered) I shall not take up time to establish this point. A question then arises,
how far that system partakes of a federal republic.—I observed in a former
letter, that it appears to be the first important step to a consolidation of the
states; that its strong tendency is to that point.[106]

2. But what do we mean by a federal republic? and what by a consolidated
government? To erect a federal republic, we must first make a number of
states on republican principles; each state with a government organized for
the internal management of its affairs: The states, as such, must unite under
a federal head, and delegate to it powers to make and execute laws in certain
enumerated cases, under certain restrictions; this head may be a single assembly, like the present congress, or the Amphictionic council;[107] or it may
consist of a legislature, with one or more branches; of an executive, and of a
judiciary. To form a consolidated, or one entire government, there must be
no state, or local governments, but all things, persons and property, must be
subject to the laws of one legislature alone; to one executive, and one judiciary. Each state government, as the government of New Jersey, &c. is a
consolidated, or one entire government, as it respects the counties, towns,
citizens and property within the limits of the state.—The state governments
are the basis, the pillar on which the federal head is placed, and the whole
together, when formed on elective principles, constitute a federal republic.
A federal republic in itself supposes state or local governments to exist, as
the body or props, on which the federal head rests, and that it cannot remain
a moment after they cease. In erecting the federal government, and always
in its councils, each state must be known as a sovereign body; but in erecting
this government, I conceive, the legislature of the state, by the expressed or
implied assent of the people, or the people of the state, under the direction
of the government of it, may accede to the federal compact: Nor do I conceive it to be necessarily a part of a confederacy of states, that each have an
equal voice in the general councils. A confederated republic being organized, each state must retain powers for managing its internal police, and all
delegate to the union power to manage general concerns: The quantity of
power the union must possess is one thing, the mode of exercising the powers given, is quite a different consideration; and it is the mode of exercising

106. *FF I* (1).

107. The *Amphyctionic Council* was the deliberative body for the Amphyctionic
League, a confederation of ancient Greek cities often cited during the founding era
as a model (for good or ill) of a confederacy of republics.

them, that makes one of the essential distinctions between one entire or consolidated government, and a federal republic; that is, however the government may be organized, if the laws of the union, in most important concerns, as in levying and collecting taxes, raising troops, &c. operate immediately upon the persons and property of individuals, and not on states, extend to organizing the militia, &c. the government, as to its administration, as to making and executing laws, is not federal, but consolidated. To illustrate my idea—the union makes a requisition, and assigns to each state its quota of men or monies wanted; each state, by its own laws and officers, in its own way, furnishes its quota: here the state governments stand between the union and individuals; the laws of the union operate only on states, as such, and federally: Here nothing can be done without the meetings of the state legislatures—but in the other case the union, though the state legislatures should not meet for years together, proceeds immediately, by its own laws and officers, to levy and collect monies of individuals, to inlist men, form armies, &c. here the laws of the union operate immediately on the body of the people, on persons and property; in the same manner the laws of one entire consolidated government operate.—These two modes are very distinct, and in their operation and consequences have directly opposite tendencies: The first makes the existence of the state governments indispensable, and throws all the detail business of levying and collecting the taxes, &c. into the hands of those governments, and into the hands, of course, of many thousand officers solely created by, and dependent on the state. The last entirely excludes the agency of the respective states, and throws the whole business of levying and collecting taxes, &c. into the hands of many thousand officers solely created by, and dependent upon the union, and makes the existence of the state government of no consequence in the case. It is true, congress in raising any given sum in direct taxes, must by the constitution, raise so much of it in one state, and so much in another, by a fixed rule, which most of the states some time since agreed to: But this does not effect the principle in question, it only secures each state against any arbitrary proportions. The federal mode is perfectly safe and eligible, founded in the true spirit of a confederated republic; there could be no possible exception to it, did we not find by experience, that the states will sometimes neglect to comply with the reasonable requisitions of the union. It being according to the fundamental principles of federal republics, to raise men and monies by requisitions, and for the states individually to organize and train the militia, I conceive, there can be no reason whatever for departing from them, except this, that the states sometimes neglect to comply with

reasonable requisitions, and that it is dangerous to attempt to compel a delinquent state by force, as it may often produce a war. We ought, therefore,
to enquire attentively, how extensive the evils to be guarded against are, and
cautiously limit the remedies to the extent of the evils. I am not about to
defend the confederation, or to charge the proposed constitution with imperfections not in it; but we ought to examine facts, and strip them of the
false colourings often given them by incautious observations, by unthinking
or designing men. We ought to premise, that laws for raising men and monies, even in consolidated governments, are not often punctually complied
with. Historians, except in extraordinary cases, but very seldom take notice
of the detail collection of taxes; but these facts we have fully proved, and well
attested; that the most energetic governments have relinquished taxes frequently, which were of many years standing. These facts amply prove, that
taxes assessed, have remained many years uncollected. I agree there have
been instances in the republics of Greece, Holland &c. in the course of
several centuries, of states neglecting to pay their quotas of requisitions; but
it is a circumstance certainly deserving of attention, whether these nations
which have depended on requisitions principally for their defence, have not
raised men and monies nearly as punctually as entire governments, which
have taxed directly; whether we have not found the latter as often distressed
for the want of troops and monies as the former. It has been said that the
Amphictionic council, and the Germanic head, have not possessed sufficient
powers to controul the members of the republic in a proper manner. Is this,
if true, to be imputed to requisitions? Is it not principally to be imputed to
the unequal powers of those members, connected with this important circumstance, that each member possessed power to league itself with foreign
powers, and powerful neighbours, without the consent of the head? After
all, has not the Germanic body a government as good as its neighbours in
general? and did not the Grecian republic remain united several centuries,
and form the theatre of human greatness? No government in Europe has
commanded monies more plentifully than the government of Holland. As
to the United States, the separate states lay taxes directly, and the union calls
for taxes by way of requisitions; and is it a fact, that more monies are due in
proportion on requisitions in the United States, than on the state taxes directly laid?—It is but about ten years since congress began to make requisitions, and in that time, the monies, &c. required, and the bounties given for
men required of the states, have amounted, specie value, to about 36 millions dollars, about 24 millions of dollars of which have been actually paid;
and a very considerable part of the 12 millions not paid, remains so not so

much from the neglect of the states, as from the sudden changes in paper money, &c. which in a great measure rendered payments of no service, and which often induced the union indirectly to relinquish one demand, by making another in a different form.[108] Before we totally condemn requisitions, we ought to consider what immense bounties the states gave, and what prodigious exertions they made in the war, in order to comply with the requisitions of congress; and if since the peace they have been delinquent, ought we not carefully to enquire, whether that delinquency is to be imputed solely to the nature of requisitions? ought it not in part to be imputed to two other causes? I mean first, an opinion, that has extensively prevailed, that the requisitions for domestic interest have not been founded on just principles; and secondly, the circumstance, that the government itself, by proposing imposts, &c. has departed virtually from the constitutional system; which proposed changes, like all changes proposed in government, produce an inattention and negligence in the execution of the government in being.

3. I am not for depending wholly on requisitions; but I mention these few facts to shew they are not so totally futile as many pretend. For the truth of many of these facts I appeal to the public records; and for the truth of the others, I appeal to many republican characters, who are best informed in the affairs of the United States. Since the peace, and till the convention reported, the wisest men in the United States generally supposed, that certain limited funds would answer the purposes of the union: and though the states are by no means in so good a condition as I wish they were, yet, I think, I may very safely affirm, they are in a better condition than they would be had congress always possessed the powers of taxation now contended for. The fact is admitted, that our federal government does not possess sufficient powers to give life and vigor to the political system; and that we experience disappointments, and several inconveniencies; but we ought carefully to distinguish those which are merely the consequences of a severe and tedious war, from those which arise from defects in the federal system. There has been an entire revolution in the United States within thirteen years, and the least we can compute the waste of labour and property at, during that period, by the war, is three hundred million of dollars. Our people are like a man just recovering from a severe fit of sickness. It was the war that disturbed the course of commerce, introduced floods of paper money, the stagnation of credit, and threw many valuable men out of steady business. From these sources our greatest evils arise;

108. See Smith speech at New York ratifying convention, June 27, 1788 (6).

men of knowledge and reflection must perceive it;—but then, have we not done more in three or four years past, in repairing the injuries of the war, by repairing houses and estates, restoring industry, frugality, the fisheries, manufactures, &c. and thereby laying the foundation of good government, and of individual and political happiness, than any people ever did in a like time; we must judge from a view of the country and facts, and not from foreign newspapers, or our own, which are printed chiefly in the commercial towns, where imprudent living, imprudent importations, and many unexpected disappointments, have produced a despondency, and a disposition to view every thing on the dark side. Some of the evils we feel, all will agree, ought to be imputed to the defective administration of the governments. From these and various considerations, I am very clearly of opinion, that the evils we sustain, merely on account of the defects of the confederation, are but as a feather in the balance against a mountain, compared with those which would, infallibly, be the result of the loss of general liberty, and that happiness men enjoy under a frugal, free, and mild government.

4. Heretofore we do not seem to have seen danger any where, but in giving power to congress, and now no where but in congress wanting powers; and, without examining the extent of the evils to be remedied, by one step, we are for giving up to congress almost all powers of any importance without limitation. The defects of the confederation are extravagantly magnified, and every species of pain we feel imputed to them: and hence it is inferred, there must be a total change of the principles, as well as forms of government: and in the main point, touching the federal powers, we rest all on a logical inference, totally inconsistent with experience and sound political reasoning.[109]

5. It is said, that as the federal head must make peace and war, and provide for the common defence, it ought to possess all powers necessary to that end: that powers unlimited, as to the purse and sword, to raise men and monies, and form the militia, are necessary to that end; and, therefore, the federal head ought to possess them. This reasoning is far more specious than solid: it is necessary that these powers so exist in the body politic, as to be called into exercise whenever necessary for the public safety; but it is by no means true, that the man, or congress of men, whose duty it more immediately is to provide for the common defence, ought to possess them without limitation. But clear it is, that if such men, or congress, be not in

109. Cf. *Federalist* 23, 31.

a situation to hold them without danger to liberty, he or they ought not to possess them. It has long been thought to be a well founded position, that the purse and sword ought not to be placed in the same hands in a free government. Our wise ancestors have carefully separated them—placed the sword in the hands of their king, even under considerable limitations, and the purse in the hands of the commons alone: yet the king makes peace and war, and it is his duty to provide for the common defence of the nation. This authority at least goes thus far—that a nation, well versed in the science of government, does not conceive it to be necessary or expedient for the man entrusted with the common defence and general tranquility, to possess unlimitedly the powers in question, or even in any considerable degree. Could he, whose duty it is to defend the public, possess in himself independently, all the means of doing it consistent with the public good, it might be convenient: but the people of England know that their liberties and happiness would be in infinitely greater danger from the king's unlimited possession of these powers, than from all external enemies and internal commotions to which they might be exposed: therefore, though they have made it his duty to guard the empire, yet they have wisely placed in other hands, the hands of their representatives, the power to deal out and controul the means. In Holland their high mightinesses must provide for the common defence, but for the means they depend, in a considerable degree, upon requisitions made on the state or local assemblies. Reason and facts evince, that however convenient it might be for an executive magistrate, or federal head, more immediately charged with the national defence and safety, solely, directly, and independently to possess all the means; yet such magistrate, or head, never ought to possess them, if thereby the public liberties shall be endangered. The powers in question never have been, by nations wise and free, deposited, nor can they ever be, with safety, any where, but in the principal members of the national system;—where these form one entire government, as in Great-Britain, they are separated and lodged in the principal members of it. But in a federal republic, there is quite a different organization; the people form this kind of government, generally, because their territories are too extensive to admit of their assembling in one legislature, or of executing the laws on free principles under one entire government. They convene in their local assemblies, for local purposes, and for managing their internal concerns, and unite their states under a federal head for general purposes. It is the essential characteristic of a confederated republic, that this head be dependant on, and kept within limited bounds by, the local governments; and it is because, in these alone, in fact, the people can be substantially assembled or represented. It is, therefore, we very universally see, in this kind of government, the congressional powers placed in a few hands, and accordingly limited, and specifically enumerated: and the local assemblies strong and well guarded, and composed of numerous members. Wise men will always place the controuling power where the people are substantially collected by their representatives. By the proposed system, the federal head will possess, without limitation, almost every species of power that can, in its exercise, tend to change the government, or to endanger liberty; while in it, I think it has been fully shewn, the people will have but the shadow of representation, and but the shadow of security for their rights and liberties. In a confederated republic, the division of representation, &c. in its nature, requires a correspondent division and deposit of powers relative to taxes and military concerns: and I think the plan offered stands quite alone, in confounding the principles of governments in themselves totally distinct. I wish not to exculpate the states for their improper neglects in not paying their quotas of requisitions; but, in applying the remedy, we must be governed by reason and facts. It will not be denied, that the people have a right to change the government when the majority chuse it, if not restrained by some existing compact—that they have a right to displace their rulers, and consequently to determine when their measures are reasonable or not—and that they have a right, at any time, to put a stop to those measures they may deem prejudicial to them, by such forms and negatives as they may see fit to provide. From all these, and many other well founded considerations, I need not mention, a question arises, what powers shall there be delegated to the federal head, to insure safety, as well as energy, in the government? I think there is a safe and proper medium pointed out by experience, by reason, and facts. When we have organized the government, we ought to give power to the union, so far only as experience and present circumstances shall direct, with a reasonable regard to time to come. Should future circumstances, contrary to our expectations, require that further powers be transferred to the union, we can do it far more easily, than get back those we may now imprudently give. The system proposed is untried: candid advocates and opposers admit, that it is, in a degree, a mere experiment, and that its organization is weak and imperfect; surely then, the safe ground is cautiously to vest power in it, and when we are sure we have given enough for ordinary exigencies, to be extremely careful how we delegate powers, which, in common cases, must necessarily be useless or abused, and of very uncertain effect in uncommon ones.

6. By giving the union power to regulate commerce, and to levy and collect taxes by imposts, we give it an extensive authority, and permanent productive funds, I believe quite as adequate to the present demands of the union, as excises and direct taxes can be made to the present demands of the separate states. The state governments are now about four times as expensive as that of the union; and their several state debts added together, are nearly as large as that of the union—Our impost duties since the peace have been almost as productive as the other sources of taxation, and when under one general system of regulations, the probability is, that those duties will be very considerably increased: Indeed the representation proposed will hardly justify giving to congress unlimited powers to raise taxes by imposts, in addition to the other powers the union must necessarily have. It is said, that if congress possess only authority to raise taxes by imposts, trade probably will be overburdened with taxes, and the taxes of the union be found inadequate to any uncommon exigencies: To this we may observe, that trade generally finds its own level, and will naturally and necessarily heave off any undue burdens laid upon it: further, if congress alone possess the impost, and also unlimited power to raise monies by excises and direct taxes, there must be much more danger that two taxing powers, the union and states, will carry excises and direct taxes to an unreasonable extent, especially as these have not the natural boundaries taxes on trade have. However, it is not my object to propose to exclude congress from raising monies by internal taxes, as by duties, excises, and direct taxes, but my opinion is, that congress, especially in its proposed organization, ought not to raise monies by internal taxes, except in strict conformity to the federal plan; that is, by the agency of the state governments in all cases, except where a state shall neglect, for an unreasonable time, to pay its quota of a requisition; and never where so many of the state legislatures as represent a majority of the people, shall formally determine an excise law or requisition is improper, in their next session after the same be laid before them. We ought always to recollect that the evil to be guarded against is found by our own experience, and the experience of others, to be mere neglect in the states to pay their quotas; and power in the union to levy and collect the neglecting states' quotas with interest, is fully adequate to the evil. By this federal plan, with this exception mentioned, we secure the means of collecting the taxes by the usual process of law, and avoid the evil of attempting to compel or coerce a state; and we avoid also a circumstance, which never yet could be, and I am fully confident never can be, admitted in a free

federal republic; I mean a permanent and continued system of tax laws of the union, executed in the bowels of the states by many thousand officers, dependent as to the assessing and collecting federal taxes, solely upon the union. On every principle then, we ought to provide, that the union render an exact account of all monies raised by imposts and other taxes; and that whenever monies shall be wanted for the purposes of the union, beyond the proceeds of the impost duties, requisitions shall be made on the states for the monies so wanted; and that the power of laying and collecting shall never be exercised, except in cases where a state shall neglect, a given time, to pay its quota. This mode seems to be strongly pointed out by the reason of the case, and spirit of the government; and I believe, there is no instance to be found in a federal republic, where the congressional powers ever extended generally to collecting monies by direct taxes or excises. Creating all these restrictions, still the powers of the union in matters of taxation, will be too unlimited; further checks, in my mind, are indispensably necessary. Nor do I conceive, that as full a representation as is practicable in the federal government, will afford sufficient security: the strength of the government, and the confidence of the people, must be collected principally in the local assemblies; every part or branch of the federal head must be feeble, and unsafely trusted with large powers. A government possessed of more power than its constituent parts will justify, will not only probably abuse it, but be unequal to bear its own burden; it may as soon be destroyed by the pressure of power, as languish and perish for want of it.

7. There are two ways further of raising checks, and guarding against undue combinations and influence in a federal system. The first is, in levying taxes, raising and keeping up armies, in building navies, in forming plans for the militia, and in appropriating monies for the support of the military, to require the attendance of a large proportion of the federal representatives, as two-thirds or three-fourths of them; and in passing laws, in these important cases, to require the consent of two-thirds or three-fourths of the members present. The second is, by requiring that certain important laws of the federal head, as a requisition or a law for raising monies by excise shall be laid before the state legislatures, and if disapproved of by a given number of them, say by as many of them as represent a majority of the people, the law shall have no effect. Whether it would be adviseable to adopt both, or either of these checks, I will not undertake to determine. We have seen them both exist in confederated republics. The first exists substantially in the confederation, and will exist in some measure in the plan proposed, as in chusing a president by the house, in expelling members; in

the senate, in making treaties, and in deciding on impeachments, and in the whole in altering the constitution. The last exists in the United Netherlands, but in a much greater extent. The first is founded on this principle, that these important measures may, sometimes, be adopted by a bare quorum of members, perhaps, from a few states, and that a bare majority of the federal representatives may frequently be of the aristocracy, or some particular interests, connections, or parties in the community, and governed by motives, views, and inclinations not compatible with the general interest.—The last is founded on this principle, that the people will be substantially represented, only in their state or local assemblies; that their principal security must be found in them; and that, therefore, they ought to have ultimately a constitutional controul over such interesting measures.

8. I have often heard it observed, that our people are well informed, and will not submit to oppressive governments; that the state governments will be their ready advocates, and possess their confidence, mix with them, and enter into all their wants and feelings. This is all true; but of what avail will these circumstances be, if the state governments, thus allowed to be the guardians of the people, possess no kind of power by the forms of the social compact, to stop, in their passage, the laws of congress injurious to the people? State governments must stand and see the law take place; they may complain and petition—so may individuals; the members of them, in extreme cases, may resist, on the principles of self-defence—so may the people and individuals.

9. It has been observed, that the people, in extensive territories, have more power, compared with that of their rulers, than in small states. Is not directly the opposite true?[110] The people in a small state can unite and act in concert, and with vigour; but in large territories, the men who govern find it more easy to unite, while people cannot; while they cannot collect the opinions of each part, while they move to different points, and one part is often played off against the other.

10. It has been asserted, that the confederate head of a republic at best, is in general weak and dependent;—that the people will attach themselves to, and support their local governments, in all disputes with the union. Admit the fact: is it any way to remove the inconvenience by accumulating powers upon a weak organization? The fact is, that the detail administration of affairs, in this mixed republic, depends principally on the local governments;

110. *Federalist* 28.

and the people would be wretched without them: and a great proportion of social happiness depends on the internal administration of justice, and on internal police. The splendor of the monarch, and the power of the government are one thing. The happiness of the subject depends on very different causes: but it is to the latter, that the best men, the greatest ornaments of human nature, have most carefully attended: it is to the former tyrants and oppressors have always aimed.

The Federal Farmer.

– XVIII –

January 25, 1788

Dear Sir,

1. I am persuaded, a federal head never was formed, that possessed half the powers which it could carry into full effect, altogether independently of the state or local governments, as the one, the convention has proposed, will possess. Should the state legislatures never meet, except merely for chusing federal senators and appointing electors, once in four and six years, the federal head may go on for ages to make all laws relative to the following subjects, and by its own courts, officers, and provisions, carry them into full effect, and to any extent it may deem for the general welfare, that is, for *raising taxes*, borrowing and coining monies, and for applying them— for forming and governing *armies* and *navies* and for directing their operations—for regulating commerce with foreign nations, and among the several states, and with the Indian tribes—for regulating *bankruptcies*, weights and measures, post-offices and post-roads, and captures on land and water— for establishing a uniform rule of naturalization, and for promoting the progress of science and useful arts—for defining and punishing piracies and felonies committed on the high seas, the offences of counterfeiting the securities and current coin of the United States, and offences against the law of nations, and for regulating all maritime concerns—for *organizing, arming* and *disciplining* the militia (the respective states training them, and appointing the officers)—for *calling them forth* when wanted, and for governing them when in the service of the union—for the *sole and exclusive government* of a federal city or town, not exceeding ten miles square, and of places ceded for forts, magazines arsenals, dock-yards, and other needful buildings—for granting letters of marque and reprisal, and making war— for regulating the *times, places,* and *manner of holding elections* for senators and representatives—for making and concluding all treaties, and carrying

them into execution—for judicially deciding all questions arising on the constitution laws, and treaties of the union, in law and equity, and questions arising on state laws also, where ambassadors, other public ministers, and consuls, where the United States, individual states, or a state, where *citizens of different states*, and where foreign states, or a *foreign subject*, are parties or party—for impeaching and trying federal officers—for deciding on elections, and for expelling members, &c. All these enumerated powers we must examine and contemplate in all their extent and various branches, and then reflect, that the federal head will have full power to make all laws whatever respecting them; and for carrying into full effect all powers vested in the union, in any department, or officers of it, by the constitution, in order to see the full extent of the federal powers, which will be supreme, and exercised by that head at pleasure, conforming to the few limitations mentioned in the constitution. Indeed, I conceive, it is impossible to see them in their full extent at present: we see vast undefined powers lodged in a weak organization, but cannot, by the enquiries of months and years, clearly discern them in all their numerous branches. These powers in feeble hands, must be tempting objects for ambition and a love of power and fame.

2. But, say the advocates, they are all necessary for forming an energetic federal government; all necessary in the hands of the union, for the common defence and general welfare. In these great points they appear to me to go from the end to the means, and from the means to the end, perpetually begging the question.[111] I think in the course of these letters, I shall sufficiently prove, that some of these powers need not be lodged in the hands of the union—that others ought to be exercised under better checks, and in part, by the agency of the states—some I have already considered, some in my mind, are not liable to objections, and the others, I shall briefly notice in this closing letter.

3. The power to controul the military forces of the country, as well as the revenues of it, requires serious attention. Here again I must premise, that a federal republic is a compound system, made up of constituent parts, each essential to the whole: we must then expect the real friends of such a system will always be very anxious for the security and preservation of each part, and to this end, that each constitutionally possess its natural portion of power and influence—and that it will constantly be an object of concern to them, to see one part armed at all points by the constitution, and in

111. Cf. *Brutus V* (4–5).

manner destructive in the end, even of its own existence, and the others left constitutionally defenceless.

4. The military forces of a free country may be considered under three general descriptions—1. The militia. 2. the navy—and 3. the regular troops—and the whole ought ever to be, and understood to be, in strict subordination to the civil authority; and that regular troops, and select corps, ought not to be kept up without evident necessity. Stipulations in the constitution to this effect, are perhaps, too general to be of much service, except merely to impress on the minds of the people and soldiery, that the military ought ever to be subject to the civil authority, &c. But particular attention, and many more definite stipulations, are highly necessary to render the military safe, and yet useful in a free government; and in a federal republic, where the people meet in distinct assemblies, many stipulations are necessary to keep a part from transgressing, which would be unnecessary checks against the whole met in one legislature, in one entire government.—A militia, when properly formed, are in fact the people themselves, and render regular troops in a great measure unnecessary. The powers to form and arm the militia, to appoint their officers, and to command their services, are very important; nor ought they in a confederated republic to be lodged, solely, in any one member of the government. First, the constitution ought to secure a genuine and guard against a select militia, by providing that the militia shall always be kept well organized, armed, and disciplined, and include, according to the past and general usage of the states, all men capable of bearing arms; and that all regulations tending to render this general militia useless and defenceless, by establishing select corps of militia, or distinct bodies of military men, not having permanent interests and attachments in the community to be avoided. I am persuaded, I need not multiply words to convince you of the value and solidity of this principle, as it respects general liberty, and the duration of a free and mild government: having this principle well fixed by the constitution, then the federal head may prescribe a general uniform plan, on which the respective states shall form and train the militia, appoint their officers and solely manage them, except when called into the service of the union, and when called into that service, they may be commanded and governed by the union. This arrangement combines energy and safety in it; it places the sword in the hands of the solid interest of the community, and not in the hands of men destitute of property, of principle, or of attachment to the society and government, who often form the select corps of peace or ordinary establishments: by it, the militia are the people, immediately under the management of the state

governments, but on a uniform federal plan, and called into the service, command, and government of the union, when necessary for the common defence and general tranquility. But, say gentlemen, the general militia are for the most part employed at home in their private concerns, cannot well be called out, or be depended upon; that we must have a select militia; that is, as I understand it, particular corps or bodies of young men, and of men who have but little to do at home, particularly armed and disciplined in some measure, at the public expence, and always ready to take the field. These corps, not much unlike regular troops, will ever produce an inattention to the general militia; and the consequence has ever been, and always must be, that the substantial men, having families and property, will generally be without arms, without knowing the use of them, and defenceless; whereas, to preserve liberty, it is essential that the whole body of the people always possess arms, and be taught alike, especially when young, how to use them; nor does it follow from this, that all promiscuously must go into actual service on every occasion. The mind that aims at a select militia, must be influenced by a truly anti-republican principle; and when we see many men disposed to practice upon it, whenever they can prevail, no wonder true republicans are for carefully guarding against it. As a farther check, it may be proper to add, that the militia of any state shall not remain in the service of the union, beyond a given period, without the express consent of the state legislature.

5. As to the navy, I do not see that it can have any connection with the local governments. The want of employment for it, and the want of monies in the hands of the union, must be its proper limitation. The laws for building or increasing it, as all the important laws mentioned in a former letter, touching military and money matters, may be checked by requiring the attendance of a large proportion of the representatives, and the consent of a large proportion of those present, to pass them as before mentioned.

6. By art. 1. sect. 8. "Congress shall have *power to provide for* organizing, arming, and disciplining the militia": *power to provide for*—does this imply any more than power to prescribe a general uniform plan? And must not the respective states pass laws (but in conformity to the plan) for forming and training the militia?

In the present state of mankind, and of conducting war, the government of every nation must have power to raise and keep up regular troops: the question is, how shall this power be lodged? In an entire government, as in Great-Britain, where the people assemble by their representatives in one legislature, there is no difficulty, it is of course properly lodged in that legislature: But in a confederated republic, where the organization consists of a federal head, and local governments, there is no one part in which it can be solely, and safely lodged. By art. 1. sect. 8. "congress shall have power to raise and support armies," &c. By art. 1. sect. 10. "no state, without the consent of congress, shall keep troops, or ships of war, in time of peace." It seems fit the union should direct the raising of troops, and the union may do it in two ways; by requisitions on the states, or by direct taxes—the first is most conformable to the federal plan, and safest; and it may be improved, by giving the union power, by its own laws and officers, to raise the states quota that may neglect, and to charge it with the expence; and by giving a fixed quorum of the state legislatures power to disapprove the requisition. There would be less danger in this power to raise troops, could the state governments keep a proper controul over the purse and over the militia; but after all the precautions we can take, without evidently fettering the union too much, we must give a large accumulation of powers to it, in these and other respects. There is one check, which, I think, may be added with great propriety—that is, no land forces shall be kept up, but by legislative acts annually passed by congress, and no appropriation of monies for their support shall be for a longer term than one year. This is the constitutional practice in Great-Britain, and the reasons for such checks in the United States appear to be much stronger. We may also require that these acts be passed by a special majority, as before mentioned. There is another mode still more guarded, and which seems to be founded in the true spirit of a federal system: it seems proper to divide those powers we can with safety, lodge them in no one member of the government alone; yet substantially to preserve their use, and to ensure duration to the government, by modifying the exercise of them—it is to empower congress to raise troops by direct levies, not exceeding a given number, say 2000 in time of peace, and 12,000 in a time of war, and for such further troops as may be wanted, to raise them by requisitions qualified as before mentioned. By the above recited clause no state shall keep troops, &c. in time of peace—this clearly implies, it may do it in time of war: this must be on the principle, that the union cannot defend all parts of the republic, and suggests an idea very repugnant to the general tendency of the system proposed, which is to disarm the state governments: a state in a long war may collect forces sufficient to take the field against the neighbouring states. This clause was copied from the confederation, in which it was of more importance than in the plan proposed, because under this the separate states, probably, will have but small revenues.

7. By article 1. section 8. congress shall have power to establish uniform laws on the subject of bankruptcies, throughout the United States. It is to be observed, that the separate states have ever been in possession of the power, and in the use of it, of making bankrupt laws, militia laws, and laws in some other cases, respecting which, the new constitution, when adopted, will give the union power to legislate, &c.—but no words are used by the constitution to exclude the jurisdiction of the several states, and whether they will be excluded or not, or whether they and the union will have concurrent jurisdiction or not, must be determined by inference; and from the nature of the subject; if the power, for instance, to make uniform laws on the subject of bankruptcies, is in its nature indivisible, or incapable of being exercised by two legislatures independently, or by one in aid of the other, then the states are excluded, and cannot legislate at all on the subject, even though the union should neglect or find it impracticable to establish uniform bankrupt laws. How far the union will find it practicable to do this, time only can fully determine. When we consider the extent of the country, and the very different ideas of the different parts in it, respecting credit, and the mode of making men's property liable for paying their debts, we may, I think, with some degree of certainty, conclude that the union never will be able to establish such laws; but if practicable, it does not appear to me, on further reflection, that the union ought to have the power;[112] it does not appear to me to be a power properly incidental to a federal head, and, I believe, no one ever possessed it; it is a power that will immediately and extensively interfere with the internal police of the separate states, especially with their administering justice among their own citizens. By giving this power to the union, we greatly extend the jurisdiction of the federal judiciary, as all questions arising on bankrupt laws, being laws of the union, even between citizens of the same state, may be tried in the federal courts; and I think it may be shewn, that by the help of these laws, actions between citizens of different states, and the laws of the federal city, aided by no overstrained judicial fictions, almost all civil causes may be drawn into those courts. We must be sensible how cautious we ought to be in extending unnecessarily the jurisdiction of those courts, for reasons I need not repeat. This article of power too, will considerably increase, in the hands of the union, an accumulation of powers, some of a federal and some of an unfederal nature, too large without it.

8. The constitution provides, that congress shall have the sole and exclu-

112. Cf. *FF I* (10).

sive government of what is called the federal city, a place not exceeding ten miles square, and of all places ceded for forts, dock-yards, &c. I believe this is a novel kind of provision in a federal republic; it is repugnant to the spirit of such a government, and must be founded in an apprehension of a hostile disposition between the federal head and the state governments; and it is not improbable, that the sudden retreat of congress from Philadelphia, first gave rise to it.—With this apprehension, we provide, the government of the union shall have secluded places, cities, and castles of defence, which no state laws whatever shall invade. When we attentively examine this provision in all its consequences, it opens to view scenes almost without bounds. A federal, or rather a national city, ten miles square, containing a hundred square miles, is about four times as large as London; and for forts, magazines, arsenals, dock-yards, and other needful buildings, congress may possess a number of places or towns in each state. It is true, congress cannot have them unless the state legislatures cede them; but when once ceded, they never can be recovered, and though the general temper of the legislatures may be averse to such cessions, yet many opportunities and advantages may be taken of particular times and circumstances of complying assemblies, and of particular parties, to obtain them. It is not improbable, that some considerable towns or places, in some intemperate moments, or influenced by anti-republican principles, will petition to be ceded for the purposes mentioned in the provision. There are men, and even towns, in the best republics, which are often fond of withdrawing from the government of them, whenever occasion shall present. The case is still stronger; if the provision in question holds out allurements to attempt to withdraw, the people of a state must ever be subject to state as well as federal taxes; but the federal city and places will be subject only to the latter, and to them by no fixed proportion, nor of the taxes raised in them, can the separate states demand any account of congress.—These doors opened for withdrawing from the state governments entirely, may, on other accounts, be very alluring and pleasing to those anti-republican men who prefer a place under the wings of courts.

9. If a federal town be necessary for the residence of congress and the public officers, it ought to be a small one, and the government of it fixed on republican and common law principles, carefully enumerated and established by the constitution. It is true, the states, when they shall cede places, may stipulate, that the laws and government of congress in them, shall always be formed on such principles; but it is easy to discern, that the stipulations of a state, or of the inhabitants of the place ceded, can

be of but little avail against the power and gradual encroachments of the union. The principles ought to be established by the federal constitution, to which all the states are parties; but in no event can there be any need of so large a city and places for forts, &c. totally exempted from the laws and jurisdictions of the state governments. If I understand the constitution, the laws of congress, constitutionally made, will have complete and supreme jurisdiction to all federal purposes, on every inch of ground in the United States, and exclusive jurisdiction on the high seas, and this by the highest authority, the consent of the people. Suppose ten acres at West-Point shall be used as a fort of the union, or a sea port town as a dock-yard, the laws of the union in those places respecting the navy, forces of the union, and all federal objects, must prevail, be noticed by all judges and officers, and executed accordingly: and I can discern no one reason for excluding from these places, the operation of state laws, as to mere state purposes; for instance, for the collection of state taxes in them, recovering debts, deciding questions of property arising within them on state laws, punishing, by state laws, theft, trespasses, and offences committed in them by mere citizens against the state laws.

10. The city, and all the places in which the union shall have this exclusive jurisdiction, will be immediately under one entire government, that of the federal head; and be no part of any state, and consequently no part of the United States. The inhabitants of the federal city and places, will be as much exempt from the laws and controul of the state governments, as the people of Canada or Nova Scotia will be. Neither the laws of the states respecting taxes, the militia, crimes or property, will extend to them; nor is there a single stipulation in the constitution, that the inhabitants of this city, and these places, shall be governed by laws founded on principles of freedom. All questions, civil and criminal, arising on the laws of these places, which must be the laws of congress, must be decided in the federal courts; and also, all questions that may, by such judicial fictions as these courts may consider reasonable, be supposed to arise within this city, or any of these places, may be brought into these courts; and by a very common legal fiction, any personal contract may be supposed to have been made in any place. A contract made in Georgia may be supposed to have been made in the federal city, in Pennsylvania; the courts will admit the fiction, and not in these cases, make it a serious question, where it was in fact made. Every suit in which an inhabitant of a federal district may be a party, of course may be instituted in the federal courts—also, every suit in which it may be alledged, and not denied, that a party in it is an inhabitant of such

a district—also, every suit to which a foreign state or subject, the union, a state, citizens of different states, in fact, or by reasonable legal fictions, may be a party or parties: And thus, by means of bankrupt laws, federal districts, &c. almost all judicial business, I apprehend may be carried into the federal courts, without essentially departing from the usual course of judicial proceedings.[113] The courts in Great Britain have acquired their powers, and extended, very greatly, their jurisdictions by such fictions and suppositions as I have mentioned. The constitution, in these points, certainly involves in it principles, and almost hidden cases, which may unfold, and in time exhibit consequences we hardly think of. The power of naturalization, when viewed in connection with the judicial powers and cases, is, in my mind, of very doubtful extent. By the constitution itself, the citizens of each state will be naturalized citizens of every state, to the general purposes of instituting suits, claiming the benefits of the laws, &c. And in order to give the federal courts jurisdiction of an action, between citizens of the same state, in common acceptation, may not a court allow the plaintiff to say, he is a citizen of one state, and the defendant a citizen of another, without carrying legal fictions so far, by any means, as they have been carried by the courts of King's Bench and Exchequer, in order to bring causes within their cognizance?—Further, the federal city and districts, will be totally distinct from any state, and a citizen of a state will not of course be a subject of any of them; and to avail himself of the privileges and immunities of them, must he not be naturalized by congress in them? and may not congress make any proportion of the citizens of the states naturalized subjects of the federal city and districts, and thereby entitle them to sue or defend, in all cases, in the federal courts? I have my doubts, and many sensible men, I find, have their doubts, on these points; and we ought to observe, they must be settled in the courts of law, by their rules, distinctions, and fictions. To avoid many of these intricacies and difficulties, and to avoid the undue and unnecessary extension of the federal judicial powers, it appears to me, that no federal districts ought to be allowed, and no federal city or town, except perhaps a small town, in which the government shall be republican, but in which congress shall have no jurisdiction over the inhabitants, but in common with the other inhabitants of the states. Can the union want, in such a town, any thing more than a right to the soil on which it may set its buildings, and extensive jurisdiction over the federal buildings, and property, its own members, officers, and servants in it? As to all federal objects, the union

113. Cf. *Brutus XII* (3–5).

will have complete jurisdiction over them, of course any where, and every where. I still think, that no actions ought to be allowed to be brought in the federal courts, between citizens of different states, at least, unless the cause be of very considerable importance: that no action against a state government, by any citizen or foreigner, ought to be allowed; and no action, in which a foreign subject is party, at least, unless it be of very considerable importance, ought to be instituted in the federal courts—I confess, I can see no reason whatever, for a foreigner, or for citizens of different states, carrying sixpenny causes into the federal courts; I think the state courts will be found by experience, to be bottomed on better principles, and to administer justice better than the federal courts.

11. The difficulties and dangers I have supposed, will result from so large a federal city, and federal districts, from the extension of the federal judicial powers, &c. are not, I conceive, merely possible, but probable. I think, pernicious political consequences will follow from them, and from the federal city especially, for very obvious reasons, a few of which I will mention.

12. We must observe, that the citizens of a state will be subject to state as well as federal taxes, and the inhabitants of the federal city and districts, only to such taxes as congress may lay—We are not to suppose all our people are attached to free government, and the principles of the common law, but that many thousands of them will prefer a city governed, not on republican principles—This city, and the government of it, must indubitably take their tone from the characters of the men, who from the nature of its situation and institution, must collect there. This city will not be established for productive labour, for mercantile, or mechanic industry; but for the residence of government, its officers and attendants. If hereafter it should ever become a place of trade and industry, in the early periods of its existence, when its laws and government must receive their fixed tone, it must be a mere court, with its appendages, the executive, congress, the law courts, gentlemen of fortune and pleasure, with all the officers, attendants, suitors, expectants and dependants on the whole, however brilliant and honourable this collection may be, if we expect it will have any sincere attachments to simple and frugal republicanism, to that liberty and mild government, which is dear to the laborious part of a free people, we most assuredly deceive ourselves. This early collection will draw to it men from all parts of the country, of a like political description: we see them looking towards the place already.

13. Such a city, or town, containing a hundred square miles, must soon

be the great, the visible, and dazzling centre, the mistress of fashions, and the fountain of politics. There may be a free or shackled press in this city, and the streams which may issue from it may overflow the country, and they will be poisonous or pure, as the fountain may be corrupt or not. But not to dwell on a subject that must give pain to the virtuous friends of freedom, I will only add, can a free and enlightened people create a common head so extensive, so prone to corruption and slavery, as this city probably will be, when they have it in their power to form one pure and chaste, frugal and republican?

14. Under the confederation congress has no power whereby to govern its own officers and servants; a federal town, in which congress might have special jurisdiction, might be expedient; but under the new constitution, without a federal town, congress will have all necessary powers of course over its officers and servants; indeed it will have a complete system of powers to all the federal purposes mentioned in the constitution; so that the reason for a federal town under the confederation, will by no means exist under the constitution.—Even if a trial by jury should be admitted in the federal city, what man, with any state attachments or republican virtue about him, will submit to be tried by a jury of it?

15. I might observe more particularly upon several other parts of the constitution proposed; but it has been uniformly my object in examining a subject so extensive, and difficult in many parts to be illustrated, to avoid unimportant things, and not to dwell upon points not very material. The rule for apportioning requisitions on the states, having some time since been agreed to by eleven states, I have viewed as settled. The stipulation that congress, after twenty one years may prohibit the importation of slaves, is a point gained, if not so favourable as could be wished for. As monopolies in trade perhaps, can in no case be useful, it might not be amiss to provide expressly against them. I wish the power to reprieve and pardon was more cautiously lodged, and under some limitations. I do not see why congress should be allowed to consent that a person may accept a present, office, or title of a foreign prince, &c. As the state governments, as well as the federal, are essential parts of the system, why should not the oath taken by the officers be expressly to support the whole? As to debts due to and from the union, I think the constitution intends, on examining art. 4. sect. 8. and art. 6. that they shall stand on the same ground under the constitution as under the confederation. In the article respecting amendments, it is stipulated, that no state shall ever be deprived of its equal vote in the senate without its consent; and that alterations may be made by the consent of three-fourths

of the states. Stipulations to bind the majority of the people may serve one purpose, to prevent frequent motions for change; but these attempts to bind the majority, generally give occasion for breach of contract. The states all agreed about seven years ago, that the confederation should remain unaltered, unless every state should agree to alterations: but we now see it agreed by the convention, and four states, that the old confederacy shall be destroyed, and a new one, of nine states, be erected, if nine only shall come in. Had we agreed, that a majority should alter the confederation, a majority's agreeing would have bound the rest: but now we must break the old league, unless all the states agree to alter, or not proceed with adopting the constitution. Whether the adoption by nine states will not produce a nearly equal and dangerous division of the people for and against the constitution—whether the circumstances of the country were such as to justify the hazarding a probability of such a situation, I shall not undertake to determine. I shall leave it to be determined hereafter, whether nine states, under a new federal compact, can claim the benefits of any treaties made with a confederation of thirteen, under a distinct compact and form of existence—whether the new confederacy can recover debts due to the old confederacy, or the arrears of taxes due from the states excluded.

16. It has been well observed, that our country is extensive, and has no external enemies to press the parts together: that, therefore, their union must depend on strong internal ties. I differ with the gentlemen who make these observations only in this, they hold the ties ought to be strengthened by a considerable degree of internal consolidation, and my object is to form them and strengthen them, on pure federal principles. Whatever may be the fate of many valuable and necessary amendments in the constitution proposed, the ample discussion and respectable opposition it will receive, will have a good effect—they will operate to produce a mild and prudent administration, and to put the wheels of the whole system in motion on proper principles—they will evince, that true republican principles and attachments are still alive and formidable in this country. These, in view, I believe, even men quite disposed to make a bad use of the system, will long hesitate before they will resolve to do it. A majority, from a view of our situation, and influenced by many considerations, may acquiese in the adoption of this constitution; but, it is evident that a very great majority of the people of the United States think it, in many parts, an unnecessary and unadviseable departure from true republican and federal principles.

The Federal Farmer.

Essays of Brutus

—I—

18 October 1787

To the Citizens of the State of New-York.

1. When the public is called to investigate and decide upon a question in which not only the present members of the community are deeply interested, but upon which the happiness and misery of generations yet unborn is in great measure suspended, the benevolent mind cannot help feeling itself peculiarly interested in the result.

2. In this situation, I trust the feeble efforts of an individual, to lead the minds of the people to a wise and prudent determination, cannot fail of being acceptable to the candid and dispassionate part of the community. Encouraged by this consideration, I have been induced to offer my thoughts upon the present important crisis of our public affairs.

3. Perhaps this country never saw so critical a period in their political concerns. We have felt the feebleness of the ties by which these United-States are held together, and the want of sufficient energy in our present confederation, to manage, in some instances, our general concerns. Various expedients have been proposed to remedy these evils, but none have succeeded. At length a Convention of the states has been assembled, they have formed a constitution which will now, probably, be submitted to the people to ratify or reject, who are the fountain of all power, to whom alone it of right belongs to make or unmake constitutions, or forms of government, at their pleasure. The most important question that was ever proposed to your decision, or to the decision of any people under heaven, is before you, and you are to decide upon it by men of your own election, chosen specially for this purpose. If the constitution, offered to your acceptance, be a wise one, calculated to preserve the invaluable blessings of liberty, to secure the inestimable rights of mankind, and promote human happiness, then, if you accept it, you will lay a lasting foundation of happiness for millions yet unborn; generations to come will rise up and call you blessed. You may rejoice in the prospects of this vast extended continent becoming filled with freemen, who will assert the dignity of human nature. You may

From the *New York Journal*, October 18, 1787.

solace yourselves with the idea, that society, in this favoured land, will fast advance to the highest point of perfection;[1] the human mind will expand in knowledge and virtue, and the golden age be, in some measure, realised. But if, on the other hand, this form of government contains principles that will lead to the subversion of liberty if it tends to establish a despotism, or, what is worse, a tyrannic aristocracy; then, if you adopt it, this only remaining assylum for liberty will be shut up, and posterity will execrate your memory.

4. Momentous then is the question you have to determine, and you are called upon by every motive which should influence a noble and virtuous mind, to examine it well, and to make up a wise judgment. It is insisted, indeed, that this constitution must be received, be it ever so imperfect. If it has its defects, it is said, they can be best amended when they are experienced. But remember, when the people once part with power, they can seldom or never resume it again but by force. Many instances can be produced in which the people have voluntarily increased the powers of their rulers; but few, if any, in which rulers have willingly abridged their authority. This is a sufficient reason to induce you to be careful, in the first instance, how you deposit the powers of government.

5. With these few introductory remarks, I shall proceed to a consideration of this constitution:

The first question that presents itself on the subject is, whether a confederated government be the best for the United States or not? Or in other words, whether the thirteen United States should be reduced to one great republic, governed by one legislature, and under the direction of one executive and judicial; or whether they should continue thirteen confederated republics, under the direction and controul of a supreme federal head for certain defined national purposes only?

6. This enquiry is important, because, although the government reported by the convention does not go to a perfect and entire consolidation, yet it approaches so near to it, that it must, if executed, certainly and infallibly terminate in it.[2]

7. This government is to possess absolute and uncontroulable power, legislative, executive and judicial, with respect to every object to which it

---

1. See "Address by a Plebeian to the People of the State of New York, 1788" (hereafter "Plebian"), paragraph 35, in this volume.
2. See *Federal Farmer* (hereafter *FF*) I (9–10); *Plebeian* (16).

extends, for by the last clause of section 8th, article 1st, it is declared "that the Congress shall have power to make all laws which shall be necessary and proper for carrying into execution the foregoing powers, and all other powers vested by this constitution, in the government of the United States; or in any department or office thereof." And by the 6th article, it is declared "that this constitution, and the laws of the United States, which shall be made in pursuance thereof, and the treaties made, or which shall be made, under the authority of the United States, shall be the supreme law of the land; and the judges in every state shall be bound thereby, any thing in the constitution, or law of any state to the contrary notwithstanding." It appears from these articles that there is no need of any intervention of the state governments, between the Congress and the people, to execute any one power vested in the general government, and that the constitution and laws of every state are nullified and declared void, so far as they are or shall be inconsistent with this constitution, or the laws made in pursuance of it, or with treaties made under the authority of the United States.[3]—The government then, so far as it extends, is a complete one, and not a confederation. It is as much one complete government as that of New-York or Massachusetts, has as absolute and perfect powers to make and execute all laws, to appoint officers, institute courts, declare offences, and annex penalties, with respect to every object to which it extends, as any other in the world. So far therefore as its powers reach, all ideas of confederation are given up and lost.[4] It is true this government is limited to certain objects, or to speak more properly, some small degree of power is still left to the states, but a little attention to the powers vested in the general government, will convince every candid man, that if it is capable of being executed, all that is reserved for the individual states must very soon be annihilated, except so far as they are barely necessary to the organization of the general government. The powers of the general legislature extend to every case that is of the least importance—there is nothing valuable to human nature, nothing dear to freemen, but what is within its power. It has authority to make laws which will affect the lives, the liberty, and property of every man in the United States; nor can the constitution or laws of any state, in any way prevent or impede the full and complete execution of every power given. The legislative power is competent to lay taxes, duties, imposts, and excises;[5]

3. See *FF IV* (7).
4. See *FF I* (10, 13).
5. For fuller discussion, see *Brutus V–VIII*.

there is no limitation to this power, unless it be said that the clause which directs the use to which those taxes, and duties shall be applied, may be said to be a limitation: but this is no restriction of the power at all, for by this clause they are to be applied to pay the debts and provide for the common defence and general welfare of the United States; but the legislature have authority to contract debts at their discretion; they are the sole judges of what is necessary to provide for the common defence, and they only are to determine what is for the general welfare; this power therefore is neither more nor less, than a power to lay and collect taxes, imposts, and excises, at their pleasure; not only is the power to lay taxes unlimited, as to the amount they may require, but it is perfect and absolute to raise them in any mode they please.[6] No state legislature, or any power in the state governments, have any more to do in carrying this into effect, than the authority of one state has to do with that of another. In the business therefore of laying and collecting taxes, the idea of confederation is totally lost, and that of one entire republic is embraced. It is proper here to remark, that the authority to lay and collect taxes is the most important of any power that can be granted; it connects with it almost all other powers, or at least will in process of time draw all other after it; it is the great mean of protection, security, and defence, in a good government, and the great engine of oppression and tyranny in a bad one.[7] This cannot fail of being the case, if we consider the contracted limits which are set by this constitution, to the state governments, on this article of raising money. No state can emit paper money—lay any duties, or imposts, on imports, or exports, but by consent of the Congress; and then the net produce shall be for the benefit of the United States: the only mean therefore left, for any state to support its government and discharge its debts, is by direct taxation; and the United States have also power to lay and collect taxes, in any way they please. Every one who has thought on the subject, must be convinced that but small sums of money can be collected in any country, by direct taxes, when the foederal government begins to exercise the right of taxation in all its parts, the legislatures of the several states will find it impossible to raise monies to support their governments. Without money they cannot be supported, and they must dwindle away, and, as before observed, their powers absorbed in that of the general government.

6. See *Brutus V* (4).
7. See *Brutus V* (9–11); cf. *FF IV* (9).

8. It might be here shewn, that the power in the federal legislative, to raise and support armies at pleasure, as well in peace as in war, and their controul over the militia, tend, not only to a consolidation of the government, but the destruction of liberty.[8]—I shall not, however, dwell upon these, as a few observations upon the judicial power of this government, in addition to the preceding, will fully evince the truth of the position.

9. The judicial power of the United States is to be vested in a supreme court, and in such inferior courts as Congress may from time to time ordain and establish.[9] The powers of these courts are very extensive; their jurisdiction comprehends all civil causes, except such as arise between citizens of the same state; and it extends to all cases in law and equity arising under the constitution. One inferior court must be established, I presume, in each state, at least, with the necessary executive officers appendant thereto. It is easy to see, that in the common course of things, these courts will eclipse the dignity, and take away from the respectability, of the state courts. These courts will be, in themselves, totally independent of the states, deriving their authority from the United States, and receiving from them fixed salaries; and in the course of human events it is to be expected, that they will swallow up all the powers of the courts in the respective states.

10. How far the clause in the 8th section of the 1st article may operate to do away all idea of confederated states, and to effect an entire consolidation of the whole into one general government, it is impossible to say. The powers given by this article are very general and comprehensive, and it may receive a construction to justify the passing almost any law. A power to make all laws, which shall be *necessary and proper*, for carrying into execution, all powers vested by the constitution in the government of the United States, or any department or officer thereof, is a power very comprehensive and definite [indefinite?], and may, for ought I know, be exercised in a such manner as entirely to abolish the state legislatures.[10] Suppose the legislature of a state should pass a law to raise money to support their government and pay the state debt, may the Congress repeal this law, because it may prevent the collection of a tax which they may think proper and necessary to lay, to provide for the general welfare of the United States? For all laws made, in pursuance of this constitution, are the supreme law of the land, and the judges in every state shall be bound thereby, any thing in the constitution

8. See *Brutus VIII–X*.
9. See *Brutus XI–XV* on the judiciary.
10. See *FF IV* (7).

or laws of the different states to the contrary notwithstanding.—By such a law, the government of a particular state might be overturned at one stroke, and thereby be deprived of every means of its support.

11. It is not meant, by stating this case, to insinuate that the constitution would warrant a law of this kind; or unnecessarily to alarm the fears of the people, by suggesting, that the federal legislature would be more likely to pass the limits assigned them by the constitution, than that of an individual state, further than they are less responsible to the people. But what is meant is, that the legislature of the United States are vested with the great and uncontroulable powers, of laying and collecting taxes, duties, imposts, and excises; of regulating trade, raising and supporting armies, organizing, arming, and disciplining the militia, instituting courts, and other general powers. And are by this clause invested with the power of making all laws, *proper and necessary*, for carrying all these into execution; and they may so exercise this power as entirely to annihilate all the state governments, and reduce this country to one single government. And if they may do it, it is pretty certain they will; for it will be found that the power retained by individual states, small as it is, will be a clog upon the wheels of the government of the United States; the latter therefore will be naturally inclined to remove it out of the way. Besides, it is a truth confirmed by the unerring experience of ages, that every man, and every body of men, invested with power, are ever disposed to increase it, and to acquire a superiority over every thing that stands in their way. This disposition, which is implanted in human nature, will operate in the federal legislature to lessen and ultimately to subvert the state authority, and having such advantages, will most certainly succeed, if the federal government succeeds at all. It must be very evident then, that what this constitution wants of being a complete consolidation of the several parts of the union into one complete government, possessed of perfect legislative, judicial, and executive powers, to all intents and purposes, it will necessarily acquire in its exercise and operation.

12. Let us now proceed to enquire, as I at first proposed, whether it be best the thirteen United States should be reduced to one great republic, or not? It is here taken for granted, that all agree in this, that whatever government we adopt, it ought to be a free one; that it should be so framed as to secure the liberty of the citizens of America, and such an one as to admit of a full, fair, and equal representation of the people. The question then will be, whether a government thus constituted, and founded on such principles, is practicable, and can be exercised over the whole United States, reduced into one state?

13. If respect is to be paid to the opinion of the greatest and wisest men who have ever thought or wrote on the science of government, we shall be constrained to conclude, that a free republic cannot succeed over a country of such immense extent, containing such a number of inhabitants, and these encreasing in such rapid progression as that of the whole United States. Among the many illustrious authorities which might be produced to this point, I shall content myself with quoting only two. The one is the baron de Montesquieu, spirit of laws, chap. xvi. vol. I book VIII. "It is natural to a republic to have only a small territory, otherwise it cannot long subsist. In a large republic there are men of large fortunes, and consequently of less moderation; there are trusts too great to be placed in any single subject; he has interest of his own; he soon begins to think that he may be happy, great and glorious, by oppressing his fellow citizens; and that he may raise himself to grandeur on the ruins of his country. In a large republic, the public good is sacrificed to a thousand views; it is subordinate to exceptions, and depends on accidents. In a small one, the interest of the public is easier perceived, better understood, and more within the reach of every citizen; abuses are of less extent, and of course are less protected." Of the same opinion is the marquis Beccarari.[11]

14. History furnishes no example of a free republic, any thing like the extent of the United States. The Grecian republics were of small extent; so also was that of the Romans. Both of these, it is true, in process of time, extended their conquests over large territories of country; and the consequence was, that their governments were changed from that of free governments to those of the most tyrannical that ever existed in the world.

15. Not only the opinion of the greatest men, and the experience of mankind, are against the idea of an extensive republic, but a variety of reasons may be drawn from the reason and nature of things, against it. In every government, the will of the sovereign is the law. In despotic governments, the supreme authority being lodged in one, his will is law, and can be as easily expressed to a large extensive territory as to a small one. In a pure democracy the people are the sovereign, and their will is declared by themselves; for this purpose they must all come together to deliberate, and decide. This kind of government cannot be exercised, therefore, over a country of any considerable extent; it must be confined to a single city, or at least limited to such bounds as that the people can conveniently assemble, be able to

11. Beccaria, *An Essay on Crimes and Punishments*, chap. 26 ("Of the Spirit of Family in States"); cf. *FF VI* (6).

debate, understand the subject submitted to them, and declare their opinion concerning it.

16. In a free republic, although all laws are derived from the consent of the people, yet the people do not declare their consent by themselves in person, but by representatives, chosen by them, who are supposed to know the minds of their constituents, and to be possessed of integrity to declare this mind.

17. In every free government, the people must give their assent to the laws by which they are governed. This is the true criterion between a free government and an arbitrary one. The former are ruled by the will of the whole, expressed in any manner they may agree upon; the latter by the will of one, or a few. If the people are to give their assent to the laws, by persons chosen and appointed by them, the manner of the choice and the number chosen, must be such, as to possess, be disposed, and consequently qualified to declare the sentiments of the people; for if they do not know, or are not disposed to speak the sentiments of the people, the people do not govern, but the sovereignty is in a few. Now, in a large extended country, it is impossible to have a representation, possessing the sentiments, and of integrity, to declare the minds of the people, without having it so numerous and unwieldly, as to be subject in great measure to the inconveniency of a democratic government.[12]

18. The territory of the United States is of vast extent; it now contains near three millions of souls, and is capable of containing much more than ten times that number. Is it practicable for a country, so large and so numerous as they will soon become, to elect a representation, that will speak their sentiments, without their becoming so numerous as to be incapable of transacting public business? It certainly is not.

19. In a republic, the manners, sentiments, and interests of the people should be similar. If this be not the case, there will be a constant clashing of opinions; and the representatives of one part will be continually striving against those of the other.[13] This will retard the operations of government, and prevent such conclusions as will promote the public good. If we apply this remark to the condition of the United States, we shall be convinced that it forbids that we should be one government. The United States includes a variety of climates. The productions of the different parts of the union are very variant, and their interests, of consequence, diverse. Their

12. On representation, see *Brutus III* and *IV*; cf. *FF II* (1).
13. See *FF VIII* (7) and, of course, *Federalist* 10.

manners and habits differ as much as their climates and productions; and their sentiments are by no means coincident. The laws and customs of the several states are, in many respects, very diverse, and in some opposite; each would be in favor of its own interests and customs, and, of consequence, a legislature, formed of representatives from the respective parts, would not only be too numerous to act with any care or decision, but would be composed of such heterogenous and discordant principles, as would constantly be contending with each other.[14]

20. The laws cannot be executed in a republic, of an extent equal to that of the United States, with promptitude.

21. The magistrates in every government must be supported in the execution of the laws, either by an armed force, maintained at the public expence for that purpose; or by the people turning out to aid the magistrate upon his command, in case of resistance.[15]

22. In despotic governments, as well as in all the monarchies of Europe, standing armies are kept up to execute the commands of the prince or the magistrate, and are employed for this purpose when occasion requires: But they have always proved the destruction of liberty, and are abhorrent to the spirit of a free republic.[16] In England, where they depend upon the parliament for their annual support, they have always been complained of as oppressive and unconstitutional, and are seldom employed in executing of the laws; never except on extraordinary occasions, and then under the direction of a civil magistrate.

23. A free republic will never keep a standing army to execute its laws. It must depend upon the support of its citizens. But when a government is to receive its support from the aid of the citizens, it must be so constructed as to have the confidence, respect, and affection of the people. Men who, upon the call of the magistrate, offer themselves to execute the laws, are influenced to do it either by affection to the government, or from fear; where a standing army is at hand to punish offenders, every man is actuated by the latter principle, and therefore, when the magistrate calls, will obey: but, where this is not the case, the government must rest for its support upon the confidence and respect which the people have for their government and laws. The body of the people being attached, the government will always be sufficient to support and execute its laws, and to operate upon the fears

14. See *FF I* (14).
15. See *FF II* (4), *III* (1), *VII* (1–4); *Brutus IV* (5–6).
16. See *Brutus II* (10), *IX* (5–15), *X* (18); *FF III* (16), *XIII* (13).

of any faction which may be opposed to it, not only to prevent an opposition to the execution of the laws themselves, but also to compel the most of them to aid the magistrate; but the people will not be likely to have such confidence in their rulers, in a republic so extensive as the United States, as necessary for these purposes. The confidence which the people have in their rulers, in a free republic, arises from their knowing them, from their being responsible to them for their conduct, and from the power they have of displacing them when they misbehave: but in a republic of the extent of this continent, the people in general would be acquainted with very few of their rulers: the people at large would know little of their proceedings, and it would be extremely difficult to change them. The people in Georgia and New-Hampshire would not know one another's mind, and therefore could not act in concert to enable them to effect a general change of representatives. The different parts of so extensive a country could not possibly be made acquainted with the conduct of their representatives, nor be informed of the reasons upon which measures were founded. The consequence will be, they will have no confidence in their legislature, suspect them of ambitious views, be jealous of every measure they adopt, and will not support the laws they pass. Hence the government will be nerveless and inefficient, and no way will be left to render it otherwise, but by establishing an armed force to execute the laws at the point of the bayonet—a government of all others the most to be dreaded.[17]

24. In a republic of such vast extent as the United-States, the legislature cannot attend to the various concerns and wants of its different parts. It cannot be sufficiently numerous to be acquainted with the local condition and wants of the different districts, and if it could, it is impossible it should have sufficient time to attend to and provide for all the variety of cases of this nature, that would be continually arising.[18]

25. In so extensive a republic, the great officers of government would soon become above the controul of the people, and abuse their power to the purpose of aggrandizing themselves, and oppressing them. The trust committed to the executive offices, in a country of the extent of the United-States, must be various and of magnitude. The command of all the troops and navy of the republic, the appointment of officers, the power of pardoning offences, the collecting of all the public revenues, and the power of expending them, with a number of other powers, must be lodged and

17. *FF II* (9).
18. See *FF I* (14).

exercised in every state, in the hands of a few. When these are attended with great honor and emolument, as they always will be in large states, so as greatly to interest men to pursue them, and to be proper objects for ambitious and designing men, such men will be ever restless in their pursuit after them. They will use the power, when they have acquired it, to the purposes of gratifying their own interest and ambition, and it is scarcely possible, in a very large republic, to call them to account for their misconduct, or to prevent their abuse of power.[19]

26. These are some of the reasons by which it appears, that a free republic cannot long subsist over a country of the great extent of these states. If then this new constitution is calculated to consolidate the thirteen states into one, as it evidently is, it ought not to be adopted.

27. Though I am of opinion, that it is a sufficient objection to this government, to reject it, that it creates the whole union into one government, under the form of a republic, yet if this objection was obviated, there are exceptions to it, which are so material and fundamental, that they ought to determine every man, who is a friend to the liberty and happiness of mankind, not to adopt it. I beg the candid and dispassionate attention of my countrymen while I state these objections—they are such as have obtruded themselves upon my mind upon a careful attention to the matter, and such as I sincerely believe are well founded. There are many objections, of small moment, of which I shall take no notice—perfection is not to be expected in any thing that is the production of man—and if I did not in my conscience believe that this scheme was defective in the fundamental principles—in the foundation upon which a free and equal government must rest—I would hold my peace.

Brutus.

– II –

1 November 1787

To the Citizens of the State of New-York.

1. I flatter myself that my last address established this position, that to reduce the Thirteen States into one government, would prove the destruction of your liberties.

2. But lest this truth should be doubted by some, I will now proceed to consider its merits.

19. See *FF XIV* (7).

3. Though it should be admitted, that the arguments against reducing all the states into one consolidated government, are not sufficient fully to establish this point; yet they will, at least, justify this conclusion, that in forming a constitution for such a country, great care should be taken to limit and define its powers, adjust its parts, and guard against an abuse of authority. How far attention has been paid to these objects, shall be the subject of future enquiry. When a building is to be erected which is intended to stand for ages, the foundation should be firmly laid. The constitution proposed to your acceptance, is designed not for yourselves alone, but for generations yet unborn. The principles, therefore, upon which the social compact is founded, ought to have been clearly and precisely stated, and the most express and full declaration of rights to have been made—But on this subject there is almost an entire silence.

4. If we may collect the sentiments of the people of America, from their own most solemn declarations, they hold this truth as self evident, that all men are by nature free.[20] No one man, therefore, or any class of men, have a right, by the law of nature, or of God, to assume or exercise authority over their fellows. The origin of society then is to be sought, not in any natural right which one man has to exercise authority over another, but in the united consent of those who associate. The mutual wants of men, at first dictated the propriety of forming societies; and when they were established, protection and defence pointed out the necessity of instituting government. In a state of nature every individual pursues his own interest; in this pursuit it frequently happened, that the possessions or enjoyments of one were sacrificed to the views and designs of another; thus the weak were a prey to the strong, the simple and unwary were subject to impositions from those who were more crafty and designing. In this state of things, every individual was insecure; common interest therefore directed, that government should be established, in which the force of the whole community should be collected, and under such directions, as to protect and defend every one who composed it. The common good, therefore, is the end of civil government, and common consent, the foundation on which it is established. To effect this end, it was necessary that a certain portion of natural liberty should be surrendered, in order, that what remained should be preserved: how great a proportion of natural freedom is necessary to be yielded by individuals, when they submit to government, I shall not now

20. "Brutus" is, of course, part paraphrasing, part interpreting the Declaration of Independence.

enquire. So much, however, must be given up, as will be sufficient to enable those, to whom the administration of the government is committed, to establish laws for the promoting the happiness of the community, and to carry those laws into effect. But it is not necessary, for this purpose, that individuals should relinquish all their natural rights. Some are of such a nature that they cannot be surrendered. Of this kind are the rights of conscience, the right of enjoying and defending life, etc. Others are not necessary to be resigned, in order to attain the end for which government is instituted, these therefore ought not to be given up. To surrender them, would counteract the very end of government, to wit, the common good.[21] From these observations it appears, that in forming a government on its true principles, the foundation should be laid in the manner I before stated, by expressly reserving to the people such of their essential natural rights, as are not necessary to be parted with.[22] The same reasons which at first induced mankind to associate and institute government, will operate to influence them to observe this precaution. If they had been disposed to conform themselves to the rule of immutable righteousness, government would not have been requisite. It was because one part exercised fraud, oppression, and violence on the other, that men came together, and agreed that certain rules should be formed, to regulate the conduct of all, and the power of the whole community lodged in the hands of rulers to enforce an obedience to them. But rulers have the same propensities as other men; they are as likely to use the power with which they are vested for private purposes, and to the injury and oppression of those over whom they are placed, as individuals in a state of nature are to injure and oppress one another. It is therefore as proper that bounds should be set to their authority, as that government should have at first been instituted to restrain private injuries.[23]

5. This principle, which seems so evidently founded in the reason and nature of things, is confirmed by universal experience. Those who have governed, have been found in all ages ever active to enlarge their powers and abridge the public liberty. This has induced the people in all countries, where any sense of freedom remained, to fix barriers against the encroachments of their rulers. The country from which we have derived our origin, is an eminent example of this. Their magna charta and bill of rights have long been the boast, as well as the security, of that nation. I need say no

---

21. For *FF*'s science of rights, see *VI* (15–23).
22. *Brutus IX* (1).
23. See *Brutus IV* (1–3), *XVI* (1).

more, I presume, to an American, than, that this principle is a fundamental one, in all the constitutions of our own states; there is not one of them but what is either founded on a declaration or bill of rights, or has certain express reservation of rights interwoven in the body of them. From this it appears, that at a time when the pulse of liberty beat high and when an appeal was made to the people to form constitutions for the government of themselves, it was their universal sense, that such declarations should make a part of their frames of government. It is therefore the more astonishing, that this grand security, to the rights of the people, is not to be found in this constitution.

6. It has been said, in answer to this objection, that such declarations of rights, however requisite they might be in the constitutions of the states, are not necessary in the general constitution, because, "in the former case, every thing which is not reserved is given, but in the latter the reverse of the proposition prevails, and every thing which is not given is reserved."[24] It requires but little attention to discover, that this mode of reasoning is rather specious than solid. The powers, rights, and authority, granted to the general government by this constitution, are as complete, with respect to every object to which they extend, as that of any state government—It reaches to every thing which concerns human happiness—Life, liberty, and property, are under its controul. There is the same reason, therefore, that the exercise of power, in this case, should be restrained within proper limits, as in that of the state governments. To set this matter in a clear light, permit me to instance some of the articles of the bills of rights of the individual states, and apply them to the case in question.

7. For the security of life, in criminal prosecutions, the bills of rights of most of the states have declared, that no man shall be held to answer for a crime until he is made fully acquainted with the charge brought against him; he shall not be compelled to accuse, or furnish evidence against himself—The witnesses against him shall be brought face to face, and he shall be fully heard by himself or counsel. That it is essential to the security of life and liberty, that trial of facts be in the vicinity where they happen. Are not provisions of this kind as necessary in the general government, as in that of a particular state? The powers vested in the new Congress extend in many cases to life; they are authorised to provide for the punishment

24. James Wilson, "Address to the Citizens of Philadelphia," in John Bach Mc-Master and Frederick Stone, *Pennsylvania and the Federal Constitution, 1787–1788* (Lancaster, 1888).

of a variety of capital crimes, and no restraint is laid upon them in its exercise, save only, that "the trial of all crimes, except in cases of impeachment, shall be by jury; and such trial shall be in the state where the said crimes shall have been committed." No man is secure of a trial in the county where he is charged to have committed a crime; he may be brought from Niagara to New-York, or carried from Kentucky to Richmond for trial for an offence, supposed to be committed. What security is there, that a man shall be furnished with a full and plain description of the charges against him? That he shall be allowed to produce all proof he can in his favor? That he shall see the witnesses against him face to face, or that he shall be fully heard in his own defence by himself or counsel?

8. For the security of liberty it has been declared, "that excessive bail should not be required, nor excessive fines imposed, nor cruel or unusual punishments inflicted—That all warrants, without oath or affirmation, to search suspected places, or seize any person, his papers or property, are grievous and oppressive."[25]

9. These provisions are as necessary under the general government as under that of the individual states; for the power of the former is as complete to the purpose of requiring bail, imposing fines, inflicting punishments, granting search warrants, and seizing persons, papers, or property, in certain cases, as the other.

10. For the purpose of securing the property of the citizens, it is declared by all the states, "that in all controversies at law, respecting property, the ancient mode of trial by jury is one of the best securities of the rights of the people, and ought to remain sacred and inviolable."[26]

11. Does not the same necessity exist of reserving this right, under this national compact, as in that of these states? Yet nothing is said respecting it. In the bills of rights of the states it is declared, that a well regulated militia is the proper and natural defence of a free government—That as standing armies in time of peace are dangerous, they are not to be kept up, and that the military should be kept under strict subordination to, and controuled by the civil power.

12. The same security is as necessary in this constitution, and much

25. The quotation is from the Maryland Constitution of 1776, Declaration of Rights, Arts. 22–23.

26. The quotation is from the North Carolina Constitution, Declaration of Rights, Art. 14.

more so; for the general government will have the sole power to raise and to pay armies, and are under no controul in the exercise of it; yet nothing of this is to be found in this new system.

13. I might proceed to instance a number of other rights, which were as necessary to be reserved, such as, that elections should be free, that the liberty of the press should be held sacred; but the instances adduced, are sufficient to prove, that this argument is without foundation.—Besides, it is evident, that the reason here assigned was not the true one, why the framers of this constitution omitted a bill of rights; if it had been, they would not have made certain reservations, while they totally omitted others of more importance. We find they have, in the 9th section of the 1st article, declared, that the writ of habeas corpus shall not be suspended, unless in cases of rebellion—that no bill of attainder, or expost facto law, shall be passed—that no title of nobility shall be granted by the United States, &c. If every thing which is not given is reserved, what propriety is there in these exceptions?[27] Does this constitution any where grant the power of suspending the habeas corpus, to make expost facto laws, pass bills of attainder, or grant titles of nobility? It certainly does not in express terms. The only answer that can be given is, that these are implied in the general powers granted. With equal truth it may be said, that all the powers, which the bills of right, guard against the abuse of, are contained or implied in the general ones granted by this constitution.

14. So far it is from being true, that a bill of rights is less necessary in the general constitution than in those of the states, the contrary is evidently the fact.—This system, if it is possible for the people of America to accede to it, will be an original compact; and being the last, will, in the nature of things, vacate every former agreement inconsistent with it. For it being a plan of government received and ratified by the whole people, all other forms, which are in existence at the time of its adoption, must yield to it. This is expressed in positive and unequivocal terms, in the 6th article, "That this constitution and the laws of the United States, which shall be made in pursuance thereof, and all treaties made, or which shall be made, under the authority of the United States, shall be the supreme law of the land; and the judges in every state shall be bound thereby, any thing in the *constitution*, or laws of any state, *to the contrary* notwithstanding.

27. See *FF IV* (9–10), *XVI* (1–2).

15. "The senators and representatives before-mentioned, and the members of the several state legislatures, and all executive and judicial officers, both of the United States, and of the several states, shall be bound, by oath or affirmation, to support this constitution."

16. It is therefore not only necessarily implied thereby, but positively expressed, that the different state constitutions are repealed and entirely done away, so far as they are inconsistent with this, with the laws which shall be made in pursuance thereof, or with treaties made, or which shall be made, under the authority of the United States; of what avail will the constitutions of the respective states be to preserve the rights of its citizens? Should they be plead, the answer would be, the constitution of the United States, and the laws made in pursuance thereof, is the supreme law, and all legislatures and judicial officers, whether of the general or state governments, are bound by oath to support it. No priviledge, reserved by the bills of rights, or secured by the state government, can limit the power granted by this, or restrain any laws made in pursuance of it. It stands therefore on its own bottom, and must receive a construction by itself without any reference to any other—And hence it was of the highest importance, that the most precise and express declarations and reservations of rights should have been made.

17. This will appear the more necessary, when it is considered, that not only the constitution and laws made in pursuance thereof, but all treaties made, or which shall be made, under the authority of the United States, are the supreme law of the land, and supersede the constitutions of all the states. The power to make treaties, is vested in the president, by and with the advice and consent of two thirds of the senate. I do not find any limitation, or restriction, to the exercise of this power. The most important article in any constitution may therefore be repealed, even without a legislative act. Ought not a government, vested with such extensive and indefinite authority, to have been restricted by a declaration of rights? It certainly ought.

18. So clear a point is this, that I cannot help suspecting, that persons who attempt to persuade people, that such reservations were less necessary under this constitution than under those of the states, are wilfully endeavouring to deceive, and to lead you into an absolute state of vassalage.

Brutus.

– III –

15 November 1787

To the Citizens of the State of New-York.

1. In the investigation of the constitution, under your consideration, great care should be taken, that you do not form your opinions respecting it, from unimportant provisions, or fallacious appearances.

2. On a careful examination, you will find, that many of its parts, of little moment, are well formed; in these it has a specious resemblance of a free government—but this is not sufficient to justify the adoption of it—the gilded pill, is often found to contain the most deadly poison.

3. You are not however to expect, a perfect form of government, any more than to meet with perfection in man; your views therefore, ought to be directed to the main pillars upon which a free government is to rest; if these are well placed, on a foundation that will support the superstructure, you should be satisfied, although the building may want a number of orna-ments, which, if your particular tastes were gratified, you would have added to it: on the other hand, if the foundation is insecurely laid, and the main supports are wanting, or not properly fixed, however the fabric may be decorated and adorned, you ought to reject it.[28]

4. Under these impressions, it has been my object to turn your attention to the principal defects in this system.

5. I have attempted to shew, that a consolidation of this extensive con-tinent, under one government, for internal, as well as external purposes, which is evidently the tendency of this constitution, cannot succeed, without a sacrifice of your liberties; and therefore that the attempt is not only pre-posterous, but extremely dangerous; and I have shewn, independent of this, that the plan is radically defective in a fundamental principle, which ought to be found in every free government; to wit, a declaration of rights.

6. I shall now proceed to take a nearer view of this system, to examine its parts more minutely, and shew that the powers are not properly deposited, for the security of public liberty.

7. The first important object that presents itself in the organization of this government, is the legislature. This is to be composed of two branches; the first to be called the general assembly, and is to be chosen by the people

28. See *FF V* (2–4).

of the respective states, in proportion to the number of their inhabitants, and is to consist of sixty five members, with powers in the legislature to encrease the number, not to exceed one for every thirty thousand inhabitants. The second branch is to be called the senate, and is to consist of twenty-six members, two of which are to be chosen by the legislatures of each of the states.

8. In the former of these there is an appearance of justice, in the appointment of its members—but if the clause, which provides for this branch, be stripped of its ambiguity, it will be found that there is really no equality of representation, even in this house.

9. The words are "representatives and direct taxes, shall be apportioned among the several states, which may be included in this union, according to their respective numbers, which shall be determined by adding to the whole number of free persons, including those bound to service for a term of years, and excluding Indians not taxed, three fifths of all other persons."—What a strange and unnecessary accumulation of words are here used to conceal from the public eye, what might have been expressed in the following concise manner. Representatives are to be proportioned among the states respectively, according to the number of freemen and slaves inhabiting them, counting five slaves for three free men.[29]

10. "In a free state," says the celebrated Montesquieu, "every man, who is supposed to be a free agent, ought to be concerned in his own government, therefore the legislature should reside in the whole body of the people, or their representatives."[30] But it has never been alledged that those who are not free agents, can, upon any rational principle, have any thing to do in government, either by themselves or others. If they have no share in government, why is the number of members in the assembly, to be increased on their account? Is it because in some of the states, a considerable part of the property of the inhabitants consists in a number of their fellow men, who are held in bondage, in defiance of every idea of benevolence, justice, and religion, and contrary to all the principles of liberty, which have been publickly avowed in the late glorious revolution? If this be a just ground for representation, the horses in some of the states, and the oxen in others, ought to be represented—for a great share of property in some of them, consists in these animals; and they have as much controul over their own

29. See Smith speech, June 20, 1788 (8).

30. Montesquieu, *Spirit of the Laws* XI, chap. 6. The same passage is quoted by *FF VII* (6) and is paraphrased in Smith speech, June 20, 1788 (8) and in *Brutus XVI* (2).

actions, as these poor unhappy creatures, who are intended to be described in the above recited clause, by the words, "all other persons." By this mode of apportionment, the representatives of the different parts of the union, will be extremely unequal; in some of the southern states, the slaves are nearly equal in number to the free men; and for all these slaves, they will be entitled to a proportionate share in the legislature—this will give them an unreasonable weight in the government, which can derive no additional strength, protection, nor defence from the slaves, but the contrary. Why then should they be represented? What adds to the evil is, that these states are to be permitted to continue the inhuman traffic of importing slaves, until the year 1808—and for every cargo of these unhappy people, which unfeeling, unprincipled, barbarous, and avaricious wretches, may tear from their country, friends and tender connections, and bring into those states, they are to be rewarded by having an increase of members in the general assembly.

11. There appears at the first view a manifest inconsistency, in the apportionment of representatives in the senate, upon the plan of a consolidated government.[31] On every principle of equity, and propriety, representation in a government should be in exact proportion to the numbers, or the aids afforded by the persons represented. How unreasonable, and unjust then is it, that Delaware should have a representation in the senate, equal to Massachusetts, or Virginia? The latter of which contains ten times her numbers, and is to contribute to the aid of the general government in that proportion? This article of the constitution will appear the more objectionable, if it is considered, that the powers vested in this branch of the legislature are very extensive, and greatly surpass those lodged in the assembly, not only for general purposes, but, in many instances, for the internal police of the states. The other branch of the legislature, in which, if in either, a faint spark of democracy is to be found, should have been properly organized and established—but upon examination you will find, that this branch does not possess the qualities of a just representation, and that there is no kind of security, imperfect as it is, for its remaining in the hands of the people.

12. It has been observed, that the happiness of society is the end of government—that every free government is founded in compact; and that, because it is impracticable for the whole community to assemble, or when

---

31. Cf. *Brutus XVI* (4); *FF III* (5), *XI* (1).

assembled, to deliberate with wisdom, and decide with dispatch, the mode of legislating by representation was devised.[32]

13. The very term, representative, implies, that the person or body chosen for this purpose, should resemble those who appoint them—a representation of the people of America, if it be a true one, must be like the people. It ought to be so constituted, that a person, who is a stranger to the country, might be able to form a just idea of their character, by knowing that of their representatives. They are the sign—the people are the thing signified. It is absurd to speak of one thing being the representative of another, upon any other principle. The ground and reason of representation, in a free government, implies the same thing. Society instituted government to promote the happiness of the whole, and this is the great end always in view in the delegation of powers. It must then have been intended, that those who are placed instead of the people, should possess their sentiments and feelings, and be governed by their interests, or, in other words, should bear the strongest resemblance of those in whose room they are substituted. It is obvious, that for an assembly to be a true likeness of the people of any country, they must be considerably numerous.—One man, or a few men, cannot possibly represent the feelings, opinions, and characters of a great multitude. In this respect, the new constitution is radically defective.—The house of assembly, which is intended as a representation of the people of America, will not, nor cannot, in the nature of things, be a proper one—sixty-five men cannot be found in the United States, who hold the sentiments, possess the feelings, or are acquainted with the wants and interests of this vast country. This extensive continent is made up of a number of different classes of people; and to have a proper representation of them, each class ought to have an opportunity of choosing their best informed men for the purpose; but this cannot possibly be the case in so small a number. The state of New-York, on the present apportionment, will send six members to the assembly: I will venture to affirm, that number cannot be found in the state, who will bear a just resemblance to the several classes of people who compose it. In this assembly, the farmer, merchant, mecanick, and other various orders of people, ought to be represented according to their respective weight and numbers; and the representatives ought to be intimately acquainted with the wants, understand the interests of the several orders in the society, and feel a proper sense and becoming zeal to promote their prosperity. I cannot conceive that any six men in this

32. *Brutus II* (3–4); *FF II* (1).

state can be found properly qualified in these respects to discharge such important duties: but supposing it possible to find them, is there the least degree of probability that the choice of the people will fall upon such men? According to the common course of human affairs, the natural aristocracy of the country will be elected.[33] Wealth always creates influence, and this is generally much increased by large family connections: this class in society will for ever have a great number of dependents; besides, they will always favour each other—it is their interest to combine—they will therefore constantly unite their efforts to procure men of their own rank to be elected—they will concenter all their force in every part of the state into one point, and by acting together, will most generally carry their election. It is probable, that but few of the merchants, and those the most opulent and ambitious, will have a representation from their body—few of them are characters sufficiently conspicuous to attract the notice of the electors of the state in so limited a representation. The great body of the yeomen of the country cannot expect any of their order in this assembly—the station will be too elevated for them to aspire to—the distance between the people and their representatives, will be so very great, that there is no probability that a farmer, however respectable, will be chosen—the mechanicks of every branch, must expect to be excluded from a seat in this Body—It will and must be esteemed a station too high and exalted to be filled by any but the first men in the state, in point of fortune; so that in reality there will be no part of the people represented, but the rich, even in that branch of the legislature, which is called the democratic.—The well born, and highest orders in life, as they term themselves, will be ignorant of the sentiments of the midling class of citizens, strangers to their ability, wants, and difficulties, and void of sympathy, and fellow feeling. This branch of the legislature will not only be an imperfect representation, but there will be no security in so small a body, against bribery, and corruption—It will consist at first, of sixty-five, and can never exceed one for every thirty thousand inhabitants; a majority of these, that is, thirty-three, are a quorum, and a majority of which, or seventeen, may pass any law—so that twenty-five men, will have the power to give away all the property of the citizens of these states—what security therefore can there be for the people, where their liberties and property are at the disposal of so few men? It will literally be a government in the hands of the few to oppress and plunder the many. You may conclude

33. Cf. *FF VII* (5); Smith speeches, June 21, 1788 (15–20), and June 23, 1788 (21–22).

with a great degree of certainty, that it, like all others of a similar nature, will be managed by influence and corruption, and that the period is not far distant, when this will be the case, if it should be adopted; for even now there are some among us, whose characters stand high in the public estimation, and who have had a principal agency in framing this constitution, who do not scruple to say, that this is the only practicable mode of governing a people, who think with that degree of freedom which the Americans do[34]—this government will have in their gift a vast number of offices of great honor and emolument. The members of the legislature are not excluded from appointments; and twenty-five of them, as the case may be, being secured, any measure may be carried.

14. The rulers of this country must be composed of very different materials from those of any other, of which history gives us any account, if the majority of the legislature are not, before many years, entirely at the devotion of the executive—and these states will soon be under the absolute domination of one, or a few, with the fallacious appearance of being governed by men of their own election.

15. The more I reflect on this subject, the more firmly am I persuaded, that the representation is merely nominal—a mere burlesque; and that no security is provided against corruption and undue influence. No free people on earth, who have elected persons to legislate for them, ever reposed that confidence in so small a number. The British house of commons consists of five hundred and fifty-eight members; the number of inhabitants in Great-Britain, is computed at eight millions—this gives one member for a little more than fourteen thousand, which exceeds double the proportion this country can ever have: and yet we require a larger representation in proportion to our numbers, than Great-Britain, because this country is much more extensive, and differs more in its productions, interests, manners, and habits. The democratic branch of the legislatures of the several states in the union consists, I believe at present, of near two thousand; and this number was not thought too large for the security of liberty by the framers of our state constitutions: some of the states may have erred in this respect, but the difference between two thousand, and sixty-five, is so very great, that it will bear no comparison.

16. Other objections offer themselves against this part of the constitution—I shall reserve them for a future paper, when I shall shew, defective as

34. Cf. *FF III* (14).

this representation is, no security is provided, that even this shadow of the right, will remain with the people.[35]

Brutus.

– IV –

29 November 1787

To the People of the State of New-York.

1. There can be no free government where the people are not possessed of the power of making the laws by which they are governed, either in their own persons, or by others substituted in their stead.

2. Experience has taught mankind, that legislation by representatives is the most eligible, and the only practicable mode in which the people of any country can exercise this right, either prudently or beneficially. But then, it is a matter of the highest importance, in forming this representation, that it be so constituted as to be capable of understanding the true interests of the society for which it acts, and so disposed as to pursue the good and happiness of the people as its ultimate end. The object of every free government is the public good, and all lesser interests yield to it. That of every tyrannical government, is the happiness and aggrandisement of one, or a few, and to this the public felicity, and every other interest must submit.—The reason of this difference in these governments is obvious. The first is so constituted as to collect the views and wishes of the whole people in that of their rulers, while the latter is so framed as to separate the interests of the governors from that of the governed. The principle of self love, therefore, that will influence the one to promote the good of the whole, will prompt the other to follow its own private advantage. The great art, therefore, in forming a good constitution, appears to be this, so to frame it, as that those to whom the power is committed shall be subject to the same feelings, and aim at the same objects as the people do, who transfer to them their authority. There is no possible way to effect this but by an equal, full and fair representation; this, therefore, is the great desideratum in politics. However fair an appearance any government may make, though it may possess a thousand plausible articles and be decorated with ever so many ornaments, yet if it is deficient in this essential principle of a full and just representation of the people, it will be only like a painted sepulcher—For, without this it cannot be a free government; let the administration of it be good or ill, it

35. *Brutus IV* (1–10).

still will be a government, not according to the will of the people, but according to the will of a few.

3. To test this new constitution then, by this principle, is of the last importance—It is to bring it to the touch-stone of national liberty, and I hope I shall be excused, if, in this paper, I pursue the subject commenced in my last number, to wit, the necessity of an equal and full representation in the legislature.—In that, I showed that it was not equal, because the smallest states are to send the same number of members to the senate as the largest, and, because the slaves, who afford neither aid or defence to the government, are to encrease the proportion of members. To prove that it was not a just or adequate representation, it was urged, that so small a number could not resemble the people, or possess their sentiments and dispositions. That the choice of members would commonly fall upon the rich and great, while the middling class of the community would be excluded. That in so small a representation there was no security against bribery and corruption.[36]

4. The small number which is to compose this legislature, will not only expose it to the danger of that kind of corruption, and undue influence, which will arise from the gift of places of honor and emolument, or the more direct one of bribery, but it will also subject it to another kind of influence no less fatal to the liberties of the people, though it be not so flagrantly repugnant to the principles of rectitude. It is not to be expected that a legislature will be found in any country that will not have some of its members, who will pursue their private ends, and for which they will sacrifice the public good. Men of this character are, generally, artful and designing, and frequently possess brilliant talents and abilities; they commonly act in concert, and agree to share the spoils of their country among them; they will keep their object ever in view, and follow it with constancy. To effect their purpose, they will assume any shape, and, Proteus like, mould themselves into any form[37]—where they find members proof against direct bribery or gifts of offices, they will endeavor to mislead their minds by specious and false reasoning, to impose upon their unsuspecting honesty by an affectation of zeal for the public good; they will form juntos, and hold out-door meetings; they will operate upon the good nature of their opponents, by a thousand little attentions, and teize them into compliance by the earnestness of solicitation. Those who are acquainted with the manner of conducting business

36. *FF V* (2), *VI* (11, 14); Smith speech, June 20, 1788 (9).
37. Proteus: a mythical being who could change shape at will.

in public assemblies, know how prevalent art and address are in carrying a measure, even over men of the best intentions, and of good understanding. The firmest security against this kind of improper and dangerous influence, as well as all other, is a strong and numerous representation: in such a house of assembly, so great a number must be gained over, before the private views of individuals could be gratified that there could be scarce a hope of success. But in the foederal assembly, seventeen men are all that is necessary to pass a law. It is probable, it will seldom happen that more than twenty-five will be requisite to form a majority, when it is considered what a number of places of honor and emolument will be in the gift of the executive, the powerful influence that great and designing men have over the honest and unsuspecting, by their art and address, their soothing manners and civilities, and their cringing flattery, joined with their affected patriotism; when these different species of influence are combined, it is scarcely to be hoped that a legislature, composed of so small a number, as the one proposed by the new constitution,[38] will long resist their force.[39]

5. A farther objection against the feebleness of the representation is, that it will not possess the confidence of the people. The execution of the laws in a free government must rest on this confidence, and this must be founded on the good opinion they entertain of the framers of the laws.[40] Every government must be supported, either by the people having such an attachment to it, as to be ready, when called upon, to support it, or by a force at the command of the government, to compel obedience. The latter mode destroys every idea of a free government; for the same force that may be employed to compel obedience to good laws, might, and probably would be used to wrest from the people their constitutional liberties.—Whether it is practicable to have a representation for the whole union sufficiently numerous to obtain that confidence which is necessary for the purpose of internal taxation, and other powers to which this proposed government extends, is an important question. I am clearly of opinion, it is not, and therefore I have stated this in my first number, as one of the reasons against going into an entire consolidation of the states—one of the most capital errors in the system, is that of extending the powers of the foederal government to objects to which it is not adequate, which it cannot exercise without endangering public liberty, and which it is not necessary they should

38. Cf. *FF III* (14).
39. *FF VII* (8).
40. See note 15 above.

possess, in order to preserve the union and manage our national concerns; of this, however, I shall treat more fully in some future paper[41]—But, however this may be, certain it is, that the representation in the legislature is not so formed as to give reasonable ground for public trust.

6. In order for the people safely to repose themselves on their rulers, they should not only be of their own choice. But it is requisite they should be acquainted with their abilities to manage the public concerns with wisdom. They should be satisfied that those who represent them are men of integrity, who will pursue the good of the community with fidelity; and will not be turned aside from their duty by private interest, or corrupted by undue influence; and that they will have such a zeal for the good of those whom they represent, as to excite them to be diligent in their service; but it is impossible the people of the United States should have sufficient knowledge of their representatives, when the numbers are so few, to acquire any rational satisfaction on either of these points. The people of this state will have very little acquaintance with those who may be chosen to represent them; a great part of them will, probably, not know the characters of their own members, much less that of a majority of those who will compose the foederal assembly; they will consist of men, whose names they have never heard, and whose talents and regard for the public good, they are total strangers to; and they will have no persons so immediately of their choice so near them, of their neighbours and of their own rank in life, that they can feel themselves secure in trusting their interests in their hands.[42] The representatives of the people cannot, as they now do, after they have passed laws, mix with the people, and explain to them the motives which induced the adoption of any measure, point out its utility, and remove objections or silence unreasonable clamours against it.—The number will be so small that but a very few of the most sensible and respectable yeomanry of the country can ever have any knowledge of them: being so far removed from the people, their station will be elevated and important, and they will be considered as ambitious and designing. They will not be viewed by the people as part of themselves, but as a body distinct from them, and having separate interests to pursue; the consequence will be, that a perpetual jealousy will exist in the minds of the people against them; their conduct will be narrowly watched; their measures scrutinized; and their laws opposed, evaded, or reluctantly obeyed. This is natural, and exactly corre-

41. *Brutus V–X*; cf. *FF VII* (11); Smith speech, June 27, 1788 (38–40).
42. *FF VII* (7).

sponds with the conduct of individuals towards those in whose hands they intrust important concerns. If the person confided in, be a neighbour with whom his employer is intimately acquainted, whose talents, he knows, are sufficient to manage the business with which he is charged, his honesty and fidelity unsuspected, and his friendship and zeal for the service of this principal unquestionable, he will commit his affairs into his hands with unreserved confidence, and feel himself secure; all the transactions of the agent will meet with the most favorable construction, and the measures he takes will give satisfaction. But, if the person employed be a stranger, whom he has never seen, and whose character for ability or fidelity he cannot fully learn—If he is constrained to choose him, because it was not in his power to procure one more agreeable to his wishes, he will trust him with caution, and be suspicious of all his conduct.

7. If then this government should not derive support from the good will of the people, it must be executed by force, or not executed at all; either case would lead to the total destruction of liberty.—The convention seemed aware of this, and have therefore provided for calling out the militia to execute the laws of the union. If this system was so framed as to command that respect from the people, which every good free government will obtain, this provision was unnecessary—the people would support the civil magistrate. This power is a novel one, in free governments—these have depended for the execution of the laws on the Posse Comitatus,[43] and never raised an idea, that the people would refuse to aid the civil magistrate in executing those laws they themselves had made. I shall now dismiss the subject of the incompetency of the representation, and proceed, as I promised, to shew, that, impotent as it is, the people have no security that they will enjoy the exercise of the right of electing this assembly, which, at best, can be considered but as the shadow of representation.

8. By section 4, article I, the Congress are authorized, at any time, by law, to make, or alter, regulations respecting the time, place, and manner of holding elections for senators and representatives, except as to the places of choosing senators. By this clause the right of election itself, is, in a great measure, transferred from the people to their rulers.—One would think, that if any thing was necessary to be made a fundamental article of the original compact, it would be, that of fixing the branches of the legislature, so as to put it out of its power to alter itself by modifying the election of its

43. Cf. *FF III* (16), also *Plebeian* (23).

own members at will and pleasure. When a people once resign the privilege of a fair election, they clearly have none left worth contending for.[44]

9. It is clear that, under this article, the foederal legislature may institute such rules respecting elections as to lead to the choice of one description of men. The weakness of the representation, tends but too certainly to confer on the rich and *well-born*, all honours; but the power granted in this article, may be so exercised, as to secure it almost beyond a possibility of controul. The proposed Congress may make the whole state one district, and direct, that the capital (the city of New-York, for instance) shall be the place for holding the election; the consequence would be, that none but men of the most elevated rank in society would attend, and they would as certainly choose men of their own class; as it is true what the *Apostle Paul* saith, that "no man ever yet hated his own flesh, but nourisheth and cherisheth it."[45]— They may declare that those members who have the greatest number of votes, shall be considered as duly elected; the consequence would be that the people, who are dispersed in the interior parts of the state, would give their votes for a variety of candidates, while any order, or profession, residing in populous places, by uniting their interests, might procure whom they pleased to be chosen—and by this means the representatives of the state may be elected by one tenth part of the people who actually vote. This may be effected constitutionally, and by one of those silent operations which frequently takes place without being noticed, but which often produces such changes as entirely to alter a government, subvert a free constitution, and rivet the chains on a free people before they perceive they are forged. Had the power of regulating elections been left under the direction of the state legislatures, where the people are not only nominally but substantially represented, it would have been secure; but if it was taken out of their hands, it surely ought to have been fixed on such a basis as to have put it out of the power of the foederal legislature to deprive the people of it by law. Provision should have been made for marking out the states into districts, and for choosing, by a majority of votes, a person out of each of them of permanent property and residence in the district which he was to represent.[46]

10. If the people of America will submit to a constitution that will vest in

44. Cf. *FF XII* (16–17).
45. Ephesians 5:29.
46. *FF XII* (7–14).

the hands of any body of men a right to deprive them by law of the privilege of a fair election, they will submit to almost any thing. Reasoning with them will be in vain, they must be left until they are brought to reflection by feeling oppression—they will then have to wrest from their oppressors, by a strong hand, that which they now possess, and which they may retain if they will exercise but a moderate share of prudence and firmness.

11. I know it is said that the dangers apprehended from this clause are merely imaginary, that the proposed general legislature will be disposed to regulate elections upon proper principles, and to use their power with discretion, and to promote the public good. On this, I would observe, that constitutions are not so necessary to regulate the conduct of good rulers as to restrain that of bad ones.—Wise and good men will exercise power so as to promote the public happiness under any form of government. If we are to take it for granted, that those who administer the government under this system, will always pay proper attention to the rights and interests of the people, nothing more was necessary than to say who should be invested with the powers of government, and leave them to exercise it at will and pleasure. Men are apt to be deceived both with respect to their own dispositions and those of others. Though this truth is proved by almost every page of the history of nations, to wit, that power, lodged in the hands of rulers to be used at discretion, is almost always exercised to the oppression of the people, and the aggrandizement of themselves; yet most men think if it was lodged in their hands they would not employ it in this manner.—Thus when the prophet *Elisha* told *Hazael*, "I know the evil that thou wilt do unto the children of Israel; their strong holds wilt thou set on fire, and their young men, wilt thou slay with the sword, and wilt dash their children, and rip up their women with child." Hazael had no idea that he ever should be guilty of such horrid cruelty, and said to the prophet, "Is thy servant a dog that he should do this great thing." Elisha answered, "The Lord hath shewed me that thou shalt be king of Syria."[47] The event proved, that Hazael only wanted an opportunity to perpetrate these enormities without restraint, and he had a disposition to do them, though he himself knew it not.

Brutus.

47. 2 Kings 8:13.

– V –

13 December 1787

To the People of the State of New-York.

1. It was intended in this Number to have prosecuted the enquiry into the organization of this new system; particularly to have considered the dangerous and premature union of the President and Senate, and the mixture of legislative, executive, and judicial powers in the Senate.

2. But there is such an intimate connection between the several branches in whom the different species of authority is lodged, and the powers with which they are invested, that on reflection it seems necessary first to proceed to examine the nature and extent of the powers granted to the legislature.[48]

3. This enquiry will assist us the better to determine, whether the legislature is so constituted, as to provide proper checks and restrictions for the security of our rights, and to guard against the abuse of power—For the means should be suited to the end; a government should be framed with a view to the objects to which it extends: if these be few in number, and of such a nature as to give but small occasion or opportunity to work oppression in the exercise of authority, there will be less need of a numerous representation, and special guards against abuse, than if the powers of the government are very extensive, and include a great variety of cases.[49] It will also be found necessary to examine the extent of these powers, in order to form a just opinion how far this system can be considered as a confederation, or a consolidation of the states. Many of the advocates for, and most of the opponents to this system, agree that the form of government most suitable for the United States, is that of a confederation.[50] The idea of a confederated government is that of a number of independent states entering into a compact, for the conducting certain general concerns, in which they have a common interest, leaving the management of their internal and local affairs to their separate governments. But whether the system

---

48. It is tempting to think that Brutus's change of plan was prompted by the fact that *The Federalist* series of essays was about to examine the powers to be lodged in the new government before turning to the particular structures proposed in the Constitution. *Federalist* 23, the first to deal with powers, appeared December 18, 1787. See *Brutus VI* and *VII* for Brutus's extended consideration of *Federalist* 23.

49. See *Brutus VI* (3).

50. See *FF XVII* (1).

proposed is of this nature cannot be determined without a strict enquiry into the powers proposed to be granted.

4. This constitution considers the people of the several states as one body corporate, and is intended as an original compact, it will therefore dissolve all contracts which may be inconsistent with it. This not only results from its nature, but is expressly declared in the *6th article* of it. The design of the constitution is expressed in the preamble, to be, "in order to form a more perfect union, to establish justice, insure domestic tranquility, provide for the common defence, promote the general welfare, and secure the blessings of liberty to ourselves and posterity." These are the ends this government is to accomplish, and for which it is invested with certain powers, among these is the power "to make all laws which are *necessary and proper* for carrying into execution the foregoing powers, and *all other* powers vested by this constitution in the government of the United States, or in any department or officer thereof." It is a rule in construing a law to consider the objects the legislature had in view in passing it, and to give it such an explanation as to promote their intention. The same rule will apply in explaining a constitution. The great objects then are declared in this preamble in general and indefinite terms to be to provide for the common defence, promote the general welfare, and an express power being vested in the legislature to make all laws which shall be necessary and proper for carrying into execution all the powers vested in the general government. The inference is natural that the legislature will have an authority to make all laws which they shall judge necessary for the common safety, and to promote the general welfare. This amounts to a power to make laws at discretion: No terms can be found more indefinite than these, and it is obvious, that the legislature alone must judge what laws are proper and necessary for the purpose. It may be said, that this way of explaining the constitution, is torturing and making it speak what it never intended. This is far from my intention, and I shall not even insist upon this implied power, but join issue with those who say we are to collect the idea of the powers given from the express words of the clauses granting them; and it will not be difficult to shew that the same authority is expressly given which is supposed to be implied in the forgoing paragraphs.[51]

5. In the 1st article, 8th section, it is declared, "that Congress shall have power to lay and collect taxes, duties, imposts and excises, to pay the debts, and provide for the common defence, and general welfare of the United

51. See *FF IV* (4–7).

States." In the preamble, the intent of the constitution, among other things, is declared to be to provide for the common defence, and promote the general welfare, and in this clause the power is in express words given to Congress "to provide for the common defence, and general welfare."—And in the last paragraph of the same section there is an express authority to make all laws which shall be necessary and proper for carrying into execution this power. It is therefore evident, that the legislature under this constitution may pass any law which they may think proper. It is true the 9th section restrains their power with respect to certain objects. But these restrictions are very limited, some of them improper, some unimportant, and others not easily understood, as I shall hereafter shew. It has been urged that the meaning I give to this part of the constitution is not the true one, that the intent of it is to confer on the legislature the power to lay and collect taxes, etc. in order to provide for the common defence and general welfare.[52] To this I would reply, that the meaning and intent of the constitution is to be collected from the words of it, and I submit to the public, whether the construction I have given it is not the most natural and easy. But admitting the contrary opinion to prevail, I shall nevertheless, be able to shew, that the same powers are substantially vested in the general government, by several other articles in the constitution. It invests the legislature with authority to lay and collect taxes, duties, imposts and excises, in order to provide for the common defence, and promote the general welfare, and to pass all laws which shall be necessary and proper for carrying this power into effect. To comprehend the extent of this authority, it will be requisite to examine 1st. what is included in this power to lay and collect taxes, duties, imposts and excises.

6. [2d] What is implied in the authority, to pass all laws which shall be necessary and proper for carrying this power into execution.

7. [3d] What limitation, if any, is set to the exercise of this power by the constitution.

8. [1st] To detail the particulars comprehended in the general terms, taxes, duties, imposts and excises, would require a volume, instead of a single piece in a news-paper. Indeed it would be a task far beyond my ability, and to which no one can be competent, unless possessed of a mind capable of comprehending every possible source of revenue; for they extend to every possible way of raising money, whether by direct or indirect taxation. Under this clause may be imposed a poll-tax, a land-tax, a tax on houses and

52. See *Brutus VI* (15–16); *FF III* (16), *IV* (17), *V* (1–2), *VI* (5–12).

buildings, on windows and fire places, on cattle and on all kinds of personal property:—It extends to duties on all kinds of goods to any amount, to tonnage and poundage on vessels, to duties on written instruments, newspapers, almanacks, and books:—It comprehends an excise on all kinds of liquors, spirits, wines, cyder, beer, etc. and indeed takes in duty or excise on every necessary or conveniency of life; whether of foreign or home growth or manufactory. In short, we can have no conception of any way in which a government can raise money from the people, but what is included in one or other of three general terms. We may say then that this clause commits to the hands of the general legislature every conceivable source of revenue within the United States. Not only are these terms very comprehensive, and extend to a vast number of objects, but the power to lay and collect has great latitude; it will lead to the passing a vast number of laws, which may affect the personal rights of the citizens of the states, expose their property to fines and confiscation, and put their lives in jeopardy: it opens a door to the appointment of a swarm of revenue and excise officers to pray [*sic*] upon the honest and industrious part of the community, eat up their substance, and riot on the spoils of the country.

9. [2d] We will next enquire into what is implied in the authority to pass all laws which shall be necessary and proper to carry this power into execution.

10. It is, perhaps, utterly impossible fully to define this power. The authority granted in the first clause can only be understood in its full extent, by descending to all the particular cases in which a revenue can be raised; the number and variety of these cases are so endless, and as it were infinite, that no man living has, as yet, been able to reckon them up. The greatest geniuses in the world have been for ages employed in the research, and when mankind had supposed that the subject was exhausted they have been astonished with the refined improvements that have been made in modern times, and especially in the English nation on the subject—If then the objects of this power cannot be comprehended, how is it possible to understand the extent of that power which can pass all laws which shall be necessary and proper for carrying it into execution? It is truly incomprehensible. A case cannot be conceived of, which is not included in this power. It is well known that the subject of revenue is the most difficult and extensive in the science of government. It requires the greatest talents of a statesman, and the most numerous and exact provisions of the legislature. The command of the revenues of a state gives the command of every thing in it.—He that has the purse will have the sword, and they that have

both, have every thing; so that the legislature having every source from which money can be drawn under their direction, with a right to make all laws necessary and proper for drawing forth all the resource of the country, would have, in fact, all power.

11. Were I to enter into the detail, it would be easy to shew how this power in its operation, would totally destroy all the powers of the individual states.[53] But this is not necessary for those who will think for themselves, and it will be useless to such as take things upon trust, nothing will awaken them to reflection, until the iron hand of oppression compel them to it.

12. I shall only remark, that this power, given to the federal legislature, directly annihilates all the powers of the state legislatures. There cannot be a greater solecism in politics than to talk of power in a government, without the command of any revenue. It is as absurd as to talk of an animal without blood, or the subsistence of one without food. Now the general government having in their controul every possible source of revenue, and authority to pass any law they may deem necessary to draw them forth, or to facilitate their collection; no source of revenue is therefore left in the hands of any state. Should any state attempt to raise money by law, the general government may repeal or arrest it in the execution, for all their laws will be the supreme law of the land: If then any one can be weak enough to believe that a government can exist without having the authority to raise money to pay a door-keeper to their assembly, he may believe that the state government can exist, should this new constitution take place.[54]

13. It is agreed by most of the advocates of this new system, that the government which is proper for the United States should be a confederated one; that the respective states ought to retain a portion of their sovereignty, and that they should preserve not only the forms of their legislatures, but also the power to conduct certain internal concerns. How far the powers to be retained by the states shall extend, is the question; we need not spend much time on this subject, as it respects this constitution, for a government without the power to raise money is one only in name. It is clear that the legislatures of the respective states must be altogether dependent on the will of the general legislature, for the means of supporting their government. The legislature of the United States will have a right to exhaust every source of revenue in every state, and to annul all laws of the states which may stand in the way of effecting it; unless therefore we can suppose the

53. Also see *Brutus VI* (3).
54. Cf. *FF III* (16).

state governments can exist without money to support the officers who execute them, we must conclude they will exist no longer than the general legislature choose they should. Indeed the idea of any government existing, in any respect, as an independent one, without any means of support in their own hands, is an absurdity. If therefore, this constitution has in view, what many of its framers and advocates say it has, to secure and guarantee to the separate states the exercise of certain powers of government, it certainly ought to have left in their hands some sources of revenue. It should have marked the line in which the general government should have raised money, and set bounds over which they should not pass, leaving to the separate states other means to raise supplies for the support of their governments, and to discharge their respective debts. To this it is objected, that the general government ought to have power competent to the purposes of the union; they are to provide for the common defence, to pay the debts of the United States, support foreign ministers, and the civil establishment of the union, and to do these they ought to have authority to raise money adequate to the purpose. On this I observe, that the state governments have also contracted debts, they require money to support their civil officers, and how this is to be done, if they give to the general government a power to raise money in every way in which it can possibly be raised, with such a controul over the state legislatures as to prohibit them, whenever the general legislature may think proper, from raising any money.[55] It is again objected that it is very difficult, if not impossible, to draw the line of distinction between the powers of the general and state governments on this subject. The first, it is said, must have the power of raising the money necessary for the purposes of the union, if they are limited to certain objects the revenue may fall short of a sufficiency for the public exigencies, they must therefore have discretionary power. The line may be easily and accurately drawn between the powers of the two governments on this head. The distinction between external and internal taxes, is not a novel one in this country, it is a plain one, and easily understood.[56] The first includes impost duties on all imported goods; this species of taxes it is proper should be laid by the general government; many reasons might be urged to shew that no danger is to be apprehended from their exercise of it. They may be collected in few places, and from few hands with certainty and expedition. But few officers are necessary to be imployed in collecting them, and there is no

55. Cf. *FF III* (16).
56. Cf. *FF III* (13).

danger of oppression in laying them, because, if they are laid higher than trade will bear, the merchants will cease importing, or smuggle their goods. We have therefore sufficient security, arising from the nature of the thing, against burdensome and intolerable impositions from this kind of tax. But the case is far otherwise with regard to direct taxes; these include poll taxes, land taxes, excises, duties on written instruments, on every thing we eat, drink, or wear; they take hold of every species of property, and come home to every man's house and packet. These are often so oppressive, as to grind the face of the poor, and render the lives of the common people a burden to them. The great and only security the people can have against oppression from this kind of taxes, must rest in their representatives. If they are sufficiently numerous to be well informed of the circumstances, and ability of those who send them, and have a proper regard for the people, they will be secure. The general legislature, as I have shewn in a former paper, will not be thus qualified, and therefore, on this account, ought not to exercise the power of direct taxation. If the power of laying imposts will not be sufficient, some other specific mode of raising a revenue should have been assigned the general government; many may be suggested in which their power may be accurately defined and limited, and it would be much better to give them authority to lay and collect a duty on exports, not to exceed a certain rate per cent, than to have surrendered every kind of resource that the country has, to the complete abolition of the state governments, and which will introduce such an infinite number of laws and ordinances, fines and penalties, courts, and judges, collectors, and excisemen, that when a man can number them, he may enumerate the stars of Heaven.

14. I shall resume this subject in my next, and by an induction of particulars shew, that this power, in its exercise, will subvert all state authority, and will work to the oppression of the people, and that there are no restrictions in the constitution that will soften its rigour, but rather the contrary.

Brutus.

– VI –

27 December 1787

1. It is an important question, whether the general government of the United States should be so framed, as to absorb and swallow up the state governments? or whether, on the contrary, the former ought not to be confined to certain defined national objects, while the latter should retain all the powers which concern the internal police of the states?

2. I have, in my former papers, offered a variety of arguments to prove, that a simple free government could not be exercised over this whole continent, and that therefore we must either give up our liberties and submit to an arbitrary one, or frame a constitution on the plan of confederation. Further reasons might be urged to prove this point—but it seems unnecessary, because the principal advocates of the new constitution admit of the position. The question therefore between us, this being admitted, is, whether or not this system is so formed as either directly to annihilate the state governments, or that in its operation it will certainly effect it.[57] If this is answered in the affirmative, then the system ought not to be adopted, without such amendments as will avoid this consequence. If on the contrary it can be shewn, that the state governments are secured in their rights to manage the internal police of the respective states, we must confine ourselves in our enquiries to the organization of the government and the guards and provisions it contains to prevent a misuse or abuse of power. To determine this question, it is requisite, that we fully investigate the nature, and the extent of the powers intended to be granted by this constitution to the rulers.

3. In my last number I called your attention to this subject, and proved, as I think, uncontrovertibly, that the powers given the legislature under the 8th section of the 1st article, had no other limitation than the discretion of the Congress. It was shewn, that even if the most favorable construction was given to this paragraph, that the advocates for the new constitution could wish, it will convey a power to lay and collect taxes, imposts, duties, and excises, according to the discretion of the legislature, and to make all laws which they shall judge proper and necessary to carry this power into execution. This I shewed would totally destroy all the power of the state governments. To confirm this, it is worth while to trace the operation of the government in some particular instances.

4. The general government is to be vested with authority to levy and collect taxes, duties, and excises; the separate states have also power to impose taxes, duties, and excises, except that they cannot lay duties on exports and imports without the consent of Congress. Here then the two governments have concurrent jurisdiction; both may lay impositions of this kind. But then the general government have superadded to this power, authority to make all laws which shall be necessary and proper for carrying the foregoing power into execution. Suppose then that both governments should lay taxes, duties, and excises, and it should fall so heavy on the people that

57. Cf. *FF I* (13).

they would be unable, or be so burdensome that they would refuse to pay them both—would it not be necessary that the general legislature should suspend the collection of the state tax? It certainly would. For, if the people could not, or would not pay both, they must be discharged from the tax to the state, or the tax to the general government could not be collected.— The conclusion therefore is inevitable, that the respective state governments will not have the power to raise one shilling in any way, but by the permission of the Congress. I presume no one will pretend, that the states can exercise legislative authority, or administer justice among their citizens for any length of time, without being able to raise a sufficiency to pay those who administer their governments.

5. If this be true, and if the states can raise money only by permission of the general government, it follows that the state governments will be dependent on the will of the general government for their existence.

6. What will render this power in Congress effectual and sure in its operation is, that the government will have complete judicial and executive authority to carry all their laws into effect, which will be paramount to the judicial and executive authority of the individual states: in vain therefore will be all interference of the legislatures, courts, or magistrates of any of the states on the subject; for they will be subordinate to the general government, and engaged by oath to support it, and will be constitutionally bound to submit to their decisions.

7. The general legislature will be empowered to lay any tax they chuse, to annex any penalties they please to the breach of their revenue laws; and to appoint as many officers as they may think proper to collect the taxes. They will have authority to farm the revenues and to vest the farmer general, with his subalterns, with plenary powers to collect them, in any way which to them may appear eligible. And the courts of law, which they will be authorized to institute, will have cognizance of every case arising under the revenue laws, the conduct of all the officers employed in collecting them; and the officers of these courts will execute their judgments. There is no way, therefore, of avoiding the destruction of the state governments, whenever the Congress please to do it, unless the people rise up, and, with a strong hand, resist and prevent the execution of constitutional laws. The fear of this, will, it is presumed, restrain the general government, for some time, within proper bounds; but it will not be many years before they will have a revenue, and force, at their command, which will place them above any apprehensions on that score.

8. How far the power to lay and collect duties and excises, may operate to dissolve the state governments, and oppress the people, it is impossible to say. It would assist us much in forming a just opinion on this head, to consider the various objects to which this kind of taxes extend, in European nations, and the infinity of laws they have passed respecting them. Perhaps, if leisure will permit, this may be essayed in some future paper.[58]

9. It was observed in my last number, that the power to lay and collect duties and excises, would invest the Congress with authority to impose a duty and excise on every necessary and convenience of life. As the principal object of the government, in laying a duty or excise, will be, to raise money, it is obvious, that they will fix on such articles as are of the most general use and consumption; because, unless great quantities of the article, on which the duty is laid, is used, the revenue cannot be considerable. We may therefore presume, that the articles which will be the object of this species of taxes will be either the real necessaries of life; or if not these, such as from custom and habit are esteemed so. I will single out a few of the productions of our own country, which may, and probably will, be of the number.

10. Cider is an article that most probably will be one of those on which an excise will be laid, because it is one, which this country produces in great abundance, which is in very general use, is consumed in great quantities, and which may be said too not to be a real necessary of life. An excise on this would raise a large sum of money in the United States. How would the power, to lay and collect an excise on cider, and to pass all laws proper and necessary to carry it into execution, operate in its exercise? It might be necessary, in order to collect the excise on cider, to grant to one man, in each county, an exclusive right of building and keeping cider-mills, and oblige him to give bonds and security for payment of the excise; or, if this was not done, it might be necessary to license the mills, which are to make this liquor, and to take from them security, to account for the excise; or, if otherwise, a great number of officers must be employed, to take account of the cider made, and to collect the duties on it.

11. Porter, ale, and all kinds of malt-liquors, are articles that would probably be subject also to an excise. It would be necessary, in order to collect such an excise, to regulate the manufactory of these, that the quantity made might be ascertained or otherwise security could not be had for the payment of the excise. Every brewery must then be licensed, and of-

58. Brutus does not reach this question.

ficers appointed, to take account of its product, and to secure the payment of the duty, or excise, before it is sold. Many other articles might be named, which would be objects of this species of taxation, but I refrain from enumerating them. It will probably be said, by those who advocate this system, that the observations already made on this head, are calculated only to inflame the minds of the people, with the apprehension of dangers merely imaginary. That there is not the least reason to apprehend, the general legislature will exercise their power in this manner. To this I would only say, that these kinds of taxes exist in Great Britain, and are severely felt. The excise on cider and perry, was imposed in that nation a few years ago, and it is in the memory of every one, who read the history of the transaction, what great tumults it occasioned.

12. This power, exercised without limitation, will introduce itself into every corner of the city, and country—It will wait upon the ladies at their toilett, and will not leave them in any of their domestic concerns; it will accompany them to the ball, the play, and the assembly; it will go with them when they visit, and will, on all occasions, sit beside them in their carriages, nor will it desert them even at church; it will enter the house of every gentleman, watch over his cellar, wait upon his cook in the kitchen, follow the servants into the parlour, preside over the table, and note down all he eats or drinks; it will attend him to his bed-chamber, and watch him while he sleeps; it will take cognizance of the professional man in his office, or his study; it will watch the merchant in the counting-house, or in his store; it will follow the mechanic to his shop, and in his work, and will haunt him in his family, and in his bed; it will be a constant companion of the industrious farmer in all his labour, it will be with him in the house, and in the field, observe the toil of his hands, and the sweat of his brow; it will penetrate into the most obscure cottage; and finally, it will light upon the head of every person in the United States. To all these different classes of people, and in all these circumstances, in which it will attend them, the language in which it will address them, will be GIVE! GIVE!

13. A power that has such latitude, which reaches every person in the community in every conceivable circumstance, and lays hold of every species of property they possess, and which has no bounds set to it, but the discretion of those who exercise it, I say, such a power must necessarily, from its very nature, swallow up all the power of the state governments.

14. I shall add but one other observation on this head, which is this—It appears to me a solecism, for two men, or bodies of men, to have unlimited power respecting the same object. It contradicts the scripture maxim,

which saith, "no man can serve two masters,"[59] the one power or the other must prevail, or else they will destroy each other, and neither of them effect their purpose. It may be compared to two mechanic powers, acting upon the same body in opposite directions, the consequence would be, if the powers were equal, the body would remain in a state of rest, or if the force of the one was superior to that of the other, the stronger would prevail, and overcome the resistance of the weaker.

15. But it is said, by some of the advocates of this system, "That the idea that Congress can levy taxes at pleasure, is false, and the suggestion wholly unsupported: that the preamble to the constitution is declaratory of the purposes of the union, and the assumption of any power not necessary to establish justice, &c. to provide for the common defence, &c. will be un-constitutional. Besides, in the very clause which gives the power of levying duties and taxes, the purposes to which the money shall be appropriated, are specified, viz. to pay the debts, and provide for the common defence and general welfare."* I would ask those, who reason thus, to define what ideas are included under the terms, to provide for the common defence and general welfare? Are these terms definite, and will they be understood in the same manner, and to apply to the same cases by every one? No one will pretend they will. It will then be matter of opinion, what tends to the general welfare; and the Congress will be the only judges in the matter. To provide for the general welfare, is an abstract proposition, which mankind differ in the explanation of, as much as they do on any political or moral proposition that can be proposed; the most opposite measures may be pursued by different parties, and both may profess, that they have in view the general welfare; and both sides may be honest in their professions, or both may have sinister views. Those who advocate this new constitution declare, they are influenced by a regard to the general welfare; those who oppose it, declare they are moved by the same principle; and I have no doubt but a number on both sides are honest in their professions; and yet nothing is more certain than this, that to adopt this constitution, and not to adopt it, cannot both of them be promotive of the general welfare.

16. It is as absurd to say, that the power of Congress is limited by these general expressions, "to provide for the common safety, and general welfare," as it would be to say, that it would be limited, had the constitution

59. Matthew 6:24; Luke 16:13.
* Vide an examination into the leading principles of the federal constitution, printed in Philadelphia, Page 34.

said they should have power to lay taxes, &c. at will and pleasure. Were this authority given, it might be said, that under it the legislature could not do injustice, or pursue any measures, but such as were calculated to promote the public good, and happiness. For every man, rulers as well as others, are bound by the immutable laws of God and reason, always to will what is right. It is certainly right and fit, that the governors of every people should provide for the common defence and general welfare; every government, therefore, in the world, even the greatest despot, is limited in the exercise of his power. But however just this reasoning may be, it would be found, in practice, a most pitiful restriction. The government would always say, their measures were designed and calculated to promote the public good; and there being no judge between them and the people, the rulers themselves must, and would always, judge for themselves.

17. There are others of the favourers of this system, who admit, that the power of the Congress under it, with respect to revenue, will exist without limitation, and contend, that so it ought to be.

18. It is said, "The power to raise armies, to build and equip fleets, and to provide for their support, ought to exist without limitation, because it is impossible to foresee, or to define, the extent and variety of national exigencies, or the correspondent extent and variety of the means which may be necessary to satisfy them."

19. This, it is said, "is one of those truths which, to correct and unprejudiced minds, carries its own evidence along with it. It rests upon axioms as simple as they are universal: the means ought to be proportioned to the end; the person, from whose agency the attainment of any end is expected, ought to possess the means by which it is to be attained."*

20. This same writer insinuates, that the opponents to the plan promulgated by the convention, manifests a want of candor, in objecting to the extent of the powers proposed to be vested in this government; because he asserts, with an air of confidence, that the powers ought to be unlimited as to the object to which they extend; and that this position, if not self-evident, is at least clearly demonstrated by the foregoing mode of reasoning. But with submission to this author's better judgment, I humbly conceive his reasoning will appear, upon examination, more specious than solid. The means, says the gentleman, ought to be proportioned to the end: admit the proposition to be true it is then necessary to enquire, what is the end of the government of the United States, in order to draw any just conclusions from

* Vide the Federalist, No. 23.

it. Is this end simply to preserve the general government, and to provide for the common defence and general welfare of the union only? certainly not: for beside this, the state governments are to be supported, and provision made for the managing such of their internal concerns as are allotted to them. It is admitted, "that the circumstances of our country are such, as to demand a compound, instead of a simple, a confederate, instead of a sole government," that the objects of each ought to be pointed out, and that each ought to possess ample authority to execute the powers committed to them. The government then, being complex in its nature, the end it has in view is so also; and it is as necessary, that the state governments should possess the means to attain the ends expected from them, as for the general government. Neither the general government, nor the state governments, ought to be vested with all the powers proper to be exercised for promoting the ends of government. The powers are divided between them—certain ends are to be attained by the one, and other certain ends by the other; and these, taken together, include all the ends of good government. This being the case, the conclusion follows, that each should be furnished with the means, to attain the ends, to which they are designed.

21. To apply this reasoning to the case of revenue; the general government is charged with the care of providing for the payment of the debts of the United States; supporting the general government, and providing for the defence of the union. To obtain these ends, they should be furnished with means. But does it thence follow, that they should command all the revenues of the United States! Most certainly it does not. For if so, it will follow, that no means will be left to attain other ends, as necessary to the happiness of the country, as those committed to their care. The individual states have debts to discharge; their legislatures and executives are to be supported, and provision is to be made for the administration of justice in the respective states. For these objects the general government has no authority to provide; nor is it proper it should. It is clear then, that the states should have the command of such revenues, as to answer the ends they have to obtain. To say, "that the circumstances that endanger the safety of nations are infinite,"[60] and from hence to infer, that all the sources of revenue in the states should be yielded to the general government, is not conclusive reasoning: for the Congress are authorized only to controul in general concerns, and not regulate local and internal ones; and these are as essentially requisite to be provided for as those. The peace and happiness of

60. *Federalist* 23.

a community is as intimately connected with the prudent direction of their domestic affairs, and the due administration of justice among themselves, as with a competent provision for their defence against foreign invaders, and indeed more so.

22. Upon the whole, I conceive, that there cannot be a clearer position than this, that the state governments ought to have an uncontroulable power to raise a revenue, adequate to the exigencies of their governments; and, I presume, no such power is left them by this constitution.

Brutus.

– VII –

3 January 1788

1. The result of our reasoning in the two preceeding numbers is this, that in a confederated government, where the powers are divided between the general and the state government, it is essential to its existence, that the revenues of the country, without which no government can exist, should be divided between them, and so apportioned to each, as to answer their respective exigencies, as far as human wisdom can effect such a division and apportionment.

2. It has been shewn, that no such allotment is made in this constitution, but that every source of revenue is under the controul of the Congress; it therefore follows, that if this system is intended to be a complex and not a simple, a confederate and not an entire consolidated government, it contains in it the sure seeds of its own dissolution.—One of two things must happen—Either the new constitution will become a mere *nudum pactum,*[61] and all the authority of the rulers under it be cried down, as has happened to the present confederation—Or the authority of the individual states will be totally supplanted, and they will retain the mere form without any of the powers of government.—To one or the other of these issues, I think, this new government, if it is adopted, will advance with great celerity.

3. It is said, I know, that such a separation of the sources of revenue, cannot be made without endangering the public safety—"unless (says a writer) it can be shewn that the circumstances which may affect the public safety are reducible within certain determinate limits; unless the contrary of this position can be fairly and rationally disputed; it must be admitted as a nec-

61. *Nudum pactum:* "naked contract," a nonenforceable agreement.

essary consequence, that there can be no limitation of that authority which is to provide for the defence and protection of the community, &c."*

4. The pretended demonstration of this writer will instantly vanish, when it is considered, that the *protection and defence* of the community is not intended to be entrusted *solely* into the hands of the general government, and by his own confession it ought not to be. It is true this system commits to the general government the protection and defence of the community against foreign force and invasion, against piracies and felonies on the high seas, and against insurrections among ourselves. They are also authorised to provide for the administration of justice in certain matters of a general concern, and in some that I think are not so. But it ought to be left to the state governments to provide for the protection and defence of the citizen against the hand of private violence, and the wrongs done or attempted by individuals to each other—Protection and defence against the murderer, the robber, the thief, the cheat, and the unjust person, is to be derived from the respective state governments.—The just way of reasoning therefore on this subject is this, the general government is to provide for the protection and defence of the community against foreign attacks, &c., they therefore ought to have authority sufficient to effect this, so far as is consistent with the providing for our internal protection and defence. The state governments are entrusted with the care of administring justice among its [sic] citizens, and the management of other internal concerns, they ought therefore to retain power adequate to the end. The preservation of internal peace and good order, and the due administration of law and justice, ought to be the first care of every government.—The happiness of a people depends infinitely more on this than it does upon all that glory and respect which nations acquire by the most brilliant martial achievements—and I believe history will furnish but few examples of nations who have duly attended to these, who have been subdued by foreign invaders. If a proper respect and submission to the laws prevailed over all orders of men in our country; and if a spirit of public and private justice, oeconomy and industry influenced the people, we need not be under any apprehensions but what they would be ready to repel any invasion that might be made on the country. And more than this, I would not wish from them—A defensive war is the only one I think justifiable—I do not make these observations to prove, that a government ought not to be authorised to provide

* Federalist, No. 2 3.

for the protection and defence of a country against external enemies, but to shew that this is not the most important, much less the only object of their care.

5. The European governments are almost all of them framed, and administered with a view to arms, and war, as that in which their chief glory consists; they mistake the end of government—it was designed to save men's lives, not to destroy them. We ought to furnish the world with an example of a great people, who in their civil institutions hold chiefly in view, the attainment of virtue, and happiness among ourselves. Let the monarchs, in Europe, share among them the glory of depopulating countries, and butchering thousands of their innocent citizens, to revenge private quarrels, or to punish an insult offered to a wife, a mistress, or a favorite: I envy them not the honor, and I pray heaven this country may never be ambitious of it. The czar Peter the great,[62] acquired great glory by his arms; but all this was nothing, compared with the true glory which he obtained, by civilizing his rude and barbarous subjects, diffusing among them knowledge, and establishing, and cultivating the arts of life: by the former he desolated countries, and drenched the earth with human blood: by the latter he softened the ferocious nature of his people, and pointed them to the means of human happiness. The most important end of government then, is the proper direction of its internal policy, and oeconomy; this is the province of the state governments, and it is evident, and is indeed admitted, that these ought to be under their controul. Is it not then preposterous, and in the highest degree absurd, when the state governments are vested with powers so essential to the peace and good order of society, to take from them the means of their own preservation?

6. The idea, that the powers of congress in respect to revenue ought to be unlimited, "because the circumstances which may affect the public safety are not reducible to certain determinate limits," is novel, as it relates to the government of the united states. The inconveniencies which resulted from the feebleness of the present confederation was discerned, and felt soon after its adoption. It was soon discovered, that a power to require money, without either the authority or means to enforce a collection of it, could not be relied upon either to provide for the common defence, the discharge of the national debt, or for support of government. Congress therefore, so early as February 1781, recommended to the states to invest them with a

---

62. Peter the Great (1672–1725), the founder of modern Russia. As Brutus says, he was both a great conqueror and a great reformer.

power to levy an impost of five per cent ad valorem,[63] on all imported goods, as a fund to be appropriated to discharge the debts already contracted, or which should hereafter be contracted for the support of the war, to be continued until the debts should be fully and finally discharged. There is not the most distant idea held out in this act, that an unlimited power to collect taxes, duties and excises was necessary to be vested in the united states, and yet this was a time of the most pressing danger and distress. The idea then was, that if certain definite funds were assigned to the union, which were certain in their natures, productive, and easy of collection, it would enable them to answer their engagements, and provide for their defence, and the impost of five per cent was fixed upon for the purpose.

7. This same subject was revived in the winter and spring of 1783, and after a long consideration of the subject, and many schemes were proposed; the result was, a recommendation of the revenue system of April 1783; this system does not suggest an idea that it was necessary to grant the United States unlimited authority in matters of revenue. A variety of amendments were proposed to this system, some of which are upon the journals of Congress, but it does not appear that any of them proposed to invest the general government with discretionary power to raise money. On the contrary, all of them limit them to certain definite objects, and fix the bounds over which they could not pass. This recommendation was passed at the conclusion of the war, and was founded on an estimate of the whole national debt. It was computed, that one million and an half of dollars, in addition to the impost, was a sufficient sum to pay the annual interest of the debt, and gradually to abolish the principal.—Events have proved that their estimate was sufficiently liberal, as the domestic debt appears upon its being adjusted to be less than it was computed, and since this period a considerable portion of the principal of the domestic debt has been discharged by the sale of the western lands. It has been constantly urged by Congress, and by individuals, ever since, until lately, that had this revenue been appropriated by the states, as it was recommended, it would have been adequate to every exigency of the union. Now indeed it is insisted, that all the treasures of the country are to be under the controul of that body, whom we are to appoint to provide for our protection and defence against foreign enemies. The debts of the several states, and the support of the governments of them are to trust to fortune and accident. If the union should not have occasion for all the money they can raise, they will leave a portion for the state, but

63. Ad valorem: according to the value.

this must be a matter of mere grace and favor. Doctrines like these would not have been listened to by any state in the union, at a time when we were pressed on every side by a powerful enemy, and were called upon to make greater exertions than we have any reason to expect we shall ever be again. The ability and character of the convention, who framed the proferred constitution, is sounded forth and reiterated by every declaimer and writer in its favor, as a powerful argument to induce its adoption. But are not the patriots who guided our councils in the perilous times of the war, entitled to equal respect. How has it happened, that none of these perceived a truth, which it is pretended is capable of such clear demonstration, that the power to raise a revenue should be deposited in the general government without limitation? Were the men so dull of apprehension, so incapable of reasoning as not to be able to draw the inference? The truth is, no such necessity exists. It is a thing practicable, and by no means so difficult as is pretended, to limit the powers of the general government in respect to revenue, while yet they may retain reasonable means to provide for the common defence.

8. It is admitted, that human wisdom cannot foresee all the variety of circumstances that may arise to endanger the safety of nations—and it may with equal truth be added, that the power of a nation, exerted with its utmost vigour, may not be equal to repel a force with which it may be assailed, much less may it be able, with its ordinary resources and power, to oppose an extraordinary and unexpected attack;—but yet every nation may form a rational judgment, what force will be competent to protect and defend it, against any enemy with which it is probable it may have to contend. In extraordinary attacks, every country must rely upon the spirit and special exertions of its inhabitants—and these extraordinary efforts will always very much depend upon the happiness and good order the people experience from a wise and prudent administration of their internal government. The states are as capable of making a just estimate on this head, as perhaps any nation in the world.—We have no powerful nation in our neighbourhood; if we are to go to war, it must either be with the Aboriginal natives, or with European nations. The first are so unequal to a contest with this whole continent, that they are rather to be dreaded for the depredations they may make on our frontiers, than for any impression they will ever be able to make on the body of the country. Some of the European nations, it is true, have provinces bordering upon us, but from these, unsupported by their European forces, we have nothing to apprehend; if any of them should attack us, they will have to transport their armies across the atlantic, at immense expence, while we should defend ourselves in our own country,

which abounds with every necessary of life. For defence against any assault, which there is any probability will be made upon us, we may easily form an estimate.

9. I may be asked to point out the sources, from which the general government could derive a sufficient revenue, to answer the demands of the union. Many might be suggested, and for my part, I am not disposed to be tenacious of my own opinion on the subject. If the object be defined with precision, and will operate to make the burden fall any thing nearly equal on the different parts of the union, I shall be satisfied.

10. There is one source of revenue, which it is agreed, the general government ought to have the sole controul of. This is an impost upon all goods imported from foreign countries.[64] This would, of itself, be very productive, and would be collected with ease and certainty.—It will be a fund too, constantly encreasing—for our commerce will grow, with the productions of the country; and these, together with our consumption of foreign goods, will encrease with our population. It is said, that the impost will not produce a sufficient sum to satisfy the demands of the general government; perhaps it would not. Let some other then, equally well defined, be assigned them:—that this is practicable is certain, because such particular objects were proposed by some members of Congress when the revenue system of April 1783, was agitated in that body. It was then moved, that a tax at the rate of _____ ninetieths[65] of a dollar on surveyed land, and a house tax of half a dollar on a house, should be granted to the United States. I do not mention this, because I approve of raising a revenue in this mode. I believe such a tax would be difficult in its collection, and inconvenient in its operation. But it shews, that it has heretofore been the sense of some of those, who now contend, that the general government should have unlimited authority in matters of revenue, that their authority should be definite and limitted on that head.—My own opinion is, that the objects from which the general government should have authority to raise a revenue, should be of such a nature, that the tax should be raised by simple laws, with few officers, with certainty and expedition, and with the least interference with the internal police of the states.—Of this nature is the impost on imported goods—and it appears to me that a duty on exports, would also be of this nature—and therefore, for ought I can discover, this would be the best source of revenue to grant the general government. I know

64. Cf. *FF III* (13), *XVII* (6).
65. The space is left blank by Brutus.

neither the Congress nor the state legislatures will have authority under the new constitution to raise a revenue in this way.[66] But I cannot perceive the reason of the restriction. It appears to me evident, that a tax on articles exported, would be as nearly equal as any that we can expect to lay, and it certainly would be collected with more ease and less expence than any direct tax. I do not however, contend for this mode, it may be liable to well founded objections that have not occurred to me. But this I do contend for, that some mode is practicable, and that limits must be marked between the general government, and the states on this head, or if they be not, either the Congress in the exercise of this power, will deprive the state legislatures of the means of their existence, or the states by resisting the constitutional authority of the general government, will render it nugatory.

Brutus.

– VIII –

10 January 1788

1. The next powers vested by this constitution in the general government, which we shall consider, are those, which authorise them to "borrow money on the credit of the United States, and to raise and support armies." I take these two together and connect them with the power to lay and collect taxes, duties, imposts and excises, because their extent, and the danger that will arise from the exercise of these powers, cannot be fully understood, unless they are viewed in relation to each other.[67]

2. The power to borrow money is general and unlimited, and the clause so often before referred to, authorises the passing any laws proper and necessary to carry this into execution. Under this authority, the Congress may mortgage any or all the revenues of the union, as a fund to loan money upon, and it is probably, in this way, they may borrow of foreign nations, a principal sum, the interest of which will be equal to the annual revenues of the country.—By this means, they may create a national debt, so large, as to exceed the ability of the country ever to sink. I can scarcely contemplate a greater calamity that could befal this country, than to be loaded with a

66. Article I, section 9, of the Constitution prohibits Congress from laying export duties. Article I, section 10, prohibits the states from doing so without the consent of Congress except so far as "absolutely necessary for executing its inspection laws."

67. See *FF III* (12–20); *Plebeian* (24).

debt exceeding their ability ever to discharge. If this be a just remark, it is unwise and improvident to vest in the general government a power to borrow at discretion, without any limitation or restriction.

3. It may possibly happen that the safety and welfare of the country may require, that money be borrowed, and it is proper when such a necessity arises that the power should be exercised by the general government.—But it certainly ought never to be exercised, but on the most urgent occasions, and then we should not borrow of foreigners if we could possibly avoid it.

4. The constitution should therefore have so restricted, the exercise of this power as to have rendered it very difficult for the government to practise it. The present confederation requires the assent of nine states to exercise this, and a number of the other important powers of the confederacy— and it would certainly have been a wise provision in this constitution, to have made it necessary that two thirds of the members should assent to borrowing money—when the necessity was indispensable, this assent would always be given, and in no other cause ought it to be.

5. The power to raise armies, is indefinite and unlimited, and authorises the raising forces, as well in peace as in war. Whether the clause which impowers the Congress to pass all laws which are proper and necessary, to carry this into execution, will not authorise them to impress men for the army, is a question well worthy consideration? If the general legislature deem it for the general welfare to raise a body of troops, and they cannot be procured by voluntary enlistments, it seems evident, that it will be proper and necessary to effect it, that men be impressed from the militia to make up the deficiency.

6. These powers taken in connection, amount to this: that the general government have unlimitted authority and controul over all the wealth and all the force of the union. The advocates for this scheme, would favor the world with a new discovery, if they would shew, what kind of freedom or independency is left to the state governments, when they cannot command any part of the property or of the force of the country, but at the will of the Congress. It seems to me as absurd, as it would be to say, that I was free and independent, when I had conveyed all my property to another, and was tenant to will to him, and had beside, given an indenture of myself to serve him during life.—The power to keep up standing armies in time of peace, has been justly objected, to this system, as dangerous and improvident. The advocates who have wrote in its favor, have some of them ridiculed the objection, as though it originated in the distempered brain of its opponents, and others have taken pains to shew, that it is a power that was proper to be

granted to the rulers in this constitution. That you may be enabled to form a just opinion on this subject, I shall first make some remarks, tending to prove, that this power ought to be restricted, and then animadvert on the arguments which have been adduced to justify it.

7. I take it for granted, as an axiom in politic, that the people should never authorise their rulers to do any thing, which if done, would operate to their injury.

8. It seems equally clear, that in a case where a power, if given and exercised, will generally produce evil to the community, and seldom good—and which, experience has proved, has most frequently been exercised to the great injury, and very often to the total destruction of the government; in such a case, I say, this power, if given at all, should if possible be so restricted, as to prevent the ill effect of its operation.

9. Let us then enquire, whether standing armies in time of peace, would be ever beneficial to our country—or if in some extraordinary cases, they might be necessary; whether it is not true, that they have generally proved a scourge to a country, and destructive of their liberty.[68]

10. I shall not take up much of your time in proving a point, in which the friends of liberty, in all countries, have so universally agreed. The following extract from Mr. Pultney's speech, delivered in the house of commons of Great-Britain, on a motion for reducing the army, is so full to the point, and so much better than any thing I can say, that I shall be excused for inserting it.[69] He says, "I have always been, and always shall be against a standing army of any kind; to me it is a terrible thing, whether under that of a parliamentary, or any other designation; a standing army is still a standing army by whatever name it is called; they are a body of men distinct from the body of the people; they are governed by different laws, and blind obedience, and an entire submission to the orders of their commanding officer, is their only principle; the nations around us, sir, are already enslaved, and have been enslaved by those very means; by means of their standing armies they have every one lost their liberties; it is indeed impossible that the liberties of the people in any country can be preserved where a numerous standing army is kept up. Shall we then take our measures from the example of our neighbours? No, sir, on the contrary, from their misfortunes we ought to learn to avoid those rocks upon which they have split.

68. *FF III* (16), *XIII* (3).

69. *Cobbett's Parliamentary History of England* (London, 1811), VIII, 172–73, 904–10. (Storing, II, 449, n68)

11. "It signifies nothing to tell me that our army is commanded by such gentlemen as cannot be supposed to join in any measures for enslaving their country; it may be so; I have a very good opinion of many gentlemen now in the army; I believe they would not join in any such measures; but their lives are uncertain, nor can we be sure how long they will be kept in command, they may all be dismissed in a moment, and proper tools of power put in their room. Besides, sir, we know the passions of men, we know how dangerous it is to trust the best of men with too much power. Where was a braver army than that under Jul. Caesar? Where was there ever an army that had served their country more faithfully? That army was commanded generally by the best citizens of Rome, by men of great fortune and figure in their country, yet that army enslaved their country. The affections of the soldiers towards their country, the honor and integrity of the under officers, are not to be depended on. By the military law the administration of justice is so quick, and the punishment so severe, that neither the officer nor soldier dare dispute the orders of his supreme commander; he must not consult his own inclination. If an officer were commanded to pull his own father out of this house, he must do it; he dares not disobey; immediate death would be the sure consequence of the least grumbling: and if an officer were sent into the court of request, accompanied by a body of musketeers with screwed bayonets, and with orders to tell us what we ought to do, and how we were to vote: I know what would be the duty of this house; I know it would be our duty to order the officer to be hanged at the door of the lobby; but I doubt, sir, I doubt much, if such a spirit could be found in the house, or in any house of commons that will ever be in England.

12. "Sir, I talk not of imaginary things? I talk of what has happened to an English house of commons, from an English army; not only from an English army, but an army that was raised by that very house of commons, an army that was paid by them, and an army that was commanded by generals appointed by them; therefore do not let us vainly imagine, that an army, raised and maintained by authority of parliament, will always be so submissive to them. If an army be so numerous as to have it in their power to overawe the parliament, they will be submissive as long as the parliament does nothing to disoblige their favourite general; but when that case happens, I am afraid, that in place of the parliament's dismissing the army, the army will dismiss the parliament."—If this great man's reasoning be just, it follows, that keeping up a standing army, would be in the highest degree dangerous to the liberty and happiness of the community—and if so, the

general government ought not to have authority to do it; for no government should be empowered to do that which if done, would tend to destroy public liberty.

Brutus.

– IX –

17 January 1788

1. The design of civil government is to protect the rights and promote the happiness of the people. For this end, rulers are invested with powers. But we cannot from hence justly infer that these powers should be unlimited. There are certain rights which mankind possess, over which government ought not to have any controul, because it is not necessary they should, in order to attain the end of its institution. There are certain things which rulers should be absolutely prohibited from doing, because, if they should do them, they would work an injury, not a benefit to the people. Upon the same principles of reasoning, if the exercise of a power, is found generally or in most cases to operate to the injury of the community, the legislature should be restricted in the exercise of that power, so as to guard, as much as possible, against the danger. These principles seem to be the evident dictates of common sense, and what ought to give sanction to them in the minds of every American, they are the great principles of the late revolution, and those which governed the framers of all our state constitutions. Hence we find, that all the state constitutions, contain either formal bills of rights, which set bounds to the powers of the legislature, or have restrictions for the same purpose in the body of the constitutions. Some of our new political Doctors, indeed, reject the idea of the necessity, or propriety of such restrictions in any elective government, but especially in the general one.

2. But it is evident, that the framers of this new system were of a contrary opinion, because they have prohibited the general government, the exercise of some powers, and restricted them in that of others.

3. I shall adduce two instances, which will serve to illustrate my meaning, as well as to confirm the truth of the preceeding remark.

4. In the 9th section, it is declared, "no bill of attainder shall be passed." This clause takes from the legislature all power to declare a particular person guilty of a crime by law. It is proper the legislature should be deprived of the exercise of this power, because it seldom is exercised to the benefit of the community, but generally to its injury.

5. In the same section it is provided, that "the privilege of the writ of habeas corpus shall not be suspended, unless when in cases of rebellion and invasion, the public safety may require it." This clause limits the power of the legislature to deprive a citizen of the right of habeas corpus, to particular cases viz. those of rebellion and invasion; the reason is plain, because in no other cases can this power be exercised for the general good.

6. Let us apply these remarks to the case of standing armies in times of peace. If they generally prove the destruction of the happiness and liberty of the people, the legislature ought not to have power to keep them up, or if they had, this power should be so restricted, as to secure the people against the danger arising from the exercise of it.

7. That standing armies are dangerous to the liberties of a people was proved in my last number—If it was necessary, the truth of the position might be confirmed by the history of almost every nation in the world. A cloud of the most illustrious patriots of every age and country, where freedom has been enjoyed, might be adduced as witnesses in support of the sentiment. But I presume it would be useless, to enter into a laboured argument, to prove to the people of America, a position, which has so long and so generally been received by them as a kind of axiom.

8. Some of the advocates for this new system controvert this sentiment, as they do almost every other that has been maintained by the best writers on free government.—Others, though they will not expressly deny, that standing armies in times of peace are dangerous, yet join with these in maintaining, that it is proper the general government should be vested with the power to do it. I shall now proceed to examine the arguments they adduce in support of their opinions.

9. A writer, in favor of this system, treats this objection as a ridiculous one. He supposes it would be as proper to provide against the introduction of Turkish janizaries, or against making the Alcoran a rule of faith.

10. From the positive, and dogmatic manner, in which this author delivers his opinions, and answers objections made to his sentiments—one would conclude, that he was some pedantic pedagogue who had been accustomed to deliver his dogmas to pupils, who always placed implicit faith in what he delivered.

11. But, why is this provision so ridiculous? because, says this author, it is unnecessary. But, why is it unnecessary? "because, the principles and habits, as well as the power of the Americans are directly opposed to standing armies; and there is as little necessity to guard against them by positive constitutions, as to prohibit the establishment of the Mahometan religion."

It is admitted then, that a standing army in time of peace, is an evil. I ask then, why should this government be authorised to do evil? If the principles and habits of the people of this country are opposed to standing armies in time of peace, if they do not contribute to the public good, but would endanger the public liberty and happiness, why should the government be vested with the power? No reason can be given, why rulers should be authorised to do, what, if done, would oppose the principles and habits of the people, and endanger the public safety, but there is every reason in the world, that they should be prohibited from the exercise of such a power. But this author supposes, that no danger is to be apprehended from the exercise of this power, because, if armies are kept up, it will be by the people themselves, and therefore, to provide against it, would be as absurd as for a man to "pass a law in his family, that no troops should be quartered in his family by his consent."[70] This reasoning supposes, that the general government is to be exercised by the people of America themselves—But such an idea is groundless and absurd. There is surely a distinction between the people and their rulers, even when the latter are representatives of the former.—They certainly are not identically the same, and it cannot be disputed, but it may and often does happen, that they do not possess the same sentiments or pursue the same interests. I think I have shewn, that as this government is constituted, there is little reason to expect, that the interest of the people and their rulers will be the same.

12. Besides, if the habits and sentiments of the people of America are to be relied upon, as the sole security against the encroachment of their rulers, all restrictions in constitutions are unnecessary; nothing more is requisite, than to declare who shall be authorized to exercise the powers of government, and about this we need not be very careful—for the habits and principles of the people will oppose every abuse of power. This I suppose to be the sentiments of this author, as it seems to be of many of the advocates of this new system. An opinion like this, is as directly opposed to the principles and habits of the people of America, as it is to the sentiments of every writer of reputation on the science of government, and repugnant to the principles of reason and common sense.[71]

70. A Citizen of North America [Noah Webster], "An Examination into the Leading Principles of the Federal Constitution," in *Friends of the Constitution*, edited by Colleen A. Sheehan and Gary L. McDowell (Indianapolis: Liberty Fund, 1998), 393.

71. See *FF X* (1).

13. The idea that there is no danger of the establishment of a standing army, under the new constitution, is without foundation.

14. It is a well known fact, that a number of those who had an agency in producing this system, and many of those who it is probable will have a principal share in the administration of the government under it, if it is adopted, are avowedly in favour of standing armies. It is a language common among them, "That no people can be kept in order, unless the government have an army to awe them into obedience; it is necessary to support the dignity of government, to have a military establishment."[72] And there will not be wanting a variety of plausible reason to justify the raising one, drawn from the danger we are in from the Indians on our frontiers, or from the European provinces in our neighbourhood. If to this we add, that an army will afford a decent support, and agreeable employment to the young men of many families, who are too indolent to follow occupations that will require care and industry, and too poor to live without doing any business, we can have little reason to doubt, but that we shall have a large standing army, as soon as this government can find money to pay them, and perhaps sooner.[73]

15. A writer, who is the boast of the advocates of this new constitution, has taken great pains to shew, that this power was proper and necessary to be vested in the general government.

16. He sets out with calling in question the candour and integrity of those who advance the objection, and with insinuating, that it is their intention to mislead the people, by alarming their passions, rather than to convince them by arguments addressed to their understandings.[74]

17. The man who reproves another for a fault, should be careful that he himself be not guilty of it. How far this writer has manifested a spirit of candour, and has pursued fair reasoning on this subject, the impartial public will judge, when his arguments pass before them in review.

18. He first attempts to shew, that this objection is futile and disingenuous, because the power to keep up standing armies, in time of peace, is vested, under the present government, in the legislature of every state in the union, except two. Now this is so far from being true, that it is expressly declared, by the present articles of confederation, that no body of forces

---

72. Cf. *FF II* (9).
73. *FF III* (16).
74. *Federalist* 24.

"shall be kept up by any state, in time of peace, except such number only, as in the judgment of the United States in Congress assembled, shall be deemed requisite to garrison the forts necessary for the defence of such state."[75] Now, was it candid and ingenuous to endeavour to persuade the public, that the general government had no other power than your own legislature have on this head; when the truth is, your legislature have no authority to raise and keep up any forces?

19. He next tells us, that the power given by this constitution, on this head, is similar to that which Congress possess under the present confederation. As little ingenuity is manifested in this representation as in that of the former.

20. I shall not undertake to enquire whether or not Congress are vested with a power to keep up a standing army in time of peace; it has been a subject warmly debated in Congress, more than once, since the peace; and one of the most respectable states in the union, were so fully convinced that they had no such power, that they expressly instructed their delegates to enter a solemn protest against it on the journals of Congress, should they attempt to exercise it.

21. But should it be admitted that they have the power, there is such a striking dissimilarity between the restrictions under which the present Congress can exercise it, and that of the proposed government, that the comparison will serve rather to shew the impropriety of vesting the proposed government with the power, than of justifying it.

22. It is acknowledged by this writer, that the powers of Congress, under the present confederation, amount to little more than that of recommending. If they determine to raise troops, they are obliged to effect it through the authority of the state legislatures. This will, in the first instance, be a most powerful restraint upon them, against ordering troops to be raised. But if they should vote an army, contrary to the opinion and wishes of the people, the legislatures of the respective states would not raise them. Besides, the present Congress hold their places at the will and pleasure of the legislatures of the states who send them, and no troops can be raised, but by the assent of nine states out of the thirteen. Compare the power proposed to be lodged in the legislature on this head, under this constitution, with that vested in the present Congress, and every person of the least discernment, whose understanding is not totally blinded by prejudice, will perceive, that they bear no analogy to each other. Under the present

75. Articles of Confederation, Art. 6.

confederation, the representatives of nine states, out of thirteen, must assent to the raising of troops, or they cannot be levied: under the proposed constitution, a less number than the representatives of two states, in the house of representatives, and the representatives of three states and an half in the senate, with the assent of the president, may raise any number of troops they please. The present Congress are restrained from an undue exercise of this power, from this consideration, they know that the state legislatures, through whose authority it must be carried into effect, would not comply with the requisition for the purpose, if it was evidently opposed to the public good: the proposed constitution authorizes the legislature to carry their determinations into execution, without the intervention of any other body between them and the people. The Congress under the present form are amenable to, and removable by, the legislatures of the respective states, and are chosen for one year only: the proposed constitution does not make the members of the legislature accountable to, or removeable by the state legislatures at all; and they are chosen, the one house for six, and the other for two years; and cannot be removed until their time of service is expired, let them conduct themselves ever so badly.—The public will judge, from the above comparison, how just a claim this writer has to that candour he affects to possess. In the mean time, to convince him, and the advocates for this system, that I possess some share of candor, I pledge myself to give up all opposition to it, on the head of standing armies, if the power to raise them be restricted as it is in the present confederation; and I believe I may safely answer, not only for myself, but for all who make the objection, that they will be satisfied with less.

Brutus.

– X –

24 January 1788

To the People of the State of New-York.

1. The liberties of a people are in danger from a large standing army, not only because the rulers may employ them for the purposes of supporting themselves in any usurpations of power, which they may see proper to exercise, but there is great hazard, that an army will subvert the forms of the government, under whose authority, they are raised, and establish one, according to the pleasure of their leader.

2. We are informed, in the faithful pages of history, of such events frequently happening.—Two instances have been mentioned in a former

paper.[76] They are so remarkable, that they are worthy of the most careful attention of every lover of freedom.—They are taken from the history of the two most powerful nations that have ever existed in the world; and who are the most renowned, for the freedom they enjoyed, and the excellency of their constitutions:—I mean Rome and Britain.

3. In the first, the liberties of the commonwealth was destroyed, and the constitution overturned, by an army, lead by Julius Cesar, who was appointed to the command, by the constitutional authority of that commonwealth. He changed it from a free republic, whose fame had sounded, and is still celebrated by all the world, into that of the most absolute despotism. A standing army effected this change, and a standing army supported it through a succession of ages, which are marked in the annals of history, with the most horrid cruelties, bloodshed, and carnage;—The most devilish, beastly, and unnatural vices, that ever punished or disgraced human nature.

4. The same army, that in Britain, vindicated the liberties of that people from the encroachments and despotism of a tyrant king, assisted Cromwell, their General, in wresting from the people, that liberty they had so dearly earned.

5. You may be told, these instances will not apply to our case:—But those who would persuade you to believe this, either mean to deceive you, or have not themselves considered the subject.

6. I firmly believe, no country in the world had ever a more patriotic army, than the one which so ably served this country, in the late war.

7. But had the General who commanded them, been possessed of the spirit of a Julius Cesar or a Cromwell, the liberties of this country, had in all probability, terminated with the war; or had they been maintained, might have cost more blood and treasure, than was expended in the conflict with Great-Britain. When an anonimous writer addressed the officers of the army at the close of the war, advising them not to part with their arms, until justice was done them—the effect it had is well known.[77] It affected them

76. *Brutus VIII* (11–12).
77. The reference is to the so-called Newburgh conspiracy of 1783, an effort to rally the army to stand up to Congress over back pay. The "conspiracy" was blunted by George Washington's speech to the officers in Newburgh on March 15, 1783, in which Washington, groping for his eyeglasses in order to read a letter to the officers, famously said, "I have grown gray in the service of my country and now feel myself growing blind." His speech, calling the officers to "reason and virtue," effectively ended the danger.

like an electric shock. He wrote like Cesar; and had the commander in chief, and a few more officers of rank, countenanced the measure, the desperate resolution had been taken, to refuse to disband. What the consequences of such a determination would have been, heaven only knows.—The army were in the full vigor of health and spirits, in the habit of discipline, and possessed of all our military stores and apparatus. They would have acquired great accessions of strength from the country.—Those who were disgusted at our republican forms of government (for such there then were, of high rank among us) would have lent them all their aid.—We should in all probability have seen a constitution and laws, dictated to us, at the head of an army, and at the point of a bayonet, and the liberties for which we had so severely struggled, snatched from us in a moment. It remains a secret, yet to be revealed, whether this measure was not suggested, or at least countenanced, by some, who have had great influence in producing the present system.[78]—Fortunately indeed for this country, it had at the head of the army, a patriot as well as a general; and many of our principal officers, had not abandoned the characters of citizens, by assuming that of soldiers, and therefore, the scheme proved abortive. But are we to expect, that this will always be the case? Are we so much better than the people of other ages and of other countries, that the same allurements of power and greatness, which led them aside from their duty, will have no influence upon men in our country? Such an idea, is wild and extravagant.—Had we indulged such a delusion, enough has appeared in a little time past, to convince the most credulous, that the passion for pomp, power and greatness, works as powerfully in the hearts of many of our better sort, as it ever did in any country under heaven.—Were the same opportunity again to offer, we should very probably be grossly disappointed, if we made dependence, that all who then rejected the overture, would do it again.

8. From these remarks, it appears, that the evil to be feared from a large standing army in time of peace, does not arise solely from the apprehension, that the rulers may employ them for the purpose of promoting their own ambitious views, but that equal, and perhaps greater danger, is to be

---

78. It was suspected then (as now) that Robert Morris and others who favored a more nationalist frame of government were somewhere behind the conspiracy. It is sometimes thought that Alexander Hamilton was also involved. In the New York context of the *Brutus* letters, it is very likely that Hamilton is the target of Brutus's insinuation.

apprehended from their overturning the constitutional powers of the government, and assuming the power to dictate any form they please.

9. The advocates for power, in support of this right in the proposed government, urge that a restraint upon the discretion of the legislatures, in respect to military establishments in time of peace, would be improper to be imposed, because they say, it will be necessary to maintain small garrisons on the frontiers, to guard against the depredations of the Indians, and to be prepared to repel any encroachments or invasions that may be made by Spain or Britain.[79]

10. The amount of this argument striped of the abundant verbages with which the author has dressed it, is this:

11. It will probably be necessary to keep up a small body of troops to garrison a few posts, which it will be necessary to maintain, in order to guard against the sudden encroachments of the Indians, or of the Spaniards and British; and therefore, the general government ought to be invested with power to raise and keep up a standing army in time of peace, without restraint; at their discretion.

12. I confess, I cannot perceive that the conclusion follows from the premises. Logicians say, it is not good reasoning to infer a general conclusion from particular premises: though I am not much of a Logician, it seems to me, this argument is very like that species of reasoning.

13. When the patriots in the parliament in Great-Britain, contended with such force of argument, and all the powers of eloquence, against keeping up standing armies in time of peace, it is obvious, they never entertained an idea, that small garrisons on their frontiers, or in the neighbourhood of powers, from whom they were in danger of encroachments, or guards, to take care of public arsenals would thereby be prohibited.

14. The advocates for this power farther urge that it is necessary, because it may, and probably will happen, that circumstances will render it requisite to raise an army to be prepared to repel attacks of an enemy, before a formal declaration of war, which in modern times has fallen into disuse.[80] If the constitution prohibited the raising an army, until a war actually commenced, it would deprive the government of the power of providing for the defence of the country, until the enemy were within our territory. If the restriction is not to extend to the raising armies in cases of emergency, but only to the keeping them up, this would leave the matter to the discretion

79. *Federalist* 24.
80. *Federalist* 25.

of the legislature; and they might, under the pretence that there was danger of an invasion, keep up the army as long as they judged proper—and hence it is inferred, that the legislature should have authority to raise and keep up an army without any restriction. But from these premises nothing more will follow than this, that the legislature should not be so restrained, as to put it out of their power to raise an army, when such exigencies as are instanced shall arise. But it does not thence follow, that the government should be empowered to raise and maintain standing armies at their discretion as well in peace as in war. If indeed, it is impossible to vest the general government with the power of raising troops to garrison the frontier posts, to guard arsenals, or to be prepared to repel an attack, when we saw a power preparing to make one, without giving them a general and indefinite authority, to raise and keep up armies, without any restriction or qualification, then this reasoning might have weight; but this has not been proved nor can it be.

15. It is admitted that to prohibit the general government, from keeping up standing armies, while yet they were authorised to raise them in case of exigency, would be an insufficient guard against the danger. A discretion of such latitude would give room to elude the force of the provision.

16. It is also admitted that an absolute prohibition against raising troops, except in cases of actual war, would be improper; because it will be requisite to raise and support a small number of troops to garrison the important frontier posts, and to guard arsenals; and it may happen, that the danger of an attack from a foreign power may be so imminent, as to render it highly proper we should raise an army, in order to be prepared to resist them. But to raise and keep up forces for such purposes and on such occasions, is not included in the idea, of keeping up standing armies in times of peace.

17. It is a thing very practicable to give the government sufficient authority to provide for these cases, and at the same time to provide a reasonable and competent security against the evil of a standing army—a clause to the following purpose would answer the end:

18. As standing armies in time of peace are dangerous to liberty, and have often been the means of overturning the best constitutions of government, no standing army, or troops of any description whatsoever, shall be raised or kept up by the legislature, except so many as shall be necessary for guards to the arsenals of the United States, or for garrisons to such posts on the frontiers, as it shall be deemed absolutely necessary to hold, to secure the inhabitants, and facilitate the trade with the Indians: unless when the United States are threatened with an attack or invasion from some foreign power, in which case the legislature shall be authorised to raise an army to

be prepared to repel the attack; provided that no troops whatsoever shall be raised in time of peace, without the assent of two thirds of the members, composing both houses of the legislature.

19. A clause similar to this would afford sufficient latitude to the legislature to raise troops in all cases that were really necessary, and at the same time competent security against the establishment of that dangerous engine of despotism a standing army.

20. The same writer who advances the arguments I have noticed, makes a number of other observations with a view to prove that the power to raise and keep up armies, ought to be discretionary in the general legislature; some of them are curious; he instances the raising of troops in Massachusetts and Pennsylvania, to shew the necessity of keeping a standing army in time of peace;[81] the least reflection must convince every candid mind that both these cases are totally foreign to his purpose—Massachusetts raised a body of troops for six months, at the expiration of which they were to disband of course; this looks very little like a standing army. But beside, was that commonwealth in a state of peace at that time? So far from it that they were in the most violent commotions and contents, and their legislature had formally declared that an unnatural rebellion existed within the state.[82] The situation of Pennsylvania was similar; a number of armed men had levied war against the authority of the state, and openly avowed their intention of withdrawing their allegiance from it.[83] To what purpose examples are brought, of states raising troops for short periods in times of war or insurrections, on a question concerning the propriety of keeping up standing armies in times of peace, the public must judge.

21. It is farther said, that no danger can arise from this power being lodged in the hands of the general government, because the legislatures will be a check upon them, to prevent their abusing it.[84]

22. This is offered, as what force there is in it will hereafter receive a more particular examination. At present, I shall only remark, that it is difficult to conceive how the state legislatures can, in any case, hold a check over the general legislature, in a constitutional way. The latter has, in every instance to which their powers extend, complete controul over the former.

81. Ibid.
82. The reference is to Shays' Rebellion, an armed debtors' movement in 1786–87.
83. The reference is to events in Pennsylvania's Wyoming Valley, where a movement to secede from the state gained supporters in 1787.
84. *Federalist* 26.

The state legislatures can, in no case, by law, resolution, or otherwise, of right, prevent or impede the general government, from enacting any law, or executing it, which this constitution authorizes them to enact or execute. If then the state legislatures check the general legislatures [*sic*], it must be by exciting the people to resist constitutional laws. In this way every individual, or every body of men, may check any government, in proportion to the influence they may have over the body of the people. But such kinds of checks as these, though they sometimes correct the abuses of government, oftner destroy all government.[85]

23. It is further said, that no danger is to be apprehended from the exercise of this power, because it is lodged in the hands of representatives of the people; if they abuse it, it is in the power of the people to remove them, and chuse others who will pursue their interests.[86] Not to repeat what has been said before, That it is unwise in any people, to authorize their rulers to do, what, if done, would prove injurious—I have, in some former numbers, shewn, that the representation in the proposed government will be a mere shadow without the substance.[87] I am so confident that I am well founded in this opinion, that I am persuaded, if it was to be adopted or rejected, upon a fair discussion of its merits, without taking into contemplation circumstances extraneous to it, as reasons for its adoption, nineteen-twentieths of the sensible men in the union would reject it on this account alone; unless its powers were confined to much fewer objects than it embraces.

Brutus.

– XI –

31 January 1788

1. The nature and extent of the judicial power of the United States, proposed to be granted by this constitution, claims our particular attention.

2. Much has been said and written upon the subject of this new system on both sides, but I have not met with any writer, who has discussed the judicial powers with any degree of accuracy. And yet it is obvious, that we can form but very imperfect ideas of the manner in which this government will work, or the effect it will have in changing the internal police and mode of distributing justice at present subsisting in the respective states, without

85. See *FF X* (2); Smith speech June 25, 1788 (31).
86. *Federalist* 26.
87. *Brutus I, III, IV.*

a thorough investigation of the powers of the judiciary and of the manner in which they will operate. This government is a complete system, not only for making, but for executing laws. And the courts of law, which will be constituted by it, are not only to decide upon the constitution and the laws made in pursuance of it, but by officers subordinate to them to execute all their decisions. The real effect of this system of government, will therefore be brought home to the feelings of the people, through the medium of the judicial power. It is, moreover, of great importance, to examine with care the nature and extent of the judicial power, because those who are to be vested with it, are to be placed in a situation altogether unprecedented in a free country. They are to be rendered totally independent, both of the people and the legislature, both with respect to their offices and salaries. No errors they may commit can be corrected by any power above them, if any such power there be, nor can they be removed from office for making ever so many erroneous adjudications.

3. The only causes for which they can be displaced, is, conviction of treason, bribery, and high crimes and misdemeanors.[88]

4. This part of the plan is so modelled, as to authorise the courts, not only to carry into execution the powers expressly given, but where these are wanting or ambiguously expressed, to supply what is wanting by their own decisions.

5. That we may be enabled to form a just opinion on this subject, I shall, in considering it,

[1st] Examine the nature and extent of the judicial powers—and
[2d] Enquire, whether the courts who are to exercise them, are so constituted as to afford reasonable ground of confidence, that they will exercise them for the general good.

6. With a regard to the nature and extent of the judicial powers, I have to regret my want of capacity to give that full and minute explanation of them that the subject merits. To be able to do this, a man should be possessed of a degree of law knowledge far beyond what I pretend to. A number of hard words and technical phrases are used in this part of the system, about the meaning of which gentlemen learned in the law differ.

7. Its advocates know how to avail themselves of these phrases. In a num-

---

88. U.S. Constitution, Art. 3, sect. 1; Art. 1, sects. 2 and 3; Art. 2, sect. 4.

ber of instances, where objections are made to the powers given to the judicial, they give such an explanation to the technical terms as to avoid them.

8. Though I am not competent to give a perfect explanation of the powers granted to this department of the government, I shall yet attempt to
trace some of the leading features of it, from which I presume it will appear,
that they will operate to a total subversion of the state judiciaries, if not, to
the legislative authority of the states.

9. In article 3d, sect. 2d, it is said, "The judicial power shall extend to
all cases in law and equity arising under this constitution, the laws of the
United States, and treaties made, or which shall be made, under their authority, &c."

10. The first article to which this power extends, is, all cases in law and
equity arising under this constitution.

11. What latitude of construction this clause should receive, it is not easy
to say. At first view, one would suppose, that it meant no more than this,
that the courts under the general government should exercise, not only the
powers of courts of law, but also that of courts of equity, in the manner in
which those powers are usually exercised in the different states. But this
cannot be the meaning, because the next clause authorises the courts to
take cognizance of all cases in law and equity arising under the laws of the
United States; this last article, I conceive, conveys as much power to the
general judicial as any of the state courts possess.

12. The cases arising under the constitution must be different from those
arising under the laws, or else the two clauses mean exactly the same thing.

13. The cases arising under the constitution must include such, as bring
into question its meaning, and will require an explanation of the nature and
extent of the powers of the different departments under it.

14. This article, therefore, vests the judicial with a power to resolve all
questions that may arise on any case on the construction of the constitution, either in law or in equity.

15. [1st] They are authorised to determine all questions that may arise
upon the meaning of the constitution in law. This article vests the courts
with authority to give the constitution a legal construction, or to explain
it according to the rules laid down for construing a law.—These rules
give a certain degree of latitude of explanation. According to this mode
of construction, the courts are to give such meaning to the constitution as
comports best with the common, and generally received acceptation of the
words in which it is expressed, regarding their ordinary and popular use,

rather than their grammatical propriety. Where words are dubious, they will be explained by the context. The end of the clause will be attended to, and the words will be understood, as having a view to it; and the words will not be so understood as to bear no meaning or a very absurd one.

16. [2d] The judicial are not only to decide questions arising upon the meaning of the constitution in law, but also in equity.

17. By this they are empowered, to explain the constitution according to the reasoning spirit of it, without being confined to the words or letter.

18. "From this method of interpreting laws (says Blackstone) by the reason of them, arises what we call equity"; which is thus defined by Grotius, "the correction of that, wherein the law, by reason of its universality, is deficient"; for since in laws all cases cannot be foreseen, or expressed, it is necessary, that when the decrees of the law cannot be applied to particular cases, there should some where be a power vested of defining those circumstances, which had they been foreseen the legislator would have expressed; and these are the cases, which according to Grotius, "lex non exacte definit, sed arbitrio boni viri permittet."[89]

19. The same learned author observes, "That equity, thus depending essentially upon each individual case, there can be no established rules and fixed principles of equity laid down, without destroying its very essence, and reducing it to a positive law."[90]

20. From these remarks, the authority and business of the courts of law, under this clause, may be understood.

21. They will give the sense of every article of the constitution, that may from time to time come before them. And in their decisions they will not confine themselves to any fixed or established rules, but will determine, according to what appears to them, the reason and spirit of the constitution. The opinions of the supreme court, whatever they may be, will have the force of law; because there is no power provided in the constitution, that can correct their errors, or controul their adjudications. From this court there is no appeal. And I conceive the legislature themselves, cannot set aside a judgment of this court, because they are authorised by the constitution to decide in the last resort. The legislature must be controuled by the

89. "The law does not define exactly, but allows the decision of good men."
90. William Blackstone, *Commentaries on the Laws of England* (Chicago, University of Chicago Press, 1979), I, 61–62. The quotations from Grotius are taken from Blackstone.

constitution, and not the constitution by them. They have therefore no more right to set aside any judgment pronounced upon the construction of the constitution, than they have to take from the president, the chief command of the army and navy, and commit it to some other person. The reason is plain; the judicial and executive derive their authority from the same source, that the legislature do theirs; and therefore in all cases, where the constitution does not make the one responsible to, or controulable by the other, they are altogether independent of each other.

22. The judicial power will operate to effect, in the most certain, but yet silent and imperceptible manner, what is evidently the tendency of the constitution:—I mean, an entire subversion of the legislative, executive and judicial powers of the individual states. Every adjudication of the supreme court, on any question that may arise upon the nature and extent of the general government, will affect the limits of the state jurisdiction. In proportion as the former enlarge the exercise of their powers, will that of the latter be restricted.

23. That the judicial power of the United States, will lean strongly in favour of the general government, and will give such an explanation to the constitution, as will favour an extension of its jurisdiction, is very evident from a variety of considerations.

24. [1st] The constitution itself strongly countenances such a mode of construction. Most of the articles in this system, which convey powers of any considerable importance, are conceived in general and indefinite terms, which are either equivocal, ambiguous, or which require long definitions to unfold the extent of their meaning. The two most important powers committed to any government, those of raising money, and of raising and keeping up troops, have already been considered, and shewn to be unlimited by any thing but the discretion of the legislature.[91] The clause which vests the power to pass all laws which are proper and necessary, to carry the powers given into execution, it has been shewn, leaves the legislature at liberty, to do every thing, which in their judgment is best.[92] It is said, I know, that this clause confers no power on the legislature, which they would not have had without it[93]—though I believe this is not the fact, yet, admitting it to be,

91. *Brutus V–X.*
92. *Brutus I* (7, 10–11), *V* (3); *FF IV* (7).
93. *Federalist* 33.

it implies that the constitution is not to receive an explanation strictly, according to its letter; but more power is implied than is expressed. And this clause, if it is to be considered, as explanatory of the extent of the powers given, rather than giving a new power, is to be understood as declaring, that in construing any of the articles conveying power, the spirit, intent and design of the clause, should be attended to, as well as the words in their common acceptation.

25. This constitution gives sufficient colour for adopting an equitable construction, if we consider the great end and design it professedly has in view—these appear from its preamble to be, "to form a more perfect union, establish justice, insure domestic tranquility, provide for the common defence, promote the general welfare, and secure the blessings of liberty to ourselves and posterity." The design of this system is here expressed, and it is proper to give such a meaning to the various parts, as will best promote the accomplishment of the end; this idea suggests itself naturally upon reading the preamble, and will countenance the court in giving the several articles such a sense, as will the most effectually promote the ends the constitution had in view—how this manner of explaining the constitution will operate in practice, shall be the subject of future enquiry.

26. [2d] Not only will the constitution justify the courts in inclining to this mode of explaining it, but they will be interested in using this latitude of interpretation. Every body of men invested with office are tenacious of power; they feel interested, and hence it has become a kind of maxim, to hand down their offices, with all its rights and privileges, unimpared to their successors; the same principle will influence them to extend their power, and increase their rights; this of itself will operate strongly upon the courts to give such a meaning to the constitution in all cases where it can possibly be done, as will enlarge the sphere of their own authority. Every extension of the power of the general legislature, as well as of the judicial powers, will increase the powers of the courts; and the dignity and importance of the judges, will be in proportion to the extent and magnitude of the powers they exercise. I add, it is highly probable the emolument of the judges will be increased, with the increase of the business they will have to transact and its importance. From these considerations the judges will be interested to extend the powers of the courts, and to construe the constitution as much as possible, in such a way as to favour it; and that they will do it, appears probable.

27. [3d] Because they will have precedent to plead, to justify them in it. It is well known, that the courts in England, have by their own authority,

extended their jurisdiction far beyond the limits set them in their original institution, and by the laws of the land.

28. The court of exchequer is a remarkable instance of this. It was originally intended principally to recover the king's debts, and to order the revenues of the crown. It had a common law jurisdiction, which was established merely for the benefit of the king's accomptants. We learn from Blackstone, that the proceedings in this court are grounded on a writ called quo minus, in which the plaintiff suggests, that he is the king's farmer or debtor, and that the defendant hath done him the damage complained of, by which he is less able to pay the king.[94] These suits, by the statute of Rutland, are expressly directed to be confined to such matters as specially concern the king, or his ministers in the exchequer. And by the articuli super cartas,[95] it is enacted, that no common pleas be thenceforth held in the exchequer contrary to the form of the great charter: but now any person may sue in the exchequer. The surmise of being debtor to the king being matter of form, and mere words of course; and the court is open to all the nation.

29. When the courts will have a precedent before them of a court which extended its jurisdiction in opposition to an act of the legislature, is it not to be expected that they will extend theirs, especially when there is nothing in the constitution expressly against it? and they are authorised to construe its meaning, and are not under any controul?

30. This power in the judicial, will enable them to mould the government, into almost any shape they please.—The manner in which this may be effected we will hereafter examine.

Brutus.

– XII –

7 February 1788

1. In my last, I shewed, that the judicial power of the United States under the first clause of the second section of article eight, would be authorized to explain the constitution, not only according to its letter, but according to its spirit and intention; and having this power, they would strongly incline to

---

94. Blackstone, *Commentaries on the Laws of England*, III, 42.

95. The *articuli super cartas*, "articles upon charters," confirmed by Edward I of England (1300), supplemented and enforced Magna Charta, as well as the Charter of the Forest.

give it such a construction as to extend the powers of the general government, as much as possible, to the diminution, and finally to the destruction, of that of the respective states.

2. I shall now proceed to shew how this power will operate in its exercise to effect these purposes. In order to perceive the extent of its influence, I shall consider,

First. How it will tend to extend the legislative authority.

Second. In what manner it will increase the jurisdiction of the courts, and

Third. The way in which it will diminish, and destroy, both the legislative and judicial authority of the United States.

3. First. Let us enquire how the judicial power will effect an extension of the legislative authority.

Perhaps the judicial power will not be able, by direct and positive decrees, ever to direct the legislature, because it is not easy to conceive how a question can be brought before them in a course of legal discussion, in which they can give a decision, declaring, that the legislature have certain powers which they have not exercised, and which, in consequence of the determination of the judges, they will be bound to exercise. But it is easy to see, that in their adjudications they may establish certain principles, which being received by the legislature, will enlarge the sphere of their power beyond all bounds.

4. It is to be observed, that the supreme court has the power, in the last resort, to determine all questions that may arise in the course of legal discussion, on the meaning and construction of the constitution. This power they will hold under the constitution, and independent of the legislature. The latter can no more deprive the former of this right, than either of them, or both of them together, can take from the president, with the advice of the senate, the power of making treaties, or appointing ambassadors.[96]

5. In determining these questions, the court must and will assume certain principles, from which they will reason, in forming their decisions. These principles, whatever they may be, when they become fixed, by a course of decisions, will be adopted by the legislature, and will be the rule by which they will explain their own powers. This appears evident from this consideration, that if the legislature pass laws, which, in the judgment of the court, they are not authorised to do by the constitution, the court will not take notice of them; for it will not be denied, that the constitution is

96. But see *Brutus XIV* (14); *FF IV* (3).

the highest or supreme law. And the courts are vested with the supreme and uncontroulable power, to determine, in all cases that come before them, what the constitution means; they cannot, therefore, execute a law, which, in their judgment, opposes the constitution, unless we can suppose they can make a superior law give way to an inferior. The legislature, therefore, will not go over the limits by which the courts may adjudge they are confined. And there is little room to doubt but that they will come up to those bounds, as often as occasion and opportunity may offer, and they may judge it proper to do it. For as on the one hand, they will not readily pass laws which they know the courts will not execute, so on the other, we may be sure they will not scruple to pass such as they know they will give effect, as often as they may judge it proper.

6. From these observations it appears, that the judgment of the judicial, on the constitution, will become the rule to guide the legislature in their construction of their powers.

7. What the principles are, which the courts will adopt, it is impossible for us to say; but taking up the powers as I have explained them in my last number, which they will possess under this clause, it is not difficult to see, that they may, and probably will, be very liberal ones.

8. We have seen, that they will be authorized to give the constitution a construction according to its spirit and reason, and not to confine themselves to its letter.

9. To discover the spirit of the constitution, it is of the first importance to attend to the principal ends and designs it has in view. These are expressed in the preamble, in the following words, viz. "We, the people of the United States, in order to form a more perfect union, establish justice, insure domestic tranquility, provide for the common defence, promote the general welfare, and secure the blessings of liberty to ourselves and our posterity, do ordain and establish this constitution," &c. If the end of the government is to be learned from these words, which are clearly designed to declare it, it is obvious it has in view every object which is embraced by any government. The preservation of internal peace—the due administration of justice—and to provide for the defence of the community, seems to include all the objects of government; but if they do not, they are certainly comprehended in the words, "to provide for the general welfare." If it be further considered, that this constitution, if it is ratified, will not be a compact entered into by states, in their corporate capacities, but an agreement of the people of the United States, as one great body politic, no doubt can

remain, but that the great end of the constitution, if it is to be collected from the preamble, in which its end is declared, is to constitute a government which is to extend to every case for which any government is instituted, whether external or internal. The courts, therefore, will establish this as a principle in expounding the constitution, and will give every part of it such an explanation, as will give latitude to every department under it, to take cognizance of every matter, not only that affects the general and national concerns of the union, but also of such as relate to the administration of private justice, and to regulating the internal and local affairs of the different parts.

10. Such a rule of exposition is not only consistent with the general spirit of the preamble, but it will stand confirmed by considering more minutely the different clauses of it.

11. The first object declared to be in view is, "To form a perfect union." It is to be observed, it is not an union of states or bodies corporate; had this been the case the existence of the state governments, might have been secured. But it is a union of the people of the United States considered as one body, who are to ratify this constitution, if it is adopted. Now to make a union of this kind perfect, it is necessary to abolish all inferior governments, and to give the general one compleat legislative, executive and judicial powers to every purpose. The courts therefore will establish it as a rule in explaining the constitution to give it such a construction as will best tend to perfect the union or take from the state governments every power of either making or executing laws. The second object is "to establish justice." This must include not only the idea of instituting the rule of justice, or of making laws which shall be the measure or rule of right, but also of providing for the application of this rule or of administering justice under it. And under this the courts will in their decisions extend the power of the government to all cases they possibly can, or otherwise they will be restricted in doing what appears to be the intent of the constitution they should do, to wit, pass laws and provide for the execution of them, for the general distribution of justice between man and man. Another end declared is "to insure domestic tranquility." This comprehends a provision against all private breaches of the peace, as well as against all public commotions or general insurrections; and to attain the object of this clause fully, the government must exercise the power of passing laws on these subjects, as well as of appointing magistrates with authority to execute them. And the courts will adopt these ideas in their expositions. I might proceed to the other clause, in the preamble, and it would appear by a consideration of all of

them separately, as it does by taking them together, that if the spirit of this system is to be known from its declared end and design in the preamble, its spirit is to subvert and abolish all the powers of the state government, and to embrace every object to which any government extends.

12. As it sets out in the preamble with this declared intention, so it proceeds in the different parts with the same idea. Any person, who will peruse the 8th section with attention, in which most of the powers are enumerated, will perceive that they either expressly or by implication extend to almost every thing about which any legislative power can be employed. But if this equitable mode of construction is applied to this part of the constitution; nothing can stand before it.

13. This will certainly give the first clause in that article a construction which I confess I think the most natural and grammatical one, to authorise the Congress to do any thing which in their judgment will tend to provide for the general welfare, and this amounts to the same thing as general and unlimited powers of legislation in all cases.

(To be continued.)

– XII –

14 February 1788
(Continued from last Thursday's paper.)

14. This same manner of explaining the constitution, will fix a meaning, and a very important one too, to the 12th [18th?] clause of the same section, which authorises the Congress to make all laws which shall be proper and necessary for carrying into effect the foregoing powers, &c. A voluminous writer in favor of this system, has taken great pains to convince the public, that this clause means nothing: for that the same powers expressed in this, are implied in other parts of the constitution.[97] Perhaps it is so, but still this will undoubtedly be an excellent auxilliary to assist the courts to discover the spirit and reason of the constitution, and when applied to any and every of the other clauses granting power, will operate powerfully in extracting the spirit from them.

15. I might instance a number of clauses in the constitution, which, if explained in an *equitable* manner, would extend the powers of the government to every case, and reduce the state legislatures to nothing; but, I should

97. *Federalist* 33, 44.

draw out my remarks to an undue length, and I presume enough has been said to shew, that the courts have sufficient ground in the exercise of this power, to determine, that the legislature have no bounds set to them by this constitution, by any supposed right the legislatures of the respective states may have, to regulate any of their local concerns.

16. I proceed, 2d, To inquire, in what manner this power will increase the jurisdiction of the courts.

17. I would here observe, that the judicial power extends, expressly, to all civil cases that may arise save such as arise between citizens of the same state, with this exception to those of that description, that the judicial of the United States have cognizance of cases between citizens of the same state, claiming lands under grants of different states.[98] Nothing more, therefore, is necessary to give the courts of law, under this constitution, complete jurisdiction of all civil causes, but to comprehend cases between citizens of the same state not included in the foregoing exception.

18. I presume there will be no difficulty in accomplishing this. Nothing more is necessary than to set forth, in the process, that the party who brings the suit is a citizen of a different state from the one against whom the suit is brought, and there can be little doubt but that the court will take cognizance of the matter, and if they do, who is to restrain them?[99] Indeed, I will freely confess, that it is my decided opinion, that the courts ought to take cognizance of such causes, under the powers of the constitution. For one of the great ends of the constitution is, "to establish justice." This supposes that this cannot be done under the existing governments of the states; and there is certainly as good reason why individuals, living in the same state, should have justice, as those who live in different states. Moreover, the constitution expressly declares, that "the citizens of each state shall be entitled to all the privileges and immunities of citizens in the several states."[100] It will therefore be no fiction, for a citizen of one state to set forth, in a suit, that he is a citizen of another; for he that is entitled to all the privileges and immunities of a country, is a citizen of that country. And in truth, the citizen of one state will, under this constitution, be a citizen of every state.

19. But supposing that the party, who alledges that he is a citizen of another state, has recourse to fiction in bringing in his suit, it is well known, that the courts have high authority to plead, to justify them in suffering

98. U.S. Constitution, Art. 3, sect. 2.
99. Cf. *FF XVIII* (10).
100. U.S. Constitution, Art. 4, sect. 2.

actions to be brought before them by such fictions. In my last number I stated, that the court of exchequer tried all causes in virtue of such a fiction. The court of king's bench, in England, extended their jurisdiction in the same way. Originally, this court held pleas, in civil cases, only of trespasses and other injuries alledged to be committed *vi et armis*.[101] They might likewise, says Blackstone, upon the division of the *aula regia*,[102] have originally held pleas of any other civil action whatsoever (except in real actions which are now very seldom in use) provided the defendant was an officer of the court, or in the custody of the marshall or prison-keeper of this court, for breach of the peace, &c.[103] In process of time, by a fiction, this court began to hold pleas of any personal action whatsoever; it being surmised, that the defendant has been arrested for a supposed trespass that "he has never committed, and being thus in the custody of the marshall of the court, the plaintiff is at liberty to proceed against him, for any other personal injury: which surmise of being in the marshall's custody, the defendant is not at liberty to dispute." By a much less fiction, may the pleas of the courts of the United States extend to cases between citizens of the same state. I shall add no more on this head, but proceed briefly to remark, in what way this power will diminish and destroy both the legislative and judicial authority of the states.

20. It is obvious that these courts will have authority to decide upon the validity of the laws of any of the states, in all cases where they come in question before them. Where the constitution gives the general government exclusive jurisdiction, they will adjudge all laws made by the states, in such cases, void *ab initio*. Where the constitution gives them concurrent jurisdiction, the laws of the United States must prevail, because they are the supreme law. In such cases, therefore, the laws of the state legislatures must be repealed, restricted, or so construed, as to give full effect to the laws of the union on the same subject. From these remarks it is easy to see, that in proportion as the general government acquires power and jurisdiction, by the liberal construction which the judges may give the constitution, will those of the states lose its rights, until they become so trifling and unimportant, as not to be worth having. I am much mistaken, if this system will

101. "By force and arms."

102. "The hall of the king," the hall in which William the Conqueror personally dispensed justice as king. The hall could be anywhere the king was in residence at the time. It was later replaced by the creation of the central courts at Westminster.

103. Blackstone, *Commentaries on the Laws of England*, III, 42.

not operate to effect this with as much celerity, as those who have the administration of it will think prudent to suffer it. The remaining objections to the judicial power shall be considered in a future paper.

Brutus.

– XIII –

21 February 1788

1. Having in the two preceding numbers, examined the nature and tendency of the judicial power, as it respects the explanation of the constitution, I now proceed to the consideration of the other matters, of which it has cognizance.—The next paragraph extends its authority, to all cases, in law and equity, arising under the laws of the United States. This power, as I understand it, is a proper one. The proper province of the judicial power, in any government, is, as I conceive, to declare what is the law of the land. To explain and enforce those laws, which the supreme power or legislature may pass; but not to declare what the powers of the legislature are. I suppose the cases in equity, under the laws, must be so construed, as to give the supreme court not only a legal, but equitable jurisdiction of cases which may be brought before them, or in other words, so as to give them, not only the powers which are now exercised by our courts of law, but those also, which are now exercised by our court of chancery. If this be the meaning, I have no other objection to the power, than what arises from the undue extension of the legislative power. For, I conceive that the judicial power should be commensurate with the legislative. Or, in other words, the supreme court should have authority to determine questions arising under the laws of the union.

2. The next paragraph which gives a power to decide in law and equity, on all cases arising under treaties, is unintelligible to me. I can readily comprehend what is meant by deciding a case under a treaty. For as treaties will be the law of the land, every person who have rights or privileges secured by treaty, will have aid of the courts of law, in recovering them. But I do not understand, what is meant by equity arising under a treaty. I presume every right which can be claimed under a treaty, must be claimed by virtue of some article or clause contained in it, which gives the right in plain and obvious words; or at least, I conceive, that the rules for explaining treaties, are so well ascertained, that there is no need of having recourse to an equitable construction. If under this power, the courts are to explain treaties, according to what they conceive are their spirit, which

is nothing less than a power to give them whatever extension they may judge proper, it is a dangerous and improper power. The cases affecting ambassadors, public ministers, and consuls—of admiralty and maritime jurisdiction; controversies to which the United States are a party, and controversies between states, it is proper should be under the cognizance of the courts of the union, because none but the general government, can, or ought to pass laws on their subjects. But, I conceive the clause which extends the power of the judicial to controversies arising between a state and citizens of another state, improper in itself, and will, in its exercise, prove most pernicious and destructive.

3. It is improper, because it subjects a state to answer in a court of law, to the suit of an individual. This is humiliating and degrading to a government, and, what I believe, the supreme authority of no state ever submitted to.

4. The states are now subject to no such actions. All contracts entered into by individuals with states, were made upon the faith and credit of the states; and the individuals never had in contemplation any compulsory mode of obliging the government to fulfil its engagements.

5. The evil consequences that will flow from the exercise of this power, will best appear by tracing it in its operation. The constitution does not direct the mode in which an individual shall commence a suit against a state or the manner in which the judgment of the court shall be carried into execution, but it gives the legislature full power to pass all laws which shall be proper and necessary for the purpose. And they certainly must make provision for these purposes, or otherwise the power of the judicial will be nugatory. For, to what purpose will the power of a judicial be, if they have no mode, in which they can call the parties before them? Or of what use will it be, to call the parties to answer, if after they have given judgment, there is no authority to execute the judgment? We must, therefore, conclude, that the legislature will pass laws which will be effectual in this head. An individual of one state will then have a legal remedy against a state for any demand he may have against a state to which he does not belong. Every state in the union is largely indebted to individuals. For the payment of these debts they have given notes payable to the bearer. At least this is the case in this state. Whenever a citizen of another state becomes possessed of one of these notes, he may commence an action in the supreme court of the general government; and I cannot see any way in which he can be prevented from recovering. It is easy to see, that when this once happens, the notes of the state will pass rapidly from the hands of citizens of the state to those of other states.

6. And when the citizens of other states possess them, they may bring suits against the state for them, and by this means, judgments and executions may be obtained against the state for the whole amount of the state debt. It is certain the state, with the utmost exertions it can make, will not be able to discharge the debt she owes, under a considerable number of years, perhaps with the best management, it will require twenty or thirty years to discharge it. This new system will protract the time in which the ability of the state will enable them to pay off their debt, because all the funds of the state will be transferred to the general government, except those which arise from internal taxes.

7. The situation of the states will be deplorable. By this system, they will surrender to the general government, all the means of raising money, and at the same time, will subject themselves to suits at law, for the recovery of the debts they have contracted in effecting the revolution.

8. The debts of the individual states will amount to a sum, exceeding the domestic debt of the United States; these will be left upon them, with power in the judicial of the general government, to enforce their payment, while the general government will possess an exclusive command of the most productive funds, from which the states can derive money, and a command of every other source of revenue paramount to the authority of any state.

9. It may be said that the apprehension that the judicial power will operate in this manner is merely visionary, for that the legislature will never pass laws that will work these effects. Or if they were disposed to do it, they cannot provide for levying an execution on a state, for where will the officer find property whereon to levy?

10. To this I would reply, if this is a power which will not or cannot be executed, it was useless and unwise to grant it to the judicial. For what purpose is a power given which it is imprudent or impossible to exercise? If it be improper for a government to exercise a power, it is improper they should be vested with it. And it is unwise to authorise a government to do what they cannot effect.

11. As to the idea that the legislature cannot provide for levying an execution on a state, I believe it is not well founded. I presume the last paragraph of the 8th section of article 1, gives the Congress express power to pass any laws they may judge proper and necessary for carrying into execution the power vested in the judicial department. And they must exercise this power, or otherwise the courts of justice will not be able to carry into effect the authorities with which they are invested. For the constitution

does not direct the mode in which the courts are to proceed, to bring parties before them, to try causes, or to carry the judgment of the courts into execution. Unless they are pointed out by law, how are these to proceed, in any of the cases of which they have cognizance? They have the same authority to establish regulations in respect to these matters, where a state is a party, as where an individual is a party. The only difficulty is, on whom shall process be served, when a state is a party, and how shall execution be levied. With regard to the first, the way is easy, either the executive or legislative of the state may be notified, and upon proof being made of the service of the notice, the court may proceed to a hearing of the cause. Execution may be levied on any property of the state, either real or personal. The treasury may be seized by the officers of the general government, or any lands the property of the state, may be made subject to seizure and sale to satisfy any judgment against it. Whether the estate of any individual citizen may not be made answerable for the discharge of judgments against the state, may be worth consideration. In some corporations this is the case.

12. If the power of the judicial under this clause will extend to the cases above stated, it will, if executed, produce the utmost confusion, and in its progress, will crush the states beneath its weight. And if it does not extend to these cases, I confess myself utterly at a loss to give it any meaning. For if the citizen of one state, possessed of a written obligation, given in pursuance of a solemn act of the legislature, acknowledging a debt due to the bearer, and promising to pay it, cannot recover in the supreme court, I can conceive of no case in which they can recover. And it appears to me ridiculous to provide for obtaining judgment against a state, without giving the means of levying execution.

Brutus.

– XIV –

28 February 1788

1. The second paragraph of sect. 2d. art. 3, is in these words: "In all cases affecting ambassadors, other public ministers and consuls, and those in which a state shall be a party, the supreme court shall have original jurisdiction. In all the other cases before mentioned, the supreme court shall have appellate jurisdiction, both as to law and fact, with such exceptions, and under such regulations as the Congress shall make."

2. Although it is proper that the courts of the general government should

have cognizance of all matters affecting ambassadors, foreign ministers, and consuls; yet I question much the propriety of giving the supreme court original jurisdiction in all cases of this kind.

3. Ambassadors, and other public ministers, claim, and are entitled by the law of nations, to certain privileges, and exemptions, both for their persons and their servants.

4. The meanest servant of an ambassador is exempted by the law of nations from being sued for debt. Should a suit be brought against such an one by a citizen, through inadvertency or want of information, he will be subject to an action in the supreme court. All the officers concerned in issuing or executing the process will be liable to like actions. Thus may a citizen of a state be compelled, at great expence and inconveniency, to defend himself against a suit, brought against him in the supreme court, for inadvertently commencing an action against the most menial servant of an ambassador for a just debt.

5. The appellate jurisdiction granted to the supreme court, in this paragraph, has justly been considered as one of the most objectionable parts of the constitution: under this power, appeals may be had from the inferior courts to the supreme, in every case to which the judicial power extends, except in the few instances in which the supreme court will have original jurisdiction.

6. By this article, appeals will lie to the supreme court, in all criminal as well as civil causes. This I know, has been disputed by some; but I presume the point will appear clear to any one, who will attend to the connection of this paragraph with the one that precedes it. In the former, all the cases, to which the power of the judicial shall extend, whether civil or criminal, are enumerated. There is no criminal matter, to which the judicial power of the United States will extend; but such as are included under some one of the cases specified in this section. For this section is intended to define all the cases, of every description, to which the power of the judicial shall reach. But in all these cases it is declared, the supreme court shall have appellate jurisdiction, except in those which affect ambassadors, other public ministers and consuls, and those in which a state shall be a party. If then this section extends the power of the judicial, to criminal cases, it allows appeals in such cases. If the power of the judicial is not extended to criminal matters by this section, I ask, by what part of this system does it appear, that they have any cognizance of them?

7. I believe it is a new and unusual thing to allow appeals in criminal matters. It is contrary to the sense of our laws, and dangerous to the lives

and liberties of the citizen. As our law now stands, a person charged with a crime has a right to a fair and impartial trial by a jury of his country [county?], and their verdict is final. If he is acquitted no other court can call upon him to answer for the same crime. But by this system, a man may have had ever so fair a trial, have been acquitted by ever so respectable a jury of his country; and still the officer of the government who prosecutes, may appeal to the supreme court. The whole matter may have a second hearing. By this means, persons who may have disobliged those who execute the general government, may be subjected to intolerable oppression. They may be kept in long and ruinous confinement, and exposed to heavy and insupportable charges, to procure the attendence of witnesses, and provide the means of their defence, at a great distance from their places of residence.

8. I can scarcely believe there can be a considerate citizen of the United States, that will approve of this appellate jurisdiction, as extending to criminal cases, if they will give themselves time for reflection.

9. Whether the appellate jurisdiction as it respects civil matters, will not prove injurious to the rights of the citizens, and destructive of those privileges which have ever been held sacred by Americans, and whether it will not render the administration of justice intolerably burthensome, intricate, and dilatory, will best appear, when we have considered the nature and operation of this power.

10. It has been the fate of this clause, as it has of most of those, against which unanswerable objections have been offered, to be explained different ways, by the advocates and opponents to the constitution. I confess I do not know what the advocates of the system, would make it mean, for I have not been fortunate enough to see in any publication this clause taken up and considered. It is certain however, they do not admit the explanation which those who oppose the constitution give it, or otherwise they would not so frequently charge them with want of candor, for alledging that it takes away the trial by jury; appeals from an inferior to a superior court, as practised in the civil law courts, are well understood. In these courts, the judges determine both on the law and the fact; and appeals are allowed from the inferior to the superior courts, on the whole merits: the superior tribunal will re-examine all the facts as well as the law, and frequently new facts will be introduced, so as many times to render the cause in the court of appeals very different from what it was in the court below.

11. If the appellate jurisdiction of the supreme court, be understood in the above sense, the term is perfectly intelligible. The meaning then is, that

in all the civil causes enumerated, the supreme court shall have authority to re-examine the whole merits of the case, both with respect to the facts and the law which may arise under it, without the intervention of a jury; that this is the sense of this part of the system appears to me clear, from the express words of it, "in all the other cases before mentioned, the supreme court shall have appellate jurisdiction, both as to law and fact, &c." Who are the supreme court? Does it not consist of the judges? and they are to have the same jurisdiction of the fact as they are to have of the law. They will therefore have the same authority to determine the fact as they will have to determine the law, and no room is left for a jury on appeals to the supreme court.

12. If we understand the appellate jurisdiction in any other way, we shall be left utterly at a loss to give it a meaning; the common law is a stranger to any such jurisdiction: no appeals can lie from any of our common law courts, upon the merits of the case; the only way in which they can go up from an inferior to a superior tribunal is by habeas corpus before a hearing, or by certiorari, or writ of error, after they are determined in the subordinate courts; but in no case, when they are carried up, are the facts re-examined, but they are always taken as established in the inferior courts.

(To be continued.)

– XIV –

6 March 1788

(Continued.)

13. It may still be insisted that this clause does not take away the trial by jury on appeals, but that this may be provided for by the legislature, under that paragraph which authorises them to form regulations and restrictions for the court in the exercise of this power.

14. The natural meaning of this paragraph seems to be no more than this, that Congress may declare, that certain cases shall not be subject to the appellate jurisdiction, and they may point out the mode in which the court shall proceed in bringing up the causes before them, the manner of their taking evidence to establish the facts, and the method of the courts proceeding. But I presume they cannot take from the court the right of deciding on the fact, any more than they can deprive them of the right of determining on the law, when a cause is once before them; for they have the same jurisdiction as to fact, as they have as to the law. But supposing the Congress may under this clause establish the trial by jury on appeals, it

does not seem to me that it will render this article much less exceptionable. An appeal from one court and jury, to another court and jury, is a thing altogether unknown in the laws of our state, and in most of the states in the union. A practice of this kind prevails in the eastern states; actions are there commenced in the inferior courts, and an appeal lies from them on the whole merits to the superior courts: the consequence is well known, very few actions are determined in the lower courts; it is rare that a case of any importance is not carried by appeal to the supreme court, and the jurisdiction of the inferior courts is merely nominal; this has proved so burthensome to the people in Massachusetts, that it was one of the principal causes which excited the insurrection in that state, in the year past; very few sensible and moderate men in that state but what will admit, that the inferior courts are almost entirely useless, and answer very little purpose, save only to accumulate costs against the poor debtors who are already unable to pay their just debts.

15. But the operation of the appellate power in the supreme judicial of the United States, would work infinitely more mischief than any such power can do in a single state.

16. The trouble and expence to the parties would be endless and intolerable. No man can say where the supreme court are to hold their sessions, the presumption is, however, that it must be at the seat of the general government: in this case parties must travel many hundred miles, with their witnesses and lawyers, to prosecute or defend a suit; no man of midling fortune, can sustain the expence of such a law suit, and therefore the poorer and midling class of citizens will be under the necessity of submitting to the demands of the rich and the lordly, in cases that will come under the cognizance of this court. If it be said, that to prevent this oppression, the supreme court will set in different parts of the union, it may be replied, that this would only make the oppression somewhat more tolerable, but by no means so much as to give a chance of justice to the poor and midling class. It is utterly impossible that the supreme court can move into so many different parts of the Union, as to make it convenient or even tolerable to attend before them with witnesses to try causes from every part of the United states; if to avoid the expence and inconvenience of calling witnesses from a great distance, to give evidence before the supreme court, the expedient of taking the deposition of witnesses in writing should be adopted, it would not help the matter. It is of great importance in the distribution of justice that witnesses should be examined face to face, that the parties should have the fairest opportunity of cross examining them in order to bring out the

whole truth; there is something in the manner in which a witness delivers his testimony which cannot be committed to paper, and which yet very frequently gives a complexion to his evidence, very different from what it would bear if committed to writing, besides the expence of taking written testimony would be enormous; those who are acquainted with the costs that arise in the courts, where all the evidence is taken in writing, well know that they exceed beyond all comparison those of the common law courts, where witnesses are examined viva voce.

17. The costs accruing in courts generally advance with the grade of the court; thus the charges attending a suit in our common pleas, is much less than those in the supreme court, and these are much lower than those in the court of chancery; indeed the costs in the last mentioned court, are in many cases so exorbitant and the proceedings so dilatory that the suitor had almost as well give up his demand as to prosecute his suit. We have just reason to suppose, that the costs in the supreme general court will exceed either of our courts; the officers of the general court will be more dignified than those of the states, the lawyers of the most ability will practice in them, and the trouble and expence of attending them will be greater. From all these considerations, it appears, that the expence attending suits in the supreme court will be so great, as to put it out of the power of the poor and midling class of citizens to contest a suit in it.

18. From these remarks it appears, that the administration of justice under the powers of the judicial will be dilatory; that it will be attended with such an heavy expence as to amount to little short of a denial of justice to the poor and middling class of people who in every government stand most in need of the protection of the law; and that the trial by jury, which has so justly been the boast of our fore fathers as well as ourselves is taken away under them.

19. These extraordinary powers in this court are the more objectionable, because there does not appear the least necessity for them, in order to secure a due and impartial distribution of justice.

20. The want of ability or integrity, or a disposition to render justice to every suitor, has not been objected against the courts of the respective states: so far as I have been informed, the courts of justice in all the states, have ever been found ready, to administer justice with promptitude and impartiality according to the laws of the land. It is true in some of the states, paper money has been made, and the debtor authorised to discharge his debts with it, at a depreciated value, in others, tender laws have been passed, obliging the creditor to receive on execution other property than money in

discharge of his demand, and in several of the states laws have been made unfavorable to the creditor and tending to render property insecure.

21. But these evils have not happened from any defect in the judicial departments of the states; the courts indeed are bound to take notice of these laws, and so will the courts of the general government be under obligation to observe the laws made by the general legislature not repugnant to the constitution; but so far have the judicial been from giving undue latitude of construction to laws of this kind, that they have invariably strongly inclined to the other side. All the acts of our legislature, which have been charged with being of this complexion, have uniformly received the strictest construction by the judges, and have been extended to no cases but to such as came within the strict letter of the law. In this way, have our courts, I will not say evaded the law, but so limited it in its operation as to work the least possible injustice: the same thing has taken place in Rhode-Island, which has justly rendered herself infamous, by her tenaciously adhering to her paper money system. The judges there gave a decision, in opposition to the words of the Statute, on this principle, that a construction according to the words of it, would contradict the fundamental maxims of their laws and constitution.[104]

22. No pretext therefore, can be formed, from the conduct of the judicial courts which will justify giving such powers to the supreme general court, for their decisions have been such as to give just ground of confidence in them, that they will firmly adhere to the principles of rectitude, and there is no necessity of lodging these powers in the courts, in order to guard against the evils justly complained of, on the subject of security of property under this constitution. For it has provided, "that no state shall emit bills of credit, or make any thing but gold and silver coin a tender in payment of debts." It has also declared, that "no state shall pass any law impairing the obligation of contracts."[105]—These prohibitions give the most perfect security against those attacks upon property which I am sorry to say some of the states have but too wantonly made, by passing laws sanctioning fraud in the debtor against his creditor. For "this constitution will be the supreme law of the land, and the judges in every state will be bound thereby; any thing in the constitution and laws of any state to the contrary notwithstanding."[106]

104. *Trevett v. Weeden* (1786). This case is frequently cited as an important state precedent for the power of judicial review.

105. U.S. Constitution, Art. 1, sect. 10.

106. U.S. Constitution, Art. 6.

23. The courts of the respective states might therefore have been securely trusted, with deciding all cases between man and man, whether citizens of the same state or of different states, or between foreigners and citizens, and indeed for ought I see every case that can arise under the constitution or laws of the United States, ought in the first instance to be tried in the court of the state, except those which might arise between states, such as respect ambassadors, or other public ministers, and perhaps such as call in question the claim of lands under grants from different states. The state courts would be under sufficient controul, if writs of error were allowed from the state courts to the supreme court of the union, according to the practice of the courts in England and of this state, on all cases in which the laws of the union are concerned, and perhaps to all cases in which a foreigner is a party.

24. This method would preserve the good old way of administering justice, would bring justice to every man's door, and preserve the inestimable right of trial by jury. It would be following, as near as our circumstances will admit, the practice of the courts in England, which is almost the only thing I would wish to copy in their government.

25. But as this system now stands, there is to be as many inferior courts as Congress may see fit to appoint, who are to be authorised to originate and in the first instance to try all the cases falling under the description of this article;[107] there is no security that a trial by jury shall be had in these courts, but the trial here will soon become, as it is in Massachusetts' inferior courts, mere matter of form; for an appeal may be had to the supreme court on the whole merits. This court is to have power to determine in law and in equity, on the law and the fact, and this court is exalted above all other power in the government, subject to no controul, and so fixed as not to be removeable, but upon impeachment, which I shall hereafter shew, is much the same thing as not to be removeable at all.

26. To obviate the objections made to the judicial power it has been said, that the Congress, in forming the regulations and exceptions which they are authorised to make respecting the appellate jurisdiction, will make provision against all the evils which are apprehended from this article. On this I would remark, that this way of answering the objection made to the power, implies an admission that the power is in itself improper without restraint, and if so, why not restrict it in the first instance.

27. The just way of investigating any power given to a government, is to

107. U.S. Constitution, Art. 3, sect. 1.

examine its operation supposing it to be put in exercise. If upon enquiry, it appears that the power, if exercised, would be prejudicial, it ought not to be given. For to answer objections made to a power given to a government, by saying it will never be exercised, is really admitting that the power ought not to be exercised, and therefore ought not to be granted.

Brutus.

– XV[108] –

20 March 1788

1. I said in my last number, that the supreme court under this constitution would be exalted above all other power in the government, and subject to no controul. The business of this paper will be to illustrate this, and to shew the danger that will result from it. I question whether the world ever saw, in any period of it, a court of justice invested with such immense powers, and yet placed in a situation so little responsible. Certain it is, that in England, and in the several states, where we have been taught to believe, the courts of law are put upon the most prudent establishment, they are on a very different footing.

2. The judges in England, it is true, hold their offices during their good behaviour, but then their determinations are subject to correction by the house of lords; and their power is by no means so extensive as that of the proposed supreme court of the union.—I believe they in no instance assume the authority to set aside an act of parliament under the idea that it is inconsistent with their constitution. They consider themselves bound to decide according to the existing laws of the land, and never undertake to controul them by adjudging that they are inconsistent with the constitution—much less are they vested with the power of giving an *equitable* construction to the constitution.

3. The judges in England are under the controul of the legislature, for they are bound to determine according to the laws passed by them. But the judges under this constitution will controul the legislature, for the supreme

---

108. The original text has a parenthetical label, "continued," as for the March 13 continuation of essay XIV. This is most probably a printer's error, based on the previous week's installment, or, less likely, an error by Brutus himself, confusing the continuation of the paper, as in the previous week, and the continuation of the topic, the judiciary. It will be noted that Brutus opens this paper by referring to his "last number," indicating clearly that he does not see this one as a continuation of the previous installment.

court are authorised in the last resort, to determine what is the extent of the powers of the Congress; they are to give the constitution an explanation, and there is no power above them to set aside their judgment. The framers of this constitution appear to have followed that of the British, in rendering the judges independent, by granting them their offices during good behaviour, without following the constitution of England, in instituting a tribunal in which their errors may be corrected; and without adverting to this, that the judicial under this system have a power which is above the legislative, and which indeed transcends any power before given to a judicial by any free government under heaven.

4. I do not object to the judges holding their commissions during good behaviour. I suppose it a proper provision provided they were made properly responsible. But I say, this system has followed the English government in this, while it has departed from almost every other principle of their jurisprudence, under the idea, of rendering the judges independent; which, in the British constitution, means no more than that they hold their places during good behaviour, and have fixed salaries, they have made the judges *independent*, in the fullest sense of the word. There is no power above them, to controul any of their decisions. There is no authority that can remove them, and they cannot be controuled by the laws of the legislature. In short, they are independent of the people, of the legislature, and of every power under heaven. Men placed in this situation will generally soon feel themselves independent of heaven itself. Before I proceed to illustrate the truth of these assertions, I beg liberty to make one remark—Though in my opinion the judges ought to hold their offices during good behaviour, yet I think it is clear, that the reasons in favour of this establishment of the judges in England, do by no means apply to this country.

5. The great reason assigned, why the judges in Britain ought to be commissioned during good behaviour, is this, that they may be placed in a situation, not to be influenced by the crown, to give such decisions, as would tend to increase its powers and prerogatives. While the judges held their places at the will and pleasure of the king, on whom they depended not only for their offices, but also for their salaries, they were subject to every undue influence. If the crown wished to carry a favorite point, to accomplish which the aid of the courts of law was necessary, the pleasure of the king would be signified to the judges. And it required the spirit of a martyr, for the judges to determine contrary to the king's will.—They were absolutely dependent upon him both for their offices and livings. The king, holding his office during life, and transmitting it to his posterity as an inheritance,

has much stronger inducements to increase the prerogatives of his office than those who hold their offices for stated periods, or even for life. Hence the English nation gained a great point, in favour of liberty. When they obtained the appointment of the judges, during good behaviour, they got from the crown a concession, which deprived it of one of the most powerful engines with which it might enlarge the boundaries of the royal prerogative and encroach on the liberties of the people. But these reasons do not apply to this country, we have no hereditary monarch; those who appoint the judges do not hold their offices for life, nor do they descend to their children. The same arguments, therefore, which will conclude in favor of the tenor of the judge's offices for good behaviour, lose a considerable part of their weight when applied to the state and condition of America. But much less can it be shewn, that the nature of our government requires that the courts should be placed beyond all account more independent, so much so as to be above controul.

6. I have said that the judges under this system will be *independent* in the strict sense of the word: To prove this I will shew—That there is no power above them that can controul their decisions, or correct their errors. There is no authority that can remove them from office for any errors or want of capacity, or lower their salaries, and in many cases their power is superior to that of the legislature.

7. [1st] There is no power above them that can correct their errors or controul their decisions—The adjudications of this court are final and irreversible, for there is no court above them to which appeals can lie, either in error or on the merits.—In this respect it differs from the courts in England, for there the house of lords is the highest court, to whom appeals, in error, are carried from the highest of the courts of law.

8. [2d] They cannot be removed from office or suffer a diminution of their salaries, for any error in judgement or want of capacity.

9. It is expressly declared by the constitution,—"That they shall at stated times receive a compensation for their services which shall not be diminished during their continuance in office."

10. The only clause in the constitution which provides for the removal of the judges from office, is that which declares, that "the president, vice-president, and all civil officers of the United States, shall be removed from office, on impeachment for, and conviction of treason, bribery, or other high crimes and misdemeanors."[109] By this paragraph, civil officers, in

---

109. U.S. Constitution, Art. 2, sect. 4.

which the judges are included, are removable only for crimes. Treason and bribery are named, and the rest are included under the general terms of high crimes and misdemeanors.—Errors in judgement, or want of capacity to discharge the duties of the office, can never be supposed to be included in these words, *high crimes and misdemeanors*. A man may mistake a case in giving judgment, or manifest that he is incompetent to the discharge of the duties of a judge, and yet give no evidence of corruption or want of integrity. To support the charge, it will be necessary to give in evidence some facts that will shew, that the judges commited the error from wicked and corrupt motives.

11. [3d] The power of this court is in many cases superior to that of the legislature. I have shewed, in a former paper, that this court will be authorised to decide upon the meaning of the constitution, and that, not only according to the natural and obvious meaning of the words, but also according to the spirit and intention of it.[110] In the exercise of this power they will not be subordinate to, but above the legislature. For all the departments of this government will receive their powers, so far as they are expressed in the constitution, from the people immediately, who are the source of power. The legislature can only exercise such powers as are given them by the constitution, they cannot assume any of the rights annexed to the judicial, for this plain reason, that the same authority which vested the legislature with their powers, vested the judicial with theirs—both are derived from the same source, both therefore are equally valid, and the judicial hold their powers independently of the legislature, as the legislature do of the judicial.—The supreme court then have a right, independent of the legislature, to give a construction to the constitution and every part of it, and there is no power provided in this system to correct their construction or do it away. If, therefore, the legislature pass any law, inconsistent with the sense the judges put upon the constitution, they will declare it void; and therefore in this respect their power is superior to that of the legislature. In England the judges are not only subject to have their decisions set aside by the house of lords, for error, but in cases where they give an explanation to the laws or constitution of the country, contrary to the sense of the parliament, though the parliament will not set aside the judgement of the court, yet, they have authority, by a new law, to explain a former one, and by this means to prevent a reception of such decisions. But no such power

110. *Brutus XI.*

is in the legislature. The judges are supreme—and no law, explanatory of the constitution, will be binding on them.

12. From the preceding remarks, which have been made on the judicial powers proposed in this system, the policy of it may be fully developed.

13. I have, in the course of my observation on this constitution, affirmed and endeavored to shew, that it was calculated to abolish entirely the state governments, and to melt down the states into one entire government, for every purpose as well internal and local, as external and national. In this opinion the opposers of the system have generally agreed—and this has been uniformly denied by its advocates in public. Some individuals, indeed, among them, will confess, that it has this tendency, and scruple not to say, it is what they wish; and I will venture to predict, without the spirit of prophecy, that if it is adopted without amendments, or some such precautions as will ensure amendments immediately after its adoption, that the same gentlemen who have employed their talents and abilities with such success to influence the public mind to adopt this plan, will employ the same to persuade the people, that it will be for their good to abolish the state governments as useless and burdensome.

14. Perhaps nothing could have been better conceived to facilitate the abolition of the state governments than the constitution of the judicial. They will be able to extend the limits of the general government gradually, and by insensible degrees, and to accommodate themselves to the temper of the people. Their decisions on the meaning of the constitution will commonly take place in cases which arise between individuals, with which the public will not be generally acquainted; one adjudication will form a precedent to the next, and this to a following one. These cases will immediately affect individuals only; so that a series of determinations will probably take place before even the people will be informed of them. In the mean time all the art and address of those who wish for the change will be employed to make converts to their opinion. The people will be told, that their state officers, and state legislatures are a burden and expence without affording any solid advantage, for that all the laws passed by them, might be equally well made by the general legislature. If to those who will be interested in the change, be added, those who will be under their influence, and such who will submit to almost any change of government, which they can be persuaded to believe will ease them of taxes, it is easy to see, the party who will favor the abolition of the state governments would be far from being inconsiderable.—In this situation, the general legislature, might pass one law after another, extending the general and abridging the state jurisdic-

tions, and to sanction their proceedings would have a course of decisions of the judicial to whom the constitution has committed the power of explaining the constitution.—If the states remonstrated, the constitutional mode of deciding upon the validity of the law, is with the supreme court, and neither people, nor state legislatures, nor the general legislature can remove them or reverse their decrees.

15. Had the construction of the constitution been left with the legislature, they would have explained it at their peril; if they exceed their powers, or sought to find, in the spirit of the constitution, more than was expressed in the letter, the people from whom they derived their power could remove them, and do themselves right; and indeed I can see no other remedy that the people can have against their rulers for encroachments of this nature. A constitution is a compact of a people with their rulers; if the rulers break the compact, the people have a right and ought to remove them and do themselves justice; but in order to enable them to do this with the greater facility, those whom the people chuse at stated periods, should have the power in the last resort to determine the sense of the compact; if they determine contrary to the understanding of the people, an appeal will lie to the people at the period when the rulers are to be elected, and they will have it in their power to remedy the evil; but when this power is lodged in the hands of men independent of the people, and of their representatives, and who are not, constitutionally, accountable for their opinions, no way is left to controul them but *with a high hand and an outstretched arm.*

Brutus.

– XVI –

10 April 1788

1. When great and extraordinary powers are vested in any man, or body of men, which in their exercise, may operate to the oppression of the people, it is of high importance that powerful checks should be formed to prevent the abuse of it.

2. Perhaps no restraints are more forcible, than such as arise from responsibility to some superior power.—Hence it is that the true policy of a republican government is, to frame it in such manner, that all persons who are concerned in the government, are made accountable to some superior for their conduct in office.—This responsibility should ultimately rest with the People. To have a government well administered in all its parts, it is requisite the different departments of it should be separated and lodged

as much as may be in different hands. The legislative power should be in one body, the executive in another, and the judicial in one different from either—But still each of these bodies should be accountable for their conduct. Hence it is impracticable, perhaps, to maintain a perfect distinction between these several departments—For it is difficult, if not impossible, to call to account the several officers in government, without in some degree mixing the legislative and judicial. The legislature in a free republic are chosen by the people at stated periods, and their responsibility consists, in their being amenable to the people.[111] When the term, for which they are chosen, shall expire, who will then have opportunity to displace them if they disapprove of their conduct—but it would be improper that the judicial should be elective, because their business requires that they should possess a degree of law knowledge, which is acquired only by a regular education, and besides it is fit that they should be placed, in a certain degree in an independent situation, that they may maintain firmness and steadiness in their decisions. As the people therefore ought not to elect the judges, they cannot be amenable to them immediately, some other mode of amenability must therefore be devised for these, as well as for all other officers which do not spring from the immediate choice of the people: this is to be effected by making one court subordinate to another, and by giving them cognizance of the behaviour of all officers; but on this plan we at last arrive at some supreme, over whom there is no power to controul but the people themselves. This supreme controling power should be in the choice of the people, or else you establish an authority independent, and not amenable at all, which is repugnant to the principles of a free government. Agreeable to these principles I suppose the supreme judicial ought to be liable to be called to account, for any misconduct, by some body of men, who depend upon the people for their places; and so also should all other great officers in the State, who are not made amenable to some superior officers. This policy seems in some measure to have been in view of the framers of the new system, and to have given rise to the institution of a court of impeachments—How far this Court will be properly qualified to execute the trust which will be reposed in them, will be the business of a future paper to investigate.[112] To prepare the way to do this, it shall be the busi-

---

111. See *Brutus III* (10), where Brutus quotes Montesquieu as an authority for this notion. Also see *FF VII* (6).

112. Brutus never did write the paper presenting his views on this question. *XVI* is the last paper he published, but he clearly was projecting more essays.

ness of this, to make some remarks upon the constitution and powers of the Senate, with whom the power of trying impeachments is lodged.

3. The following things may be observed with respect to the constitution of the Senate.

[1st] They are to be elected by the legislatures of the States and not by the people, and each State is to be represented by an equal number.

[2d] They are to serve for six years, except that one third of those first chosen are to go out of office at the expiration of two years, one third at the expiration of four years, and one third at the expiration of six years, after which this rotation is to be preserved, but still every member will serve for the term of six years.

[3d] If vacancies happen by resignation or otherwise, during the recess of the legislature of any State, the executive is authorised to make temporary appointments until the next meeting of the legislature.

[4] No person can be a senator who has not arrived to the age of thirty years, been nine years a citizen of the United States, and who is not at the time he is elected an inhabitant of the State for which he is elected.

4. The apportionment of members of Senate among the States is not according to numbers, or the importance of the States; but is equal. This, on the plan of a consolidated government, is unequal and improper; but is proper on the system of confederation—on this principle I approve of it. It is indeed the only feature of any importance in the constitution of a confederated government. It was obtained after a vigorous struggle of that part of the Convention who were in favor of preserving the state governments. It is to be regretted, that they were not able to have infused other principles into the plan, to have secured the government of the respective states, and to have marked with sufficient precision the line between them and the general government.

5. The term for which the senate are to be chosen, is in my judgment too long, and no provision being made for a rotation will, I conceive, be of dangerous consequence.

6. It is difficult to fix the precise period for which the senate should be chosen. It is a matter of opinion, and our sentiments on the matter must be formed, by attending to certain principles. Some of the duties which are to be performed by the senate, seem evidently to point out the propriety of their term of service being extended beyond the period of that of the

assembly. Besides as they are designed to represent the aristocracy of the country, it seems fit they should possess more stability, and so continue a longer period than that branch who represent the democracy. The business of making treaties and some other which it will be proper to commit to the senate, requires that they should have experience, and therefore that they should remain some time in office to acquire it.—But still it is of equal importance that they should not be so long in office as to be likely to forget the hand that formed them, or be insensible of their interests. Men long in office are very apt to feel themselves independent and to form and pursue interests separate from those who appointed them. And this is more likely to be the case with the senate, as they will for the most part of the time be absent from the state they represent, and associate with such company as will possess very little of the feelings of the middling class of people. For it is to be remembered that there is to be a *federal city*, and the inhabitants of it will be the great and the mighty of the earth. For these reasons I would shorten the term of their service to four years. Six years is a long period for a man to be absent from his home, it would have a tendency to wean him from his constituents.

7. A rotation in the senate, would also in my opinion be of great use. It is probable that senators once chosen for a state will, as the system now stands, continue in office for life. The office will be honorable if not lucrative. The persons who occupy it will probably wish to continue in it, and therefore use all their influence and that of their friends to continue in office.—Their friends will be numerous and powerful, for they will have it in their power to confer great favors; besides it will before long be considered as disgraceful not to be re-elected. It will therefore be considered as a matter of delicacy to the character of the senator not to return him again.—Every body acquainted with public affairs knows how difficult it is to remove from office a person who is [has?] long been in it. It is seldom done except in cases of gross misconduct. It is rare that want of competent ability procures it. To prevent this inconvenience I conceive it would be wise to determine, that a senator should not be eligible after he had served for the period assigned by the constitution for a certain number of years; perhaps three would be sufficient. A farther benefit would be derived from such an arrangement; it would give opportunity to bring forward a greater number of men to serve their country, and would return those, who had served, to their state, and afford them the advantage of becoming better acquainted with the condition and politics of their constituents. It farther appears to me proper, that the legislatures should retain the right which they

now hold under the confederation, of recalling their members. It seems an evident dictate of reason, that when a person authorises another to do a piece of business for him, he should retain the power to displace him, when he does not conduct according to his pleasure. This power in the state legislatures, under confederation, has not been exercised to the injury of the government, nor do I see any danger of its being so exercised under the new system. It may operate much to the public benefit.[113]

8. These brief remarks are all I shall make on the organization of the senate. The powers with which they are invested will require a more minute investigation.

9. This body will possess a strange mixture of legislative, executive and judicial powers, which in my opinion will in some cases clash with each other.

10. [1] They are one branch of the legislature, and in this respect will possess equal powers in all cases with the house of representatives; for I consider the clause which gives the house of representatives the right of originating bills for raising a revenue as merely nominal, seeing the senate be authorised to propose or concur with amendments.

11. [2] They are a branch of the executive in the appointment of ambassadors and public ministers, and in the appointment of all other officers, not otherwise provided for; whether the forming of treaties, in which they are joined with the president, appertains to the legislative or the executive part of the government, or to neither, is not material.

12. [3] They are part of the judicial, for they form the court of impeachments. It has been a long established maxim, that the legislative, executive and judicial departments in government should be kept distinct. It is said, I know, that this cannot be done. And therefore that this maxim is not just, or at least that it should only extend to certain leading features in a government. I admit that this distinction cannot be perfectly preserved. In a due ballanced government, it is perhaps absolutely necessary to give the executive qualified legislative powers, and the legislative or a branch of them judicial powers in the last resort. It may possibly also, in some special cases, be adviseable to associate the legislature, or a branch of it, with the executive, in the exercise of acts of great national importance. But still the maxim is a good one, and a separation of these powers should be sought as far as is practicable. I can scarcely imagine that any of the advocates of the

113. See *Brutus III* (11) for his earlier objections to state equality in the Senate. *FF* displayed the exact same change of mind: *FF III* (5) and *XI* (1).

system will pretend, that it was necessary to accumulate all these powers in the senate.[114]

13. There is a propriety in the senate's possessing legislative powers; this is the principal end which should be held in view in their appointment. I need not here repeat what has so often and ably been advanced on the subject of a division of the legislative power into two branches—The arguments in favor of it I think conclusive. But I think it equally evident, that a branch of the legislature should not be invested with the power of appointing officers. This power in the senate is very improperly lodged for a number of reasons—These shall be detailed in a future number.

Brutus.

Address by a Plebeian to the People of the State of New York, 1788

Friends and Fellow Citizens,

1. The advocates for the proposed new constitution, having been beaten off the field of argument, on its merits, have now taken new ground. They admit it is liable to well-founded objections—that a number of its articles ought to be amended; that if alterations do not take place, a door will be left open for an undue administration, and encroachments on the liberties of the people; and many of them go so far as to say, if it should continue for any considerable period, in its present form, it will lead to a subversion of our equal republican forms of government.—But still, although they admit this, they urge that it ought to be adopted, and that we should confide in procuring the necessary alterations after we have received it. Most of the leading characters, who advocate its reception, now profess their readiness to concur with those who oppose it, in bringing about the most material amendments contended for, provided they will first agree to accept the proffered system as it is. These concessions afford strong evidence, that the opposers of the constitution have reason on their side, and that they have not been influenced, in the part they have taken, by the mean and unworthy motives of selfish and private interests with which they have been illiberally

114. Cf. *FF XI* (11–13); Smith speech, June 25, 1788 (1).

From *The Complete Anti-Federalist*, vol. 6, edited by Herbert J. Storing (Chicago: University of Chicago Press, 1981), 128–47.

charged.—As the favourers of the constitution seem, if their professions are sincere, to be in a situation similar to that of Agrippa, when he cried out upon Paul's preaching,—"almost thou persuadest me to be a christian," I cannot help indulging myself in expressing the same wish which St. Paul uttered on that occasion, "Would to God you were not only almost, but altogether such an one as I am."[1] But alas, as we hear no more of Agrippa's christianity after this interview with Paul, so it is much to be feared, that we shall hear nothing of amendments from most of the warm advocates for adopting the new government, after it gets into operation. When the government is once organized, and all the offices under it filled, the inducements which our great men will have to support it, will be much stronger than they are now to urge its reception. Many of them will then hold places of great honour and emolument, and others will then be candidates for such places. It is much harder to relinquish honours or emoluments, which we have in possession, than to abandon the pursuit of them, while the attainment is held in a state of uncertainty.—The amendments contended for as necessary to be made, are of such a nature, as will tend to limit and abridge a number of the powers of the government. And is it probable, that those who enjoy these powers will be so likely to surrender them after they have them in possession, as to consent to have them restricted in the act of granting them? Common sense says—they will not.

2. When we consider the nature and operation of government, the idea of receiving a form radically defective, under the notion of making the necessary amendments, is evidently absurd.

3. Government is a compact entered into by mankind, in a state of society, for the promotion of their happiness. In forming this compact, common sense dictates, that no articles should be admitted that tend to defeat the end of its institution. If any such are proposed, they should be rejected. When the compact is once formed and put into operation, it is too late for individuals to object. The deed is executed—the conveyance is made—and the power of reassuming the right is gone, without the consent of the parties.—Besides, when a government is once in operation, it acquires strength by habit, and stability by exercise. If it is tolerably mild in its administration, the people sit down easy under it, be its principles and forms ever so repugnant to the maxims of liberty.—It steals, by insensible degrees, one right from the people after another, until it rivets its powers so as to put it beyond the ability of the community to restrict or limit

1. Acts 26:28, 29.

it.[2] The history of the world furnishes many instances of a people's increasing the powers of their rulers by persuasion, but I believe it would be difficult to produce one in which the rulers have been persuaded to relinquish their powers to the people. Wherever this has taken place, it has always been the effect of compulsion. These observations are so well-founded, that they are become a kind of axioms in politics; and the inference to be drawn from them is equally evident, which is this,—that in forming a government, care should be taken not to confer powers which it will be necessary to take back; but if you err at all, let it be on the contrary side, because it is much easier, as well as safer, to enlarge the powers of your rulers, if they should prove not sufficiently extensive, than it is to abridge them if they should be too great.[3]

4. It is agreed, the plan is defective—that some of the powers granted, are dangerous—others not well defined—and amendments are necessary. Why then not amend it? why not remove the cause of danger, and, if possible, even the apprehension of it? The instrument is yet in the hands of the people; it is not even signed, sealed, and delivered, and they have power to give it any form they please.

5. But it is contended, adopt it first, and then amend it. I ask, why not amend, and then adopt it? Most certainly the latter mode of proceeding is more consistent with our ideas of prudence in the ordinary concerns of life. If men were about entering into a contract respecting their private concerns, it would be highly absurd in them to sign and seal an instrument containing stipulations which are contrary to their interests and wishes, under the expectation, that the parties, after its execution, would agree to make alterations agreeable to their desires.—They would insist upon the exceptionable clauses being altered before they would ratify the contract. And is a compact for the government of ourselves and our posterity of less moment than contracts between individuals? Certainly not. But to this reasoning, which at first view would appear to admit of no reply, a variety of objections are made, and a number of reasons urged for adopting the system, and afterwards proposing amendments.—Such as have come under my observation, I shall state, and remark upon.

6. It is insisted, that the present situation of our country is such, as not to admit of a delay in forming a new government, or of time sufficient to

2. Cf. *FF IV* (17), *VI* (5).
3. See *Brutus VI–VII*.

deliberate and agree upon the amendments which are proper, without in-
volving ourselves in a state of anarchy and confusion.

7. On this head, all the powers of rhetoric, and arts of description, are
employed to paint the condition of this country, in the most hideous and
frightful colours. We are told, that agriculture is without encouragement;
trade is languishing; private faith and credit are disregarded, and public
credit is prostrate; that the laws and magistrates are contemned and set at
nought; that a spirit of licentiousness is rampant, and ready to break over
every bound set to it by the government; that private embarrassments and
distresses invade the house of every man of middling property, and insecurity threatens every man in affluent circumstances: in short, that we are in a
state of the most grievous calamity at home, and that we are contemptible
abroad, the scorn of foreign nations, and the ridicule of the world. From
this high-wrought picture, one would suppose, that we were in a condition
the most deplorable of any people upon earth. But suffer me, my countrymen, to call your attention to a serious and sober estimate of the situation
in which you are placed, while I trace the embarrassments under which you
labour, to their true sources. What is your condition? Does not every man
sit under his own vine and under his own fig-tree, having none to make
him afraid? Does not every one follow his calling without impediments and
receive the reward of his well-earned industry? The farmer cultivates his
land, and reaps the fruit which the bounty of heaven bestows on his honest
toil. The mechanic is exercised in his art, and receives the reward of his
labour. The merchant drives his commerce, and none can deprive him of
the gain he honestly acquires; all classes and callings of men amongst us are
protected in their various pursuits, and secured by the laws in the possession and enjoyment of the property obtained in those pursuits. The laws
are as well executed as they ever were, in this or any other country. Neither
the hand of private violence, nor the more to be dreaded hand of legal oppression, are reached out to distress us.[4]

8. It is true, many individuals labour under embarrassments, but these
are to be imputed to the unavoidable circumstances of things, rather than
to any defect in our governments. We have just emerged from a long and
expensive war. During its existence few people were in a situation to encrease their fortunes, but many to diminish them. Debts contracted before
the war were left unpaid while it existed, and these were left a burden too

4. Cf. *FF I* (2).

heavy to be borne at the commencement of peace. Add to these, that when the war was over, too many of us, instead of reassuming our old habits of frugality and industry, by which alone every country must be placed in a prosperous condition, took up the profuse use of foreign commodities. The country was deluged with articles imported from abroad, and the cash of the country has been sent out to pay for them, and still left us labouring under the weight of a huge debt to persons abroad. These are the true sources to which we are to trace all the private difficulties of individuals: But will a new government relieve you from these? The advocates for it have not yet told you how it will do it—And I will venture to pronounce, that there is but one way in which it can be effected, and that is by industry and oeconomy; limit your expences within your earnings; sell more than you buy, and every thing will be well on this score. Your present condition is such as is common to take place after the conclusion of a war. Those who can remember our situation after the termination of the war preceding the last, will recollect that our condition was similar to the present, but time and industry soon recovered us from it. Money was scarce, the produce of the country much lower than it has been since the peace, and many individuals were extremely embarrassed with debts; and this happened, although we did not experience the ravages, desolations, and loss of property, that were suffered during the late war.

9. With regard to our public and national concerns, what is there in our condition that threatens us with any immediate danger? We are at peace with all the world; no nation menaces us with war; Nor are we called upon by any cause of sufficient importance to attack any nation. The state governments answer the purposes of preserving the peace, and providing for present exigencies. Our condition as a nation is in no respect worse than it has been for several years past. Our public debt has been lessened in various ways, and the western territory, which has always been relied upon as a productive fund to discharge the national debt, has at length been brought to market, and a considerable part actually applied to its reduction. I mention these things to shew, that there is nothing special, in our present situation, as it respects our national affairs, that should induce us to accept the proffered system, without taking sufficient time to consider and amend it. I do not mean by this, to insinuate, that our government does not stand in need of a reform. It is admitted by all parties, that alterations are necessary in our federal constitution, but the circumstances of our case do by no means oblige us to precipitate this business, or require that we should adopt

a system materially defective. We may safely take time to deliberate and amend, without in the mean time hazarding a condition, in any considerable degree, worse than the present.[5]

10. But it is said that if we postpone the ratification of this system until the necessary amendments are first incorporated, the consequence will be a civil war among the states. On this head weak minds are alarmed with being told, that the militia of Connecticut and Massachusetts on the one side, and of New Jersey and Pennsylvania on the other, will attack us with hostile fury; and either destroy us from off the face of the earth, or at best divide us between the two states adjoining us on either side. The apprehension of danger is one of the most powerful incentives to human action, and is therefore generally excited on political questions: But still, a prudent man, though he foreseeth the evil and avoideth it, yet he will not be terrified by imaginary dangers. We ought therefore to enquire what ground there is to fear such an event?—There can be no reason to apprehend, that the other states will make war with us for not receiving the constitution proposed, until it is amended, but from one of the following causes: either that they will have just cause to do it, or that they may have a disposition to do it. We will examine each of these:—That they will have no just cause to quarrel with us for not acceding, is evident, because we are under no obligation to do it, arising from any existing compact or previous stipulation. The confederation is the only compact now existing between the states: By the terms of it, it cannot be changed without the consent of every one of the parties to it. Nothing therefore can be more unreasonable than for part of the states to claim of the others, as matter of right, an accession to a system to which they have material objections. No war can therefore arise from this principle, but on the contrary, it is to be presumed, it will operate strongly the opposite way.—The states will reason on the subject in the following manner: On this momentuous question, every state has an indubitable right to judge for itself: This is secured to it by solemn compact, and if any of our sister states disagree with us upon the question, we ought to attend to their objections, and accommodate ourselves as far as possible to the amendments they propose.

11. As to the inclination of the states to make war with us, for declining to accede, until it is amended, this is highly improbable, not only because such a procedure would be most unjust and unreasonable in itself, but for various other reasons.

5. Cf. *FF I* (1–2).

12. The idea of a civil war amongst the states is abhorrent to the principles and feelings of almost every man of every rank in the union. It is so obvious to every one of the least reflection, that in such an event we should hazard the loss of all things, without the hope of gaining anything, that the man who should entertain a thought of this kind, would be justly deemed more fit to be shut up in Bedlam, than to be reasoned with. But the idea of one or more states attacking another, for insisting upon alterations in this system, before it is adopted, is more extravagant still; it is contradicting every principle of liberty which has been entertained by the states, violating the most solemn compact, and taking from the state the right of deliberation. Indeed to suppose, that a people, entertaining such refined ideas of the rights of human nature as to be induced to wage war with the most powerful nation on earth, upon a speculative point, and from the mere apprehension of danger only, should so far be lost to their own feelings and principles, as to deny to their brethren, who were associated with them in the arduous conflict, the right of free deliberation on a question of the first importance to their political happiness and safety, is equally an insult to the character of the people of America, and to common sense, and could only be suggested by a vicious heart and a corrupt mind.

13. The idea of being attacked by the other states, will appear visionary and chimerical, if we consider that tho' several of them have adopted the new constitution, yet the opposition to it has been numerous and formidable. The eastern states from whom we are told we have most to fear, should a civil war be blown up, would have full employ to keep in awe those who are opposed to it in their own governments. Massachusetts, after a long and dubious contest in their convention, has adopted it by an inconsiderable majority, and in the very act has marked it with a stigma in its present form. No man of candour, judging from their public proceedings, will undertake to say, on which side the majority of the people are. Connecticut, it is true, have acceded to it, by a large majority of their convention; but it is a fact well known, that a large proportion of the yeomanry of the country are against it:—And it is equally true, that a considerable part of those who voted for it in the convention, wish to see it altered. In both these states the body of the common people, who always do the fighting of a country, would be more likely to fight against than for it: Can it then be presumed, that a country, divided among themselves, upon a question where even the advocates for it, admit the system they contend for needs amendments, would make war upon a sister state, who only insist that that should be done before they receive it, which it is granted ought to be done

after, and where it is confessed no obligation lies upon them by compact to do it? Can it, I say, be imagined, that in such a case they would make war on a sister state? The idea is preposterous and chimerical.

14. It is further urged, we must adopt this plan because we have no chance of getting a better. This idea is inconsistent with the principles of those who advance it. They say, it must be altered, but it should be left until after it is put in operation. But if this objection is valid, the proposal of altering, after it is received, is mere delusion.

15. It is granted, that amendments ought to be made; that the exceptions taken to the constitution, are grounded on just principles, but it is still insisted, that alterations are not to be attempted until after it is received: But why not? Because it is said, there is no probability of agreeing in amendments previous to the adoption, but they may be easily made after it. I wish to be informed what there is in our situation or circumstances that renders it more probable that we shall agree in amendments better after, than before submitting to it? No good reason has as yet been given; it is evident none can be given: On the contrary, there are several considerations which induce a belief, that alterations may be obtained with more ease before, than after its reception, and if so, every one must agree, it is much the safest. The importance of preserving an union, and of establishing a government equal to the purpose of maintaining that union, is a sentiment deeply impressed on the mind of every citizen of America. It is now no longer doubted, that the confederation, in its present form, is inadequate to that end: Some reform in our government must take place. In this, all parties agree: It is therefore to be presumed, that this object will be pursued with ardour and perseverance, until it is attained by all parties.[6] But when a government is adopted that promises to effect this, we are to expect the ardour of many, yea, of most people, will be abated;—their exertions will cease, or be languid, and they will sit down easy, although they may see, that the constitution which provides for this, does not sufficiently guard the rights of the people, or secure them against the encroachments of their rulers. The great end they had in view, the security of the union, they will consider effected, and this will divert their attention from that which is equally interesting, safety to their liberties. Besides, the human mind cannot continue intensely engaged for any great length of time upon one object. As after a storm, a calm generally succeeds, so after the minds

6. *FF I* (1); *Brutus I* (3).

of a people have been ardently employed upon a subject, especially upon that of government, we commonly find that they become cool and inattentive: Add to this, that those in the community who urge the adoption of this system, because they hope by it to be raised above the common level of their fellow citizens; because they expect to be among the number of the few who will be benefitted by it, will more easily be induced to consent to the amendments before it is received than afterwards. Before its reception they will be inclined to be pliant and condescending; if they cannot obtain all they wish, they will consent to take less. They will yield part to obtain the rest. But when the plan is once agreed to, they will be tenacious of every power, they will strenuously contend to retain all they have got; this is natural to human nature, and it is consonant to the experience of mankind. For history affords us no examples of persons once possessed of power, resigning it willingly.[7]

16. The reasonings made use of to persuade us, that no alterations can be agreed upon previous to the adoption of the system, are as curious as they are futile. It is alledged, that there was great diversity of sentiments in forming the proposed constitution; that it was the effect of mutual concessions and a spirit of accommodation, and from hence it is inferred, that farther changes cannot be hoped for. I should suppose that the contrary inference was the fair one. If the convention, who framed this plan, were possessed of such a spirit of moderation and condescension, as to be induced to yield to each other certain points, and to accommodate themselves to each other's opinions, and even prejudices, there is reason to expect, that this same spirit will continue and prevail in a future convention, and produce an union of sentiments on the points objected to. There is more reason to hope for this, because the subject has received a full discussion, and the minds of the people much better known than they were when the convention sat. Previous to the meeting of the convention, the subject of a new form of government had been little thought of, and scarcely written upon at all. It is true, it was the general opinion, that some alterations were requisite in the federal system. This subject had been contemplated by almost every thinking man in the union. It had been the subject of many well-written essays, and was the anxious wish of every true friend to America. But it never was in the contemplation of one in a thousand of those who had reflected on the matter, to have an entire change in the nature of our federal government—to

7. Cf. *Brutus I* (4).

alter it from a confederation of states, to that of one entire government, which will swallow up that of the individual states.[8] I will venture to say, that the idea of a government similar to the one proposed, never entered the mind of the legislatures who appointed the convention, and of but very few of the members who composed it, until they had assembled and heard it proposed in that body: much less had the people any conception of such a plan until after it was promulgated. While it was agitated, the debates of the convention were kept an impenetrable secret, and no opportunity was given for well informed men to offer their sentiments upon the subject. The system was therefore never publicly discussed, nor indeed could be, because it was not known to the people until after it was proposed. Since that, it has been the object of universal attention—it has been thought of by every reflecting man—been discussed in a public and private manner, in conversation and in print; its defects have been pointed out, and every objection to it stated; able advocates have written in its favour, and able opponents have written against it. And what is the result? It cannot be denied but that the general opinion is, that it contains material errors, and requires important amendments. This then being the general sentiment, both of the friends and foes of the system, can it be doubted, that another convention would concur in such amendments as would quiet the fears of the opposers, and effect a great degree of union on the subject?—An event most devoutly to be wished. But it is farther said, that there can be no prospect of procuring alterations before it is acceded to, because those who oppose it do not agree among themselves with respect to the amendments that are necessary. To this I reply, that this may be urged against attempting alterations after it is received, with as much force as before; and therefore, if it concludes any thing, it is, that we must receive any system of government proposed to us, because those who object to it do not entirely concur in their objections. But the assertion is not true to any considerable extent. There is a remarkable uniformity in the objections made to the constitution, on the most important points. It is also worthy of notice, that very few of the matters found fault with in it, are of a local nature, or such as affect any particular state; on the contrary, they are such as concern the principles of general liberty, in which the people of New-Hampshire, New-York, and Georgia are equally interested.

8. *Brutus I* (6–11).

17. It would be easy to shew, that in the leading and most important objections that have been made to the plan, there has been, and is an entire concurrence of opinion among writers, and in public bodies throughout the United States.

18. I have not time fully to illustrate this by a minute narration of particulars; but to prove that this is the case, I shall adduce a number of important instances.

19. It has been objected to the new system, that it is calculated to, and will effect such a consolidation of the States, as to supplant and overturn the state governments. In this the minority of Pennsylvania, the opposition in Massachusetts, and all the writers of any ability or note in Philadelphia, New-York, and Boston concur.[9] It may be added, that this appears to have been the opinion of the Massachusetts convention, and gave rise to that article in the amendments proposed, which confines the general government to the exercise only of powers expressly given.[10]

20. It has been said, that the representation in the general legislature is too small to secure liberty, or to answer the intention of representation. In this there is an union of sentiments in the opposers.[11]

21. The constitution has been opposed, because it gives to the legislature an unlimited power of taxation, both with respect to direct and indirect taxes, a right to lay and collect taxes, duties, imposts, and excises of every kind and description, and to any amount. In this, there has been as general a concurrence of opinion as in the former.[12]

22. The opposers to the constitution have said that it is dangerous, because the judicial power may extend to many cases which ought to be reserved to the decision of the State courts, and because the right of trial by jury is not secured in the judicial courts of the general government, in civil cases. All the opposers are agreed in this objection.[13]

23. The power of the general legislature to alter and regulate the time, place, and manner of holding elections, has been stated as an argument against the adoption of the system. It has been urged, that this power will

---

9. See *FF I* (1) and passim; *Brutus I* (1ff.).

10. See Elliott, II, 177.

11. See, e.g., *FF II* (1), *III* (2–3), *V* (1–2), *VI* (11–12), *VII–XII, XV* (8); *Brutus I* (14–16), *IV.*

12. See, e.g., *Brutus V–VI.*

13. See, e.g., *Brutus XI; FF II* (5), *IV* (13–14).

place in the hands of the general government, the authority, whenever they shall be disposed, and a favourable opportunity offers, to deprive the body of the people, in effect, of all share in the government. The opposers to the constitution universally agree in this objection, and of such force is it, that most of its ardent advocates admit its validity, and those who have made attempts to vindicate it, have been reduced to the necessity of using the most trifling arguments to justify it.[14]

24. The mixture of legislative, judicial, and executive powers in the senate;[15] the little degree of responsibility under which the great officers of government will be held;[16] and the liberty granted by the system to establish and maintain a standing army, without any limitation or restriction,[17] are also objected to the constitution; and in these, there is a great degree of unanimity of sentiment in the opposers.

25. From these remarks it appears, that the opponents to the system accord in the great and material points on which they wish amendments. For the truth of the assertion, I appeal to the protest of the minority of the convention of Pennsylvania,[18] to all the publications against the constitution, and to the debates of the convention of Massachusetts. As a higher authority than these, I appeal to the amendments proposed by the Massachusetts convention; these are to be considered as the sense of that body upon the defects of the system.[19] And it is a fact, which I will venture to assert, that a large majority of that convention were of opinion, that a number of additional alterations ought to be made. Upon reading the articles which they propose as amendments, it will appear, that they object to indefinite powers in the legislature—to the power of laying direct taxes—to the authority of regulating elections—to the extent of the judicial powers, both as it respects the inferior courts and the appellate jurisdiction—to the smallness of the representation, etc.—It is admitted, that some writers have advanced objections that others have not noticed—that exceptions have been taken by some, that have not been insisted upon by others, and it is probable,

14. See, e.g., *Brutus IV* (8); *FF III* (16).

15. See, e.g., *Brutus XVI* (8–13).

16. See *FF VIII* (9).

17. See *Brutus VIII* (5–6); *FF III* (12–20).

18. Address of the Minority of the Pennsylvania House of Representatives, October 4, 1787, in Storing, III, 11–16.

19. For the amendments proposed by the Massachusetts convention, see Elliott, II, 176–77.

that some of the opponents may approve what others will reject. But still these differences are on matters of small importance, and of such a nature as the persons who hold different opinions will not be tenacious of. Perfect uniformity of sentiment on so great a political subject is not to be expected. Every sensible man is impressed with this idea, and is therefore prepared to make concessions and accommodate on matters of small importance. It is sufficient that we agree in the great leading principles, which relate to the preservation of public liberty and private security. And on these I will venture to affirm we are as well agreed, as any people ever were on a question of this nature. I dare pronounce, that were the principal advocates for the proposed plan to write comments upon it, they would differ more in the sense they would give the constitution, than those who oppose it do, in the amendments they would wish. I am justified in this opinion, by the sentiments advanced by the different writers in favour of the constitution.

26. It is farther insisted, that six states have already adopted the constitution; that probably nine will agree to it; in which case it will be put in operation. That it is unreasonable to expect that those states which have acceded to it, will reconsider the subject in compliance with the wishes of a minority.

27. To perceive the force of this objection, it is proper to review the conduct and circumstances of the states which have acceded it. It cannot be controverted, that Connecticut and New-Jersey were very much influenced in their determinations on the question, by local considerations. The duty of impost laid by this state, has been a subject of complaint by those states. The new constitution transfers the power of imposing these duties from the state to the general government, and carries the proceeds to the use of the union, instead of that of those state. This is a popular matter with the people of those states, and at the same time, is not advanced by the sensible opposers to the system in this state as an objection to it.—To excite in the minds of the people of these states an attachment to the new system, the amount of the revenue arising from our impost has been magnified to a much larger sum than it produces; it has been stated to amount to from sixty to eighty thousand pounds lawful money: and a gentleman of high eminence in Connecticut has lent the authority of his name to support it.[20] It has been said, that Connecticut pays a third of this sum annually for impost, and Jersey nearly as much. It has farther been asserted, that the avails of the impost were applied to the separate use of the state of New-York. By

20. See Elliott, II, 189, 192.

these assertions the people have been grossly imposed upon, for neither of them are true.

28. The amount of the revenue from impost for two years past, has not exceeded fifty thousand pounds currency, per annum, and a draw-back of duties is allowed by law, upon all goods exported to either of the before-mentioned states, in casks or packages unbroken.

29. The whole of this sum, and more, has been paid into the federal treasury for the support of the government of the union. All the states therefore have actually derived equal benefit with the state of New-York, from the impost. It may be said, I know, that this state has obtained credit for the amount, upon the requisitions of Congress: It is admitted; but still it is a fact, that other states, and especially those who complain, have paid no part of the monies required of them, and have scarcely made an effort to do it. The fact therefore is, that they have received as much advantage from the impost of this state, as we ourselves have. The proposed constitution directs to no mode, in which the deficiencies of states on former requisitions, are to be collected, but seems to hold out the idea, that we are to start anew, and all past payments be forgotten. It is natural to expect, that selfish motives will have too powerful an influence on men's minds, and that too often, they will shut the eyes of a people to their best and true interest. The people of those states have been persuaded to believe, that this new constitution will relieve them from the burden of taxes, by providing for all the exigencies of the union, by duties which can be raised only in the neighbouring states. When they come to be convinced, that this promise is a mere delusion, as they assuredly will, by finding the continental tax-gatherer knocking at their doors, if not before, they will be among the first to urge amendments, and perhaps the most violent to obtain them. But notwithstanding the local prejudices which operate upon the people of these states, a considerable part of them wish for amendments. It is not to be doubted, that a considerable majority of the people of Connecticut wish for them, and many in Jersey have the same desires, and their numbers are increasing: It cannot be disputed, that amendments would accord with the sentiments of a great majority in Massachusetts, or that they would be agreeable to the greater part of the people of Pennsylvania: There is no reason to doubt but that they would be agreeable to Delaware and Georgia—If then, the states who have already ratified the constitution, are desirous to have alterations made in it, what reason can be assigned why they should not cordially meet with overtures for that purpose from any state, and concur in appointing a convention to effect it? Mankind are easily induced to

fall upon measures to obtain an object agreeable to them. In this case, the states would not only be moved by this universal principle of human nature, but by the strong and powerful motive of uniting all the states under a form of government agreeable to them.

30. I shall now dismiss the consideration of objections made to attempting alterations previous to the adoption of the plan, but before I close, I beg your indulgence, while I make some remarks on the splendid advantages, which the advocates for this system say are to be derived from it.—Hope and fear are two of the most active principles of our nature: We have considered how the latter is addressed on this occasion, and with how little reason: It will appear that the promises it makes, are as little to be relied upon, as its threatenings. We are amused with the fair prospects that are to open, when this government is put into operation—Agriculture is to flourish, and our fields to yield an hundred fold—Commerce is to expand her wings, and bear our productions to all the ports in the world—Money is to pour into our country through every channel—Arts and manufactures are to rear their heads, and every mechanic find full employ—Those who are in debt, are to find easy means to procure money to pay them—Public burdens and taxes are to be lightened, and yet all our public debts are soon to be discharged.—With such vain and delusive hopes are the minds of many honest and well meaning people fed, and by these means are they led inconsiderately to contend for a government, which is made to promise what it cannot perform; while their minds are diverted from contemplating its true nature, or considering whether it will not endanger their liberties, and work oppression.

31. Far be it from me to object to granting the general government the power of regulating trade, and of laying imposts and duties for that purpose, as well as for raising a revenue: But it is as far from me to flatter people with hopes of benefits to be derived from such a change in our government, which can never be realized. Some advantages may accrue from vesting in one general government, the right to regulate commerce, but it is a vain delusion to expect any thing like what is promised. The truth is, this country buys more than it sells: It imports more than it exports. There are too many merchants in proportion to the farmers and manufacturers. Until these defects are remedied, no government can relieve us. Common sense dictates, that if a man buys more than he sells, he will remain in debt; the same is true of a country.—And as long as this country imports more goods than she exports—the overplus must be paid for in money or not paid at all. These few remarks may convince us, that the radical remedy for

the scarcity of cash is frugality and industry. Earn much and spend little, and you will be enabled to pay your debts, and have money in your pockets; and if you do not follow this advice, no government that can be framed, will relieve you.

32. As to the idea of being relieved from taxes by this government, it is an affront to common sense, to advance it. There is no complaint made against the present confederation more justly founded than this, that it is incompetent to provide the means to discharge our national debt, and to support the national government. Its inefficacy to these purposes, which was early seen and felt, was the first thing that suggested the necessity of changing the government; other things, it is true, were afterwards found to require alterations; but this was the most important, and accordingly we find, that while in some other things the powers of this government seem to be in some measure limited, on the subject of raising money, no bounds are set to it. It is authorised to raise money to any amount, and in any way it pleases. If then, the capital embarrassment in our present government arises from the want of money, and this constitution effectually authorises the raising of it, how are the taxes to be lessened by it? Certainly money can only be raised by taxes of some kind or other; it must be got either by additional impositions on trade, by excise, or by direct taxes, or what is more probable, by all together. In either way, it amounts to the same thing, and the position is clear, that as the necessities of the nation require more money than is now raised, the taxes must be enhanced. This you ought to know, and prepare yourself to submit to.—Besides, how is it possible that the taxes can be decreased when the expences of your government will be greatly advanced? It does not require any great skill in politics, or ability at calculation to shew, that the new government will cost more money to administer it, than the present. I shall not descend to an estimate of the cost of a federal town, the salaries of the president, vice-president, judges, and other great officers of state, nor calculate the amount of the pay the legislature will vote themselves, or the salaries that will be paid the innumerable revenue and subordinate officers. The bare mention of these things is sufficient to convince you, that the new government will be vastly more expensive than the old: And how is the money to answer these purposes to be obtained? It is obvious, it must be taken out of the pockets of the people, by taxes, in some mode or other.

33. Having remarked upon the arguments which have been advanced, to induce you to accede to this government, without amendments, and I trust

refuted them, suffer me to close with an address dedicated by the affection of a brother, and the honest zeal of a lover of his country.

———

Friends, countrymen, and fellow-citizens,

34. The present is the most important crisis at which you ever have arrived. You have before you a question big with consequences, unutterably important to yourselves, to your children, to generations yet unborn, to the cause of liberty and of mankind; every motive of religion and virtue, of private happiness and public good, of honour and dignity, should urge you to consider coolly and determine wisely.[21]

35. Almost all the governments that have arisen among mankind, have sprung from force and violence. The records of history inform us of none that have been the result of cool and dispassionate reason and reflection: It is reserved for this favoured country to exhibit to mankind the first example.[22]—This opportunity is now given us, and we are to exercise our rights in the choice of persons to represent us in convention, to deliberate and determine upon the constitution proposed: It will be to our everlasting disgrace to be indifferent on such a subject, for it is impossible, we can contemplate any thing that relates to the affairs of this life of half the importance.

36. You have heard that both sides on this great question, agree, that there are in it great defects; yet the one side tell you, choose such men as will adopt it, and then amend it—while the other say, amend previous to its adoption.—I have stated to you my reasons for the latter, and I think they are unanswerable.—Consider you the common people, the yeomanry of the country, for to such I principally address myself, you are to be the principal losers, if the constitution should prove oppressive. When a tyranny is established, there are always masters as well as slaves; the great and the well-born are generally the former, and the middling class the latter—Attempts have been made, and will be repeated, to alarm you with the fear of consequences; but reflect, there are consequences on both sides, and none can be apprehended more dreadful, than entailing on ourselves and posterity a government which will raise a few to the height of human greatness and wealth, while it will depress the many to the extreme of poverty and

21. Cf. *Brutus I* (4).
22. Cf. *Brutus I* (3).

wretchedness. Consequences are under the controul of that all-wise and all-powerful being, whose providence directs the affairs of men: Our part is to act right, and we may then have confidence that the consequences will be favourable. The path in which you should walk is plain and open before you; be united as one man, and direct your choice to such men as have been uniform in their opposition to the proposed system in its present form, or without proper alterations: In men of this description you have reason to place confidence, while on the other hand, you have just cause to distrust those who urge the adoption of a bad constitution, under which the delusive expectation of making amendments after it is acceded to. Your jealousy of such characters should be the more excited, when you consider that the advocates for the constitution have shifted their ground. When men are uniform in their opinions, it affords evidence that they are sincere: When they are shifting, it gives reason to believe, they do not change from conviction. It must be recollected, that when this plan was first announced to the public, its supporters cried it up as the most perfect production of human wisdom: It was represented either as having no defects, or if it had, they were so trifling and inconsiderable, that they served only, as the shades in a fine picture, to set off the piece to the greater advantage. One gentleman in Philadelphia went so far, in the ardour of his enthusiasm in its favour, as to pronounce, that the men who formed it were as really under the guidance of Divine Revelation, as was Moses, the Jewish lawgiver.[23] Their language is now changed; the question has been discussed; the objections to the plan ably stated, and they are admitted to be unanswerable. The same men who held it almost perfect, now admit it is very imperfect; that it is necessary it should be amended. The only question between us, is simply this: Shall we accede to a bad constitution, under the uncertain prospect of getting it amended, after we have received it, or shall we amend it before we adopt it? Common sense will point out which is the most rational, which is the most secure line of conduct. May heaven inspire you with wisdom, union, moderation and firmness, and give you hearts to make a proper estimate of your invaluable privileges, and preserve them to you, to be transmitted to your posterity unimpaired, and may they be maintained in this our country, while Sun and Moon endure.

A Plebeian

23. This is a reference to a speech by Benjamin Rush before the Pennsylvania ratifying convention. (Storing, VI, 147, n21.)

Postscript

37. Since the foregoing pages have been put to the press, a pamphlet has appeared, entitled, "An address to the people of the state of New-York, on the subject of the new constitution, &c."[24] Upon a cursory examination of this performance (for I have not had leisure to give it more than a cursory examination) it appears to contain little more than declamation and observations that have been often repeated by the advocates of the new constitution.

An attentive reader will readily perceive, that almost every thing deserving the name of an argument in this publication, has received consideration, and, I trust, a satisfactory answer in the preceding remarks, so far as they apply to prove the necessity of an immediate adoption of the plan, without amendments.

38. I shall therefore only beg the patience of my readers, while I make a few very brief remarks on this piece.

39. The author introduces his observations with a short history of the revolution, and of the establishment of the present existing federal government. He draws a frightful picture of our condition under the present confederation. The whole of what he says on that head, stripped of its artificial colouring, amounts to this, that the existing system is rather recommendatory than coercive, or that Congress have not, in most cases, the power of enforcing their own resolves. This he calls "a new and wonderful system." However "wonderful" it may be, it certainly is not "new." For most of the *federal governments* that have been in the world, have been of the same nature.—The United Netherlands are governed on the same plan. There are other governments also now existing, which are in a similar condition with our's, with regard to several particulars, on account of which this author denominates it "new and wonderful."—The king of Great-Britain "may make war, but has not power to raise money to carry it on." He may borrow money, but is without the means of repayment, etc. For these he is dependent on his parliament. But it is needless to add on this head, because it is admitted that the powers of the general government ought to be increased in several of the particulars this author instances. But these things are mentioned to shew, that the outcry made against the confederation, as being a system new, unheard of, and absurd, is really without foundation.

24. "Plebeian" is referring to an anonymously published pamphlet by John Jay, "An Address to the People of the State of New York on the Subject of the Constitution Agreed upon at Philadelphia," 1788. (Storing, VI, 147, n22.)

40. The author proceeds to depicture our present condition in the high-wrought strains common to his party.—I shall add nothing to what I have said on this subject in the former part of this pamphlet, but will only observe, that his imputing our being kept out of the possession of the western posts, and our want of peace with the Algerines, to the defects in our present government, is much easier said than proved. The British keep possession of these posts, because it subserves their interest, and probably will do so, until they perceive that we have gathered strength and resources sufficient to assert our rights with the sword. Let our government be what it will, this cannot be done without time and patience. In the present exhausted situation of the country, it would be madness in us, had we ever so perfect a government, to commence a war for the recovery of these posts.—With regard to the Algerines, there are but two ways in which their ravages can be prevented. The one is, by a successful war against them, and the other is by treaty. The powers of Congress under the confederation are completely competent either to declare war against them, or to form treaties. Money, it is true, is necessary to do both these. This only brings us to this conclusion, that the great defect in our present government, is the want of powers to provide money for the public exigencies. I am willing to grant *reasonable* powers on this score, but not unlimited ones; commercial treaties may be made under the present powers of Congress. I am persuaded we flatter ourselves with advantages which will result from them, that will never be realized. I know of no benefits that we receive from any that have yet been formed.

41. This author tells us, "it is not his design to investigate the merits of the plan, nor of the objections made to it." It is well he did not undertake it, for if he had, from the specimen he has given, the cause he assumes would not have probably gained much strength by it.

42. He however takes notice of two or three of the many objections brought against the plan.

43. "We are told," says he among other strange things, "that the liberty of the press is left insecure by the proposed constitution, and yet that constitution says neither more nor less about it, than the constitution of the state of New-York does. We are told it deprives us of trial by jury, whereas the fact is, that it expressly secures it in certain cases, and takes it away in none, etc. It is absurd to construe the silence of this, or of our own constitution relative to a great number of our rights into a total extinction of them; silence and a blank paper neither grant nor take away anything."

44. It may be a strange thing to this author to hear the people of America

anxious for the preservation of their rights, but those who understand the true principles of liberty, are no strangers to their importance. The man who supposes the constitution, in any part of it, is like a blank piece of paper, has very erroneous ideas of it. He may be assured every clause has a meaning, and many of them such extensive meaning, as would take a volume to unfold. The suggestion, that the liberty of the press is secure, because it is not in express words spoken of in the constitution, and that the trial by jury is not taken away, because it is not said in so many words and let-ters it is so, is puerile and unworthy of a man who pretends to reason. We contend, that by the indefinite powers granted to the general government, the liberty of the press may be restricted by duties, etc. and therefore the constitution ought to have stipulated for its freedom.[25] The trial by jury, in all civil cases is left at the discretion of the general government, except in the supreme court on the appellate jurisdiction, and in this I affirm it is taken away, not by express words, but by fair and legitimate construction and inference; for the supreme court have expressly given them an appel-late jurisdiction, in every case to which their powers extend (with two or three exceptions) both as to *law and fact*. The court are the judges; every man in the country, who has served as a juror, knows, that there is a distinc-tion between the court and the jury, and that the lawyers in their pleading, make the distinction. If the court, upon appeals, are to determine both the law and the fact, there is no room for a jury, and the right of trial in this mode is taken away.[26]

45. The author manifests equal levity in referring to the constitution of this state, to shew that it was useless to stipulate for the liberty of the press, or to insert a bill of rights in the constitution. With regard to the first, it is perhaps an imperfection in our constitution that the liberty of the press is not expressly reserved; but still there was not equal necessity of making this reservation in our State as in the general Constitution, for the common and statute law of England, and the laws of the colony are established, in which this privilege is fully defined and secured. It is true, a bill of rights is not prefixed to our constitution, as it is in that of some of the states; but still this author knows, that many essential rights are reserved in the body of it; and I will promise, that every opposer of this system will be satisfied, if the stipulations that they contend for are agreed to, whether they are prefixed, affixed, or inserted in the body of the constitution, and that they will not

---

25. Cf. *FF IV* (14).
26. Cf. *FF XV* (6); *Brutus XIV* (9).

contend which way this is done, if it be but done. I shall add but one re-mark, and that is upon the hackneyed argument introduced by the author, drawn from the character and ability of the framers of the new constitution. The favourers of this system are not very prudent in bringing this forward. It provokes to an investigation of characters, which is an invidious task. I do not wish to detract from their merits, but I will venture to affirm, that twenty assemblies of equal number might be collected, equally respectable both in point of ability, integrity, and patriotism. Some of the characters which compose it I revere; others I consider as of small consequence, and a number are suspected of being great public defaulters, and to have been guilty of notorious peculation and fraud, with regard to public property in the hour of our distress. I will not descend to personalities, nor would I have said so much on the subject, had it not been in self defence. Let the constitution stand on its own merits. If it be good, it stands not in need of great men's names to support it. If it be bad, their names ought not to sanction it.

Speeches of Melancton Smith at the New York
Ratifying Convention, 1788

1. Mr. SMITH again rose. He most heartily concurred in sentiment with the honorable gentleman who opened the debate yesterday, that the discussion of the important question now before them ought to be entered on with a spirit of patriotism;[1] with minds open to conviction; with a determination to form opinions only on the merits of the question, from those evidences which should appear in the course of the investigation.

2. How far the general observations made by the honorable gentleman accorded with these principles, he left to the House to determine.

3. It was not, he said, his intention to follow that gentleman through all his remarks—he should only observe, that what had been advanced did not appear to him to apply to the subject under consideration.

4. He was as strongly impressed with the necessity of a Union, as any one could be: He would seek it with as much ardor. In the discussion of this subject, he was disposed to make every reasonable concession, and indeed to sacrifice every thing for a Union, except the liberties of his country, than which he could contemplate no greater misfortune. But he hoped we were not reduced to the necessity of sacrificing or even endangering our liberties to preserve the Union. If that was the case, the alternative was dreadful. But he would not now say that the adoption of the Constitution would endanger our liberties; because that was the point to be debated, and the

From *Debates on the Adoption of the Federal Constitution*, vol. 2, edited by Jonathan Elliot (Salem, N.H.: Ayer, 1987), 222–29.
    1. The reference is to the speech of Robert Livingston on June 19, 1788.

premises should be laid down previously to the drawing of any conclusion. He wished that all observations might be confined to this point; and that declamation and appeals to the passions might be omitted.

5. Why, said he, are we told of our weaknesses?[2] Of the defenceless condition of the southern parts of our state? Of the exposed situation of our capital? Of Long Island, surrounded by water, and exposed to the incursions of our neighbours in Connecticut? Of Vermont having separated from us and assumed the powers of a distinct government; And of the North-West part of our state being in the hands of a foreign enemy?—Why are we to be alarmed with apprehensions that the Eastern states are inimical, and disinclined to form alliances with us? He was sorry to find that such suspicions were entertained. He believed that no such disposition existed in the Eastern states. Surely it could not be supposed that those states would make war upon us for exercising the rights of freemen, deliberating and judging for ourselves, on a subject the most interesting that ever came before any assembly. If a war with our neighbour was to be the result of not acceding, there was no use in debating here; we had better receive their dictates, if we were unable to resist them. The defects of the old Confederation needed as little proof as the necessity of an Union: But there was no proof in all this, that the proposed Constitution was a good one. Defective as the Old Confederation is, he said, no one could deny but it was possible we might have a worse government. But the question was not whether the present Confederation be a bad one; but whether the proposed Constitution be a good one.

6. It had been observed, that no examples of Federal Republics had succeeded. It was true that the antient confederated Republics were all destroyed—so were those which were not confederated; and all antient Governments of every form had shared the same fate. Holland had undoubtedly experienced many evils from the defects in her government; but with all these defects, she yet existed; she had under her confederacy made a principal figure among the nations of Europe, and he believed few countries had experienced a greater share of internal peace and prosperity. The Germanic Confederacy was not the most pertinent example to produce on this occasion:—Among a number of absolute Princes who consider their subjects as their property, whose will is law, and to whose ambition there are no bounds, it was no difficult task to discover other causes from which the convulsions in that country rose, than the defects of their Confedera-

2. Cf. *FF I* (1), *VI* (4); *Plebeian* (6); *Brutus I* (2).

tion. Whether a Confederacy of States under any form be a practicable Government, was a question to be discussed in the course of investigating this Constitution.

7. He was pleased that this early in the debate, the honorable gentleman had himself shewn, that the intent of the Constitution was not a Confederacy, but a reduction of all the states into a consolidated government. He hoped the gentleman would be complaisant enough to exchange names with those who disliked the Constitution, as it appeared from his own concession that they were Federalists, and those who advocated it Anti-Federalists. He begged leave, however, to remind the gentleman, that Montesquieu, with all the examples of modern and antient Republics in view, gives it as his opinion, that a confederated Republic has all the internal advantages of a Republic, with the external force of a Monarchical Government.[3] He was happy to find an officer of such high rank recommending to the other officers of Government, and to those who are members of the Legislature, to be unbiassed by any motives of interest or state importance.[4] Fortunately for himself, he was out of the verge of temptations of this kind, not having the honor to hold any office under the state. But then he was exposed, in common with other gentlemen of the Convention, to another temptation, against which he thought it necessary that we should be equally guarded:—If, said he, this constitution is adopted, there will be a number of honorable and lucrative offices to be filled, and we ought to be cautious lest an expectancy of some of them should influence us to adopt without due consideration.

8. We may wander, said he, in the fields of fancy without end, and gather flowers as we go: It may be entertaining—but it is of little service to the discovery of truth:—We may on one side compare the scheme advocated by our opponents to *golden images, with feet part of iron and part of clay;* and on the other, *to a beast dreadful and terrible, and strong exceedingly, having great iron teeth, which devours, breaks in pieces, and stamps the residue with his feet:* And after all, said he, we shall find that both these allusions are taken from the same *vision;* and their true meaning must be discovered by sober reasoning.

He would agree with the honorable gentleman, that perfection in any system of government was not to be looked for. If that was the object, the debates on the one before them might soon be closed.—But he would ob-

3. Montesquieu, *Spirit of the Laws*, IX, chap. 1.
4. Livingston was chancellor of the state of New York.

serve that this observation applied with equal force against changing any systems—especially against material and radical changes.—Fickleness and inconstancy, he said, were characteristic of a free people; and in framing a Constitution for them, it was, perhaps the most difficult thing to correct this spirit, and guard against the evil effects of it—he was persuaded it could not be altogether prevented without destroying their freedom—it would be like, attempting to correct a small indisposition in the habit of the body, by fixing the patient in a confirmed consumption.—This fickle and inconstant spirit was the more dangerous in bringing about changes in the government. The instance that had been adduced by the gentleman from sacred history, was an example in point to prove this: The nation of Israel having received a form of civil government from Heaven, enjoyed it for a considerable period; but at length labouring under pressures, which were brought upon them by their own misconduct and imprudence, instead of imputing their misfortunes to their true causes, and making a proper improvement of their calamities, by a correction of their errors, they imputed them to a defect in their constitution; they rejected their Divine Ruler, and asked Samuel to make them a King to judge them, like other nations. Samuel was grieved at their folly; but still, by the command of God, he hearkened to their voice; tho' not until he had solemnly declared unto them the manner in which the King should reign over them. "This, (says Samuel) shall be the manner of the King that shall reign over you. He will take your sons and appoint them for himself, for his chariots, and for his horsemen, and some shall run before his chariots; and he will appoint him captains over thousands, and captains over fifties, and will set them to clear his ground, and to reap his harvest, and to make his instruments of war, and instruments of his chariots. And he will take your daughters to be confectionaries, and to be cooks, and to be bakers. And he will take your fields, and your vine yards, and your olive yards, even the best of them, and give them to his servants. And he will take the tenth of your seed, and of your vineyards, and give to his officers and to his servants. And he will take your men servants and your maid servants, and your goodliest young men, and your asses, and put them to his work. He will take the tenth of your sheep: And ye shall be his servants. And ye shall cry out in that day, because of your King which ye have chosen you; and the Lord will not hear you in that day."[5] How far this was applicable to the subject he would not now say; it

5. 1 Samuel 8:11–18.

could be better judged of when they had gone through it.—On the whole he wished to take up this matter with candor and deliberation.

9. He would now proceed to state his objections to the clause just read, (section 2 of article 1, clause 3).[6] His objections were comprised under three heads: 1st the rule of apportionment is unjust; 2d. there is no precise number fixed on below which the house shall not be reduced; 3d. it is inadequate. In the first place, the rule of apportionment of the representatives is to be according to the whole number of the white inhabitants, with three fifths of all others; that is in plain English, each state is to send Representatives in proportion to the number of freemen, and three fifths of the slaves it contains.[7] He could not see any rule by which slaves are to be included in the ratio of representation. The principle of a representation, being that every free agent should be concerned in governing himself, it was absurd to give that power to a man who could not exercise it—slaves have no will of their own: The very operation of it was to give certain privileges to those people who were so wicked as to keep slaves. He knew it would be admitted that this rule of apportionment was founded on unjust principles, but that it was the result of accommodation; which he supposed we should be under the necessity of admitting, if we meant to be in union with the Southern States, though utterly repugnant to his feelings. In the second place, the number was not fixed by the Constitution, but left at the discretion of the Legislature; perhaps he was mistaken; it was his wish to be informed. He understood from the Constitution, that sixty-five Members were to compose the House of Representatives for three years; that after that time a census was to be taken, and the numbers to be ascertained by the Legislature on the following principles: 1st, they shall be apportioned to the respective States according to numbers; 2d, each state shall have one at least; 3d, they shall never exceed one to every thirty thousand. If this was the case, the first Congress that met might reduce the number below what it now is; a power inconsistent with every principle of a free government, to leave it to the discretion of the rulers to determine the number of representatives of the people. There was no kind of security except in the integrity of the men who were entrusted; and if you have no other security, it is idle to contend about Constitutions. In the third place, supposing Congress should declare that there should be one representative for every thirty

6. The New York ratifying convention had resolved to go through the Constitution clause by clause.

7. Cf. *Brutus III* (9–10).

thousand of the people, in his opinion it would be incompetent to the great purposes of representation. It was, he said, the fundamental principle of a free government, that the people should make the laws by which they were to be governed: He who is controlled by another is a slave; and that government which is directed by the will of any one or a few, or any number less than is the will of the community, is a government for slaves.

10. The new point was, how was the will of the community to be expressed? It was not possible for them to come together; the multitude would be too great: In order, therefore to provide against this inconvenience, the scheme of representation had been adopted, by which the people deputed others to represent them. Individuals entering into society became one body, and that body ought to be animated by one mind; and he conceived that every form of government should have that complexion. It was true that notwithstanding all the experience we had from others, it had not appeared that the experiment of representation had been fairly tried: there was something like it in the ancient republics, in which, being of small extent, the people could easily meet together, though instead of deliberating, they only considered of those things which were submitted to them by their magistrates. In Great Britain representation had been carried much farther than in any government we knew of, except our own; but in that country it now had only a name. America was the only country, in which the first fair opportunity had been offered. When we were Colonies, our representation was better than any that was then known: Since the revolution we had advanced still nearer to perfection. He considered it as an object, of all others the most important, to have it fixed on its true principle; yet he was convinced that it was impracticable to have such a representation in a consolidated government. However, said he, we may approach a great way towards perfection by encreasing the representation and limiting the powers of Congress.[8] He considered that the great interests and liberties of the people could only be secured by the State Governments. He admitted, that if the new government was only confined to great national objects, it would be less exceptionable; but it extended to every thing dear to human nature. That this was the case could be proved without any long chain of reasoning:—for that power which had both the purse and the sword, had the government of the whole country, and might extend its powers to any and to every object. He had already observed, that by the true doctrine of representation, this principle was established—that the representative must be chosen by the free will of

8. Cf. *Brutus IV* (5); *FF III*.

the majority of his constituents: It therefore followed that the representative should be chosen from small districts. This being admitted, he would ask, could 65 men, for 3,000,000, or 1 for 30,000, be chosen in this manner? Would they be possessed of the requisite information to make happy the great number of souls that were spread over this extensive country?—There was another objection to the clause: If great affairs of government were trusted to a few men, they would be more liable to corruption. Corruption, he knew, was unfashionable amongst us, but he supposed that Americans were like other men; and tho' they had hitherto displayed great virtues, still they were men; and therefore such steps should be taken as to prevent the possibility of corruption. We were now in that stage of society, in which we could deliberate with freedom;—how long it might continue, God only knew! Twenty years hence, perhaps, these maxims might become unfashionable; we already hear, said he, in all parts of the country, gentlemen ridiculing that spirit of patriotism and love of liberty, which carried us through all our difficulties in times of danger.—When patriotism was already nearly hooted out of society, ought we not to take some precautions against the progress of corruption?

11. He had one more observation to make, to shew that the representation was insufficient—Government, he said, must rest for its execution, on the good opinion of the people, for if it was made in heaven, and had not the confidence of the people, it could not be executed: that this was proved, by the example given by the gentleman, of the Jewish theocracy. It must have a good setting out, or the instant it takes place there is an end of liberty. He believed that the inefficacy of the old Confederation, had arisen from that want of confidence; and this caused in a great degree by the continual declamation of gentlemen of importance against it from one end of the continent to the other, who had frequently compared it to a rope of sand. It had pervaded every class of citizens, and their misfortunes, the consequences of idleness and extravagance, were attributed to the defects of that system. At the close of the war, our country had been left in distress; and it was impossible that any government on earth could immediately retrieve it; it must be time and industry alone that could effect it. He said he would pursue these observations no further at present,—And concluded with making the following motion:

"*Resolved*, That it is proper that the number of representatives be fixed at the rate of one for every twenty thousand inhabitants, to be ascertained on the principles mentioned in the second section of the first article of the Constitution, until they amount to three hundred; after which they shall be apportioned among the States, in proportion to the number of inhabitants of the States respectively: And that before the first enumeration shall be made, the several States shall be entitled to chuse double the number of representatives for that purpose, mentioned in the Constitution."[9]

– SATURDAY, JUNE 21, 1788 –

1. Mr. M. SMITH. I had the honor yesterday of submitting an amendment to the clause under consideration, with some observations in support of it. I hope I shall be indulged in making some additional remarks in reply to what has been offered by the honorable gentleman from New-York.[10]

2. He has taken up much time in endeavouring to prove that the great defect in the old confederation was, that it operated upon states instead of individuals. It is needless to dispute concerning points on which we do not disagree: It is admitted that the powers of the general government ought to operate upon individuals to a certain degree.[11] How far the powers should extend, and in what cases to individuals is the question. As the different parts of the system will come into view in the course of our investigation, an opportunity will be afforded to consider this question; I wish at present to confine myself to the subject immediately under the consideration of the committee. I shall make no reply to the arguments offered by the hon. gentleman to justify the rule of apportionment fixed by this clause: For though I am confident they might be easily refuted, yet I am persuaded we must yield this point, in accommodation to the southern states. The amendment therefore proposes no alteration to the clause in this respect.

3. The honorable gentleman says, that the clause by obvious construction fixes the representation. I wish not to torture words or sentences. I perceive no such obvious construction. I see clearly, that on one hand the representatives cannot exceed one for thirty thousand inhabitants; and on the other, that whatever larger number of inhabitants may be taken for the rule of apportionment, each state shall be entitled to send one representative. Every thing else appears to me in the discretion of the legislature.

9. Cf. *FF IX* (6).

From *Debates on the Adoption of the Federal Constitution*, vol. 2, edited by Jonathan Elliot (Salem, N.H.: Ayer, 1987), 243–51.

10. Alexander Hamilton is the "honorable gentleman" to whom Smith refers.

11. Cf. *FF I* (11–14), *V* (4); *Brutus I*.

If there be any other limitation, it is certainly implied. Matters of such moment should not be left to doubtful construction. It is urged that the number of representatives will be fixed at one for 30,000, because it will be the interest of the larger states to do it. I cannot discern the force of this argument.—To me it appears clear, that the relative weight of influence of the different states will be the same, with the number of representatives at 65 as at 600, and that of the individual members greater. For each member's share of power will decrease as the number of the house of representatives increases.—If therefore this maxim be true, that men are unwilling to relinquish powers which they once possess, we are not to expect that the house of representatives will be inclined to enlarge the numbers. The same motive will operate to influence the president and senate to oppose the increase of the number of representatives; for in proportion as the weight of the house of representatives is augmented, they will feel their own diminished: It is therefore of the highest importance that a suitable number of representatives should be established by the constitution.

4. It has been observed by an honorable member, that the eastern states insisted upon a small representation on the principles of oeconomy.—This argument must have no weight in the mind of a considerate person. The difference of expence, between supporting a house of representatives sufficiently numerous, and the present proposed one would be about 20 or 30,000 dollars per annum. The man who would seriously object to this expence, to secure his liberties, does not deserve to enjoy them. Besides, by increasing the number of representatives, we open a door for the admission of the substantial yeomanry of our country; who, being possessed of the habits of oeconomy, will be cautious of imprudent expenditures, by which means a much greater saving will be made of public money than is sufficient to support them. A reduction of the number of the state legislatures might also be made, by which means there might be a saving of expence much more than sufficient for the purpose of supporting the general legislature.—For, as under this system all the powers of legislation relating to our general concerns, are vested in the general government, the powers of the state legislatures will be so curtailed, as to render it less necessary to have them so numerous as they now are.

5. But an honorable gentleman has observed, that it is a problem that cannot be solved, what the proper number is which ought to compose the house of representatives, and calls upon me to fix the number. I admit this is a question that will not admit of a solution with mathematical certainty—few political questions will—yet we may determine with cer-

tainty that certain numbers are too small or too large. We may be sure that ten is too small, and a thousand too large a number[12]—every one will allow that the first number is too small to possess the sentiments, be influenced by the interests of the people, or secure against corruption: A thousand would be too numerous to be capable of deliberating.

6. To determine whether the number of representatives proposed by this Constitution is sufficient, it is proper to examine the qualifications which this house ought to possess, in order to exercise their powers discreetly for the happiness of the people. The idea that naturally suggests itself to our minds, when we speak of representatives is, that they resemble those they represent; they should be a true picture of the people; possess the knowledge of their circumstances and their wants; sympathize in all their distresses, and be disposed to seek their true interests. The knowledge necessary for the representatives of a free people, not only comprehends extensive political and commercial information, such as is acquired by men of refined education, who have leisure to attain to high degrees of improvement, but it should also comprehend that kind of acquaintance with the common concerns and occupations of the people, which men of the middling class of life are in general more competent to, than those of a superior class. To understand the true commercial interests of a country, not only requires just ideas of the general commerce of the world, but also, and principally, a knowledge of the productions of your own country and their value, what your soil is capable of producing, the nature of your manufactures, and the capacity of the country to increase both. To exercise the power of laying taxes, duties and excises with discretion, requires something more than an acquaintance with the abstruse parts of the system of finance. It calls for a knowledge of the circumstances and ability of the people in general, a discernment how the burdens imposed will bear upon the different classes.

7. From these observations results this conclusion that the number of representatives should be so large, as that while it embraces the men of the first class, it should admit those of the middling class of life. I am convinced that this Government is so constituted, that the representatives will generally be composed of the first class in the community, which I shall distinguish by the name of the natural aristocracy of the country.[13] I do not mean to give offence by using this term. I am sensible this idea is treated by many gentlemen as chimerical. I shall be asked what is meant by the

12. Cf. *FF VII* (6), *IX* (6).
13. Cf. *Brutus III* (13), *IV* (5–7); *FF VII* (6–9).

natural aristocracy—and told that no such distinction of classes of men exists among us. It is true it is our singular felicity that we have no legal or hereditary distinctions of this kind; but still there are real differences: Every society naturally divides itself into classes. The author of nature has bestowed on some greater capacities than on others—birth, education, talents and wealth, create distinctions among men as visible and of as much influence as titles, stars and garters. In every society, men of this class will command a superior degree of respect—and if the government is so constituted as to admit but few to exercise the powers of it, it will, according to the natural course of things, be in their hands. Men in the middling class, who are qualified as representatives, will not be so anxious to be chosen as those of the first. When the number is so small the office will be highly elevated and distinguished—the stile in which the members live will probably be high—circumstances of this kind, will render the place of a representative not a desirable one to sensible, substantial men, who have been used to walk in the plain and frugal paths of life.

8. Besides, the influence of the great will generally enable them to succeed in elections—it will be difficult to combine a district of country containing 30 or 40,000 inhabitants, frame your election laws as you please, in any one character; unless it be in one of conspicuous, military, popular, civil or legal talents. The great easily form associations; the poor and middling class form them with difficulty. If the elections be by plurality, as probably will be the case in this state, it is almost certain, none but the great will be chosen—for they easily unite their interest—The common people will divide, and their divisions will be promoted by the others. There will be scarcely a chance of their uniting, in any other but some great man, unless in some popular demagogue, who will probably be destitute of principle. A substantial yeoman of sense and discernment, will hardly ever be chosen. From these remarks it appears that the government will fall into the hands of the few and the great. This will be a government of oppression. I do not mean to declaim against the great, and charge them indiscriminately with want of principle and honesty.—The same passions and prejudices govern all men. The circumstances in which men are placed in a great measure give a cast to the human character. Those in middling circumstances, have less temptation—they are inclined by habit and the company with whom they associate, to set bounds to their passions and appetites—if this is not sufficient, the want of means to gratify them will be a restraint—they are obliged to employ their time in their respective callings—hence the substantial yeomanry of the country are more temperate, of better morals

and less ambition than the great. The latter do not feel for the poor and middling class; the reasons are obvious—they are not obliged to use the same pains and labour to procure property as the other.—They feel not the inconveniences arising from the payment of small sums. The great consider themselves above the common people—entitled to more respect—do not associate with them—they fancy themselves to have a right of pre-eminence in every thing. In short, they possess the same feelings, and are under the influence of the same motives, as an hereditary nobility. I know the idea that such a distinction exists in this country is ridiculed by some—But I am not the less apprehensive of danger from their influence on this account—Such distinctions exist all the world over—have been taken notice of by all writers on free government—and are founded in the nature of things. It has been the principal care of free governments to guard against the encroachments of the great. Common observation and experience prove the existence of such distinctions. Will any one say, that there does not exist in this country the pride of family, of wealth, of talents; and that they do not command influence and respect among the common people? Congress, in their address to the inhabitants of the province of Quebec, in 1775, state this distinction in the following forcible words quoted from the Marquis Beccaria. "In every human society, there is an essay continually tending to confer on one part the height of power and happiness, and to reduce the other to the extreme of weakness and misery. The intent of good laws is to oppose this effort, and to diffuse their influence universally and equally."[14] We ought to guard against the government being placed in the hands of this class—They cannot have that sympathy with their constituents which is necessary to connect them closely to their interest: Being in the habit of profuse living, they will be profuse in the public expences. They find no difficulty in paying their taxes, and therefore do not feel public burthens: Besides if they govern, they will enjoy the emoluments of the government. The middling class, from their frugal habits, and feeling themselves the public burdens, will be careful how they increase them.

9. But I may be asked, would you exclude the first class in the community, from any share in legislation? I answer by no means—they would be more dangerous out of power than in it—they would be factious—discontented and constantly disturbing the government—it would also be unjust—they have their liberties to protect as well as others—and the largest share of

---

14. *Journals of the Continental Congress*, I, 105–13. The address quotes from the introduction to Beccaria's *Essay on Crimes and Punishments*. See *FF VII* (9).

property. But my idea is, that the Constitution should be so framed as to admit this class, together with a sufficient number of the middling class to controul them. You will then combine the abilities and honesty of the community—a proper degree of information, and a disposition to pursue the public good. A representative body, composed principally of respectable yeomanry is the best possible security to liberty.—When the interest of this part of the community is pursued, the public good is pursued; because the body of every nation consists of this class. And because the interest of both the rich and the poor are involved in that of the middling class. No burden can be laid on the poor, but what will sensibly affect the middling class. Any law rendering property insecure, would be injurious to them.—When therefore this class in society pursue their own interest, they promote that of the public, for it is involved in it.

10. In so small a number of representatives, there is great danger from corruption and combination. A great politician has said that every man has his price: I hope this is not true in all its extent—But I ask the gentleman to inform, what government there is, in which it has not been practised? Notwithstanding all that has been said of the defects in the Constitution of the antient Confederacies in the Grecian Republics, their destruction is to be imputed more to this cause than to any imperfection in their forms of government. This was the deadly poison that effected their dissolution. This is an extensive country, increasing in population and growing in consequence. Very many lucrative offices will be in the grant of the government, which will be the object of avarice and ambition. How easy will it be to gain over a sufficient number, in the bestowment of these offices, to promote the views and purposes of those who grant them! Foreign corruption is also to be guarded against. A system of corruption is known to be the system of government in Europe. It is practised without blushing. And we may lay it to our account it will be attempted amongst us. The most effectual as well as natural security against this, is a strong democratic branch in the legislature frequently chosen, including in it a number of the substantial, sensible yeomanry of the country. Does the house of representatives answer this description? I confess, to me they hardly wear the complexion of a democratic branch—they appear the mere shadow of representation. The whole number in both houses amounts to 91—Of these 46 make a quorum; and 24 of those being secured, may carry any point. Can the liberties of three millions of people be securely trusted in the hands of 24 men? Is it prudent to commit to so small a number the decision of the great questions which will come before them? Reason revolts at the idea.

11. The honorable gentleman from New York has said that 65 members in the house of representatives are sufficient for the present situation of the country, and taking it for granted that they will increase as one for 30,000, in 25 years they will amount to 200. It is admitted by this observation that the number fixed in the Constitution, is not sufficient without it is augmented. It is not declared that an increase shall be made, but is left at the discretion of the legislature, by the gentleman's own concession; therefore the Constitution is imperfect. We certainly ought to fix in the Constitution those things which are essential to liberty. If any thing falls under this description, it is the number of the legislature. To say, as this gentleman does, that our security is to depend upon the spirit of the people, who will be watchful of their liberties, and not suffer them to be infringed, is absurd. It would equally prove that we might adopt any form of government. I believe were we to create a despot, he would not immediately dare to act the tyrant; but it would not be long before he would destroy the spirit of the people, or the people would destroy him. If our people have a high sense of liberty, the government should be congenial to this spirit—calculated to cherish the love of liberty, while yet it had sufficient force to restrain licentiousness. Government operates upon the spirit of the people, as well as the spirit of the people operates upon it—and if they are not conformable to each other, the one or the other will prevail. In a less time than 25 years, the government will receive its tone. What the spirit of the country may be at the end of that period, it is impossible to foretell: Our duty is to frame a government friendly to liberty and the rights of mankind, which will tend to cherish and cultivate a love of liberty among our citizens. If this government becomes oppressive it will be by degrees: It will aim at its end by disseminating sentiments of government opposite to republicanism; and proceed from step to step in depriving the people of a share in the government. A recollection of the change that has taken place in the minds of many in this country in the course of a few years, ought to put us upon our guard. Many who are ardent advocates for the new system, reprobate republican principles as chimerical and such as ought to be expelled from society. Who would have thought ten years ago, that the very men who risqued their lives and fortunes in support of republican principles, would now treat them as the fictions of fancy?—A few years ago we fought for liberty—We framed a general government on free principles—We placed the state legislatures, in whom the people have a full and fair representation, between Congress and the people. We were then, it is true, too cautious; and too much restricted the powers of the general government. But now it is proposed to

go into the contrary, and a more dangerous extreme; to remove all barriers; to give the New Government free access to our pockets, and ample command of our persons; and that without providing for a genuine and fair representation of the people. No one can say what the progress of the change of sentiment may be in 25 years. The same men who now cry up the necessity of an energetic government, to induce a compliance with this system, may in much less time reprobate this in as severe terms as they now do the confederation, and may as strongly urge the necessity of going as far beyond this, as this is beyond the confederation.—Men of this class are increasing—they have influence, talents and industry—It is time to form a barrier against them. And while we are willing to establish a government adequate to the purposes of the union, let us be careful to establish it on the broad basis of equal liberty.

– MONDAY, JUNE 23, 1788 –

1. Honorable Mr. SMITH. I did not intend to make any more observations on this article. Indeed, I have heard nothing today, which has not been suggested before, except the polite reprimand I have received for my declamation. I should not have risen again, but to examine who has proved himself the greatest declaimer.[15] The gentleman wishes me to describe what I meant, by representing the feelings of the people. If I recollect right, I said the representative ought to understand, and govern his conduct by the true interest of the people.—I believe I stated this idea precisely. When he attempts to explain my ideas, he explains them away to nothing; and instead of answering, he distorts, and then sports with them. But he may rest assured that, in the present spirit of the Convention, to irritate is not the way to conciliate. The gentleman, by the false gloss he has given to my argument, makes me an enemy to the rich: This is not true. All I said, was, that mankind were influenced, in a great degree, by interests and prejudices:—That men, in different ranks of life, were exposed to different temptations—and that ambition was more peculiarly the passion of the rich and great. The gentleman supposes the poor have less sympathy with the sufferings of their

From *Debates on the Adoption of the Federal Constitution*, vol. 2, edited by Jonathan Elliot (Salem, N.H.: Ayer, 1987), 280–82.

15. The reference is to a speech by Chancellor Livingston, who spoke against the need for "representing the feelings of the people" (Elliot, II, 275–76).

fellow creatures; for that those who feel most distress themselves, have the least regard to the misfortunes of others:—Whether this be reasoning or declamation, let all who hear us determine. I observed that the rich were more exposed to those temptations, which rank and power hold out to view; that they were more luxurious and intemperate, because they had more fully the means of enjoyment; that they were more ambitious, because more in the hope of success. The gentleman says my principle is not true; for that a poor man will be as ambitious to be a constable, as a rich man to be a governor:—But he will not injure his country so much by the party he creates to support his ambition.

2. The next object of the gentleman's ridicule is my idea of an aristocracy; and he indeed has done me the honor, to rank me in the order. If then I am an aristocrat, and yet publicly caution my countrymen against the encroachments of the aristocrats, they will surely consider me as one of their most disinterested friends. My idea of aristocracy is not new:—it is embraced by many writers on government:—I would refer the gentleman for a definition of it to the honorable *John Adams*, one of our natural aristocrats.[16] This writer will give him a description the most ample and satisfactory. But I by no means intended to carry my idea of it to such a ridiculous length as the gentleman would have me; nor will any of my expressions warrant the construction he imposes on them. My argument was, that in order to have a true and genuine representation, you must receive the middling class of people into your government—such as compose the body of this assembly. I observed, that a representation from the United States could not be so constituted, as to represent completely the feelings and interests of the people; but that we ought to come as near this object as possible. The gentlemen say, that the exactly proper number of representatives is so indeterminate and vague, that it is impossible for them to ascertain it with any precision. But surely they are able to see the distinction between twenty and thirty. I acknowledge that a complete representation would make the legislature too numerous; and therefore, it is our duty to limit the powers, and form checks on the government, in proportion to the smallness of the number.

3. The honorable gentleman next animadverts on my apprehensions of corruption, and instances the present Congress, to prove an absurdity in my argument. But is this fair reasoning? There are many material checks to

16. See *FF VII* (6), *IV* (12); *Brutus III* (13); Adams, *Defence*, letter 25.

the operations of that body, which the future Congress will not have. In the first place, they are chosen annually:—What more powerful check! They are subject to recal: Nine states must agree to any important resolution, which will not be carried into execution, till it meets the approbation of the people in the state legislatures. Admitting what he says, that they have pledged their faith to support the acts of Congress; yet, if these be contrary to the essential interests of the people, they ought not to be acceded to; for they are not bound to obey any law, which tends to destroy them.

4. It appears to me, that had oeconomy been a motive for making the representation small; it might have operated more properly in leaving out some of the offices which this Constitution requires. I am sensible that a great many of the common people, who do not reflect, imagine that a numerous representation involves a great expense:—But they are not aware of the real security it gives to an oeconomical management in all the departments of government.

5. The gentleman further declared, that as far his acquaintance extended, the people thought sixty-five a number fully large enough for our State Assembly; and hence inferred, that sixty-five is to two hundred and forty thousand, as sixty five is to three millions.—This is curious reasoning.

6. I feel that I have troubled the committee too long. I should not indeed have risen again upon this subject, had not my ideas been grossly misrepresented.

– Tuesday, June 24, 1788 –

1. The honorable Mr. Smith observed, that when he had the honor to address the committee on the preceding question of the representation,[17] he stated to them his idea, that it would be impossible, under the new constitution as it stands, to have such a genuine representation of the people, as would itself form a check in the government: That therefore it became our duty to provide checks of another nature. The honorable gentleman from New-York had made many pertinent observations on the propriety of giving stability to the senate. The general principles laid down, he thought

From *Debates on the Adoption of the Federal Constitution*, vol. 2, edited by Jonathan Elliot (Salem, N.H.: Ayer, 1987), 309–15.

17. On June 24, the convention turned to the consideration of Art. 1, sect. 3, concerning the Senate.

were just. He only disputed the inferences drawn from them, and their application to the proposed amendment.[18] The only question was, whether the checks attempted in the amendment were incompatible with that stability which he acknowledged was essential to good government. Mr. *Smith* said he did not rise to enter at present into the debate at large. Indisposition obliged him to beg leave of the committee to defer what he had to offer to them till the succeeding day.

Convention adjourned

– WEDNESDAY, JUNE 25 –

1. Section third was again read—when Mr. SMITH resumed his argument as follows. The amendment embraces two objects: First, that the senators shall be eligible for only six years in any term of twelve years; Second, that they shall be subject to the recall of the legislatures of their several states. It is proper that we take up these points separately. I concur with the honorable gentleman, that there is a necessity for giving this branch a greater stability than the house of representatives. I think his reasons are conclusive on this point. But, Sir, it does not follow from this position that the senators ought to hold their places during life. Declaring them ineligible during a certain term after six years, is far from rendering them less stable than is necessary. We think the amendment will place the senate in a proper medium between a fluctuating and a perpetual body. As the clause now stands, there is no doubt that the senators will hold their office perpetually; and in this situation, they must of necessity lose their dependence and attachment to the people. It is certainly inconsistent with the established principles of republicanism, that the senate should be a fixed and unchangeable body of men. There should be then some constitutional provision against this evil. A rotation I consider as the best possible mode of affecting a remedy. The

18. On June 24, the Anti-Federalist George Livingston proposed an amendment to Art. 1, sect. 3: "Resolved, that no person shall be eligible as a senator for more than six years in any term of twelve years, and that it shall be in the power of legislatures of the several states to recall their senators, or either of them, and to elect others in their stead, to serve for the remainder of the time for which the senator or senators, so recalled, were appointed." That is, he attempted to introduce two of the Anti-Federalist devices for controlling government: rotation in office and recall by state legislatures.

From *Debates on the Adoption of the Federal Constitution*, vol. 2, edited by Jonathan Elliot (Salem, N.H.: Ayer, 1987), 309–15.

amendment will not only have a tendency to defeat any plots, which may be formed against the liberty and authority of the state governments, but will be the best means to extinguish the factions which often prevail, and which are sometimes so fatal in legislative bodies. This appears to me an important consideration. We have generally found, that perpetual bodies have either combined in some scheme of usurpation, or have been torn and distracted with cabals—Both have been the source of misfortunes to the state. Most people acquainted with history will acknowledge these facts. Our Congress would have been a fine field for party spirit to act in—That body would undoubtedly have suffered all the evils of faction, had it not been secured by the rotation established by the articles of confederation. I think a rotation in the government is a very important and truly republican institution. All good republicans, I presume to say, will treat it with respect.[19]

2. It is a circumstance strongly in favor of rotation, that it will have a tendency to diffuse a more general spirit of emulation, and to bring forward into office the genius and abilities of the continent—The ambition of gaining the qualifications necessary to govern, will be in some proportion to the chance of success. If the office is to be perpetually confined to a few, other men of equal talents and virtue, but not possessed of so extensive an influence, may be discouraged from aspiring to it. The more perfectly we are versed in the political science, the more firmly will the happy principles of republicanism be supported. The true policy of constitutions will be to increase the information of the country, and disseminate the knowledge of government as universally as possible. If this be done, we shall have, in any dangerous emergency, a numerous body of enlightened citizens, ready for the call of their country. As the constitution now is, you only give an opportunity to two men to be acquainted with the public affairs. It is a maxim with me, that every man employed in a high office by the people, should from time to time return to them, that he may be in a situation to satisfy them with respect to his conduct and the measures of administration. If I recollect right, it was observed by an honorable member from New-York, that this amendment would be an infringement of the natural rights of the people.[20] I humbly conceive, if the gentleman reflects maturely on the nature of his argument, he will acknowledge its weakness. What is government itself, but a restraint upon the natural rights of the people? What constitution was ever devised, that did not operate as a restraint on their

---

19. On rotation and recall, see *FF XI* (11–13); *Brutus XVI* (6–7).
20. This argument was made by Robert Livingston. (Elliot, II, 324.)

original liberties? What is the whole system of qualifications, which take place in all free governments, but a restraint? Why is a certain age made necessary? Why a certain term of citizenship? This constitution itself, Sir, has restraints innumerable.—The amendment, it is true, may exclude two of the best men: but it can rarely happen, that the state will sustain any material loss by this. I hope and believe that we shall always have more than two men, who are capable of discharging the duty of a senator. But, if it should so happen that the state possessed only two capable men, it will be necessary they should return home, from time to time, to inspect and regulate our domestic affairs. I do not conceive the state can suffer any inconvenience. The argument indeed might have some weight were the representation very large: But as the power is to be exercised upon only two men, the apprehensions of the gentleman are entirely without foundation.

3. With respect to the second part of the amendment, I would observe that as the senators are the representatives of the state legislatures, it is reasonable and proper that they should be under their controul. When a state sends an agent commissioned to transact any business, or perform any service, it certainly ought to have a power to recall him. These are plain principles, and so far as they apply to the case under examination, they ought to be adopted by us. Form this government as you please, you must at all events lodge in it very important powers: These powers must be in the hands of a few men, so situated as to produce a small degree of responsibility. These circumstances ought to put us upon our guard; and the inconvenience of this necessary delegation of power should be corrected, by providing some suitable checks.

4. Against this part of the amendment a great deal of argument has been used, and with considerable plausibility. It is said if the amendment takes place, the senators will hold their office only during the pleasure of the state legislatures, and consequently will not possess the necessary firmness and stability. I conceive, Sir, there is a fallacy in this argument, founded upon the suspicion that the legislature of a state will possess the qualities of a mob, and be incapable of any regular conduct. I know that the impulses of the multitude are inconsistent with systematic government. The people are frequently incompetent to deliberate discussion, and subject to errors and imprudencies. Is this the complexion of the state legislatures? I presume it is not. I presume that they are never actuated by blind impulses—that they rarely do things hastily and without consideration. My apprehension is, that the power of recall would not be exercised as often as it ought. It is highly improbable that a man, in whom the state has confided, and who

has an established influence, will be recalled, unless his conduct has been notoriously wicked.—The arguments of the gentleman therefore, do not apply in this case. It is further observed, that it would be improper to give the legislatures this power, because the local interests and prejudices of the states ought not to be admitted into the general government; and that if the senator is rendered too independent of his constituents, he will sacrifice the interests of the Union to the policy of his state. Sir, the senate has been generally held up by all parties as a safe guard to the rights of the several states. In this view, the closest connection between them has been considered as necessary. But now it seems we speak a different language—We now look upon the least attachment to their states as dangerous—We are now for separating them, and rendering them entirely independent, that we may root out the last vestige of state sovereignty.

5. An honorable gentleman from New-York observed yesterday,[21] that the states would always maintain their importance and authority, on account of their superior influence over the people. To prove this influence, he mentioned the aggregate number of the state representatives throughout the continent. But I ask him, how long the people will retain their confidence for two thousand representatives, who shall meet once in a year to make laws for regulating the heighth of your fences and the repairing of your roads? Will they not by and by be saying,—Here, we are paying a great number of men for doing nothing: We had better give up all the civil business of our state with its powers to congress, who are sitting all the year round: We had better get rid of the useless burthen. That matters will come to this at last, I have no more doubt than I have of my existence. The state governments, without object or authority, will soon dwindle into insignificance, and be despised by the people themselves. I am, sir, at a loss to know how the state legislatures will spend their time. Will they make laws to regulate agriculture? I imagine this will be best regulated by the sagacity and industry of those who practise it. Another reason offered by the gentleman is, that the states will have a greater number of officers than the general government. I doubt this. Let us make a comparison. In the first place, the federal government must have a compleat set of judicial officers of different ranks throughout the continent: Then, a numerous train of executive officers, in all the branches of the revenue, both internal and external, and all the civil and military departments. Add to this, their salaries will probably be larger and better secured than those of any state of-

21. Alexander Hamilton. (Elliot, II, 304–5.)

ficers. If these numerous offices are not at once established, they are in the power of congress, and will all in time be created. Very few offices will be objects of ambition in the states. They will have no establishments at all to correspond with some of those I have mentioned—In other branches, they will have the same as congress. But I ask, what will be their comparative influence and importance? I will leave it, sir, to any man of candour, to determine whether there will not probably be more lucrative and honorable places in the gift of congress than in the disposal of the states all together. But the whole reasoning of the gentlemen rests upon the principle that the states will be able to check the general government, by exciting the people to opposition: It only goes to prove, that the state officers will have such an influence over the people, as to impell them to hostility and rebellion. This kind of check, I contend, would be a pernicious one; and certainly ought to be prevented. Checks in government ought to act silently, and without public commotion. I think that the harmony of the two powers should by all means be maintained: If it be not, the operation of government will be baneful—One or the other of the parties must finally be destroyed in the conflict. The constitutional line between the authority of each should be so obvious, as to leave no room for jealous apprehensions or violent contests.[22]

6. It is further said, that the operation of local interests should be counteracted; for which purpose, the senate should be rendered permanent. I conceive that the true interest of every state is the interest of the whole; and that if we should have a well regulated government, this idea will prevail. We shall indeed have few local interests to pursue, under the new constitution: because it limits the claims of the states by so close a line, that on their part there can be little dispute, and little worth disputing about. But, sir, I conceive that partial interests will grow continually weaker, because there are not those fundamental differences between the real interests of the several states, which will long prevent their coming together and becoming uniform.

Another argument advanced by the gentleman is, that our amendment would be the means of producing factions among the electors:—That aspiring men would misrepresent the conduct of a faithful senator; and by intrigue, procure a recall, upon false grounds, in order to make room for themselves. But, sir, men who are ambitious for places will rarely be disposed to render those places unstable. A truly ambitious man will never do

22. Cf. *Brutus X* (21–22).

this, unless he is mad. It is not to be supposed that a state will recall a man once in twenty years, to make way for another. Dangers of this kind are very remote: I think they ought not to be brought seriously into view.

7. More than one of the gentlemen have ridiculed my apprehensions of corruption. How, say they, are the people to be corrupted? By their own money? Sir, in many countries, the people pay money to corrupt themselves: why should it not happen in this? Certainly, the congress will be as liable to corruption as other bodies of men. Have they not the same frailties, and the same temptations? With respect to the corruption arising from the disposal of offices, the gentlemen have treated the argument as insignificant. But let any one make a calculation, and see whether there will not be good offices enough, to dispose of to every man who goes there, who will then freely resign his seat: for, can any one suppose, that a member of congress would not go out and relinquish his four dollars a day, for two or three thousand pounds a year? It is here objected that no man can hold an office created during the time he is in Congress—But it will be easy for a man of influence, who has in his eye a favorite office previously created and already filled, to say to his friend, who holds it—Here—I will procure you another place of more emolument, provided you will relinquish yours in favor of me. The constitution appears to be a restraint, when in fact it is none at all. I presume, sir, there is not a government in the world in which there is greater scope for influence and corruption in the disposal of offices. Sir, I will not declaim, and say all men are dishonest; but I think that, in forming a constitution, if we presume this, we shall be on the safest side.[23] This extreme is certainly less dangerous than the other. It is wise to multiply checks to a greater degree than the present state of things requires. It is said that corruption has never taken place under the old government—I believe, gentlemen hazard this assertion without proofs. That it has taken place in some degree is very probable. Many millions of money have been put into the hands of government, which have never yet been accounted for: The accounts are not yet settled, and Heaven only knows when they will be.

8. I have frequently observed a restraint upon the state governments, which Congress never can be under, construct that body as you please. It is a truth, capable of demonstration, that the nearer the representative is to his constituent, the more attached and dependent he will be—In the states, the elections are frequent, and the representatives numerous: They transact

23. Cf. *Brutus IV* (11).

business in the midst of their constituents, and every man may be called upon to account for his conduct. In this state the council of appointment are elected for one year.—The proposed constitution establishes a council of appointment who will be perpetual—Is there any comparison between the two governments in point of security? It is said that the governor of this state is always eligible: But this is not in point. The governor of this state is limited in his powers—Indeed his authority is small and insignificant, compared to that of the senate of the United States.

–Thursday June 26, 1788–

1. Mr. Smith. The gentleman misunderstands me. I did not mean the amendment to operate on the other states: they may use their discretion. The amendment is in the negative. The very design of it is to enable the states to act their discretion, without the control of Congress.[24] So the gentleman's reasoning is directly against himself.

2. If the argument had any force, it would go against proposing any amendment at all; because, says the gentleman, it would be dictating to the Union. What is the object of our consultations? For my part, I do not know, unless we are to express our sentiments of the Constitution before we adopt it. It is only exercising the privilege of freemen; and shall we be debarred from this? It is said, it is left to the discretion of the states. If this were true, it would be all we contend for. But, sir, Congress can alter as they please any mode adopted by the states. What discretion is there here? The gentleman instances the Constitution of New York, as opposed to my argument. I believe that there are now gentlemen in this house, who were members of the Convention of this state, and who were inclined for an amendment like this. It is to be regretted that it was not adopted. The fact is, as your Constitution stands, a man may have a seat in your legislature, who is not elected by a majority of his constituents. For my part, I know of no principle that ought to be more fully established than the right of election by a majority.

From *Debates on the Adoption of the Federal Constitution*, vol. 2, edited by Jonathan Elliot (Salem, N.H.: Ayer, 1987), 328.

24. Smith is speaking to an amendment of Art. 1, sect. 4, which gives Congress the power to regulate the time, manner, and place of elections for Congress. For a fuller statement of the fears that led Smith to oppose this power, see *FF XII* and *Brutus IV* (8–10).

– FRIDAY, JUNE 27TH, 1788 –

1. Section 8, was again read,—and the hon. Mr. SMITH rose. We are now come to a part of the system, which requires our utmost attention, and most careful investigation.[25] It is necessary that the powers vested in government should be precisely defined, that the people may be able to know whether it moves in the circle of the constitution. It is the more necessary in governments like the one under examination; because Congress here is to be considered as only part of a complex system. The state governments are necessary for certain local purposes; the general government for national purposes: The latter ought to rest on the former, not only in its form, but in its operations. It is therefore of the highest importance, that the line of jurisdiction should be accurately drawn. It is necessary, sir, in order to maintain harmony between the governments, and to prevent the constant interference which must either be the cause of perpetual differences, or oblige one to yield, perhaps unjustly, to the other. I conceive the system cannot operate well, unless it is so contrived, as to preserve harmony. If this be not done, in every contest, the weak must submit to the strong. The clause before us is of the greatest importance:[26] It respects the very vital principle of government: The power is the most efficient and comprehensive that can be delegated; and seems in some measure to answer for all others.[27] I believe it will appear evident, that money must be raised for the support of both governments: If therefore you give to one or the other, a power which may in its operation become exclusive; it is obvious, that one can exist only at the will of the other; and must ultimately be sacrificed.[28] The powers of the general government extend to the raising of money, in all possible ways, except by duties on exports; to the laying taxes on imports, lands, buildings, and even on persons.[29] The individual states in time will be allowed to raise no money at all: The United States will have a right to raise money from every quarter. The general government has moreover this advantage. All disputes relative to jurisdiction must be decided in a federal court.

From *Debates on the Adoption of the Federal Constitution*, vol. 2, edited by Jonathan Elliot (Salem, N.H.: Ayer, 1987), 332–37.
    25. The convention had reached Art. 1, sect. 8, the list of powers of Congress.
    26. They were specifically concerned with the power of Congress to lay taxes.
    27. Cf. *Brutus I* (7).
    28. Cf. *Brutus V* (11–14), *VI* (1–8, 13–14).
    29. Cf. *Brutus I* (7).

2. It is a general maxim, that all governments find a use for as much money as they can raise. Indeed they have commonly demands for more: Hence it is, that all, as far as we are acquainted, are in debt. I take this to be a settled truth, that they will all spend as much as their revenue; that is, will live at least up to their income. Congress will ever exercise their powers, to levy as much money as the people can pay. They will not be restrained from direct taxes, by the consideration that necessity does not require them. If they forbear, it will be because the people cannot answer their demands. There will be no possibility of preventing the clashing of jurisdictions, unless some system of accommodation is formed. Suppose taxes are laid by both governments on the same article: It seems to me impossible, that they can operate with harmony. I have no more conception that in taxation two powers can act together; than that two bodies can occupy the same place. They will therefore not only interfere; but they will be hostile to each other. Here are to be two lists of all kinds of officers—supervisors, assessors, constables, &c. imployed in this business. It is unnecessary that I should enter into a minute detail, to prove that these complex powers cannot operate peaceably together, and without one being overpowered by the other. On one day, the continental collector calls for the tax; He seizes a horse: The next day, the state collector comes, procures a replevin and retakes the horse, to satisfy the state tax. I just mention this, to shew that people will not submit to such a government, and that finally it must defeat itself.

3. It must appear evident that there will be a constant jarring of claims and interests. Now, will the states in this contest stand any chance of success? If they will, there is less necessity for our amendment.[30] But, consider the superior advantages of the general government: Consider their extensive, exclusive revenues; the vast sums of money they can command, and the means they thereby possess of supporting a powerful standing force. The states, on the contrary, will not have the command of a shilling, or a soldier. The two governments will be like two men contending for a certain property: The one has no interest but that which is the subject of the controversy; while the other has money enough to carry on the law-suit for twenty years. By this clause unlimited powers in taxation are given:

---

30. The Anti-Federalist John Williams had moved that Congress should lay no direct taxes except when the impost and excise are insufficient to meet the public exigencies and then only after requisitions on the states have been refused or neglected. (Storing, VI, 169.)

Another clause declares, that Congress shall have power to make all laws necessary to carry the constitution into effect. Nothing therefore is left to construction; but the powers are most express.[31] How far the state legislatures will be able to command a revenue, every man, on viewing the subject, can determine. If he contemplates the ordinary operation of causes, he will be convinced that the powers of the confederacy will swallow up those of the members. I do not suppose that this effect will be brought about suddenly—As long as the people feel universally and strongly attached to the state governments, Congress will not be able to accomplish it: If they act prudently, their powers will operate and be increased by degrees. The tendency of taxation, tho' it be moderate, is to lessen the attachment of the citizens—If it becomes oppressive, it will certainly destroy their confidence. While the general taxes are sufficiently heavy, every attempt of the states to enhance them, will be considered as a tyrannical act, and the people will lose their respect and affection for a government, which cannot support itself, without the most grievous impositions upon them. If the constitution is accepted as it stands, I am convinced, that in seven years as much will be said against the state governments, as is now said in favour of the proposed system.

4. Sir, I contemplate the abolition of the state constitutions as an event fatal to the liberties of America. These liberties will not be violently wrested from the people; they will be undermined and gradually consumed. On subjects of this kind we cannot be too critical. The investigation is difficult, because we have no examples to serve as guides. The world has never seen such a government over such a country.[32] If we consult authorities in this matter, they will declare the impracticability of governing a free people, on such an extensive plan. In a country, where a portion of the people live more than twelve hundred miles from the center, I think that one body cannot possibly legislate for the whole. Can the legislature frame a system of taxation that will operate with uniform advantages? Can they carry any system into execution? Will it not give occasion for an innumerable swarm of officers, to infest our country and consume our substance? People will be subject to impositions, which they cannot support, and of which their complaints can never reach the government.

5. Another idea is in my mind, which I think conclusive against a simple

31. Cf. *Brutus I* (5), *V* (3).
32. Cf. *Brutus I* (12–15).

government for the United States. It is not possible to collect a set of representatives, who are acquainted with all parts of the continent. Can you find men in Georgia who are acquainted with the situation of New-Hampshire? who know what taxes will best suit the inhabitants; and how much they are able to bear?[33] Can the best men make laws for a people of whom they are entirely ignorant? Sir, we have no reason to hold our state governments in contempt, or to suppose them incapable of acting wisely. I believe they have operated more beneficially than most people expected, who considered that those governments were erected in a time of war and confusion, when they were very liable to errors in their structure. It will be a matter of astonishment to all unprejudiced men hereafter, who shall reflect upon our situation, to observe to what a great degree good government has prevailed. It is true some bad laws have been passed in most of the states; but they arose more from the difficulty of the times, than from any want of honesty or wisdom. Perhaps there never was a government, which in the course of ten years did not do something to be repented of. As for Rhode-Island, I do not mean to justify her—She deserves to be condemned[34]— If there were in the world but one example of political depravity, it would be her's: And no nation ever merited or suffered a more genuine infamy, than a wicked administration has attached to her character. Massachusetts also has been guilty of errors: and has lately been distracted by an internal convulsion. Great-Britain, notwithstanding her boasted constitution, has been a perpetual scene of revolutions and civil war—Her parliaments have been abolished; her kings have been banished and murdered. I assert that the majority of the governments in the union have operated better than any body had reason to expect: and that nothing but experience and habit is wanting, to give the state laws all the stability and wisdom necessary to make them respectable. If these things be true, I think we ought not to exchange our condition, with a hazard of losing our state constitutions. We all agree that a general government is necessary: But it ought not to go so far, as to destroy the authority of the members. We shall be unwise, to make a new experiment in so important a matter, without some known and sure grounds to go upon. The state constitutions should be the guardians of our domestic rights and interests; and should be both the support and the check of the federal government. The want of the means of raising a general reve-

33. Cf. *Brutus I* (20).
34. Cf. *Brutus XIV* (21).

nue has been the principal cause of our difficulties. I believe no man will doubt that if our present Congress had money enough, there would be few complaints of their weakness. Requisitions have perhaps been too much condemned. What has been their actual operation? Let us attend to experience, and see if they are such poor, unproductive things, as is commonly supposed. If I calculate right, the requisitions for the ten years past, have amounted to thirty-six millions of dollars; of which twenty-four millions, or two thirds, have been actually paid. Does not this fact warrant a conclusion that some reliance is to be placed on this mode?[35] Besides, will any gentleman say that the states have generally been able to collect more than two thirds of their taxes from the people? The delinquency of some states has arisen from the fluctuations of paper money, &c. Indeed it is my decided opinion, that no government in the difficult circumstances, which we have passed thro', will be able to realize more than two thirds of the taxes it imposes. I might suggest two other considerations which have weight with me—There has probably been more money called for, than was actually wanted, on the expectation of delinquencies; and it is equally probable, that in a short course of time the increasing ability of the country will render requisitions a much more efficient mode of raising a revenue. The war left the people under very great burthens, and oppressed with both public and private debts. They are now fast emerging from their difficulties. Many individuals without doubt still feel great inconveniences; but they will find a gradual remedy.[36] Sir, has any country which has suffered distresses like ours, exhibited within a few years, more striking marks of improvement and prosperity? How its population has grown; How its agriculture, commerce, and manufactures have been extended and improved! How many forests have been cut down; How many wastes have been cleared and cultivated; How many additions have been made to the extent and beauty of our towns and cities! I think our advancement has been rapid. In a few years, it is to be hoped that we shall be relieved from our embarrassments, and, unless new calamities come upon us, shall be flourishing and happy. Some difficulties will ever occur in the collection of taxes by any mode whatever. Some states will pay more; some less. If New-York lays a tax, will not one county or district furnish more, another less than its proportion? The same will happen to the United States, as happens in New-York, and in every

35. Cf. *FF XVII* (2).
36. Cf. *FF I* (1–2).

other country.—Let them impose a duty equal and uniform—those districts, where there is plenty of money, will pay punctually: Those, in which money is scarce, will be in some measure delinquent. The idea that Congress ought to have unlimited powers, is entirely novel; I never heard it, till the meeting of this convention. The general government once called on the states, to invest them with the command of funds adequate to the exigencies of the union: but they did not ask to command all the resources of the states—They did not wish to have a controul over all the property of the people. If we now give them this controul, we may as well give up the state governments with it. I have no notion of setting the two powers at variance; nor would I give a farthing for a government, which could not command a farthing. On the whole, it appears to me probable, that unless some certain, specific source of revenue is reserved to the states, their governments, with their independency will be totally annihilated.

– TUESDAY, JULY 1, 1788 –

1. Mr. SMITH observed, that he supposed the states would have a right to lay taxes, if there was no power in the general government to control them. He acknowledged that the counties in this state had a right to collect taxes; but it was only a legislative, not a constitutional right. It was dependent and controllable. This example, he said, was a true one; and the comparison the gentleman had made was just; but it certainly operated against him. Whether, then, the general government would have a right to control the states in taxation, was a question which depended upon the construction of the Constitution. Men eminent in law had given different opinions on this point. The difference of opinion furnished, to his mind, a reason why the matter should be constitutionally explained. No such important point should be left to doubt and construction. The clause should be so formed as to render the business of legislation as simple and plain as possible. It was not to be expected that the members of the federal legislature would generally be versed in those subtilties which distinguish the profession of the law. They would not be disposed to make nice distinctions with respect to jurisdiction. He said that, from general reasoning, it must be inferred that, if the objects of the general government were without limitation, there could be no bounds set to their powers; that they had a right to seek those

From *Debates on the Adoption of the Federal Constitution*, vol. 2, edited by Jonathan Elliot (Salem, N.H.: Ayer, 1987), 377–82.

objects by all necessary laws, and by controlling every subordinate power. The means should be adequate to the end: the less should give way to the greater. General principles, therefore, clearly led to the conclusion, that the general government must have the most complete control over every power which could create the least obstacle to its operations.

2. Mr. Smith then went into an examination of the particular provisions of the Constitution, and compared them together, to prove that his remarks were not conclusions from general principles alone, but warranted by the language of the Constitution. He conceived, therefore, that the national government would have powers, on this plan, not only to lay all species of taxes, but to control and set aside every thing which should impede the collection of them. They would have power to abrogate the laws of the states, and to prevent the operation of their taxes; and all courts, before whom any disputes on these points should come, whether federal or not, would be bound by oath to give judgment according to the laws of the Union. An honorable gentleman from New York, he said, had dwelt with great attention on the idea that the state governments were necessary and useful to the general system, and that this would secure their existence.[37] Granting that they would be very convenient in the system, yet, if the gentleman's position were true, that the two governments would be rivals, we had no need to go any further than the common feelings and passions of human nature, to prove that they must be hostile, and that one or the other must be finally subverted. If they were mutually necessary to each other, how could they be rivals? For, in this case, lessening the power of the states would be only diminishing the advantages of the general government. Another source, from which the gentleman would derive security to the states, was the superior number of the state representatives. Mr. Smith apprehended, however, that this very circumstance would be an argument for abolishing them. The people would be very apt to compare their small importance and powers with the great expense of their support. He then went into an examination of another source of security which the gentleman had pointed out, that is, the great number of officers dependent on the states, and compared them with those of the United States, and concluded with observing, that he (Mr. Smith) was one who had opposed the impost: he was also opposed to the Constitution in its present form. He said, he had opposed the impost, because it gave too much power to a single body, organized as the old Congress was; and he objected to this Constitution, because it gave too much

37. The reference again is to Alexander Hamilton.

power to the general government, however it might be organized. In both, he said, he stood on the same ground, and his conduct had been uniform and consistent.

(2nd speech, same day)

3. The Hon. Mr. SMITH, after some introductory, cursory remarks, took notice of an honorable gentleman's wishes respecting a navy. He thought it would be wild and ridiculous to attempt a project of that kind for a considerable length of time, even if the treasury were full of money. He thought it was our duty to calculate for the present period, and not attempt to provide for the contingencies of two or three centuries to come. In time, events might take place which no human wisdom could foresee, and which might totally defeat and render useless these provisions. He insisted that the present state of the country alone ought to be considered. In three or four hundred years, its population might amount to a hundred millions: at this period, two or three great empires might be established, totally different from our own.

4. Mr. Smith then made some remarks upon the circular letter of the late commander-in-chief, which Mr. Duane had produced. He asked whence the American army came: how were they raised and maintained, if the complaints in this letter were well founded? how had the country been defended, and our cause supported, through so long a war, if requisitions had been so totally fruitless? He observed that one of the gentlemen had contemplated associations among the states for the purpose of resisting Congress. This was an imaginary evil. The opposers of the Constitution, he said, had been frequently charged with being governed by chimerical apprehensions, and of being too much in extremes. He asked if these suggestions were not perfectly in the same style. We had had no evidence of a disposition to combine for such purposes: we had no ground to fear they ever would. But if they were, at any time, inclined to form a league against the Union, in order to resist an oppressive tax, would they not do it, when the tax was imposed without a requisition? Would not the same danger exist, though requisitions were unknown? He thought no power ought to be given which could not be exercised. The gentleman had himself spoken of the difficulties attending general, direct taxes, and had presumed that the general government would take the state systems, and form from them the best general plan they could. But this would but partially remedy the evil. How much better would it be to give the systems of the different states their full force, by leaving to them the execution of the tax, and the power of levying it on the people!

– WEDNESDAY, JULY 2, 1788 –

1. The Hon. Mr. SMITH. Mr. Chairman, the honorable gentleman who spoke yesterday animadverted, in a very ludicrous manner, upon my arguments, and endeavored to place them in a ridiculous point of view. Perhaps it was necessary that the Convention should be diverted with something fanciful, and that they should be relieved from the tediousness of a dull debate by a few flashes of merriment. I suppose it was for this purpose that the gentleman was induced to make so handsome a display of his comic talents, to the no small entertainment of the ladies and gentlemen without the bar. It is well known that, in theatrical exhibitions, the farce succeeds the tragedy. Now, as another honorable gentleman (Mr. Duane) had, but the day before, called to our minds, in a most dismal picture, the tragic scenes of war, devastation, and bloodshed, it was entirely proper that our feelings should be relieved from the shocking impression by a light and musical play. I think the gentleman has acquitted himself admirably. However, his attack seems to have thrown him off his guard, and to have exposed him to his own weapons. The gentleman might well have turned his strictures upon his own contradictions; for, at one time, he argues that a federal republic is impracticable; at another, he argues that the proposed government is a federal republic. At one time, he says the old Confederation has no power at all, at another, he says it has nearly as many as the one proposed. He seems to be an enemy to creeds; and yet, with respect to concurrent jurisdiction, he presents us with his creed, which we are bound to believe. Let us hear it. "I believe that the general government is supreme, and that the state governments are supreme; and yet they are not two supremes, but one supreme; and this cannot be doubted." He says there is a concurrent jurisdiction in your mind, Mr. Chairman, and yet you do not concur; for the gentleman himself claims the soil, and there seems to be a difference between you. But, as the honorable gentleman considers his harangue as containing some reasoning, I shall take notice of a few remarks.

2. The gentleman has said that the committee seemed to be convinced by the arguments of an honorable member from New York. I suppose it was only a fancy of the moment that struck him, of which he can probably give no better account than the rest of us. I can only say for myself, that, the more I hear and reflect, the more convinced I am of the necessity of

From *Debates on the Adoption of the Federal Constitution*, vol. 2, edited by Jonathan Elliot (Salem, N.H.: Ayer, 1987), 392–94.

amendment. Whether the committee have received conviction can easily be settled by a vote.

3. The gentleman from Washington has said that even the state of New York was not a perfect form. In the course of my argument, I observed that the state legislatures were competent to good government, and that it was not proper to exchange governments at so great a risk. Where is the mighty contradiction? I said that the state governments were proper depositories of power, and were the proper guardians of the people. I did not say that any government was perfect, nor did I ascribe any extraordinary qualities to the states. The gentleman endeavors to fix another contradiction upon me. He charges me with saying that direct taxes are dangerous and yet impracticable. This is an egregious misrepresentation. My declaration was, that general direct taxes would be extremely difficult in the apportionment and collection, and that this difficulty would push the general government into despotic measures. The gentleman also ridicules our idea of the states losing their powers. He says this Constitution adds little or no power to the Union, and consequently takes little or nothing from the states. If this be true, what are the advocates of the system contending about? It is the reasoning among all reasoners, that nothing to something adds nothing. If the new plan does not contain any new powers, why advocate it? If it does, whence are they taken? The honorable member cannot understand our argument about the sword and the purse, and asks, Why should the states hold them? I say, the state governments ought to hold the purse, to keep people's hands out of it. With respect to the sword, I say you must handle it, through your general government; but the states must have some agency, or the people will not be willing to put their hands to it. It is observed that we must talk a great deal, and that it is necessary to support here what we have said out of doors. Sir, I conceive that we ought to talk of this subject every where. Several gentlemen have observed that it is necessary these powers should be vested in Congress, that they may have funds to pledge for the payment of debts. This argument has not the least weight in my mind. The government ought not to have it in their power to borrow with too great facility. The funds which we agree to lodge with Congress will be sufficient for as much as they ought to borrow.

4. I submit to the candor of the committee, whether any evidence of the strength of a cause is afforded, when gentlemen, instead of reasoning fairly, assert roundly, and use all the powers of ridicule and rhetoric to abuse their adversaries. Any argument may be placed in a ridiculous light, by taking only detached parts. I wish, Mr. Chairman, that ridicule may be avoided. It can only irritate the passions, and has no tendency to convince the judgment.

Smith's Speech of July 15, 1788

Friday, July 11, 1788

—Mr. JAY moved the following resolutions:—

"*Resolved,* as the opinion of this committee, that the Constitution under consideration ought to be *ratified* by this Convention.

"*Resolved,* further, as the opinion of this committee, that such parts of the said Constitution as may be thought doubtful ought to be explained, and that whatever amendment may be deemed useful, or expedient, ought to be recommended."

Mr. JAY was supported by Mr. Chancellor Livingston, and Mr. Chief Justice Morris, and opposed by Mr. Melancton Smith. The debates on this motion continued till Tuesday, the 15th of July; when Mr. SMITH moved, as an amendment, to add to the first resolution proposed by Mr. JAY, so that the same, when amended, should read as follows:

"*Resolved,* as the opinion of this committee, that the Constitution under consideration ought to be ratified by this Convention: *upon condition nevertheless,* That until a convention shall be called and convened for proposing amendments to the said constitution, the militia of this state will not be continued in service out of this state for a longer term than six weeks, without the consent of the legislature thereof: That the Congress will not make or alter any regulation in this state respecting the times, places, and manner of holding elections for senators or representatives, unless the legislature of this state should neglect or refuse to make laws or regulations for the purpose, or from any circumstance be incapable of making the same; and that, in those cases, such power will only be exercised until the legislature of this state shall make provision in the premises: That no excise will be imposed on any article of the growth, production, or manufacture of the United States, or any of them, within this state, ardent spirits excepted: And that Congress shall not lay direct taxes within this state, but when the moneys arising from the impost and excise shall be insufficient for the public exigencies; nor then, until Congress shall first have made a requisition upon this state, to assess, levy, and pay the amount of such requisition, made agreeably to the census

From *Debates on the Adoption of the Federal Constitution,* vol. 2, edited by Jonathan Elliot (Salem, N.H.: Ayer, 1987), 410–11.

fixed in the said Constitution, in such way and manner as the legislature of this state shall judge best; but in such case, if the state shall neglect or refuse to pay its proportion pursuant to such requisition, then the Congress may assess and levy this state's proportion, together with interest at the rate of six per centum, per annum, from the time at which the same was required to be paid."

Smith's Notes for a Speech on Ratification, July 17, 1788

When I laid before the Committee the propositions now before them,[1] I did sincerely believe they approved such a mode of ratification, as Cong. could and would accept—Much has been said to shew that they cannot.[2] I confess my mind is not yet convinced the constitution absolutely prohibits it—But candor at the same time obliges me to say, that there is weight in the objections—and that taken all circumstances together I believe they would not—Perhaps my wish and the wishes of those who think with me on the merits of the system, to be admitted on these terms, may have been the reason that those arguments who appear to have the force of demonstration in the minds of those Gents. who have offered them, have not yet evidence in our minds—Be that as it may I confess I see but little reason to expect that we shall be received on these terms—I presume, Sir, the object, which those who advocate this had in view, was to bring the question of amendments before the people of America, as soon as possible—To effect this was the design of the condition of the suspension of the powers, for no one apprehends that any great inconveniency will result from the exercise of these powers for some time to come—It was supposed that a stipulation to restrain the exercise [of] these powers would be an inducement to call a

Reprinted courtesy of the New York State Library, Manuscripts and Special Collections: Melancton Smith Papers, 1786–1792.

1. Reference to the proposal to ratify the Constitution on the condition that Congress suspend some of its powers with respect to New York until a second constitutional convention could be held.

2. Federalists such as Hamilton and Harrison had argued that Congress would not accept such a conditional form of ratification as valid and would instead regard it as a rejection.

Convention—The objection to this plan is that the Congress will have no authority under the Cons. to suspend any powers—If some other mode can be devised, to attain the end, we who oppose the Const[itution] wish, the bringing these amendments before the people, with equal cert[ainty?], and at the same time to avoid the object[ion]s that are made against this plan, it ought to be embraced—

We wish to be received into the union but to insure if possible a submission of the amendments proposed to the people of America—The plan proposed it is said will not admit us—if it be true we lose our object by adhering to it—The question is can a way be devised, to secure both these objects—

The plan I now have to propose, aims at both these whether it will obtain them the Committee must judge—I suspect it will not please either side of the house—I can only say it comes nearer the object, than any thing I can offer, and that in my conscience I believe it will answer the end of the side of the house in which I rank myself equal well with the other—And I think avoids all the objections of any weight made against the other. If I am mistaken I shall regret it, and can only say I propose it from the sincerest desire to accommodate—I only beg Gent. not to decide hastily but consider well—to lay aside passions and pride—I am well aware I stand on ticklish ground—That the proposition will not meet the entire approb[ation] of either side—

Those who advocate the Cons[titution] will say we must adopt or reject—with cond[ition]—this prop[osal] is still conditional—Gen. on the other side will charge me with leaving the ground I have been striving to maintain and yielding the point in dispute—To the one I shall say, it is true it is not an unconditional adoption, but—still it is such an one as avoids the objections raised against this—To the other, that though it be true I have shifted the ground, it is only to take a better position—The objects we have in view will be better attained by the system than the former—we shall better secure our admission into the union, and procure a consideration of amendments by the people of America—

I entreat both sides, not to decide hastily, to consider well before they give an opinion—to lay aside prejudices and passion and to consider from the nature of things neither side can be entirely suited.—

Before I read the proposal, I observe that they have been hastily penned and will want correction—I only aim to bring forward the Idea, shall chearfully consent that they should be moulded in any form that will retain the substance—The first part states the sentiments of the majority [upon] the

merits of the Constitution—and [it includes the?] condition on which we come in—and these are followed by,
Resolved . . .[3]

Report on Smith's Speech of July 23, 1788

New York, July 28

Eleventh Pillar!!![1]
Copy of a letter from a gentleman in Poughkeepsie,
to the Printer, dated Friday, July 25, 1788

On Wednesday the Convention finished the consideration of the amendments, and took up the proposition of adopting the Constitution with three conditions annexed. Mr. Jones moved to insert the words *in full confidence,* instead of the words *upon condition.* Mr. M. Smith rose and declared his determination to vote against a condition. He urged that however it might otherwise be presumed he was confident in his principles and conduct. He was as thoroughly convinced then as he ever had been, that the Constitution was radically defective—amendments to it had always been the object of his pursuit, and until Virginia came in, he had reason to believe they might have been obtained previous to the operation of the Government. He was now satisfied they could not, and it was equally the dictate of reason and duty to quit his first ground, and advance so far as that they might be received into the Union. He should hereafter pursue his important and favorite object of amendments, with equal zeal as before, but in a practicable way; which was only in the mode prescribed by the Constitution. On the first suggestion of the plan then under consideration, he thought it might have answered the purpose; but from the reasonings of gentlemen in opposition to it, and whose opinions alone would deservedly have vast weight in the national councils, as well as from the sentiments of persons abroad,[2] he was now persuaded the proposition would not be received, however

3. Smith then proceeded to read from his preliminary draft of a proposed mode of ratification.

From the *Independent Journal,* July 28, 1788.
    1. "Eleventh Pillar" was a reference to the state of New York, which, by ratifying the Constitution, had become the eleventh state to enter the Union.
    2. This is likely a reference to James Madison.

doubtful it might appear, considered merely as an abstract and speculative question. The thing must now be abandoned as fallacious, for if persisted in, it would certainly prove in the event, only a dreadful deception to those who were serious for joining the Union. He then placed in a striking and affecting light, the situation of this State in case we should not be received by Congress. Convultions in the Southern part, factions and discord in the rest.[3] The strength of his own party, who were seriously anxious for amending the Government, would be dissipated; their union lost—their object probably defeated—and they would, to use the simple figurative language of Scripture, be dispersed like sheep on a mountain. He therefore concluded that it was no more than a proper discharge of his public duty, as well as the most advisable way of obtaining the great end of his opposition, to vote against any proposition which would not be received as a ratification of the Constitution. . . .

I[4] have been rather particular in stating the business of Wednesday to you, because I think it is of a decisive nature; and I was so well pleased with Smith's speech, that I have given you the substance of it with fidelity, and as nearly as I could in his own language.

Yesterday Mr. Lansing moved to annex Mr. Smith's last proposition to the ratification, or the one which proposes to adopt with a reservation of a right to withdraw;[5] then Mr. Jay, and after him Mr. Hamilton, rose and declared that the reservation could answer no good purpose in itself—that it implied a distrust of the other States—that it would awaken their pride and other passions unfriendly to the object of amendments; but what was decisive against it, it was inconsistent with the Constitution, and was no ratification.

Mr. Hamilton produced and read part of a letter from a gentleman of high public distinction, containing in explicit terms his opinion that the reservation would amount to a conditional ratification, and would not be received by Congress. Mr. Duane and the Chancellor both declared their opinion to the same effect, and they all concurred in expressing an anxious wish, that since the House had proceeded so far to an accommodation, they

3. This is a reference to the possibility of New York City seceding from the rest of the state and joining the Union if the convention did not ratify the Constitution.

4. The author of this article, Gilbert Livingston, is speaking here in the first person.

5. This refers to Smith's second proposal for conditional ratification, which he made on July 17, 1788.

might now conclude the business with harmony and to the satisfaction of both parties. Mr. Smith remained silent all the day; the question was postponed till to-day.

Friday, July 25

The question was brought on this morning. Mr. Smith made a short speech, declaring his object in originally bringing forward the proposition. He had hoped it would unite both sides; but as he found it would not, and that there was no alternative between adopting and rejecting the Constitution, he should vote against the proposition. It was carried against it by a majority of three. Thank God we have now got the Constitution; I congratulate you. I will give you the yeas and nays, and you may rely on the accuracy of it.[6]

[List of nays (31) and yeas (28)]

Smith's Proposed Amendments at the New York Ratifying Convention

Wednesday, July 2, 1788

Art. 1. Respecting the organization and arming the *militia*, &c.—

"*Provided*, That the militia of any state shall not be marched out of such state without the consent of the executive thereof, nor be continued in service out of the state, without the consent of the legislature thereof, for a longer term than six weeks; and *provided*, that the power to organize, arm, and discipline the militia, shall not be construed to extend further than to prescribe the mode of arming and disciplining the same." Moved by Mr. Smith.

To the clause respecting the power of *regulating commerce*,—

"*Resolved*, as the opinion of this committee, that nothing in the said Constitution contained shall be construed to authorize Congress to grant mo-

---

6. This, again, is Livingston speaking.

From *Debates on the Adoption of the Federal Constitution*, vol. 2, edited by Jonathan Elliot (Salem, N.H.: Ayer, 1987), 406–10.

nopolies, or erect any company with exclusive advantages of commerce."
Moved by Mr. M. Smith.

Clause relating to the granting *titles of nobility*,—

"*Resolved*, as the opinion of this committee, that the Congress shall at no time consent that any person, holding any office of profit or trust in or under the United States, shall accept of any title of nobility from any king, prince, or foreign state." Moved by Mr. M. Smith.

Friday, July 4, 1788

Art. 2. Sec. 1. Clause respecting the *office of President*,—

"*Resolved*, as the opinion of this committee, that the President of the United States should hold his office during the term of seven years, and that he should not be eligible a second time." Moved by Mr. Smith.

Saturday, July 5, 1788

Art. 2. Sec. 2, Clause 2. Amendment moved by Mr. M. Smith:—

"*Resolved*, as the opinion of this committee, that the Congress should appoint, in such manner as they may think proper, a council to advise the President in the appointment of officers; that the said council should continue in office for four years; that they should keep a record of their proceedings, and sign the same, and always be responsible for their advice, and impeachable for malconduct in office; that the counsellors should have a reasonable allowance for their services, fixed by a standing law; and that no man should be elected a counsellor who shall not have attained to the age of thirty-five years, and who is not either a natural-born citizen, or has not become a citizen, before the 4th day of July, 1776."

Clause 5. Motion by Mr. M. Smith:—

"*Provided*, That all commissions, writs, and processes, shall run in the name of the people of the United States, and be tested in the name of the President of the United States, or the person holding his place for the time being, or the first judge of the court out of which the same shall issue."

Monday, July 7, 1788

To the third clause of article sixth, Mr. M. Smith moved the following addition:—

"*Resolved*, as the opinion of this committee, that all the officers of the United States ought to be bound, by oath or affirmation, not to infringe the constitutions or rights of the respective states."

After the Constitution had been gone through, Mr. M. Smith moved for the following amendment to clause 17 of sec. 8, art. 1:—

"*Resolved*, as the opinion of this committee, that the right of the Congress to exercise exclusive legislation over such district, not exceeding ten miles square, as may, by cession of particular states, and the acceptance of Congress, become the seat of the government of the United States, shall not be so exercised as to exempt the inhabitants of such district from paying the same taxes, duties, imposts, and excises, as shall be imposed on the other inhabitants of the state where such district may be, nor shall it be so exercised as to prevent the laws of the state, and all process under those laws, from extending to such district, in all cases of crimes committed without the district, or in cases of contracts made between persons residing within such district and persons residing without it. Nor shall it be so exercised, as to authorize any inhabitant of the said district to bring any suit in any court, which may be established by the Congress within the same, against any citizen or person not an inhabitant of the said district. And it is understood that the stipulations in this Constitution, respecting all essential rights, shall extend as well to this district as to the United States in general. *Resolved*, further, as the opinion of this committee, that the right of exclusive legislation, with respect to such places as may be purchased for the erection of forts, magazines, arsenals, and dock-yards, and other needful buildings, shall not be construed to authorize the Congress to make any law to prevent the laws of the states in which they may lie, from extending to such places in all civil and criminal matters, except as to such persons, as shall be in the service of the United States, nor to them with respect to crimes committed without such places."

Letters

Letter to Andrew Craigie, October 4, 1787

New York Octr. 4th. 1787

Dear Craigie,[1]

I thank you most cordially, for the few Lines you wrote me announcing your safe arrival in twenty three days. I hope you had an agreable passage to London, and that you found our Friend well. I suppose you are by this time plunged, head and ears in speculation, you must only take care that you do not pursue the plan of a famous financier in France, and I recommend to your consideration the scheme called the Mississippi scheme—apropos, now I have mentioned, the Mississippi scheme, could you not contrive one to dispose of Lands in the western Country. I think it an object worth while to sound the people on your side of the water. If they should be inclined to adventure in such a speculation, I think we could do something handsome in the business. The new Constitution is reported, I would have sent you a copy of it, with the objections I have to it, but I do not think it best to put you to cost of postage. I will do it by the Betsy for London, which sails in about ten days. You will remember, if any plan should offer, in which you

Reprinted courtesy of the American Antiquarian Society, Letters of Delegates to Congress, vol. 24, November 6, 1786–February 29, 1788: Andrew Craigie Papers.

1. Dr. Andrew Craigie (1754–1819), a physician of Boston and Cambridge, Massachusetts, was apothecary general of the Continental Army from 1775 to 1783. After 1784 he turned his attentions increasingly from the wholesale apothecary trade to land speculation, becoming involved with associates of the Ohio Company and the Scioto Company, and in 1787 went to London as agent for William Duer to confer with Daniel Parker concerning the sale of Scioto Company lands. See the *Dictionary of American Biography;* and Archer B. Hulbert, "Andrew Craigie and the Scioto Associates," *Proceedings of the American Antiquarian Society*, n.s., 23 (October 1913): 222–36.

would make more money than you want, that I am perfectly willing to take part of the burden off your shoulders.

I am, Yours sincerely, Melancton Smith

Letter to Abraham Yates, January 23, 1788

To Abraham Yates Jun. Esq.[1]
Chairman of the Committee
Albany

N.York Jany 23, 1788

Dear Sir

I have been so engaged for a long time past that I have not been able to command leisure to write to you—Indeed for sometime past, there would have been no propriety in my writing, for report here said that you were defunct, and that your funeral had been solemnized with great pomp and your pall supported by a number of illustrious characters, who I am well informed had a principal agency in producing the new Constitution.[2] What

Reprinted courtesy of The New York Public Library, Astor, Lenox, and Tilden Foundations, Manuscripts and Archives Division, Abraham Yates Jr. Papers.

1. Abraham Yates (1724–1796), a native of Albany, New York, was a delegate to Congress, 1787–88; a New York senator, 1777–90; and the mayor of Albany, 1790–96. A fiercely partisan Anti-Federalist, he wrote several essays critiquing the Constitution. See John P. Kaminski et al., eds., *Documentary History of the Ratification of the Constitution* (Madison: Wisconsin Historical Society Press, 1976–), vol. 5, Massachusetts, no. 2, p. 1088.

2. Smith refers to several items appearing in the December 18, 1787, issue of the *Northern Centinel* that were introduced by the following titles or headings: (1) "The last Words and Dying Speech of the celebrated Rough-Hewer" (i.e., Abraham Yates Jr.); (2) "The following are the Particulars of the Death and Internment of the late ROUGH-HEWER"; (3) An ELEGY on the Death of the ROUGH-HEWER: Supposed to be written by his good Friend ANARCHY"; and (4) "The following EPITAPH is inscribed on the Tomb of the Rough-Hewer." The second item listed above includes the "Order of the Procession" for the funeral, with an illustration of a coffin containing the following statements: "ROUGH-HEWER / CAME INTO EXISTENCE / 1783 / AND DIED / DECR. 11 / 1787." Kaminski et al., *Documentary History*, vol. 20, pp. 638–39.

should have taken them, so soon from Philadelphia to Albany, I was at a loss to determine, unless it was for the benefit of the *air*, or to make an establishment at the City of Lansingburgh, which I am told is a favourable situation to carry on their business.

I am happy to hear, however that you are now in the land of the living. If the report of your decease was true, and you have been restored to this mortal life, by a dismission from the regions of the dead, for a while in order to oppose the new system of government, I should be curious to hear what a number of the patriots who assisted in effecting the late revolution say about it! But perhaps, the publication concerning your death, meant to take a distinction between the rough Hewer and Abraham Yates, so that though the former might be buried, the latter might remain in Life and health—[3]

I cannot give you any news of importance to be relied upon. We have nothing authentic from the Convention of Massachusetts. Reports on all hands say, that the division in that body will be great. But on which side the majority will be time must discover. The friends to the new government in this City appear for a few days past, to despond with respect to Massachusetts. The decision of that State will certainly have great influence on the final issue of the business. If they reject it I think it cannot go down, if they accept, every effort will be used to carry it through—we have nothing from the Southward.

I wish you and Mr. Jones[4] would favour me, as your leisure and opportunities will permit, with your observations on this system, especially on the Judicial powers of it, about which very little has yet been written. It appears to me this part of the system is so framed as to *clinch* all the other powers, and to extend them in a silent and imperceptible manner to any thing and every thing, while the Court who are vested with these powers are totally independent, uncontroulable and not amenable to any other power in any decisions they may make.

What are the cases in *equity* arising under the Constitution? Will not the supreme court under this clause have a right to enlarge the extent of

---

3. "Rough Hewer" was the pseudonym Abraham Yates used in writing against the passage of the 1783 impost recommended by Congress.

4. Samuel Jones was a New York assemblyman and leader among the Clinton faction. (Brooks, 158.)

the powers of the general government and to curtail that of the States at pleasure?—

What are the cases of equity under Treaties? Will they not under this power be authorized to reverse all acts of attainder heretofore passed by the States, and to set aside all Judgements of Confiscation?

I could state a number more questions if I had time, but I am in haste—I only wish to call your attention, and that of Mr. Jones to attend critically to this part of the plan and beg your remarks upon it. We are weak here, the few that oppose it, have not leisure or ability or else want inclination to examine and explore its defects, such of you as are of the true faith at Poughkeepsie should employ all your leisure in thinking and making remarks, if you have not time to arrange them for publication, they will afford great assistance to some here who will do it, if you will forward your observations to me. I could easily lengthen my Epistle but I am in haste—remember to your room companions.

I am your [ob. ser.],
Melancton Smith

Letter to Abraham Yates, January 28, 1788

New York Jany. 28th 1788

D. Sir,

I received yours of the 18th Inst. You seem to be of opinion, that there is a majority in both houses of the Legislature against the new Constitution.[1] We have great doubts here, whether this is the case in the assembly. If it is, how can it be accounted for, that they have chosen for the Delegates, the

Reprinted courtesy of The New York Public Library, Astor, Lenox, and Tilden Foundations, Manuscripts and Archives Division, Abraham Yates Jr. Papers.

1. In the second week of January 1788, the New York state legislature was meeting to consider how to handle the newly proposed Constitution. Abraham Yates, a member of the New York State Senate, had assured Smith that the New York legislature was opposed to the Constitution and thus would be willing to delay holding a convention for as long as possible or to attach a preface to the proposed Constitution that condemned it. (De Pauw, 84–85.)

warmest advocates for the measure?² You may say they out general you, but it amounts to the same thing, whether you are defeated by the superior skill of your enemy, or by their superior strength, it is a defeat still. All sides are waiting here with anxious expectation for the determination of the Convention of Massachusetts. Both the favourers and opposers say that they have a majority. Each party speaks as they would have it, and I believe the information received from Massachusetts differs according to the sentiments of the Men who give it. In this however both sides agree that there is very great division of sentiment in the Convention, and the advocates do not pretend to hope for more than a small majority. Letters from our Friends there state that the numbers stand in the convention, 201 against the Constitution to 119 that are for it—on the other hand those who are for it say that there will be a majority in its favour and that the opposition is lessening. It is impossible in this variety of reports to form an opinion that may be relied upon. I am not sanguine. I think it best always to reckon the strength of your adversaries as much as it is. The *better sort* have means of *convincing* those who differ from them, with which I am unacquainted. And how prevalent these kind of means may be, I cannot pretend to say. I confess I fear their power. I am not able by this opportunity to answer your question relating to Morris Letter to D. Franklin, as I do not recollect the date of it, and have had no opportunity to procure the information. I believe your statement of it is nearly just. He advises that the Sum granted as a donation should be acknowledged as a debt, and included in the Obligations given to the Court of France for monies borrowed, and assigns for reason, that this country ought not to lay under obligation to any foreign power for money given. Let me hear from you as often as you can.

I am your ob. Ser.,
Melancton Smith

2. One of the first acts of the New York Assembly was to choose a new state delegation to the Continental Congress. The assembly chose Abraham Yates, an Anti-Federalist, but also Ezra L'Hommedieu, Egbert Benson, Leonard Gansevoort, and Alexander Hamilton—all Federalists. Many Anti-Federalists in New York City, Smith included, thus viewed the actions of the assembly with concern. (Ibid.)

Letter to Cornelius Schoonmaker,[1] April 6, 1788

New York April 6, 1788

Dear Sir,

When I left you at Poughkeepsie I promised to advise you as soon after my Return as the Matter could be ascertained whether the Election of a certain Friend of ours could be secured in an adjoining County.[2] I continued in the County more than a week longer than I expected, and have made Inquiry instantly after my Return. The Result is, that it is my Opinion and that of our Friend, that it will not be prudent to hazard his Election for that County, and that therefore you had best by all means put him on your Nomination.[3] We shall attempt to chuse him here, and are not without hopes that we may succeed. For we find our Strength here greater than we expected, and I have no Doubt but many of the opposite Party will vote for him notwithstanding he differs in Sentiment with them. But still we are clearly of Opinion that you ought to hold him up—For he had better be chosen in two Places, than not to be elected at all.[4] Appearances on Long Island are favorable to our Cause, and I have strong Hopes if proper Exertions are made that all will go well, Rhode Island have rejected the System,

Reprinted courtesy of the New-York Historical Society, John Lamb Papers, April 6, 1788, box 5, no. 6.

1. Cornelius Schoonmaker (1745–1796) was an Anti-Federalist from Ulster County.

2. The "friend" is Governor George Clinton. Going into the election of delegates to the New York ratifying convention, New York Anti-Federalists realized that they were strong in Ulster County. Correspondingly, they considered running Governor Clinton, a resident of Ulster, in neighboring Kings County, a Federalist stronghold, hoping that Clinton could win in Kings and thereby gain an additional seat in the convention. (Schecter, 86–87.)

3. Clinton's chances of being elected in Kings County were considered remote; furthermore, the effort to run him there might appear to be a cynical ploy. Peter Van Gaasbeek wrote to Schoonmaker, "Many people will be Cool and many will suspect A design or Trick is intended." (Ibid.)

4. The Anti-Federalists ultimately decided to run Clinton in both Ulster County and New York City.

by the Vote of the Towns, and Accounts from Virginia and North Carolina, represent that they are much opposed to it.

I am in Haste,
Your Friend,
Me S.

Letter to Nathan Dane,[1] June 28, 1788

Poughkeepsie June 28th 1788

Dear Sir,

I am favoured with yours of the 24th Inst. The accession of New Hampshire will have no other effect upon our convention, than softening them to consider what is proper to be done, in the present situation of things, if it has that—Indeed I can scarcely perceive any effect it has had—And the most I fear is that there will not be a sufficient degree of moderation in some of our most influential men, calmly to consider the circumstances in which we are, and to accommodate our decision, to these circumstances.[2] You have had too much experience in public life not to know, that pride, passion, and interested motives have great influence in all public bodies—They no doubt have their influence in this—From my own situation, perhaps, more than from any better principle, I feel none of these, except, it is probable, a wish to support the party with whom I am connected as far as is consistent with propriety. But, I know, my great object is to procure such amendments in this government, as to prevent its attaining the ends, for which it appears to me, and to you calculated—I am therefore very anxious to procure good amendments—I had rather recommend substantial

Reprinted courtesy of the Beverly Historical Society and Museum, Beverly, Massachusetts.

1. Nathan Dane (1752–1835) was an Anti-Federalist, a Massachusetts congressman, a drafter of the Northwest Ordinance of 1787, and a friend of Smith's.

2. New Hampshire ratified the Constitution on June 21, 1788, the ninth state to do so. With the ratification of New Hampshire, under Article 7 thereof, the Constitution became binding on the nine states that had ratified it.

amendments, than adopt it conditionally with unimportant ones, leaving our critical situation out of the question. I do not find these endeavors sufficiently seconded—The principal labor of managing the Controversy lies upon me—Hitherto the amendments proposed are substantial, they will continue so—but as no question is taken on any, it is questionable whether, the most important will not be yielded, under the Idea of making previous conditional amendments—When I am persuaded, if we can agree, to make the condition, a subsequent one, that is, to take place in one or two years after adoption or the ratification to become void, we can accommodate with the advocates of the constitution for more substantial amendments.[3]

I inclose you the amendments as far as they have been offered—the last has been the subject of two days debate, and will take some days more. Mr. Hamilton and the Chancellor have spoken largely in favour of the Article. Mr. Lansing and myself have advocated the amendment. The speech published for the Chancellor is the substance of what he delivered. He and I have come in contact several times—but he has ceased hostilities. He is a wretched reasoner, very frequently. Hamilton is the champion, he speaks frequently, very long and very vehemently—has, like publius, much to say not very applicable to the subject. I wish you to communicate any observations you may think useful.

Your friend and ser.
Melancton Smith

3. For the first time Smith here suggests that the New York convention should ratify the Constitution unconditionally but with the proviso that New York would withdraw from the Union if a second constitutional convention were not called within a year or two. Smith would not present this idea to the convention until July 17, 1788.

Letter to Nathan Dane, July 15, 1788

July 15, 1788

My Dear Sir,

I have received yours, and thank you for them.[1] We have gone through the proposal of amendments, and are now deliberating what to do with them. In this we do not accord in sentiments, but I am not without hopes, we shall become of one mind. I entirely accord with you in opinion, and shall if necessary avow them. Time and patience is necessary to bring our party to accord, which I ardently wish. I have no time to copy the amendments proposed nor to answer Mr. Osgood's friendly letter, for which I beg you to thank him.[2] I beg you to use your influence to defer the organization of the New Government until we decide—you may be assured, that time and great industry is requisite to bring us to act properly. My task is arduous and disagreeable. You shall hear more by the next opportunity.

I am yours,
Melancton Smith

Reprinted courtesy of the New England Historic Genealogical Society, R. Stanton Avery Special Collections Department, John Wingate Thornton Papers, MSS 95, folder 89.

1. Nathan Dane had replied to Smith in a lengthy letter on July 3, 1788. Dane agreed with the moderate tone Smith had struck in his June 28 letter and argued strenuously that New York should ratify the Constitution unconditionally and then later seek amendments. Nathan Dane to Melancton Smith, July 3, 1788. Kaminski et al., eds., *Documentary History*, vol. 18, 214–20.

2. Samuel Osgood had written Melancton Smith and Samuel Jones on July 11, 1788, offering the same advice Dane had offered. Samuel Osgood to Melancton Smith and Samuel Jones, July 11, 1788. National Park Service, Collections of Federal Hall National Memorial, New York City. Cited in ibid., vol. 18, 258, n1.

Proposed Amendments to the Constitution, July 1788

That there be a Declaration or Bill of Rights, asserting, and securing from Encroachment the essential and unalienable Rights of the People, in some such manner as the following,—

1. That all Freemen have certain essential inherent Rights, of which they can not by any Compact deprive or divest their Posterity; among which are the Enjoyment of Life and Liberty, with the means of acquiring, possessing and protecting Property, and pursuing and obtaining Happiness and Safety.

2. That all Power is naturally vested in, and consequently derived from the People, that Magistrates therefore are their Trustees and Agents, and at all times amenable to them.

3. That Government ought to be, instituted for the common Benefit, Protection and security of the People; and that whenever any Government shall be found inadequate, or contrary to these Purposes,

Reprinted courtesy of the New York State Library, Manuscripts and Special Collections: Melancton Smith Papers, 1786–1792.

Smith drafted these amendments at the New York ratifying convention. On July 19, 1788, with debate over the proper mode of ratification of the Constitution stalled, John Lansing moved that a bill of rights and amendments be debated. Governor Clinton suggested that an informal committee of four people—Smith, Robert Yates, Richard Harrison, and James Duane—be created to arrange these amendments (De Pauw, 227). Smith produced this draft in his service on the committee. He had proposed a similar version of the bill of rights to the convention on July 15 (Brooks, 206).

a Majority of the Community hath an indubitable unalienable and
indefeasible Right, to reform, alter or abolish it, and to establish
another, in such manner as shall be judged most conducive to the
public weal; and that the doctrine of non-resistance against arbitrary
Power and oppression is absurd, slavish and destructive of the Good
and Happiness of Mankind.

4. That no man or set of men, are entitled to exclusive or separate
public Emoluments or Priviledges from the Community, but in consideration of public Services; which not being descendable neither
ought the offices of Magistrate, Legislator or Judge, or any other
public office to be hereditary.

5. That the legislative executive and judicial Powers of Government
should be separate and distinct; and that the Members of the two first
may be restrained from oppression, by feeling and participating the
public Burthens, they should at fixed periods, be reduced to a private
Station, return into the mass of the People, and the vacancies be
supplied by certain and regular Elections; in which all, or any part of
the former Members to be eligible or ineligible, as the Rules of the
Constitution of Government and the Laws shall direct.

6. That the Right of the People to participate in the Legislature is the
best Security of Liberty, and the Foundation of all free Government;
for this Purpose Elections ought to be free and frequent; and all men
having sufficient Evidence of permanent common Interest with, and
attachment to the Community, ought to have the Right of Suffrage,
and no Aid, Charge, Tax or Fee can be set, rated or levied upon the
People, without their own Consent, or that of their Representatives,
so elected, nor can they be bound by any Law to which they have not,
in like manner, assented, for the public good.

7. That all Power of suspending Laws, or the Execution of Laws, by
any Authority, without Consent of the Representatives of the People
in the Legislature is injurious to their Rights, and ought not to be
exercised.

8. That in all capital or criminal Prosecutions, a man hath a right to
demand the cause and nature of his Accusation, to be confronted with
the Accusers and Witnesses, to call for Evidence and be admitted
Counsel in his favour, and to a fair and speedy Trial by an impartial

Jury of his Vicinage; without whose unanimous Consent he can not be found guilty (except in the Government of the land, and naval Forces in time of actual War, Invasion or Rebellion) nor can he be compelled to give Evidence against himself.

9. That no Freeman ought to be taken, imprisoned, or deprived of his Freehold, Liberties, Priviledges or Franchises, or outlawed or exiled, or in any manner destroyed, or deprived of his Life, Liberty or Property but by the law of the Land.

10. That every Freeman restrained of his Liberty, is entitled to a Remedy to enquire into the Lawfulness thereof, and to remove the same if unlawful, and that such Remedy ought not to be denied or delayed.

11. That in Controvercies respecting Property, and in Suits between man and man, the ancient Trial by Jury of Facts, where they arise, is one of the greatest Securities to the Rights of a free People, and ought to remain sacred and inviolable.

12. That every Freeman ought to find a certain Remedy, by Recourse to the Laws, for all Injuries or Wrongs he may receive, in his Person, Property or Character. He ought to obtain Right and Justice freely, without Sale, compleatly and without Denial, promptly and without delay; and that all Establishments or Regulations contravening these Rights are oppressive and unjust.

13. That excessive Bail ought not to be required, nor excessive Fines imposed, nor cruel and unusual Punishments inflicted.

14. That every Freeman has a Right to be secure from all unreasonable Searches and Seizures of his Person, his Papers and his Property; all warrants therefore to search suspected Places, or to seize any Freeman, his Papers or Property, without Information upon Oath (or affirmation of a Person religiously scrupulous of taking an oath) of legal and sufficient Cause, are grievous and oppressive; and all general Warrants to search suspected Places, or to apprehend any suspected Person, without specially naming or describing the Place or Person, are dangerous, and ought not to be granted.

15. That the People have a Right peaceably to assemble together to consult for their common Good, or to instruct their Representatives, and that every Freeman has a Right to petition or apply to the Legislature for Redress of Grievances.

16. That the People have a Right to Freedom of Speech, and of writing and publishing their Sentiments; that the Freedom of the Press is one of the great Bulwarks of Liberty, and ought not to be violated.

17. That the People have a Right to keep and to bear Arms. That a well regulated Militia, composed of the Body of the People, trained to arms, is the proper, natural, and safe defence of a free State. That standing Armies in time of Peace are dangerous to Liberty, and therefore ought to be avoided, as far as the Circumstances and Protection of the Community will admit; and that in all cases, the military, should be under strict Subordination to, and governed by the civil Power.

18. That no Soldier in time of Peace ought to be quartered in any House without the Consent of the Owner; and in time of war, only by the civil Magistrate in such manner as the Laws direct.

19. That any Person religiously scrupulous of bearing Arms ought to be exempted, upon payment of an Equivalent to employ another to bear Arms in his stead.

20. That Religion or the Duty which we owe to our Creator, and the manner of discharging it, can be directed only by Reason and Conviction, not by Force or Violence, and therefore all Men have an equal natural and unalienable Right, to the free Exercise of Religion according to the Dictates of Conscience, and that no particular religious Sect or Society of Christians ought to be favoured or established by Law, in preference to others.

2

That each State in the Union shall retain its Sovereignty, Freedom and Independence, and every Power, Jurisdiction and Right, which is not by this Constitution expressly delegated to the Congress of the United States.

That there shall be one Representative for every thirty thousand Persons according to the Enumeration or Census mentioned in the Constitution, until the whole number of the Representatives amounts to two hundred.

That Congress shall not exercise the Powers respecting the Regulation of Elections, vested in them by the fourth Section of the first Article of the Constitution, but in Cases when a State neglects or refuses to make the Regulations therein mentioned, or shall make Regulations subversive of the Rights of the People to a free and equal Representation in Congress agreeably to the Constitution, or shall be prevented from making Elections by Invasion or Rebellion; and in any of these Cases, such Powers shall be exercised by the Congress only until the Cause be removed.

That the Congress do not lay direct taxes, nor Excises upon any articles of the Growth, or manufactured from the Growth of any of the American States, but when the monies arising from the Duties on Imports are insufficient for the public Exigencies; nor then, until the Congress shall have first made a Requisition upon the States, to assess, levy and pay their respective Proportions of such Requisitions according to the Enumeration or Census fixed in the Constitution, in such way and manner as the Legislature of the State shall judge best; and if any State shall neglect or refuse to pay its Proportion pursuant to such Requisition, then Congress may assess and levy such States Proportion, together with Interest thereon, at the rate of six per centum per annum, from the time of payment prescribed in such Requisition.

That the Members of the Senate and House of Representatives shall be ineligible to, and incapable of holding any office under the authority of the United States, during the time for which they shall respectively be elected.

*That there shall be a constitutional responsible Council to assist in the administration of Government, with the power of chusing out of their own Body a President, who in Case of the Death, Resignation or Disability of the President of the United States, shall act, pro tempore, as Vice President, instead of a Vice President elected in the manner prescribed by the Constitution; and that the Power of making Treaties, appointing Ambassadors, other public Ministers and Consuls, Judges of the supreme Courts, and all other officers of the United States, whose appointments are not otherwise provided for by the Constitution, and which shall be established by law, be vested in the President of the United States with the assistance of the Council so to be appointed. But all Treaties so made or entered into, shall be subject to the Revision of the Senate and House of Representatives, for their Ratification and no commercial Treaty shall be ratified without the consent of two thirds of the Members present

---

* This article not yet finally agreed upon by the Committee appointed to prepare the Amendments.[1]

1. Smith's proposal of a presidential advisory council was defeated, 46–10. (Brooks, 230, n65.)

in both Houses; nor shall any Treaty ceding, contracting, restraining or suspending, the territorial Rights or Claims of the United States, or any of them, or their, or any of their Rights or Claims to fishing in the American Seas, or navigating the American Rivers be ratified, without the Consent of three fourths of the whole number of the Members of both Houses.

No navigation Law, or Law for regulating Commerce shall be passed without the Consent of two thirds of the Members present in both Houses.

No standing Army or regular Troops shall be raised or kept up in time of peace without the Consent of two thirds of the Members of both Houses.

Neither the President or Vice President of the United States or any Member of the Council shall command the Army or Navy of the United States in person without the Consent of two thirds of the Members of both Houses.

No soldier shall be enlisted for a longer Term than four years, except in time of War, and then for no longer Term than the Continuance of the War.

No mutiny Act shall be passed for any longer Term than two years.

The President of the United States, or any other officer acting under the Authority of the United States shall, upon Impeachment, be suspended from the Exercise of his Office, during his Trial.

The Judges of the federal Court shall be incapable of holding any other office, or of receiving the Profits of any other Office or Emolument under the United States or any of them.

Proposed Amendments to Articles 1–3 of the Constitution

Art. 3. Sec. 2, add: The supreme federal judicial Court shall have no jurisdiction of causes between Citizens of different States, unless the matter of dispute be of the value of 2000 Dollars at least, nor shall the federal

Reprinted courtesy of the New York State Library, Manuscripts and Special Collections: Melancton Smith Papers, 1786–1792.

These are notes Smith made for his own purposes during the New York ratifying convention. They include proposed revisions and amendments to the various articles of the Constitution.

judicial powers extend to any actions between Citizens of diff. States, when the matter in dispute is not of the value of 1600 D. at the least.

Art. 2: So amend it—that the president shall hold his office for 7 years and never after be eligible to it,[1] and so that no person shall be chosen to it—who shall not have arrived to the age of 45 years—he shall never command the Army in person without the consent of the Legislature.

Art. 1 Sect. 9, add: No man demeaning himself peaceably shall be molested on acc. of his Religion or mode of worship—The people of the U.S. shall always be entitled to the trial by Jury, according to the general usage of the Country—The freedom of the press shall never be restrained by any taxes duties or in any matter whatsoever—No soldiers shall be quartered in time of peace on any private houses without the consent of the owner—No man shall be held to answer to any offence, till the same be fully described to him, nor to furnish evidence against himself—except in the government of the Army and Navy—No person shall be tried for any offence whereby he may incur loss of life or any infamous punishment until he be first indicted by a grand Jury—every person shall have a right to produce all proofs that may be favourable to him and to meet the witnesses against him face to face—Every person shall have a right to be secure from all unreasonable searches and seizures of their houses, persons, papers and possessions and all warrants shall be deemed contrary to this right, if the foundation of them be not previously supported by Oath and there be not in them a special designation of persons and objects of search arrest or seizure—and no person shall be exiled or molested in his person or effects otherwise than by the judgment of his peers or according to the Law of the Land—General powers to decide on Law and equity or to decide on Law and fact ought not to be vested in the same judge or judges—no Companies with exclusive advantages of Commerce ought to be erected—The people have the right always to assemble and to petition the government for a redress of wrongs—The militia shall always be kept well organized armed and disciplined, and include according to the past in ages of the States all the men capable of bearing arms—and no regulations tending to render the general militia useless and defenceless by established select corps of militia or distinct bodies of military men not having permanent interests and attachments in the community shall be made—The militia shall not be subject to

1. Smith proposed this revision at the ratifying convention on Friday, July 4, 1788.

martial Law except in time of war invasion or rebellion—No State shall be subject to be sued or prosecuted in any Court of Law—and generally Congress shall exercise no power but what is expressly delegated by the Constitution—And the federal Courts shall never be entitled to Jurisdiction by fiction or collusion.

Proposed Amendments to Article 2 of the Constitution

–AMENDMENTS–

Article 2. Sect. 1

The President of the United States shall hold his office during the term of ___ years, and shall not be eligible a second time. And no person shall be eligible to that office, who has not attained to the age of 45 years.

Sect. 2.

The President of the United States shall never command the Army or Navy of the United States in Person without the consent of two thirds of both houses of the Legislature, nor shall he grant pardons for Treason, without the consent of the Legislature, but he shall have power to grant Reprieves to persons convicted of Treason until their cases are laid before the Legislature for their decision.

The United States shall from time to time be divided by the Congress into nine convenient Districts, for each of which there shall be one Counsellor elected every fourth year in each District, in the manner following—

The Electors in each District entitled to vote for Representatives shall vote for three persons for Counsellors, and the votes shall be returned to the Congress—And the federal Representatives and Senators assembled in one room, shall take the three persons who shall have the greatest number of Votes in each district, and by joint ballot and by majority of Votes shall elect one of them Counsellor for the District. The said Council

Reprinted courtesy of the New York State Library, Manuscripts and Special Collections: Melancton Smith Papers, 1786–1792.

These are notes Smith made for himself in preparation for a discussion of amending Article 2 of the Constitution.

shall keep a record of their proceedings and sign the same, and always be responsible for their advice and impeachable for malconduct in office—

The said Counsellors shall have a reasonable allowance for their services fixed by standing Laws, and no man shall be elected a Counsellor who shall not have been seven years a Citizen of the United States, and one year an Inhabitant of the District for which he shall be elected and have attained to the age of 35 years—

The President shall have power by and with the consent of the Senate to make treaties provided two thirds of the Senators concur—And he shall nominate and by and with the consent of the Council shall appoint ambassadors or—[1]

The Congress shall appoint the Commissioners of the Treasury, and the Treasurer of the United States—

Preliminary Draft of Proposed Mode of Adoption of Constitution, July 1788

Resolved that it be recommended to the Legislature of this State to request the Congress to call a Convention to consider of and propose amendments to this Constitution at their first session and that the amendments agreed to by this Convention be transmitted to such Convention when met to be laid before them.

1. Smith formally proposed this council at the New York ratifying convention on Saturday, July 5, 1788.

Reprinted courtesy of the New York State Library, Manuscripts and Special Collections: Melancton Smith Papers, 1786–1792.

After the New York Anti-Federalists had proposed all their amendments (fifty-five altogether), the convention debated the mode of ratifying the Constitution. On July 10, the Anti-Federalist John Lansing proposed a form of conditional ratification, according to which the state would ratify only after certain "conditional amendments" had been acted upon. On July 11, the Federalist John Jay proposed a form of unconditional ratification, with the additional proposal that the convention merely recommend consideration of various amendments. On July 15, Smith proposed a compromise mode of ratification according to which New York would ratify the Constitution prior to amendments being acted upon, but only on the condition that various powers of the new Congress would be temporarily suspended until a second convention were

Resolved that a Circular Letter be addressed to all the States in the Union, inclosing the foregoing, and earnestly inviting them to join with this State in requesting the Congress at their first meeting to call a Convention of the States, to consider of the amendments proposed by all the States.

We the Delegates of the People of the State of N. York duly elected in pursuance of concurrent Resolutions of the Senate and Assembly of the said State passed the ____ day of ____ and now met in Convention having fully and fairly discussed the Constitution proposed to our consideration agreed upon by the Convention held in Philadelphia on the ____ day of ____ do make known and declare.

That after the most mature deliberation they have been able to give the subject, a majority of them cannot approve the whole of the said Constitution without amendments or alterations, for the following among other reasons.

1. Because some of the most important powers granted by this Constitution are expressed in terms so general, indefinite and ambiguous as to leave the Rulers in the exercise of them to act too much at discretion.

2. Because the limits of the powers of the general and State governments are not marked out with sufficient precision, nor those of the former so defined as entirely to prevent a clashing of jurisdictions—And there is reason to fear that the State governments may be impaired by the general government in the exercise of powers granted in such general words and by implication only especially.

3. Because the Constitution gives to the Congress an indefinite and unlimited power over all the sources of Revenue in the union, by which means there is reason to fear that the individual States will be left without adequate means of discharging Debts or maintaining their civil establishments.

---

held to consider amendments. On July 17, convinced that the Federalists would not accept his proposal, Smith proposed yet another form of conditional ratification. New York would ratify on the condition that it would retain the right to withdraw from the Union if a second constitutional convention were not called within a certain period. Instead of demanding the temporary suspension of Congress's powers as a condition of ratification, the convention would now merely recommend this suspension. This document is the preliminary draft of that proposal.

4. Because the number of Representatives are not sufficiently numerous at present to possess a competent knowledge of and attachment to the Interests of their Constituents or to afford a reasonable degree of confidence, and no certain ratio of increase is fixed, but left at the discretion of the Congress.

5. Because the power of regulating the times places and manner of holding Elections, though in the first instance given to the respective State legislatures, is yet ultimately placed under the controul of the Congress, by which means they will have it too much in their power to secure their own continuance.

6. Because an improper mixture of Legislative Executive and judicial powers are lodged in the Senate. It is a maxim in a free government that the Legislative executive and judicial departments should be kept separate—though this cannot be effected in all its extent, yet it may be much nearer attained than is done in this system—For the Senate not only form one branch of the Legislature, but are also associated with the president in the exercise of the most important executive powers, and form the highest judicial court in the nation for the trial of impeachments.

7. The judicial powers in this Constitution are given in too general and indefinite terms, are so various and extensive, that they may easily be made by legal fiction to extend, too far, and absorb some of the judicial powers of the respective States. No explicit security is given for trial by Jury in common Law cases, and the ancient and usual mode of trial in criminal matters is not secured. The appellate jurisdiction both as to Law and fact may deprive the Citizen of safety from Juries and render the obtaining justice difficult, dilatory, and expensive.

For these and various other reasons this Convention would be induced not to accede to this Constitution did not other weighty considerations interpose—

But the strong attachments they feel to their sister States and their regard to the common good of the union impel them to preserve it—

This Convention have the firmest confidence in the common Councils of the people of the US and the highest expectations, that all the necessary amendments will be produced from their farther deliberations. They therefore consent with the utmost chearfullness to abide the result of such deliberations. But as some time will be necessary to effect this, the Convention will forbear to dissent from their Bretheren of the other States—They have therefore agreed to assent to ratify the said Constitution in the firmest confidence that an opportunity will be speedily given, to revise and amend the said Constitution in the mode pointed out in the 5th Article thereof, express by reserving nevertheless to this State a right to recede and withdraw from the said Constitution in case such opportunity be not given within __ years—[1]

And this Convention do recommend to the Congress that the power to lay and collect excises &c. to call out the militia &c. be not exercised or made to operate on this State, in any other manner than is proposed in the amendments recommended by this Convention until the sense of the people of the US be taken on the propriety of the amendments to the Constitution in one or the other of the modes pointed out in it.

Draft of Circular Letter

The Convention of the State of New York have had the Constitution recommended by the Convention which met in Philadelphia in Sep. last under their consideration—

A large majority of the Convention as well as of their Constituents, are of opinion that important and material alterations are necessary to be made in the system, in order to secure the Liberties of the people under it—

Under this Conviction, they would have withheld their assent to it until amendments were first agreed upon, had not important considerations interposed. But they considered the preservation of the union as essential to the public prosperity safety and happiness, that as ten of our sister States

---

1. The words "And on the express condition" appear only in the first draft of this document.

Reprinted courtesy of the New York State Library, Manuscripts and Special Collections: Melancton Smith Papers, 1786–1792.

On July 25, 1788, after ratifying the Constitution, the New York convention appointed Smith, John Lansing, and John Jay to draft a circular letter to the states explaining their decision and soliciting support for a second constitutional convention. Smith produced this draft, although the final product, which differed considerably from Smith's draft, was primarily the work of Jay. (Brooks, 222; De Pauw, 245.)

had already acceded to the system of Gov. it had become impracticable to procure amendments previous to its going into operation—They have moreover the fullest confidence that the united councils of the people of the U.S. will effect such amendments and alterations, as will render those invaluable rights and Liberties for which the people of America have so nobly contended secure, and quiet those apprehensions which so many of our virtuous Citizens entertain from the operation of the Government—

They have therefore acceded to the Constitution, but neither a regard to their own sentiments nor to those of their Constituents would permit them to do it without reserving to this State a right to withdraw from it, in case an opportunity is not afforded in ___ years to revise the system in the mode pointed out in the 5th Article—

Our opinion is that the most eligible mode of revising the Constitution will be by calling another general Convention, to consider of and propose such amendments, as will secure the liberties of the people and accord with the sentiments of the several States.

This cannot be effected unless 2/3 of the States apply to the Congress for the purpose—We therefore earnestly invite your State to join with ours in making application to the Congress to call a Convention of the States for this purpose, as soon after they meet as is convenient.

We forbear to urge the reasons which induce us to disapprove of the system in many of its parts. Our sense of its defects will best appear by the amendments we have proposed to it a Copy of which is inclosed[1]—

But besides the imperfection of the plan, other weighty reasons urge a speedy consideration of the amendments proposed to it—It is a fact notorious, that a great proportion of the people of the United States are opposed to the Constitution in its present form. It is reasonable that their fears should be quieted, we may say, that even their predjudices should be consulted—They have earned the Liberties they enjoy, by a vast expence of blood and treasures—They are entitled to a security for them, and even to have their apprehensions of danger removed—Besides it cannot be expected that a government can be exercised for the public good when such a powerful opposition exists in the community against the principles upon which it is founded—These reasons in addition to the defects in the plan are sufficient to induce a reconsideration of it.

We prefer the mode of consideration by a general Convention, because they will be able to take up the amendments proposed by all the States, and

1. See "Proposed Amendments to the Constitution, July 1788."

accommodate them as near as possible to the general sentiment—Besides it is to be presumed that on such an occasion the States would depute men in whose ability and dispositions for such a work, they could repose the fullest confidence—

The opposition made by this State to this Constitution has been represented to proceed from local attachments and from an aversion to establish a good federal government—We trust the amendments we have proposed will manifest that none of our objections have originated from those sources—Every State in the union we presume are equally interested with ourselves in obtaining them—Our attachment to the union of the States is equally ardent with that of any of our sister States—We believe their attachments to liberty is equally strong with ours—As a decisive proof of both, we chearfully consent to submit to their determinations on the propriety of the amendments to be made to this system—And have the highest confidence that they will join with us in applying to Congress to summon a Convention to consider of such as are proposed by the States—

Part Three

AFTER THE CONVENTION

Pseudonymous Essays

Essays of a Federal Republican

For the New York Journal, &c.
Number 1
Mr. Greenleaf,

The present is a most important crisis in our public affairs—It calls for the utmost attention of every patriot, and loudly admonishes the people to be active and vigilant in the exercise of their constitutional privileges.—A complete revolution will soon take place in our government.—The new constitution being adopted by eleven of the thirteen states, and an ordinance of Congress passed for carrying it into operation; nothing is now wanting but to elect the executive and legislative officers, to give it capacity to go into exercise. The period is at hand when the choice of these is to be

From the *New York Journal*, November 27, 1788; December 11, 1788; and January 1, 1789.

"Federal Republican" was the pseudonymous author of three articles in Thomas Greenleaf's *New York Journal* published November 27 and December 11, 1788, and January 1, 1789. The articles principally addressed the need for a second constitutional convention to propose amendments to the Constitution and for electing senators to the U.S. Senate who would pursue this goal.

Melancton Smith was the likely author of these essays. Alfred Young first made this suggestion in *The Democratic Republicans in New York* (1967), 123, n44. While the partisan zeal of many Anti-Federalists had cooled by this time, Smith maintained an active interest through at least early 1789 in seeing amendments proposed. (For evidence that Anti-Federalism in New York began to wane after ratification, see DePauw, 265–79. For evidence of Smith's continued efforts on behalf of amendments through January 1789, see his letters to Gilbert Livingston and John Smith.) The choice of pseudonym was likely a reference to the Federal Republican Society, which had orga-

357

made, it has commenced in several of the states, and in a short time the citizens of this state will be called upon to give their suffrages for men to exercise, great, extensive, and important powers in the legislature of the United States.[1]

It is of the highest moment that they use this right with prudence and discretion—The change which this new system of government will effect upon the police and condition of the United States, will be very material— The powers with which it vests the rulers, are very extensive and multiform—And it will require great integrity, patriotism, and prudence to direct those who administer the government, to keep within these bounds of moderation and wisdom, which will render it acceptable and a blessing to the people. It is at all times, and under all circumstances, highly proper and necessary for the people in a free government to be careful in the choice of their rulers. In an elective republic it is the most essential mean of preserving liberty and of having an administration promotive of the public good. But there are a variety of reasons to urge a more than ordinary degree of care and circumspection in the choice of persons to commence proceedings under the new system. It is not my intention to enter into an investigation of the merits of the new constitution, or to enquire whether this state pursued its true interest, and acted agreeably to sound policy in adopting it or not. The merits of the constitution has been canvassed by able men on both sides, both in print and in public debate—The system is adopted, and it is the duty of every true friend to his country to acquiesce, and to use their influence to procure such an exercise of the powers granted by it, as will promote the public good and secure public liberty—But I am persuaded the plan is imperfect, capable of great improvements, and that it needs them; and of this opinion is undoubtedly a great majority of the people of this state, and I believe of the United States—This being the case, it is especially the duty of the people to be active, vigilant, and united in the choice

---

nized to promote precisely the goals "Federal Republican" advocated and for which Smith had recently served as a principal spokesman. The January 1, 1789, essay by Federal Republican makes an argument about the proper mode of electing senators that strikingly parallels the substance and style of Smith's letter to John Smith on January 10, 1789.

1. Governor Clinton had called a special session of the legislature for early December so that it might consider "the proceedings of the convention of this state lately held at Poughkeepsie, and the ordinance of Congress for putting into operation the constitution of the United States." (De Pauw, 273.)

of such persons as they can confide in to use their endeavors to procure amendments. Besides the constitution is complicated it reaches to a variety of cases, in which it may interfere with the exercise of the powers left to the state governments—Men of prudence should therefore be chosen to exercise the powers granted by this constitution, who will act with circumspection and caution. It is my intention, if leisure will permit, in some future papers to make some farther observations on this subject, and to endeavor to shew the propriety and necessity of revising and amending the system, and to point out the duplicity of conduct and disregard to the public good of some, who now oppose any alterations in it, though previous to its adoption they declared themselves in favor of amendments.

A Federal Republican.

–DECEMBER 11, 1788–

For the New York Journal
The Federal Republican, No. 2

When men divide in sentiments on a political question, it frequently happens that they really pursue the same end by different means, or (if this is not the case) that they possess [profess?] to have the same object in view, though they follow different courses to attain it. In the first case the two opposing parties will ultimately unite when they come to understand each others views and designs, unless in the progress of the controversy passion gains the ascendancy of reason, or an attachment to a party supplies the place of a regard to the public good. In the latter case it generally falls out that the possessions of one party, or possibly of both, appear to have been adopted merely as a blind to conceal their real designs—When a favorite point is gained the cloak is cast off, and their true end is avowed.

Men of integrity, and who act from principle, ought to be on their guard, to take care that they do not suffer themselves to be actuated by party spirit in the room of a regard for the public good—It is extremely natural for mankind to wish to gain victory to the party to which they unite—Men may, and often do, take a side from a conviction that it is right; they advocate a cause in the first instance, because they are convinced truth and the public good is on its side—But it is not uncommon, that when parties run high, in the course of the controversy, they abandon the principles upon which they set out, and adhere to their party in the pursuit of measures which they reprobated as much as their opposers. What serves as a mean to promote this is, that in almost all parties, there are individuals, and frequently the leaders of the party who have in view something different from what they profess—They pretend one thing, but aim at another—They commence with fair and plausible professions, and under these form their party. In the course of the contests the passions of their adherents get inflamed, prejudices are excited, and taking advantage of these, they carry their party with them to an object, which at first a great part with them would have rejected as much as their opposers.—The truth of these remarks might be confirmed by instances adduced from the history of the greatest revolutions that have happened in the world—The annals of the English history record a notable one in the case of Cromwell. No period of the world produced men of greater abilities, or more disinterested patriots than those who were concerned in effecting that revolution. Charles the first was a tyrant—The opposition made to him was justifiable upon every principle of justice and right reason. It was right to deprive him of that sovereign power, which he received to exercise for the benefit of the people, but which he employed for his own interest and their injury—But the leaders who were concerned in effecting this, after accomplishing it by the power of the people, instead of establishing a free government, partly by force and partly by fraud, they set up one more tyranical than that from which they had been delivered. It cannot be doubted, but that Cromwell, and a number of others who were attached to him, were influenced by as bad principles as those of Charles—they were enemies to equal liberty, though they did not like Charles for a master and a tyrant, they fought to be masters and tyrants themselves. Many very honest men were either seduced to favor his scheme, persuaded to acquiesce in it, or deterred from fear of his power from opposing it.

The present condition of our own country, ought to excite our apprehensions, and put us upon our guard, lest similar events should take place among us—No revolution ever took place, that could more truly be said to be for the people, than the one which we have seen in this country—Power was in great measure opposed to it through the whole union—It originated in the purest whig principles—was supported on the broad basis of the equal rights of mankind—and the form of government which were agreed to, recognized these principles, and the administration has moved upon them. In the progress of the general government, it has appeared to the conviction of almost every man, that the powers under the confederation were not adequate to the management of the general concerns of the union. A very general concurrence of sentiment therefore took place to revise the system—For this purpose a convention of the states by their delegates assembled, and the result of their deliberations was not merely an extension of the powers, but a change of the form of government, this has been submitted to all the states, and acceded to by eleven of them. The officers are now choosing, and the system will soon be in operation. An entire revolution is about taking place without war or bloodshed. In the discussion of this great question there has been a great division of sentiments with regard to the merits of the plan proposed—It has been urged by those who were opposed to it, that the great principles of the revolution has been too little attended to in its formation—that it embraces objects not necessary to be committed to the care of a general government—that sufficient checks are not placed in it to restrain the rulers from an abuse of power—that it will annihilate the state governments on whom we must depend for the preservation of our liberties; and, that it will operate to deprive the people of those rights, which they have so dearly earned—On the other side, it has been said, that these apprehensions are imaginary—that although there are imperfections in the plan, yet, on the whole, it is a well ballanced government, and that sufficient security is afforded against every abuse by committing the power of electing their rulers to the people. To this it is replied, that very little safety will be derived from the right of the people to elect—For that this power will be rather nominal than real—that the number of representatives will be so small, and so great a number concerned in choosing them, that the influence of a few will always predominate.—It is not my design to investigate this subject, as to repeat all that has been said upon it—It is not necessary for my purpose—It has been the general opinion in this state, of both parties, if we may judge from their professions that there are defects in the plan—the same sentiment has prevailed throughout the union. And hence it is, that the most prevailing arguments that the advocates for the system have used, have been drawn, not from its merits, but from the expediency of adopting it; considering the initial situation in which the country was. The language has been, if we must have a government adopt this, and we will cordially unite in making amendments. No inducement whatever would have prevailed upon the convention of this state to have ratified the constitution, had they not had confidence that a general union would have prevailed to submit it to the revision of another general convention. It is manifest from the proceedings of the conventions of many of the other states, that the same motives influenced them. In our own state, almost every sober thinking man declared, without reserve, their wishes to have the system revised—But what is the present language of many of the leading men who advocated the adoption of the constitution? Do they now urge the necessity and propriety of another convention? Nothing is further from their present pursuit. They now say, it is wise and proper to give the government a trial. The goodness or badness of the scheme will be proved, from experiment—If it should prove defective on a trial of ten or twenty years, then we shall be better able to amend it—But if it be true that the liberties of the people are not well secured under it, in twenty years it may, and probably will be too late to secure them. What are we to think of men who hold this language after they have pledged themselves to unite in procuring another convention? Can we refrain from suspecting that they are unfriendly to equal liberty—that they have in view a system of government which they dare not avow, and which they mean to fix over the people of this country by insensible degrees, and without their perceiving it until it is accomplished? It is time for every disinterested man and real friend to his country to open his eyes, and act with decision.

All who were sincere in declaring that they wished for a re-consideration and amendments to the system will do so, and will give their voices decidedly in favor of such men to represent them as will firmly pursue the plan recommended by the convention of this state. A variety of unanswerable arguments, beside the defects in the constitution itself, point this out as the wise, prudent, and patriotic line of conduct which ought to be pursued.

A Federal Republican.

– JANUARY 1, 1789 –

For the New York Journal, &c.
The Federal Republican, No. 3

The manner in which the legislature shall exercise the power, with which they are vested by the new constitution of choosing senators, has become a matter of general conversation, and has occasioned very considerable debates in the assembly, and probably has or will create a dispute between the two houses.

As it is a question of very considerable moment, I beg to be indulged in making a few observations upon it.

There are three modes proposed; the first is, that the senators be chosen in the manner the delegates to Congress have been elected under the confederation; that is, that each house openly nominate, and in case they disagree that they then elect by ballot of the two houses assembled together. The second mode is, that in case of disagreement in both the candidates, each house elect one by ballot, and if they agree in one but disagree in the other, the two houses determine the election by joint ballots.

The third mode is, to appoint them by law, in which each house reserves a negative upon the other.

With regard to these I shall enquire, 1st. Which of them ought to have the preference upon the true principles of government and the reason of the thing.

2. Which is most consonant to our own constitution.
3. Does the new constitution fix the one mode in preference to the other.

With respect to the first point—There is no principle better established in republican governments, than this; that all power in the rulers should be derived from the people for whose benefit all government is instituted—The power is delegated either by the people immediately, or mediately through the hands of those whom they appoint. In all free republics the legislature who exercises the supreme authority, should be elected by the people and responsible to them—and no government can be secure which does not in a great degree possess this quality. In the new constitution the people choose immediately the house of assembly, which is one branch of the legislature—The senate, the other part, are to be chosen immediately by the representatives of the people in their state legislatures—The reason upon which this article is founded appears to be this: the senate is to be composed of two senators from each state. It would be a thing extremely difficult, I may say utterly impracticable for all the people in a state to unite in choosing two men. It would be impossible for them to associate together for this purpose, and extremely inconvenient to consult with each other, and very improbable that a majority would ever unite in favor of any two men. To remedy this inconveniency which resulted from the nature of the thing, the business was committed to the legislature. But if the principle be applied, that a majority of the people ought to elect, it will follow, that when they transfer the right of election to their representatives, the power ought to be exercised by a majority. Each representative should be considered as having equal power in this business, and all of them together as possessing the whole of it; and, therefore, according to this plain principle that the greater should controul the lesser, the larger number ought to elect. Hence it appears, that the first mode is the proper one. But, again, this is the only consistent and practicable mode—Either of the others are either inconsistent, or may in their operation be found impracticable. With respect to the second, which proposes, that in case of disagreement each house shall choose one. It takes from the legislature the right of choosing entirely. For no one can suppose that by any construction, either the senate or assembly can be called the legislature.

The third mode is liable to this objection, that places the majority under the controul of a small minority. The whole legislature consists of eighty-nine members, when they all attend, thirteen of this number may prevent the election of a person, or persons, in which the whole of the remaining seventy-six are united. Such a provision in a matter in which the very existence of a government is concerned, is absurd and repugnant to every just principle of politics.

It is also liable to this material objection, that if it is adopted, it may and probably will frequently defeat any election at all—By this mode, both houses are to concur. But suppose they do not, how is the difference to be determined? It cannot be done. The one or the other must recede or no election can take place. If both houses maintain their opinions, the state will be without senators, and upon the same principle the United States may be without a senate, and the government of the union may be dissolved. If it be said, that such an event can hardly be apprehended, for it can scarcely be supposed, that such a spirit of obstinancy will prevail in the two houses, as to incline them pertinaciously to adhere to their own choice, as to defeat any appointment. Supposing this to be true, it does not help the matter. For in this case a power will be placed in the hands of a few ambitious and obstinate men always to choose whom they please. Eight or ten men in the senate firmly united together, in favour of men, who will promote their views and designs, may fatigue a great majority into a compliance with their wishes, and thus instead of having the senators chosen by a free and unbiassed voice of a majority of the representatives of the people, they may be thirst [dialectical variance of "thrust"] into their seats by a small over-bearing faction against the wishes of a great majority, both by the people and their representatives.

Such a principle in government is subversive of freedom. It has a direct tendency to elevate the few, to the depression of the many, and will give a tone to the new system of government, that may accelerate the destruction of republican government. The powers of the senate are vastly great. Besides being one branch of the legislature, they possess very important executive authority, and are the highest court of judicatory in the nation. They hold their places for six years, and are not amendable to it under the controul of the states who send them. Most sensible candid men, admit that there is too great an accumulation of power and too small a degree of responsibility in this body. The convention of this state has recommended that their powers be curtailed, and their responsibility increased. But if the mode contended for, be adopted, to appoint by law, or to give the senate a negative in the choice of senators, they will be placed almost entirely beyond the controul of the people—At any rate, the people choose them at second hand through their representatives. But this will put it out of the power of the representatives of the people to choose them, and enable one third of the senate to dictate the choice or prevent ones taking place. This is so flagrantly wrong, that I can hardly conceive that any thing can be said to shew the propriety of it.

I shall now enquire which of the proposed modes of appointment is most consonant to our own constitution. On this head little doubt can be entertained. The constitution is express on the subject of appointing delegates to Congress, and the first mode is perfectly conformable to it. It is said, I know, that our constitution does not at all apply to the case, because the new system has entirely annulled the old confederation, and stands on its own foot. That no such office exists as the constitution contemplated under the name of delegates, and therefore it can be no rule to direct in this business. On this I remark, that although the new form of government has abrogated the old, that yet the senate under the new are charged with most of the important powers and duties of the Congress under the old, especially of an executive nature—and the reason of the provision for choosing delegates, applies with equal force in the one case as in the other—Under both systems they are the delegates of the state; they are to guard its sovereignty, to watch over its rights and represent its interests. Every reason therefore that could induce a choice of this method of appointing under the confederation, applies with equal force under the new government, and therefore this ought to be the mode pursued, unless the new constitution expressly points out another; this leads to the third enquiry—Does the new Constitution fix the one mode in preference to the other?

The following are the only clauses which respect the matter art 1. sect. 3. "The senate of the United States shall be composed of two senators from each state chosen by the legislature thereof for six years, &c.

Art. 1. Sect. 4. The times, places and manner of holding elections for senators and representatives shall be prescribed in each state by the legislature thereof, &c."

From these two clauses taken together the plain sense of the constitution is this, that the legislature are to elect senators at such time and place and in such manner as they shall prescribe—They are authorized to adopt any mode of election they please. All circumstances respecting the election is under their direction. Nothing in this constitution points out any mode. It only reserves a right to the Congress to alter the regulations after they are made or to make new ones. Every legislature then are left to exercise their discretion on this head, subject to such rules and restrictions as their own constitutions provide, if any exists.

The case then with respect to the legislature of New York, stands thus: The new constitution commits to their discretion the manner in which they shall exercise the right of electing senators, but their own constitution directs how this discretion shall be used, in the article providing for the election of delegates. As the reasons on which that article was founded equally applies to senators as to delegates, who differ rather in name than in thing.

But it is said, the constitution has fixed this matter, because it says that the senators shall be chosen by the legislature—When men get attached to a party, or to a sentiment, trifles light as air will have weight to support them in their opinions—Were it not for this, I can hardly imagine any sensible man would lay much stuff upon this argument. It is said the legislature consists of the senate and assembly, that they have equal rights, and therefore both must concur in the choice. I ask the gentlemen who advance this—Who choose delegates under the confederation? I believe they will answer, as every man will, the legislature. It is true that in the exercise of this power they proceeded in a different mode than that they pursued in passing laws. The nature of the case required they should and therefore the constitution provided for it—It is the same in the case before us—The legislature are to choose—the manner is left to them by the constitution. There is not the most remote evidence from the words of the constitution, that it intended to give one house a negative or the other—the expressions are the legislature shall choose, they are to hold an election for senators—The manner they are to prescribe—The idea of choosing and of electing when applied to a body of men, implies that the voice of a majority is to decide.—Had the constitution meant to give one house a negative upon the other, it would have held a different language, it would have directed that senators should have been appointed by law, and then all the formalities observed between the two houses must have been adhered to—But I shall tire your patience and that of your reader. On the whole, as the mode prescribed in the constitution for choosing delegates, is most consonant to the principles of republicanism, most rational, friendly to liberty and safety for the people—As the other modes are attended with difficulties that may defeat a representation, in the senate at all, or place the power of appointment in a faction—As this mode is directed by the constitution in the care of delegates, and equally applies to the care of senators, as the new constitution rather favours than opposes it, I am clearly of opinion it ought to be adopted, and trust it will be by our legislature.

A Federal Republican.

Essays of Lucius

– November 24, 1792 –

For the New York Journal, &c.
Mr. Greenleaf,
Is requested to re-publish the inclosed Piece from
the American Daily Advertiser.

As it appears by the public prints, that there will be a contest for the office of Vice President, which becomes vacant on the 2d of March next, and which must be supplied by the free suffrage of the people, it may not be deemed improper, in relation to those principles which should be held

From the *New York Journal* and *American Daily Advertiser,* November 24 and 28, 1792.

The essays of Lucius, originally published in the Philadelphia-based *American Daily Advertiser,* were republished on November 24 and 28, 1792, in Thomas Greenleaf's *New York Journal.* With the 1792 vice presidential election set to take place in December, Lucius defended the candidacy of George Clinton and critiqued the candidacy of John Adams on the grounds that Adams's advocacy of a government of "king, lords, and commons" differed "radically" from the principles of the American Constitution.

Melancton Smith was the likely author of these essays. Alfred Young first made this suggestion in *The Democratic Republicans in New York,* 331, n24. Smith had become one of Clinton's principal defenders in the New York Assembly. Though he had initially supported Burr for the vice presidency (see his September 30, 1792, letter to James Madison and James Monroe), after the Republican caucus settled on Clinton in October 1792, Smith pledged to actively campaign on Clinton's behalf. He was in Philadelphia for the Republican caucus on October 16 and could have placed the article in the Philadelphia paper then. His belief that an aristocratic tendency within sacred, to make some comments on the relative pretensions of those who are said to be competitors for this important station. This trait in the executive department of our government is among the most important of those which distinguish it from the monarchies of Europe; and as its preservation must, in a great measure, depend upon the political conduct of those who fill it, a candid enquiry into the characters of the competitors becomes a matter of public right. It belongs to a free people to guard themselves from injury; and to this great principle the forms of ceremony or complaisance for persons must, upon all occasions, yield. Even the competitors, therefore, however painful the scrutiny might be, should console themselves under the reflection, that upon the preservation of the principle, the safety of their country depends.

In particular circles several gentlemen have been spoken of for the office in question, but at present all others seem to be withdrawn from view, and the contest to rest solely between John Adams, Esq. and Governor Clinton. To their comparative merits, therefore, as the only competitors, I shall confine these observations.

To treat of them in the affirmative line, would be useless, as it could lead to no satisfactory conclusion; for every person will admit that, in some respects, they both possess the requisite qualifications; that both, for instance, possess an adequate capacity for the discharge of its official functions—are of sufficient age and standing in America—and have, likewise, rendered important services to their country. To fix the preferences, their merits must be viewed from a different ground. The objections which apply to each must be scanned, and he against whom the more weighty apply, rejected.

To Mr. Adams it has been objected, that he is attached to a government of king, lords, and commons; and that the allegation is true, it is to be presumed, will not be controverted. His writings, entitled, "A Defence of the American Constitutions" and "Discourses upon Davila," fully demonstrate it.[1] If it could be supposed, that doubts existed upon this point, extracts from

---

the federal government was the principal danger of the day, along with the philosophical tone of the articles, further suggests Smith's authorship. Finally, the choice of the pseudonym itself suggests Smith. Lucius was the first name of Brutus, the sixth-century B.C. Roman statesman whose name was the likely inspiration for the nom de plume of the author of the *Essays of Brutus*.

1. In *A Defence of the American Constitutions* (1787), Adams defended the importance of checks and balances and advocated a mixed government composed of democratic, aristocratic, and monarchical elements. Accordingly, he called the English

those publications should be now furnished; they shall, however, immediately, if any intimation of the kind be given. And to Mr. Clinton, an objection of a different kind—his opposition to the present constitution, before its adoption, has been urged. These, I believe, are the principal objections made to either; they are, however, those only upon which I shall make any comment. To whom, then, does the stronger one apply? On whose political principles, at the present moment, would the good people of these states, with greater propriety, bestow their sanction?

To form a sound decision upon this interesting question, two others, on which it depends, should be previously settled. First—Which of these gentlemen's political sentiments wander farthest from the present constitution? And secondly—On which side does the greater danger lie, in the progress of the government, of an undue inclination towards the form preferred by Mr. Adams, or that ascribed to Mr. Clinton?

With respect to those of Mr. Adams, it will be readily perceived, that they depart, in all the great outlines, from the present constitution. The establishment of a government of king, lords, and commons, would entirely subvert the present one, which rests on the free suffrage of the people. Two distinct orders, with hereditary rights, would be erected over them, and they reduced to a limited portion of authority only, forming a kind of balance against those higher and hostile orders.

With respect to those of Governor Clinton, it is to be observed, that they have always ranged within the republican theory. His maxim has been, to keep the government, in all its departments, essentially connected with the people. The question about the constitution involved only a modification of this principle. Besides, it is to be presumed, that many of his objections have been done away by the amendments; so that, in fact, it must be deemed, in all its parts, as nearly correspondent with his own theory, as the contrariety of sentiment, always displayed on a subject of such importance, could reasonably admit of.

The characteristic difference, then, in their political principles, simply amounts to this, that those of Mr. Adams vary radically from the constitution, in the main features of the republican system; whereas those of his

---

constitution "the most stupendous fabric of human history." In *Discourses on Davila*, a series of articles that appeared in the spring of 1790 and were eventually published as a book, he provided a translation of Davila's history of the French civil wars of the sixteenth century and, in his commentary, stressed the perils of unbridled and unbalanced democracy.

competitor harmonize with it in that essential point. In addition to which it is of importance to observe, that upon the establishment of the constitution, and prior to the adoption of amendments, Mr. Clinton's opposition ceased; and that, on the contrary, since that event, Mr. Adams has, in the discourses above alluded to, endeavored, by all the arguments in his power, to inspire, in the minds of his countrymen, a distrust of a government founded on the people alone, and to prepare them for the gradual introduction of hereditary orders in the state.

In regard to the other question, on which side does the greater danger lie, of a more probable inclination towards the subversion of the republican system, by the introduction of a government of an higher tone, or too great a relaxation of its principles, I am persuaded that no person can seriously entertain a doubt on the subject. He must be little skilled in the political balance, and the true complexion of the times, who suspects, in any degree, a preponderance of the latter evil. That the government may stand on its present ground, is certainly the wish of those to whom a contrary sentiment has been attributed: for let the objections of those who were opposed to it, where opposition was made, be examined, and it will be found that the space which separated the body of the opponents from that of its advocates, was a narrow one. That, in fact the difference, in most instances, was but trifling, and that this has been generally accommodated by the amendments. The truth of this position has been so well established by events, that to doubt it, argues a mind so inveterately blinded by prejudice or interest, that the force of truth cannot reach it. No danger then of a vibration back need be apprehended; for in truth, no person wishes it. On the other hand, it must be acquitted, that the evident tendency is in the opposite direction. A particular enumeration of those measures which contribute to give this bias, is at present unnecessary, and would certainly, in their developement, exceed the bounds of these observations. For the truth, however, of the remark, I beg leave to appeal to the judgment of every impartial and well informed American.

If, then, the good people of these states wish to preserve their government as at present, elective in its form and limited in its powers, can they hesitate in deciding to which of these gentlemen the preference should be given? An unequivocal declaration of their sentiments upon this point, thus expressed, would hereafter be felt by the candidates for public favor, and respected. It would give a republican tone to the American character, that might tend to preserve their liberties forever. No consideration of local

attachment, should interpose to defeat a measure, which their interest requires and their judgment dictates. For the security of those great principles, upon which their revolution was founded, and [their present government rests, their union should be firm, solid, and indissoluble.]

Lucius.

– NOVEMBER 28, 1792 –

For the New York Journal, &c.
Mr. Greenleaf,
Is requested to re-publish the enclosed Piece from
the American Daily Advertiser.

In my last I urged it as a sufficient reason why the public suffrage should
be withheld from Mr. Adams, at the ensuing election for the office of Vice
President, that he was the known and avowed friend to a government of
king, lords, and commons, and had, since the adoption of the present one,
endeavored by his writings to inculcate this pernicious doctrine upon the
minds of his countrymen, thereby impairing the foundation on which it
rests. And although I cannot suppose that any person acquainted with his
writings, will undertake to vindicate him against this high charge, yet it neither suits the importance nor the propriety of the enquiry, that any doubt
on the subject should, at the present moment, arrest the public mind. His
defence of the American constitutions, and discourses upon Davila, the
documents referred to, though for some time past in print, may not have
been generally perused. To place, therefore, the merits of this charge upon
their true ground, I shall now furnish, from those publications, such brief
extracts, as will, I presume, sufficiently demonstrate its truth.

In vol. 1, page 8, of the preface, we find the following passage:—"Without
three orders, and an effectual balance between them, in every American constitution, it must be destined to frequent unavoidable revolutions; if they
are *delayed a few years*, they *must* come *in time*. The United States are large
and populous nations, in comparison of the Grecian commonwealths, or
even the Swiss Cantons; and are growing every day more disproportionate,
and therefore less capable of being held together by simple governments.
Countries that encrease in population so rapidly as the states of America
did, even during such an impoverishing and destructive war as the last, are
not to be bound together by silken threads; lions, young or old, will not be
bound by cobwebs. It would be better for America, it is nevertheless agreed,

to ring all the changes with the whole set of bells, and go through all the revolutions of the Grecian states rather than establish an *absolute monarchy* among them, notwithstanding all the great and real improvements made in that kind of government."

Again, page 22.—"If Cicero & Tacitus could revisit the earth, and learn that the English nation had reduced the *great idea* to practice, and brought it nearly to perfection, by giving each division a power to defend itself by a negative; had found the most solid and durable government, *as well as the most free.*"

Again, page 25—"What is the ingredient which in England has preserved the *democratical* authority? The balance, and *that only.*"

In page 116.—"The sources of inequality, which are common to every people, and can never be altered by any, because they are founded in the constitution of nature; this natural aristocracy among mankind has been dilated on, because it is a fact essential to be considered in the institution of a government. It is a body of men which contains the greatest collection of virtues and abilities in a free government; is the brightest ornament and glory of the nation; and may always be made the greatest blessing of society, if it be judiciously managed in the constitution."

And in the next page,—"There is but one expedient yet discovered to avail the society of all the benefits from *this body of men*, which they are capable of affording, and at the same time to prevent them from undermining or invading the public liberty, and that is to throw them all, or at least the most remarkable of them, *into one assembly together* in the legislature; to keep all the executive power entirely out of their hands as a body; to create a first magistrate over them, invested with the whole executive authority; to make them dependent on that executive magistrate for all public executive employments; to give that first magistrate a negative on the legislature, by which he may defend himself and the people from all their enterprizes in the legislature; and to erect on the other side of them an impregnable barrier against them in a *house of commons*, fairly, fully, and adequately representing the people, who shall have the power of *negativing* all their attempts at encroachments in the legislature, and of withholding, both from them and the crown, all supplies by which they may be paid for their services in executive offices, or even the public service carried on to the detriment of the nation."

Page 224—"From this example (speaking of the Roman empire) as from all others, it appears that there can be no *government of laws* without *a balance*; and that there can be no balance *without three orders*, and that even three orders can never balance each other; unless each, in its department, is *independent* and *absolute.*"

Vol. 3, page 296.—The Americans have agreed with this writer in the sentiment,—"that it is but reason that the people should see that none be interested, in the supreme authority, but persons of their own election, and such as must, in a short time, return again into the same condition with themselves." This hazardous experiment they have tried; and if elections are soberly made it may answer very well; but if parties, factions, daunkenness [drunkenness], bribes, armies, and delirium, come in, as they *always have done* sooner or later, to embroil and decide every thing, the people must again have recourse to conventions, and find a remedy. Neither philosophy nor policy has yet discovered *any other cure* than by *prolonging the duration of the first magistrate and senators.* The evil may be lessened and postponed by elections for longer periods of years, until they become for life; and if this is not found an adequate remedy, there will remain no other but to make them *hereditary.* The delicacy, or the dread of unpopularity, that should induce any man to conceal this important truth, from the full view and contemplation of the people, would be a weakness, if not a vice. As to reaping the same benefit or burthen, by the laws enacted, that befalls the rest of the people, "this will be secured, whether the first magistrate and senate be elective *or hereditary,* as long as the people are an *integral part* of the legislature; can be bound by no laws to which they have not consented; and can be subjected to no tax which they have not agreed to lay."

Page 367. The people are the fountain and original of the power of king and lords, governors and senates, as well as the house of commons, or assembly of representatives; and if the people are sufficiently enlightened to see all the dangers that surround them, they will always be represented by a distinct personage, to manage the whole executive power; a distinct senate to be guardians of property, against levellers for the purpose of plunder, to be a repository of the national tradition of public maxims, customs, and manners; and to be controulers in turn, both *of kings* and their ministers on one side, and the *representatives of the people* on the other; when either discover a disposition to do wrong: and a distinct house of representatives, to be the guardians of the public purse, and to protect the people in their turn, against *both kings* and *nobles.* A science certainly comprehends all the principles in nature which belong to the subject. The principles in nature which relate to government, cannot all be known, without a knowledge of the history of mankind. The *English constitution* is the only one which has considered and provided for all cases, that are known to have generally, indeed to have always, happened, in the progress of every nation; *it is, therefore, the only scientifical government.*

–JUNE 2, 1790–

No. eight, of the discourses on Davila.

"There is a voice within us, which seems to intimate, that real merit should govern the world; and that men ought to be respected only in proportion to their talents, virtues, and services—but the question always has been, how can this arrangement be accomplished? how shall the men of merit be discovered? how shall the proportions of merit be ascertained and graduated? who shall be the judge? when the government of a great nation is in question, shall the whole nation choose? shall the whole nation vote for senators? thirty millions of votes, for example, to each senator in France? It is obvious that this would be a lottery of millions of blanks to one prize, and that the chance of having wisdom and integrity in a senator by hereditary descent, would be far better, &c."

–JULY 7, 1790.–

No. 12

Speaking of rivalries of different kinds, in society, and especially in America, he adds, "What is the natural remedy against the inconveniences and dangers of these rivalries? whether a well balanced constitution, such as that our union *purports to be*, ought not to be cordially supported, until its defects, if it has any, can be corrected by every good citizen, as our only hope of peace and ark of safety; but it shall be left to the contemplations of our state physicians to discover the causes and the remedy of that 'fever whereof our power is sick.'" One question only shall be respectively insinuated: whether equal laws, the result only of a *balanced government*, can ever be obtained and preserved without some signs or other of *distinction* and *degree?*

–JULY 21, 1790–

Americans! Rejoice, that from experience you have learned wisdom; and instead of whimsical and fanatical projects, you have adopted a *promising essay* towards a *well ordered government*, instead of following any foreign examples to return to the legislation of confusion, contemplate the means of restoring decency, honesty, and order in society by preserving and con-templating, if any thing should be found necessary to complete the *balance* of your government.

–November 30, 1790.3–

No. 23

"We see, in this instance, that the treple balance is so established by prov-idence in the constitution of nature, that order without it can never be brought out of anarchy and confusion. The laws therefore should estab-lish this equilibrium as the dictate of nature, and the ordinance of provi-dence."

By the foregoing passages, and many others which are omitted for the sake of brevity; indeed, by the just and sound construction of both perfor-mances,[2] it is obviously the doctrine of this gentleman, that a government of kings, lords, and commons, is that only, under which mankind can enjoy with certainty or duration, any degree of freedom and happiness. That even the experiment of a more popular one, or one depending essentially on the suffrage of the people; however wise the modification or distribution of its powers, is *hazardous*, and that the sooner we become convinced of its folly, and adopt the great standard which he admires, the sooner we shall attain to perfection. The people appear throughout, to be the sole object of his terror; from them, unless excluded from all influence upon the executive, and restrained to one third portion of the legislature only, balanced in the other two by an independent and hereditary king, and order of nobility, he seems to apprehend all those calamities which an uncurbed licentiousness can inflict upon society. The most turbulent ages of the world, the most calamitous eras of ancient and modern nations have been resorted to, for documents to color the odious picture, and to demonstrate that mankind cannot govern themselves. But to the outrageous abuse of power, in the hands of a few, he shows the most benevolent indulgence, and while the dread of popular authority haunts his mind, he labors for language to ex-press his horror of it, he speaks of the higher orders of government, of a king and nobility, in terms of reverence and veneration, scarcely ever used by any other writer.

There is, however, one other trait in the character of these tracts which merits attention. Mr. Adams has heretofore been represented as exemplary

2. "Both performances" refers to Adams's two books.

for his candour, and the frank exposition of his political sentiments upon all occasions. Freely as I have censured his doctrines, as pernicious to his country, and highly reprehensible for a person in his station, it would give me pleasure if I could subscribe to this opinion of his candor. But although I am persuaded, an impartial criticism of his work will lead every other person to the conclusion I have formed, yet it is a fact which must strike the mind of the most inattentive observer, that in many passages, he has appeared to shrink from the ground he had fairly taken, and even to contradict what he had already said. Aware of the precipice on which he stood, he trembled at the prospect which menaced before him!*

In my last I stated it as a proposition which could not be contested, for it could be easily demonstrated, that the only dangers to which we were exposed in the operation of the government, were those which threatened the existence of the republican system itself. If this idea is well founded; if it is even probable, should not the good people of these states guard themselves against it by every possible and wise precaution? Should they not, in any event, exclude from their councils those who entertain sentiments so radically hostile to their government, and to those principles of equality upon which it is founded?

Lucius.

---

* The English reviewers sum up the true character of his defence of the American constitutions, in the words following, "the great and leading idea which runs through the ingenius and learned work of Mr. Adams is, that a mixture of the three powers, *the regal, the aristocratical* and *the democratical* properly balanced, composes the most perfect form of government and secures the greatest degree of happiness to the greatest number of individuals."

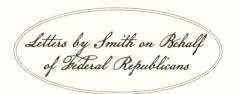

Letters by Smith on Behalf of Federal Republicans

Letter from New York City Committee of Federal Republicans to New York, November 4, 1788

To the counties within this State:

New York, November 4, 1788

Gentlemen:

The circumstances and situation of things both before, and some time after our convention had met, warranted an universal opinion among all Federal Republicans, that it was proper to adopt the new constitution only on condition that those important alterations which were considered necessary to the protection of political and civil liberty, should be made: and this was

Reprinted courtesy of the New-York Historical Society, John Lamb Papers, November 4, 1788 (to counties), box 5, no. 35.

On October 30, 1788, ten Anti-Federalists—Melancton Smith, Marinus Willett, David Gelston, John Lamb, Ezekiel Robins, Solomon Townsend, Nathaniel Lawrence, James H. Hughes, Samuel Jones, and Charles Tillinghast—met at Fraunces Tavern in New York City to form the Federal Republican Society "for the purpose of procuring a general convention to revise the Constitution." Smith moved that a committee of three people be formed "to open a correspondence with certain persons in the several states (as well as counties within the state) for the purpose of explaining the reasons which induced the adoption of the Constitution of the United States . . . , and requesting their assistance to procure the requisite amendments, by having a General Convention called." Smith, Lamb, and Hughes were appointed to serve on the committee. The following week, on November 4, the committee presented this letter, and the letter to the several states, to the group for their consideration.

Smith was probably the author of these letters. He had taken the initiative to propose the formation of this committee of correspondence. Moreover, he had suggested such a plan of correspondence a month earlier in a letter to John Lansing. Lansing wrote on October 3, 1788, "I have to acknowledge the favor of Mr. Smith's letter and am sincerely convinced that a correspondence of the plan he suggested will tend

founded not only on the defects of the Constitution, but on the anticipation that there would have been a majority in several of the State conventions of the same sentiments with our own; from whom we should have derived support. But in pursuing our opposition in this form, the sentiments and opinions of many in our Convention were changed; not, as we have reason to believe as to the principles of opposition, but as to the expediency of adopting under an alteration of circumstances, so that this State shall continue in the Union. At the same time, giving such constructions to some of its articles, and relying on the sentiments of a majority in the United States, with respect to an opinion of its defects, that the government would be restrained in the exercise of its most offensive and dangerous powers, until a new convention should have an opportunity of reconsidering and revising it, before it should have its full operation.

This alteration of sentiment with respect to a conditional adoption, and the mode of adopting it in its present manner, it is to be presumed, was caused by the reception of it by nine States successively; by which the government was capable to be put in operation; and likewise [by] the immediate and subsequent adoption of it by Virginia, perhaps one of the most influential and important States in the Union. The confidence of those who were of these sentiments was excited, because many of the most important States, had acknowledged it by small majorities; and almost all, in such a way as was expressive of its defects: and hence they considered amendments as certain; subsequent as precedent.

Thus unsupported by any of the States in the prospect of a conditional adoption, and for these reasons, it became a political calculation with them, whether it was not most for the interests of this State, under all circumstances, to continue in the Union, and trust, for the reasons aforesaid, for amendments. Unhappily, this occasioned a diversity of opinion among our friends in the convention, who were for a conditional adoption only. However, the question, as you well know, was at last carried in the way it now stands. Altho' a division took place, both within and without the convention on this point, and for these reasons, yet we hope that a confidence remains on the minds of all, that each was governed by the principles of

---

to unite the Efforts and give success to the Advocates for Amendments to the new Constitution if anything can." Finally, Smith was the only person on the committee of correspondence who had been a delegate to the New York ratifying convention. Since the letters were intended to explain what had happened at Poughkeepsie, it seems likely that they would have required the perspective of someone who had been there.

rectitude; and that the efforts and exertions of each other collectively, as well as individually, will be considered a duty in future; and made use of to obtain the great objects we have all had, and still have in view, to wit: the requisite amendments; by having a general convention called immediately, or as soon as possible after the organization of the new government.

With this design, we conceive it will be very necessary to advert to the ensuing election of members to represent this State in the assembly of the general government; and to endeavor to elect such characters as are in sentiment with us on the subject of amendments. Nor is the mode of election a matter of small importance, when it is considered that one mode may throw the balance in the hands of the advocates of an arbitrary government, while another may be favorable to equal liberty.[1] The activity and duplicity of the principal of those who have contended for unequivocal adoption, and uncontrouled exercise of the new Constitution, notwithstanding their promises to assist in procuring a convention for the purposes already mentioned, have given us just causes of suspicion, that those promises were made with a view to deceive.

To facilitate a communication of sentiment and free discussion on this subject, with you and our friends in the other counties, and thereby further the great objects of our pursuit, and oppose with success the subtle practices of the adversaries of constitutional liberty, we have formed ourselves into a society for the purpose of procuring a general convention, agreeable to the circular letter of the late convention of this State; and we beg leave to recommend to your consideration the propriety of your joining together without delay for the like design.[2]

We have only to add, that whatever diversity of sentiment may have taken place among the friends of equal liberty in our late convention, we are fully persuaded that they will unite their utmost exertions in the only mode which is now left. And should the present opportunity which is offered at the organization of the government, not be properly improved, it is highly

1. This is a reference to the debate within the New York State legislature over how the state would select its senators. See Smith's letters to John Smith for a fuller discussion of this issue.

2. This, of course, is a reference to the Federal Republican Society. While their activities in late October and November drew some attention, the society eventually dissolved. Their November 4 meeting drew only five of the original ten members, and their next meeting, on November 13, did not draw a sufficient number of members to conduct business.

probable such a favorable one will not be again presented; and the liberties of the people will then depend on the arbitrary decrees of their rulers.

In behalf of the Society, &c.

Letter from Federal Republicans to Several States, November 4, 1788

To the several States:

New York, Nov. 4, 1788

Previous to the adoption of the new constitution, a committee was formed in this place, of those who disapproved of it without essential amendments, to open a correspondence with those of the sister States, who concurred with them in sentiment; to invite them to open a communication with us and concert an union of measures. From the characters of a large majority of those who composed our convention, we had reason to expect, they would not have adopted the constitution without stipulating for such previous amendments: and of this we advised our friends. Their proceedings, containing the amendments proposed, which we do ourselves the honor to inclose you, will justify this sentiment. A small majority, however, was found who were induced from ideas of political expediency, to assent to a qualified adoption, in such manner as would admit this State into a participation of the government. It is not necessary to detail the reasons at large; nor whether they were well grounded, that influenced this measure. They may be briefly comprised in the following:

A sufficient number of states had acceded to the government, to authorize its going into operation; this being the case, it seems it was apprehended that the states who had adopted could not easily be prevailed upon to concur in any other mode to effect the requisite alterations, but the one pointed out in the Constitution itself. That if this state remained out of the Union, they might lose the opportunity of employing their influence in bringing them about. And from the dissatisfaction manifested by many of the states to the system as it stands; and from the spirit of accommodation, which it was hoped would prevail among those who approved of it; they

Reprinted courtesy of the New-York Historical Society, John Lamb Papers, November 4, 1788 (to states), box 5, no. 35.

were induced to believe that a general agreement would take place to call another Convention to consider, and recommend amendments to the objectionable parts. Though these and similar reasons, we believe influenced a majority to accede to the system, with certain declarations and explanations; yet even this, could not be obtained without an express declaration of their disapprobation of it; and agreeing to a circular letter, inviting the other states, to unite with ours in requiring a convention. In this both parties concurred unanimously.

We can with confidence assure you, that the opposition to the Constitution without amendments, has not decreased; but on the contrary, many of those who were zealous for its adoption, declare they will unite their efforts in endeavoring to have it reconsidered. But we have reason at the same time, to believe many of its most ardent advocates will use their influence and address, to prevent this. It is therefore the more necessary that the friends of equal republican government, should firmly unite in pursuing such measures, as will have a tendency to effect amendments. For this purpose, a number of gentlemen in this city, influenced by a sincere regard for constitutional liberty and the public good, have associated under the name of a society for the purpose of procuring a General Convention, agreeable to the circular letter of the late convention of this state; and have opened a correspondence with the several states; and with different parts of this state. Notwithstanding so large a part of the citizens of the United States, appear to be in sentiment, that it is necessary the constitution should be altered; in order to render the people happy, and their liberties secure under it; yet it is now evident these alterations will not be obtained without great exertions and pains to awaken the people to their interests and safety. Associations of the well informed and patriotic gentlemen in the different parts of the country, we apprehend will have the most salutary influence to effect so desirable an event; we therefore earnestly invite you to set this on foot, and to open a correspondence with us.

We have only to add that whatever diversity of sentiment may have taken place among the friends of equal liberty in our late convention we are fully persuaded that they will unite their utmost exertions to procure the amendments in the only mode that is now left. And should the opportunity, which is now offered at the organization of the government, not be properly improved, it is highly probable such a favorable one, will not be again presented; and the liberties of the people will then depend on the arbitrary decrees of their rulers.

In behalf, &c.

Letters

Letter to John Smith,[1] December 28, 1788

New York Dec. 28th 1788

Dear Sir,

I have seen in the Debates published in Childs' paper, that the great question, which it was forseen would be agitated, has come on, viz. whether the Senators should be chosen by joint ballot of both houses, or whether the one house should have a negative on the other.[2]

I consider this question as of very great importance as it affects the operation of the new government—In the investigation of the system, it appeared evidently to many of us, that it was calculated to vest very great and extensive powers in few hands, for long periods and with a small degree of responsibility—This objection applies with peculiar force against the Constitution of the Senate—They will possess powers in extent and degree not known in a single branch of a Legislature, in any free government, that I recollect—They are in the first instance not elected by the People, but by their representatives—the period of their service is for six years, and during

Reprinted courtesy of the New-York Historical Society, Misc. MSS, December 28, 1788, John Smith (1752–1816).

1. John Smith was an Anti-Federalist delegate to the New York State ratifying convention from Suffolk County. He voted with those Anti-Federalists who ratified the Constitution.

2. The New York State legislature was currently debating the method they would use for selecting U.S. senators. The two options under consideration were joint ballot of both houses of the legislature or separate ballots by each with the right to "veto" decisions by the other house. The Anti-Federalists had a majority in the legislature as a whole, but the Federalists enjoyed a majority in the Senate. Correspondingly, Smith and the rest of the Anti-Federalists preferred the joint ballot while the Federalists supported separate ballots. (Young, 124–25.)

this term they are not removable or amenable, unless for crimes—These considerations had such weight with the convention that in the amendments proposed, a number of checks are recommended to be placed upon the Senate—I am of opinion that however prudently the respective Legislatures may use their power of choosing Senators, there will be great danger of an Aristocracy or a government substantially the same, being established by means of this Body—But if the mode of election be so established, as to give the Senate a negative in the choice of Senators, It is evident the danger will be greatly increased. I do not remember that an Idea of this kind was ever suggested in our Convention. I can truly say it never entered my mind. If it had, it would more strongly confirmed [sic] me in my opposition to this part of the system. For if this mode is adopted, it will be in the power of from seven to 13 Members always to prevent an election against the sense of every other member of the Legislature. We ought to lay it to our account, that we shall always have a considerable number of high minded Gentlemen in the Senate, who will use all their influence and address to place in the Senate of the U.S. men of their own views & feelings, and the exercise of a power like this will render the office of a Senator in our Legislature much more an object of ambition than it now is. A few men will by this means have it in their power to raise men to this place in the government, that will suit their purposes, or to prevent any election at all—This last consideration, is in itself sufficient in my mind to determine that the one house ought not to exercise a negative on the other—For it appears to me an absurdity to suppose that a constitution should make such a provision for the choice of a Legislature as in its operation may destroy the body—This may be the effect of the mode contended for—If the two houses disagree, who is to decide? It cannot be done but by one or the other giving up their choice—If both adhere to their opinion, no choice can be made—As to the mode proposed by Mr. Harrison, it appears to me absurd at first blush³—It contradicts his own principles. Surely the choice of one house is not the choice of the Legislature. I know of no argument in any degree plausible that can be urged against the election in the manner that Delegates have heretofore been chosen as directed by our Constitution, but this that the new Constitution says, the choice shall be by the Legislature—This appears to me a mere play upon words, in order to make the Constitution say, what I am convinced it never intended. I would ask, who chose

3. Mr. Harrison is likely Richard Harrison, a Federalist from New York City.

Delegates under the Confederation? did not the Legislature? I presume every man would answer yes—It is a mere circumstance, whether they are chosen by the houses in their separate capacitys, or by joint ballot, and I think our own Constitution determines that Circumstance—The reason of the thing is altogether in favour of the mode hitherto pursued—When the very existence of a government depends upon the exercise of a power, common sense dictates it should be so directed as to be practicable in its execution.

I beg your pardon for [?]ing so long on your patience with this hasty scrawl—I have put my thoughts down just as they occurred. If I had time I would copy this, and make it more perfect—I mean only to suggest hints—It is a strong circumstance in favor of joint ballotting, that not only Virginia, but Maryland (whose Legislatures are said to be federal), adopted this mode and in Maryland the proposal originated with the Senate.

If you once pass a Law, giving the Senate a negative, it is not probable it will ever be altered. It is urged, I know, that if you adhere to your system, no Senators will be chosen. If they are not, let the blame be laid where it ought—according to my present Ideas. I would never recede from the plan marked out in the Constitution, were I sure no Senator would not be chosen for a Century. I beg the favour of you to write me as often as you can, and let me know the state of politics. Make my best aspects to Mr. Havens, and all friends as though named[4]—Havens loves to write, and upon condition he will write to me, he shall be entitled to half this Letter. The remaining half, will I presume be as much as you would wish—The Letter should have been a better one, if I had time but it has been written in Company, and as the subject of [this?] lies near my heart, I mean to send it by Post, promising you however, I shall do so no more, without first paying the Postage. I would have done it now but the office is upon the point of closing and the night is so stormy I cannot attend.

I am with esteem, your friend and ser.,
Melancton Smith

4. Jonathan Havens was an Anti-Federalist delegate to the New York ratifying convention from Suffolk County. Like Melancton Smith and John Smith, Havens voted to ratify the Constitution.

Letter to Gilbert Livingston,[1] January 1, 1789

N. York Jany. 1st 1789

Dear Sir,

All we hear of you is from the papers—We receive no more Letters than if there was not in the City one person who did not believe the new Constitution was of divine Original. Yet you may rest assured that a number of us retain the same sentiments respecting it we ever did, and that we are not a little interested in the issue of the business before you especially that which respects the choice of Senators[2]—You know my sentiments on the Constitution has been, that it too strongly inclines to an Aristocracy, do the best with it you can without amendments. The scheme now on foot to give the Senate a negative, will add amazing force to this tendency[3]—A few Men combining in the Senate may forever put their veto upon any choice, until it falls upon such men as would serve their purposes—This they would soon do, and by this means either embarrass the government beyond measure, or harrass the Assembly to comply with their wishes—I trust the Assembly will never yield the point, be the consequences what they may—Better have no Senators for a Century to come than establish a principle, which when once granted never can be reclaimed. For if

Reprinted courtesy of the New York State Library, Manuscripts and Special Collections. Melancton Smith Papers, 1786–1792, Letter to Gilbert Livingston, January 1, 1789: MSS 955.

1. Gilbert Livingston was an Anti-Federalist delegate to the New York State ratifying convention in Poughkeepsie. He was among the twelve Anti-Federalists who eventually voted with the Federalists for ratification. At the time the letter was written, Livingston was a representative in the New York legislature.

2. The New York legislature was debating the method it would use for selecting U.S. senators. The two options under consideration were a joint ballot of both houses of the legislature or separate ballots by each. The Anti-Federalists had a majority of the legislature as a whole, but the Federalists enjoyed a majority in the Senate. Accordingly, Smith and the rest of the Anti-Federalists preferred the joint ballot while the Federalists supported separate ballots. (Young, 124–25.)

3. The "negative" refers to the method of selecting senators through separate ballots of both houses of Congress. Each house could effectively veto the choice of the other body. (Young, 125.)

you once pass a Law or Resolution to grant the Senate the right, it will never be surrendered—It is unnecessary to urge reasons to support the sentiment—I concur substantially with those offered by the federal Republican in Greenleafs paper[4]—They might be much illustrated and enlarged. How stand our old Friends towards you.[5] Is former confidence revived, and old grudges forgotten—For the sake of the cause I wish they may—Union among ourselves is the corner Stone upon which our hopes of success in obtaining amendments must be built—The fair promises and pretensions of most of the leading men who were in favour of the new System are mere illusions—They intend to urge the execution of the plan in its present form. No reliance can be placed in any of them—We ought therefore to strive to maintain our union firm and immoveable as the mountains, to pursue the object of amendments with unremitting ardour and diligence[6]—Men may differ and will, but if they unite in the main point, they should agree to differ. Politics has consumed so much of my time and thoughts that I should be glad to lay them aside, but the establishing a good government for a great Country is an object of such moment I cannot give it up—It is a matter of too much magnitude. I view it as affecting the whole system of things to ages far remote. It may have a vast effect not only on the comfort and happiness of Men here, but may carry its influence upon the state & condition of that Kingdom which can never be moved. May we stand in our Lot in that Kingdom. Blessed be the King of it, all things are under his controul, and however great the ambition of frail mortals may be, he will conduct every event to produce the best end. For even the wrath of Man shall praise him, and the remainder will he restrain. Make my best respect

4. "Federal Republican" wrote three essays in Thomas Greenleaf's *New York Journal* in late 1788 and early 1799. On January 1, 1799, Federal Republican criticized the proposal to select senators through separate ballots and the granting of a "negative" to the two houses. Smith is the likely author of the "Federal Republican" essays. (Young, 123.)

5. Smith here inquires about the level of unity among the Anti-Federalists in Albany. The division of Anti-Federalists over whether or not to ratify the Constitution had produced a "schism" among ratifying and nonratifying Anti-Federalists that had persisted long after the summer of 1788. (Brooks, 241–42.)

6. Smith expresses here a growing concern among Anti-Federalists that the New York Federalists who had promised to consider amendments to the Constitution would not actually call a second convention. (De Pauw, 275.)

to DeWitt in particular, to Smith Havens and all friends as though named, & believe me to be in truth & sincerity[7]

Your Friend & Serv.
Melancton Smith

Tell all our friends to stand fast—

Letter to John Smith, January 10, 1789

New York Jany. 10th 1789

Dear Sir,

I thank you for your favour of the 3d. Instant. Your Letter gave me the first advice of the State of the business between the two Houses. Before now an issue must have been put to the contest. I shall be much disappointed if the Senate ultimately reject your Bill because I have the fullest conviction that the ground they have taken cannot be maintained on any principles. By their amendments, the Legislature are not to choose, in case two are to be chosen and they disagree.[1] In short in my Idea the mode of choosing Senators admits but of one alternative either they must be appointed by law, or elected by a majority of the two houses. If the Senate have rejected your Bill, it will require consideration what farther steps the Assembly ought to take. In my opinion they hitherto stand on firm ground. I wish they may maintain it, and take such other measures as will tend to vindicate themselves from blame and fix it on the majority of the Senate, should no appointment take place—It appears to me, that it would be a prudent step,

7. John DeWitt, John Smith, and Jonathan Havens were all Anti-Federalist delegates to the New York ratifying convention who had voted to ratify the Constitution. (Brooks, 254, n11.)

Reprinted courtesy of the New-York Historical Society, Misc. MSS, January 10, 1789, John Smith (1752–1816).

1. Under this mode of selecting senators, the two houses vote in separate ballots. In case of disagreement in both the candidates, each house would elect one by ballot. If they agreed in one candidate but disagreed in the other, the two houses would determine the election by joint ballots. (From *Federal Republican* no. 3, pp. 362–63 of this volume.)

for the Assembly to appoint a day to nominate Senators and to proceed on that day to the nomination, and make the Senators the offer of going to a choice in the manner directed for choosing Delegates to Congress by our Constitution. This will shew the disposition of the Assembly to elect in the usual mode, & may be the means of relieving the Governor in some measure from an embarrassment he may be under, respecting the exercise of the power of filling up the vacancies, if the Legislature should not agree to appoint.[2] I shall be sorry, if Electors should not be chosen to elect the President and vice President,[3] as it is very probable our State and Virginia would agree in the person for vice President—and by their union might very probably determine the choice.[4] I think it would be the means of promoting amendments, if a vice president was chosen who is heartily engaged in the business. If your Bill has fallen through, a question may arise whether electors can be chosen, as the day fixed by Congress for the election is passed. I am of opinion that the Legislature may yet choose. For though the Congress have the power to determine the time of choosing the electors, it does not appear that they have it exclusively. The Words are "The Congress may determine the time of chusing the electors." If the Congress do determine the time under the Constitution, it must be observed, but they may not determine the time, in which case the Legislature have power to do it. The time of holding elections for Senators it is true, has been fixed by the Congress under the old Confederation in pursuance of a resolution of the general Convention, but I presume this is to be considered as merely advisory, and therefore that it will not invalidate the choice of Electors, though made on a different day.[5] But it appears to me essential, that the Electors should meet on the same day in all the States to give their votes, for so the Constitution declares. At all events, if the two houses should

2. As a consequence of rivalry between Federalists and Anti-Federalists and between adopting and nonadopting Anti-Federalists, the New York State Senate and Assembly went through a futile series of conferences to settle on a mode of electing senators. As a result, New York went unrepresented in the Senate until July 1789, four months after it convened. (Young, 126–27.)

3. At the same time that it was deciding on the proper mode for selecting senators, the New York State legislature was also deciding on the method of choosing presidential electors.

4. Anti-Federalists in both Virginia and New York were talking of Governor George Clinton of New York as a possible candidate for vice president. (Young, 125–26.)

5. When the day set for presidential voting passed, New York had not cast a ballot. (Young, 126.)

concur in any mode of election, I think it would be best to choose electors and direct them to meet and give their votes on the day appointed for the purpose—If the votes are rejected it will not do any harm.

You seem to apprehend, that because D—— prays and J—— swears, they apply for assistance to two opposite powers in the invisible world— you need not be apprehensive of this, for I believe it might be proved that the swearing of the one has as much efficacy in engaging heaven on their side as the praying of the other, and that both are equally acceptable to the prince of the power of the air. The leaders of the federal party are in my opinion as destitute of prudence, as some of them are of true regard to Republican government. Had this not been the case, they certainly would not have taken so many steps to excite and foment discord and animosity. They ought to have known, that a majority of the Legislature were opposed to them, and therefore that the way to carry points was not by pursuing violent measures, but by manifesting a spirit of conciliation and modera-tion.[6] The success of their schemes has been answerable to the prudence with which they were laid. I cannot perceive any object they could have in view, in their address to the Governor unless it was to gratify their resent-ments, and to keep alive and inflame party spirit. The attack on their part was unprovoked, as there was nothing in his speech but what was proper and evidently correspondent to the sentiments of the convention—The consequence was, as they might have foreseen, they got severely drubbed, and many temperate men of their own party condemn them and justify the Governor[7]—Equally impolitic have they been in urging the appointment of officers, at the eve of the old Councils going out and the new ones being appointed. A person of half common sense, would have seen, if prejudice had not blinded his mind, that such conduct was not only improper in itself but would be considered as calculated to establish a party by the gift of

6. The Federalists, outnumbered in the state legislature, sought to put the choice of presidential electors in the hands of the people. When it was decided that the legislature would choose electors, Hamilton and the Federalists sought to exploit the schism between the adopting and nonadopting Anti-Federalists by proposing that each house select four electors instead of the entire legislature jointly selecting eight. When the Anti-Federalists resisted this proposal, the Federalists proposed a compromise: nominations by each house separately, followed by a joint ballot. The Anti-Federalists overcame their differences to reject this proposal as well.

7. The Federalist senate publicly criticized the governor for not having called the session earlier. (Young, 124.)

offices. And they might have seen that the Assembly would have defeated their design, as they very properly did.

I am surprized that some Gentlemen I could name, go with them such lengths—If they are Republican, how is it possible they can avoid seeing the drift of some men and reprobating them?—I have written too much but, you will impute it to my being confined for above a Week with illness. Let me hear the news.

I am yours,
Melancton Smith

P.S. I hear the Bill is rejected.

Letter to Theodore Sedgwick,[1] January 30, 1791

New York Jany. 30th 1791

Dear Sir,

I imagined that the business of Congress this session would have been conducted with great harmony and dispatch—That as the foundation for the support of public credit was laid at the last meeting, you would at this have proceeded with cordiality and union, to build upon that foundation until the superstructure was completed in all its parts[2]—But I find that the same spirit of dissension, shall I call it, division it must be called, which prevailed at the former continues, perhaps I may say rages at this session—The *excise*, the *excise*, who can submit to the *excise*[3]—It is the engine of Tyrants, the enemy to Liberty—It will subvert the rights of the free citizens of America—It is an unequal tax, and therefore most oppressive—To prove this I need only observe, that the southern States have a natural and un-

---

Reprinted courtesy of the Massachusetts Historical Society, Melancton Smith to Theodore Sedgwick, January 30, 1791, Sedgwick family papers.

1. Theodore Sedgwick was a U.S. congressman from Massachusetts. He had associated with Smith in the Continental Congress but was now one of Hamilton's leading spokesmen in the House. (Brooks, 274.)

2. Smith here refers approvingly to the funding and assumption laws passed by Congress in its previous session.

3. Hamilton had proposed an excise tax in this session of Congress.

alienable right to drink Rum and Whiskey[4]—the excise will abridge this right, if not totally destroy it—The right to drink Rum & Whiskey in the northern and middle States is less perfect, because they drink Beer & Cyder & Molasses—Can it be possible that you can agree to an excise, after what Congress has said against it to the people of Canada in 1775? Read their address![5] and then say whether any friend to freedom can be in favour of an excise! You will consider too, that they objected to an excise to be laid by the Parliament of G. Britain, in the choice of whom we had no voice, and who could have no sympathy with us, in the burdens it would create—But the present excise is proposed to be laid by men of our own choosing, our own Countrymen and friends—"Had it been an enemy that had done this we could have borne it"—But I refrain from urging any more arguments against this nefarious scheme, though a thousand might be urged of equal weight—

Will you be so good to inform me and inform me truly, whether the excise Bill, so called, will pass the respective branches of the Legislature, and also whether the Bill for the establishment of the Bank will pass—If you cannot tell me truly or certainly tell me probably—If you cannot tell me probably tell me all you know about it and all you guess about it—you will mistake much, if you suppose [I think] this good Letter, I know it is a wretched one—[You] may depend upon it I can write a better. If [you] will not believe this, I will convince you of [this] by experiment, when I have more leisure [provided] you speedily and satisfactorily answer [the] above Questions.[6]

> *I am with esteem,*
> *Your friend and Serv.,*
> *Melancton Smith*

4. Smith's argument was based on the views of Congressman James Jackson of Georgia, who attacked the excise tax on the grounds that distilled liquors in the South were "not only necessary but salutary." (Brooks, 275.)

5. In 1775 the Continental Congress had denounced the excise tax in its address to the people of Canada. (Brooks, 275.)

6. This portion of the letter is torn. The transcription of the uncertain words has been aided by Robin Brooks's transcription, in "Melancton Smith: New York Anti-Federalist, 1744–1798," diss. (University of Rochester, 1964), 275.

Letter to James Madison and James Monroe, from Melancton Smith and M. Willett,[1] September 30, 1792

New York, Sept. 30, 1792

Gent,

The republicans in this State are unanimously disposed to a change in the vice Presidency of the united States, and we have heard with pleasure that similar dispositions prevail more or less throughout all the States[2]— nothing therefore seems requisite in order to success but to unite in a candidate—Gov. Clinton and Col. Burr, and no others, to our knowledge have been thought of—So far as our knowledge of the sentiments of the republicans in this State extends it appears to us that Col. Burr would be preferred considering the men in themselves, their characters their years and their habits of life—Our known and decided attachment to Gov. Clinton, our general acquaintance with the leading characters in the republican interest in this State and our long and intimate acquaintance with both the Gentleman enables us to say this with more confidence—But two circumstances seems to have removed all hesitation on the subject from the minds of the leading characters in the republican interest here—1st Gov. Clinton does not wish to be a candidate—on this head we have had repeated conversations with him both together and apart, and he has explicitly expressed his wishes that the republicans would unite in some other person. 2nd. The office of Governor in this State is in our opinion of more importance to the republican Interest than that of vice President—Gov. Clinton has, after a great struggle become elected,[3] and that it is probable that Col. Burr would be chosen to succeed Gov. Clinton in case he should be removed, yet we think it highly improper to hazard another election at this juncture—It has

Reprinted courtesy of the Library of Congress, Washington, D.C., Manuscript Division, Papers of James Monroe, reel no. 1.

1. Marinus Willett was the sheriff of New York County and an Anti-Federalist delegate to the New York ratifying convention who had voted for ratification. (Schechter, 195.)

2. The upcoming 1792 vice presidential election provided an opportunity for opponents of the Federalist administration in both the North and the South to unite against John Adams.

3. In 1792 Clinton defeated John Jay in a closely contested election for governor that was marked by accusations of vote stealing.

been suggested to us as an objection to offering Col. Burr as a candidate
that Gov. Clinton has been generally contemplated in the southern States
and that measures have been taken accordingly—This objection we consider as of little weight, because it is within our knowledge that Col. Burr
has also been thought of within those States—because we presume that the
republicans in those States are not so exclusively attached to any one person
as to pursue his election against his own wishes the wishes of his friends
and to the prejudice of the republican Interest, and because whatever may
have been the disposition of a few individuals, we are not informed of any
measures having been taken with a view to Gov. Clinton to the northward
of Pennsylvania, but from all the information we have obtained Col. Burr
has been the only person in view in those States—We do not hesitate to
declare that in our opinion Col. Burr will receive more support in new
Jersey and in the States to the eastward of that than can be procured for
Gov. Clinton—

For the foregoing reasons we are decided in our opinion that good policy
dictates that Col. Burr should be the candidate—We wish you may concur
with us in this opinion and that you will also concur with us in soliciting
the friends of republicanism in your State and to the southward to combine with us in the support of Col. Burr. We beg at all events your candid sentiments on the subject, for it is not a particular man but a general
measure which we wish to pursue—Gov. Clinton and Col. Burr are not
Competitors—The Gov.'s friends are the friends of Col. Burr. They have
fully conversed on the subject—Though our own opinion is in favour of
Col. Burr, we are fully impressed with the necessity of union on the subject
and will concur in either of the candidates who shall appear to command
the most interest—But we hope the political situation of this State and our
views and wishes with respect to the men and the object will not be wholly
disregarded.[4]

With great respect, we are Gent.
Your Obed. Servt.
Melancton Smith
M. Willett

4. Madison and Monroe responded by diplomatically but unequivocally rejecting
Smith's suggestion and siding with Clinton. On October 16, 1792, the Republicans
met in Philadelphia and unanimously endorsed Clinton's candidacy. Smith responded
by retreating from Burr and pledging to campaign for Clinton. (Young, 329–30.)

Letter to James Monroe,[1] August 6, 1795

New York Aug 6th 1795

My dear Sir,

I with pleasure embrace the oppurtunity which offers by Mr. Gelston, the Son of our mutual friend Mr. David Gelston,[2] to revive the memory of our former friendship.—I hope you and your family enjoy health and that your situation is agreeable—Our republican friends unite in the tenderest sympathy with our french bretheren in the distresses they have endured occasioned by the scarcity of provision and by the wicked machinations of their internal enemies. We do not fear but that they will surmount all the obstacles laid in the way of their freedom and independence. The enjoyment will be more pleasant when they review the dangers and difficulties they have encountered in obtaining their freedom—The Continent is agitated from end to end with Jay's Treaty[3]—No body likes it and I believe five sixths of the people reprobate it—Persons of my political [tendency?], and these I presume you well know, are mortified, vexed and anxious—You will doubtless receive the extraordinary instrument before this reaches you— It is not known whether the president has signed it or not, though the general opinion now is that he has not, and it is hoped will not.—A certain Secretary[4] appears to be in great distress—his popularity, as well as that of the late envoy[5] has much depreciated in the State (you know I presume the latter is Governor of the State). Our friend Gov. Clinton declined stand-

---

Reprinted courtesy of the Library of Congress, Washington, D.C., Manuscript Division, Papers of James Monroe, reel no. 1.

1. James Monroe had just recently been appointed minister plenipotentiary from the United States to France.

2. David Gelston was one of the leaders of the Anti-Federalists in New York. From 1777 to 1785 he represented Suffolk County in the New York Assembly. In 1788 he had been one of the founding members of the Federal Republican Society.

3. Jay's Treaty sought to settle the brewing conflict between American merchants and Great Britain on terms that Republicans believed were largely favorable to Britain and unfavorable to France.

4. This is a reference to Alexander Hamilton, who was then the secretary of the treasury.

5. This is a reference to John Jay, who had brokered the treaty with Britain. Jay had been elected governor of New York in 1794.

ing a Candidate, his health is much impaired.[6]—The patriotic Jefferson is blessed by all good americans—He never would have disgraced his country by putting his name to an instrument like the Treaty—I need not ask your attention to young Mr. Gelston, you know his father who continues the same unshaken friend to the rights of mankind he always was—Wishing you every felicity, I am

Your Ob. Ser.,
Melancton Smith

6. In late January 1795, George Clinton issued an announcement that he would not be a candidate for governor in the 1796 election, citing his declining health. (Young, 432.)

Appendix 1

The Authorship of Two Sets of Anti-Federalist Papers:
A Computational Approach
by John Burrows[1]

A research group from the University of Notre Dame, comprising Michael Zuckert, Derek Webb, and Robert Floyd, invited me to bring the methods of computational stylistics to bear on the putative authorship of two sets of Anti-Federalist papers. These essays were published under the pseudonyms "Brutus" and "the Federal Farmer" in the course of the great public debate about the proposed Constitution of the United States of America in the late 1780s. I was aware from the first that my colleagues hypothesize that "Brutus" was Melancton Smith rather than Robert Yates and that "the Federal Farmer" was Smith rather than Richard Henry Lee, or possibly that Smith was both "Brutus" and "the Federal Farmer." But I have not seen any of their evidence and know little of the case that has previously been made—on either side—about the authorship of these papers. Such published comments as I have seen, however, lead me to believe that the matter deserves careful reappraisal and that the parallel historical and computational inquiries we are undertaking are of considerable value. My colleagues, naturally, are not responsible for any defects in my part of the inquiry.

Much the best-known contributions to the constitutional debate are the Federalist Papers, the work of Alexander Hamilton, John Jay, and James Madison. The papers are celebrated not only for the vigor with which these men put the case for the proposed Constitution but also as the occasion of a classic problem of disputed authorship. The authorship of Jay's papers has never been in dispute. Of the remainder, however, some were known to be by Hamilton, some by Madison, and some by one or the other. The

---

1. John Burrows is Professor Emeritus of Literary and Linguistic Computing, University of Newcastle, Newcastle, Australia.

stylistic evidence was assessed by Mosteller and Wallace,[2] whose study still stands after forty years as a model of what could be achieved by statistical analysis without computer assistance. Their success has allowed this particular set of texts to be used to test the effectiveness of new methods of stylistic analysis on questions of doubtful authorship. In a very thorough appraisal of new methods, Holmes and Forsyth found particular value in the application of an established statistical procedure known as principal component analysis.[3] This was among the methods employed in the course of the larger inquiry that lies behind this essay. The outcome of several trials strongly favored Melancton Smith's authorship of the texts in question and disfavored the claims of Yates and Lee.

Hamilton, Jay, and Madison had many allies and many opponents. Partisans on both sides of the debate published their views under their own names, but many others wrote under pseudonyms, often using the names of admired figures from Roman antiquity. The extensive series of papers by "Brutus" and "the Federal Farmer" were among the most notable contributions to the Anti-Federalist side of the debate, and these lie at the center of the following discussion.

Since computational stylistics, like other applications of statistical analysis, is essentially a comparison, we have assembled a corpus made up of other contributions to the debate and, where necessary, of associated writings by many of the participants. Table 1 summarizes this corpus. Our choice of texts was guided partly by availability, partly by a decision to treat four thousand words as a lower working limit for any member of the corpus, and partly by the need to be as confident as possible of the authorship of all the texts except the two sets whose authorship was in doubt. Although most of the texts were published essays, usually couched as letters to a newspaper editor, it was necessary to draw also on the personal letters and the public speeches of some authors. In literary form, the personal letters, treating chiefly the same range of constitutional questions and often coming from exchanges between convention delegates, were much like the published letters and essays. The public speeches are obviously of a different genre. Many of them, moreover, including the main body of Smith's work, are available only in the form of extensive transcripts by the shorthand reporters chosen for the various state conventions. Preliminary analyses showed that it was

2. Frederick Mosteller and David L. Wallace, *Inference and Disputed Authorship: The Federalist Papers* (New York: Springer Verlag, 1964, 2nd ed., 1984).

3. D. I. Holmes and R. S. Forsyth, "*The Federalist* Revisited: New Directions in Authorship Attribution," *Literary and Linguistic Computing* 10 (1995): 111–27.

TABLE 1. Short List of Texts

Length (no. of words)		Signatory	Literary Form
Main Set			
1	11,325	Agrippa	Papers
2	4,940	Cassius	Papers
3	5,739	Cato	Papers
4	8,072	Centinel	Papers
5	4,259	Cincinnatus	Papers
6	4,596	DemFed	Papers signed "Democratic Federalist"
7	6,448	DeWitt	Papers signed "John De Witt"
8	8,722	Grayson	Letters of William Grayson
9	27,007	Hamilton	Papers from *The Federalist*
10	7,947	ImpExam	Papers signed "Impartial Examiner"
11	8,228	Jay	Papers from *The Federalist*
12	4,060	Landholder	Papers
13	5,600	Lee1	Letters of Richard Henry Lee
14	22,568	Madison	Papers from *The Federalist*
15	11,725	Martin	Letters of Luther Martin
16	5,329	MD Farmer	Papers signed "Maryland Farmer"
17	8,234	Monroe	Letters and papers of James Monroe
18	9,675	Old Whig	Papers
19	9,214	PA Minority	"Report of Dissenting Minority"
20	8,988	Pinckney	Speeches of Charles Pinckney
21	6,983	Sherman	Letters and pseudonymous papers of Roger Sherman
22	10,328	Smith1	Melancton Smith, convention speeches
23	5,444	Webster	Papers by Noah Webster
24	7,762	Wilson	Papers of James Wilson
25	7,138	Sydney	Papers signed "Sydney" (i.e., Robert Yates)
Dubia			
26	41,436	Brutus	Papers
27	73,722	Federal Farmer	Papers
28	9,331	Plebeian	Convention speech
29	6,221	Lucius/Fed. Rep.	Papers signed "Lucius" and "Federal Republican"
Corrobative Sets			
30	5,183	Lee2	Letters of Richard Henry Lee
31	4,238	Yates	Letters and "Plan of Union" by Robert Yates
32	8,375	Smith2	Letters of Melancton Smith
33	4,525	(Smith3)	Brief summaries of speeches and comments

possible to identify and transcend this form of contamination. The fact that the authorship of speeches, as transcribed, can still be established amounts to an unexpected tribute to the accuracy of an extinct craft. In other cases, however, where speeches—some of Smith's among them—were reduced to bare summaries, authorship proved much more elusive. These were kept aside from the main analyses and used only sparingly for appropriate sorts of corroboration.

The difference of genre between Smith's speeches and the papers of Brutus and the Federal Farmer makes it a little more difficult to achieve a fair comparison but adds weight to a positive outcome. A number of Smith's hitherto unpublished letters on political matters, located by my collaborator, Derek Webb, enabled us to make up a second set of Smith's work. The fact that Lee's set is made up entirely of a selection of his letters, and does not include any speeches, nonetheless permits a comparison of Lee's known writings with the papers of Brutus and Federal Farmer. In Lee's case, too, the results could be corroborated by adding a second set of letters and keeping them aside from the initial phases of the inquiry.

In Yates's case, unfortunately, the highly appropriate papers of "Sidney" (or "Sydney"), which are acknowledged as his, could be complemented only by a handful of unpublished letters and by his "Plan of Union," which differs markedly in form from almost all the other texts. Even when the "Plan of Union" is included, Yates's group of texts remains smaller than one would wish; and his authorship of the Sidney papers may not be incontestable. The least bad solution, it seemed, was to treat the papers of Sidney as a set and the letters and "Plan of Union" as another. As will be seen, the two sets proved too different to be comfortable partners.

Excellent versions of many texts were downloaded from some of the great electronic libraries that are now available; we are especially indebted to those of the University of Chicago and the University of Virginia. A range of other texts was downloaded from sites established by organizations specializing in the constitutional history of the United States. Chiefly in order to reach the four-thousand-word threshold, some gaps were filled by keyboard entry, drawing on such printed sources as Ford's *Essays* and *Pamphlets* and Elliot's *Debates*.[4] The requirement for authenticity was breached

---

4. Paul Leicester Ford, ed., *Essays on the Constitution of the United States Published During Its Discussion by the People 1787–88* (New York: Burt Franklin, 1892; reprt. 1970); Ford, ed., *Pamphlets on . . .* (New York: Burt Franklin, 1888; reprt. 1971); Jonathan Elliot, ed., *The Debates in the Several Conventions on the Adoption of the Federal Constitution . . .* , 5 vols. (New York: Burt Franklin, 1888; undated reprint).

in two cases. It is thought that Samuel Bryan, author of the "Centinel" papers, also played some part in writing "The Address and Reasons of Dissent of the Minority of the Convention of Pennsylvania." The Centinel papers and the "Address" are included as separate members of our corpus; and Bryan's claim will be tested, in passing, by the computational evidence. "An Address to the People of the State of New York" by "a Plebeian" is said to be the work of Melancton Smith. That claim will also be tested.

All told, the main corpus comprises twenty-five authorial sets along with three main "dubia," or doubtful cases: those of Plebeian, Brutus, and Federal Farmer. A fourth, smaller dubium added at a late stage of the inquiry comprises papers of "Lucius" and of "a Federal Republican" (both from New York). These, which are regarded as Smith's work, sat comfortably as a single set. Among the supporting texts, the most important are the second, independent sets by Lee, Smith, and Yates.

Editing of the texts for the purposes of statistical analysis was kept to a minimum so that other scholars could more easily replicate our data. Passages from other writers cited by our authors were excluded from the analysis, as were such ornamental flourishes as the salutations offered at the beginning and end of letters and speeches. The ampersand symbol as an abbreviation for "et cetera" was expanded because it represents a merely adventitious difference between published letters and more formal writings. Since our software cannot deal with ligatures, the principal diphthongs were rendered as "ae" and "oe." The words "dollar" and "pound" were substituted for the usual symbols. With a single unavoidable exception, no attempt was made to standardize the spelling of the texts. The exception was a text of Noah Webster's printed as written in the full bloom of his campaign for phonetic spelling. Too little of his work was available for it to be excluded: but, as spelled, it offered quite freakish word counts. Many practitioners of computational stylistics, myself included, often find it useful to tag texts in such a way as to distinguish the different grammatical forms of such words as "so" and "that." To allow the easier replication of our data, nothing of this kind was attempted in the present inquiry.

The computational analysis of literary style is equipped to examine the full range of a writer's vocabulary, including those elements least evident to readers and least amenable to the traditional forms of literary argument. Such elements include words that occur so seldom that they usually pass unnoticed and those that occur so often that a reader makes little or nothing of them. All can yield evidence on many questions of scholarly interest, including those of disputed authorship. Take the case of the word-type "middling."[5] Within our twenty-five-author corpus, only Smith ever uses it. More conscious of social class than many of his contemporaries, and more willing than most to regard a British social vocabulary as still applicable to the America of his day, he says more than most of the other authors about the aristocracy, yeomanry, and poor. The "middling class of men" (though not, at that date, of women) accordingly have a place in his vocabulary, as have "the poor and middling classes." The immediate point of interest is that Plebeian, Brutus, and Federal Farmer all use this same term. Smith himself uses it eleven times; the others twice, thrice, and twice, respectively, in just such phrases as those quoted. As used here, the word is not unfamiliar in the British fiction and social documents of that period, yet none of the other twenty-four authors, including Lee and Yates, uses it at all.

"Middling" is a potent member of a little set of word-types occurring both in Smith and in the dubia but seldom or never in any of the other twenty-four members of our main authorial set. Among those not occurring elsewhere is "Marquis," used in reference to the political opinions of the Marquis Beccaria. The same authority (though spelled "Beccarari") is cited by Brutus. Of two references to him by Federal Farmer, one has the very sentence that Smith quotes. "Chimerical" is used by only three authors— once each by Smith, Hamilton, and Centinel. Plebeian and Federal Farmer use it twice, and "Smith3," the brief shorthand summaries of Smith's lesser contributions to the proceedings of the New York convention, uses it once. The three longer dubia all include instances of Smith's metaphor of opening or closing a door on an idea. In its only other appearance, "door" is used by James Monroe when he expresses the fear that his absence from the Bar has opened the door for his rivals.

Sometimes the correspondence between Smith and the dubia is less arbitrary than it might seem. "Fictions" and "novel" are among the words that reflect Smith's tendency to allude to literature, music, and the theatrical arts. The numbers "sixty-five" and "twenty-five" have to do with numbers of representatives, quorums, and the like in the New York convention, reflecting questions that engage Smith, Yates, Cato, Brutus, and Federal Farmer. Other members of our set who take up such technicalities were not New Yorkers and speak of other numbers. And, finally, it may be observed

5. It is often useful to distinguish between word-types and word-tokens. The many occurrences of "the" in any given text are called *word-tokens;* that is, actual appearances of the *word-type* "the." We may say, therefore, that the 10,328 word-tokens comprising our set for Smith represent 1,815 word-types. In Lee1, 5,600 represent 1,483; and in Yates's Letters and "Plan of Union," 4,238 represent 1,180.

that even at a time when most educated men used a far more Latinate vocabulary than is common nowadays, documents associated with Smith are especially rich in comparatively uncommon polysyllables.

These observations are not quite so significant as they may seem to be. In the shorter texts especially, a few changes of phraseology or a few editorial errors might alter the whole picture. A few additions to the main set of authors might well bring further instances of "middling" or "door" and further adherents of the Marquis Beccaria. Even the words themselves cannot be taken at face value. In their letters, both Yates and Smith make reference to the celebrated Governor Clinton of New York. (George Clinton is said to be the author of the vehemently Anti-Federalist papers of "Cato," a member of our set of twenty-five. He is especially fearful of undue vice presidential influence and of the possible emergence of a coterie of advisers isolating the president from the people.) The fact that no other member of our set of authors ever mentions Clinton helps to distinguish these two New Yorkers from the Virginians, Marylanders, and others, though it does nothing to distinguish them from each other. But even the broader effect hangs by a thread. All but one of Yates's references to "Clinton" are not to the governor but to a sloop of that name!

Smith's vocabulary, like that of most people, includes some truly rare words such as the obscure legal term *replevin* and the word *denned*, which does not even appear in the *Oxford English Dictionary* and may well be a misprint for "defined." These words occur neither in our main set of texts nor in any of the dubia. To take their absence as evidence that Smith wrote none of the dubia might seem whimsical. But the mere notion illustrates the danger of picking over the evidence to suit a preferred outcome.

To put such phenomena to a more valid use, I devised a series of simple rules. The first step was to tabulate the raw frequencies of the 1,815 word-types that make up Smith1. The corresponding frequencies in ten other specimens were set beside them in a Microsoft Excel spreadsheet. One of the ten specimens embraced twenty-two members of the main set of authors (excluding Smith1, Lee1, and Sidney). Smith2, Lee1, Lee2, Sidney, and Yates were left aside with the four dubia as free agents. In order to offset the immense differences of length across the range of specimens, the word-frequencies were standardized as proportions (at rates per thousand words) of the texts in which they occurred.

Table 2 summarizes the outcomes of the six tests of the data just described. In Test 1, the only requirement is that a word-type must occur in Smith1. Beyond that, the data are allowed to speak for themselves. The column headed "Types" shows how many of the 1,815 word-types occur

TABLE 2. Relative Frequency Rates of Six Sets of Word-types

	Total	Test 1: 1,815 word-types Base: Smith1 and 22 others			Test 2: 1,393 word-types Base: Smith1 and <16 others			Test 3: 346 word-types Base: Smith1 (2ex4) and <16 others		
		Types	Tokens	per 1,000	Types	Tokens	per 1,000	Types	Tokens	per 1,000
Smith1	10,328	1,815	10,328	1000	1,393	2,427	234.99	346	1,211	117.25
Main set	197,264	1,689	162,568	824.11	1,267	19,250	97.58	338	7,471	37.87
Smith2	8,375	793	7,161	855.04	411	904	107.94	151	381	45.49
Lee1	5,600	693	4,587	819.11	335	541	96.61	120	206	36.79
Lee2	5,183	617	4,283	826.36	275	502	96.86	117	208	40.13
Sidney	7,138	744	5,800	812.55	376	623	87.28	140	246	34.46
Yates	4,238	577	3,376	796.60	263	403	95.09	110	166	39.17
Plebeian	9,331	858	8,019	859.39	467	938	100.53	174	385	41.26
Brutus	41,436	1,275	36,254	874.94	854	4,131	99.70	282	1,859	44.86
F. Farmer	73,722	1,373	63,136	856.41	951	8,682	117.77	299	3,857	52.32
Lucius/FedR	6,221	733	5,399	867.87	378	680	109.31	148	282	45.33

	Total	Test 4: 258 word-types Base: Smith1(2ex2) and <16 others			Test 5: 85 word-types Base: Smith1(3ex4) and <16 others			Test 6: 55 word-types Base: Smith1(2ex2) and <5 others		
		Types	Tokens	per 1,000	Types	Tokens	per 1,000	Types	Tokens	per 1,000
Smith1	10,328	258	939	90.92	85	501	48.51	55	179	17.33
Main set	197,264	253	5,654	28.66	84	2,244	11.38	50 / 50	282	1.43
Smith2	8,375	114	288	34.39	40	94	11.22	11	15	1.79
Lee1	5,600	86	152	27.14	36	63	11.25	4	8	1.43
Lee2	5,183	86	159	30.68	30	67	12.93	4	9	1.74
Sidney	7,138	109	196	27.46	44	88	12.33	12	15	2.10
Yates	4,238	83	129	30.44	29	56	13.21	9	20	4.72
Plebeian	9,331	127	283	30.33	44	104	11.15	18	28	3.00
Brutus	41,436	209	1,419	34.25	74	668	16.12	28	72	1.74
F. Farmer	73,722	223	2,773	37.61	77	1,131	15.34	33	161	2.18
Lucius/FedR	6,221	117	222	35.69	47	93	14.95	12	19	3.05

in each of the eleven specimens. The column headed "Tokens" shows the corresponding totals of their instances. The column headed "per 1,000" shows their standardized rates of occurrence.

Since the chosen word-types are those that constitute Smith1, its perfect rate of 1,000 per 1,000 is predetermined—10,328 of 10,328 word-tokens. It is obvious that no other text, even of Smith's own authorship, will ever match it. The real point of interest in Test 1 is that Smith2 and the four dubia all show higher occurrence rates than any of the other specimens.

Provided there are none that Smith happens to eschew, Test 1 includes all the most common word-types of the language, the words everybody used all the time. This means that it has two related disadvantages for our purpose. The frequency hierarchy of English words falls away so rapidly that the standardized frequencies of the leading members can overwhelm the rest. It is possible, therefore, that the outcome of Test 1 is merely an expression (albeit a strong one) of the behavior of the most common words of all. The second disadvantage is that the most common words are to be tested by other methods in a later part of this inquiry. To exclude them for the moment allows us to make tests quite independent of those others.

Test 2, also shown in Table 2, moves in that direction. The results are set out in the same fashion as before. Instead of the full range of 1,815 word-types, however, we have the 1,393 that meet a second stipulation. Any word-type used by more than fifteen of the twenty-two authors is excluded. The effect is to exclude all the common function-words except for "she," which occurs in only eleven of the main group of twenty-two authors! The most common surviving word-type is "president," which occurs 111 times in fifteen of the twenty-two. The results for Test 2 show that the surviving word-types supply only about 10 percent of the word-tokens in most specimens, compared with the previous 80 percent or more. The gap between Smith2 and the dubia, on the one hand, and the other four free agents, on the other, is less pronounced, but the grouping is unchanged. Smith's claim continues to prevail.

Test 3 continues the exclusion of the word-types used by more than fifteen of the main set of authors. It adds a further restriction designed to exclude word-types that occur only once in Smith1 and those that occur only in a limited part of that text. This is achieved by breaking Smith1 into four equal segments and preserving only the 346 word-types that occur in two or more of them. The chosen word-types now supply only about 4 percent of each free agent. Lee2 presses close upon Plebeian, but the overall affinity between Smith2 and the four dubia remains.

The three sets of results in the lower half of Table 2 show the effect of increasingly stringent requirements. In Test 4, the fifteen-author ceiling is retained and the chosen words all appear in both halves of Smith1. The 258 word-types still supply around 3 percent of most free agents. Both Lee2 and Yates now score a little higher than Plebeian, destroying the previously consistent affinity between Smith2 and all four dubia. But neither Lee2 nor Yates matches the scores for the other three dubia. In this sense, Smith's claim on Brutus and Federal Farmer is sustained.

It is also sustained in Test 5, even though the larger pattern is broken. Lee1, Lee2, Sidney, and Yates all outscore Smith2. The test now supplies only about 1 percent of most free agents. It embraces the eighty-five word-types that occur in three out of four segments of Smith1 without exceeding the fifteen-author ceiling. Even here, however, three of the four dubia easily outscore the other free agents. And the strict requirement imposed here means that the word list is more Smith-driven than ever.

For Test 6, the word-types are required to occur in both halves of Smith1 and in no more than five of the twenty-two authors. The fifty-five of them supply only about 0.2 percent of most free agents. Three of the four dubia are among the higher scorers, and Smith2 regains its earlier advantage over Lee1 and Lee2. But Test 6 is vulnerable to adventitious effects. The letters of Robert Yates yield nine of these fifty-five word-types, twenty word-tokens, and a remarkably high rate of 4.72 per thousand. Among the twenty word-tokens, alas, there are nine instances of "committee" and four of "yesterday." It is always useful to press a statistical test to the point of collapse—and we have succeeded.

Corresponding series of tests for Sidney and Lee1 conducted in the same way showed no particular affinity for Brutus and Federal Farmer, respectively. The behavior of the three corroborative texts for Smith2, Lee2, and Yates gave further support to that outcome.

As noted earlier, the evidence of this series of tests is independent of the evidence to be assessed in the remainder of this paper. They serve, therefore, to complement the better established forms of analysis bearing on concomitant differences of frequency among the very common words. Such a complement is always worthwhile.

The value of the very common words for work like ours depends on a fact that needs illustration: the frequencies of many of them vary in consonance with each other from text to text. At its most obvious, this consonance can be seen in grammatically driven phenomena like the agreement between subject and verb or the consistency of number, mood, and tense between one verb and its neighbours. Douglas Biber's study embracing several centuries of English usage showed that the most constant and powerful stylistic contrast across a given range of texts is a complex blending of determinants. It usually sets the more extempore, speech-oriented of literary forms against the more deliberate, writing-oriented forms. The former include many plays, public speeches, and works of prose fiction. The latter include more formal, occasional, and disquisitory sorts of writing.[6] This large contrast manifests itself in different frequency rates for many of the very common words.

In speech-oriented documents one would expect, for example, to find higher than usual frequencies for personal pronouns couched in the first and second persons. In writing-oriented documents, these run far lower, giving way (as the case may be) either to third-person pronouns or to definite and indefinite articles and several of the more common prepositions. These differences, in turn, bear on the relative frequencies of the inflected auxiliary verbs and some of the connectives.

The rhetorical stance different writers adopt toward their chosen subjects affects the tense and moods of the inflected verbs and the semantic level of the more common lexical words. They may talk of what has already occurred or what they hope or fear may come to pass. They may prefer a more dignified or a more colloquial level of expression. Some of these preferences change rapidly with time, as, in the present case, when the discussion of a possible union of the states moves forward from what the convention should or should not recommend to what it has recommended and the effects of those recommendations.

Even within a set of constitutional texts that are unusually homogeneous in their main subject, however, there are inevitable differences of emphasis, which manifest themselves in the relative frequencies of many lexical words. The overall homogeneity of subject is reflected in exceptionally high frequencies for "people," "constitution," "government," and "states," as well as many other words. The differences of emphasis lead Cato, for example, to make far more use than Smith of "president" and "executive," and Yates of words pertaining to the monarchy. "Agrippa" makes far more use than Smith of words pertaining to foreign policy, especially economic policy. Luther Martin has much to say of one "committee" or another, and Alexander Hamilton of the "majority." Where Smith speaks of a "general government," others speak of it as "national" or "federal" or as the "proposed sys-

6. Douglas Biber, *Variation Across Speech and Writing* (Cambridge: Cambridge University Press, 1988).

tem." (Agrippa, forgetful that the states of the original confederation already had a neighbor to their north, speaks of a "continental government" and of its "continental" courts and laws.) Smith's frequent recourse to this use of "general" is idiosyncratic enough to make itself felt even in the third-person shorthand summaries of his lesser contributions to the New York ratifying convention. Brutus also has unusually high frequencies for this expression, as do Sherman and Yates, the latter Smith's rival as the putative Brutus.

The evidence of all the very common words, taken together, will be addressed initially by the use of the "delta procedure," a new method of my own devising. Upon making it public in 2002, I expressed the hope that others would test its efficacy.[7] In an article published in December 2004, David Hoover tested it thoroughly and found it "a valuable new tool."[8] Like me, however, he found that it errs unexpectedly at times. For that reason, I believe its best uses are in initial investigations of a range of possibilities, as here. Its particular advantage is that, unlike those yielded by principal component analysis and cluster analysis, the results for various test-pieces are quite independent of each other. Each, in turn, is tested against the same base. Each result can then be compared with others of exactly the same origin.

A little reflection indicates that, because the scores for any given specimen on a chosen set of variables will diverge in both directions from the norms for the database, an aggregate or mean divergence would comprise an arbitrary mixture of positives and negatives. Now, while the differences between positives and negatives—high scores, say, for "the" in this specimen but low ones for "I" and "me"—are most instructive, they are not the heart of the matter. An expression of difference, pure difference, is what we seek. If all the positive and negative divergences were rendered as absolute divergences, their overall aggregate or their mean could be of interest. A "delta score" is just such a mean divergence.

Table 3, which represents a small Microsoft Excel worksheet, offers a "closed version" of the procedure, bringing the top thirty words of the main set of twenty-five authors to bear on a simple question. Can we demonstrate

7. See John Burrows, "'Delta': A Measure of Stylistic Difference and a Guide to Likely Authorship," *Literary and Linguistic Computing* 17 (2002): 267–86; Burrows, "The Englishing of Juvenal: Computational Stylistics and Translated Texts," *Style* 36 (2002): 677–94; Burrows, "Questions of Authorship: Attribution and Beyond," *Computers and the Humanities* 37 (2003): 1–26.

8. David L. Hoover, "Testing Burrows's Delta," *Literary and Linguistic Computing*, 2004, 19(4): 453–75.

TABLE 3. Specimen of Delta Procedure for Three Authors and a Test-piece

1				Test-piece Lee2		Lee 1		
2						Count		30
3						Sum		20.368
4						**MEAN = "delta"**		0.679
5						STDEV		0.641
6	A B	C	D	E	F	G	H	I
8	Word	Mean	SD	Score	z-score	Score	z-score	Abs. diff.
9	1 the	7.821	1.010	8.238	0.414	6.911	−0.901	1.315
10	2 of	5.187	0.753	5.055	−0.176	5.357	0.225	0.401
11	3 to	3.432	0.511	3.627	0.381	3.643	0.412	0.031
12	4 and	3.214	0.679	3.126	−0.131	3.482	0.395	0.525
13	5 in	2.119	0.319	2.103	−0.050	1.732	−1.212	1.162
14	6 a	1.874	0.374	1.447	−1.141	1.554	−0.856	0.285
15	7 be	1.553	0.375	2.142	1.572	2.089	1.433	0.140
16	8 that	1.549	0.374	2.199	1.741	2.393	2.258	0.517
17	9 it	1.318	0.351	1.138	−0.513	1.929	1.740	2.253
18	10 is	1.308	0.370	1.331	0.062	1.232	−0.206	0.268
19	11 by	0.889	0.195	1.061	0.883	0.768	−0.617	1.501
20	12 as	0.853	0.213	1.254	1.886	0.661	−0.903	2.789
21	13 this	0.848	0.246	0.907	0.239	0.911	0.255	0.016
22	14 will	0.802	0.293	0.637	−0.566	0.500	−1.032	0.467
23	15 which	0.758	0.225	0.482	−1.222	0.518	−1.064	0.158
24	16 for	0.773	0.154	0.868	0.619	1.036	1.709	1.090
25	17 their	0.754	0.218	0.386	−1.688	0.536	−1.001	0.687
26	18 have	0.749	0.174	0.579	−0.977	0.589	−0.917	0.060
27	19 they	0.724	0.232	0.540	−0.791	0.375	−1.503	0.712
28	20 are	0.692	0.213	0.309	−1.799	0.464	−1.069	0.730
29	21 not	0.692	0.130	0.579	−0.868	0.679	−0.100	0.768
30	22 with	0.614	0.200	0.540	−0.370	0.786	0.859	1.229
31	23 or	0.563	0.186	0.521	−0.224	0.607	0.239	0.463
32	24 government	0.524	0.243	0.424	−0.412	0.286	−0.984	0.572
33	25 from	0.522	0.101	0.579	0.563	0.536	0.136	0.427
34	26 but	0.497	0.124	0.521	0.189	0.429	−0.554	0.744
35	27 I	0.493	0.432	0.849	0.825	0.839	0.802	0.022
36	28 on	0.439	0.162	0.347	−0.568	0.411	−0.177	0.391
37	29 states	0.437	0.272	0.521	0.307	0.411	−0.098	0.404
38	30 we	0.426	0.236	0.193	−0.987	0.250	−0.745	0.242

Note: Analysis based on the thirty most common words of the main set of texts.

		Smith 1			Sidney		
1							
2				30			30
3				35.756			27.100
4				**1.192**			**0.903**
5				0.818			0.607
6	A B	J	K	L	M	N	O
8	Word	Score	z-score	Abs. diff.	Score	z-score	Abs. diff.
9	1 the	7.698	−0.122	0.536	9.190	1.356	0.942
10	2 of	4.454	−0.974	0.798	5.352	0.218	0.394
11	3 to	3.486	0.104	0.277	3.965	1.042	0.661
12	4 and	2.130	−1.598	1.467	3.923	1.044	1.175
13	5 in	1.888	−0.723	0.673	2.256	0.428	0.478
14	6 a	2.179	0.814	1.955	1.709	−0.440	0.700
15	7 be	1.966	1.102	0.470	1.051	−1.340	2.912
16	8 that	1.820	0.727	1.014	1.779	0.617	1.124
17	9 it	1.617	0.851	1.364	1.275	−0.124	0.389
18	10 is	1.704	1.071	1.009	0.813	−1.342	1.403
19	11 by	0.668	−1.128	2.011	0.757	−0.675	1.559
20	12 as	1.007	0.724	1.162	0.981	0.601	1.285
21	13 this	1.152	1.236	0.997	0.672	−0.713	0.952
22	14 will	1.588	2.681	3.247	0.672	−0.443	0.122
23	15 which	0.474	−1.257	0.035	0.434	−1.435	0.213
24	16 for	0.755	−0.116	0.735	0.743	−0.199	0.818
25	17 their	0.678	−0.350	1.338	0.841	0.396	2.085
26	18 have	0.862	0.650	1.626	0.785	0.206	1.183
27	19 they	0.900	0.761	1.552	0.560	−0.705	0.087
28	20 are	0.707	0.069	1.869	0.532	−0.750	1.050
29	21 not	1.017	2.502	3.369	0.728	0.284	1.152
30	22 with	0.465	−0.748	0.378	0.728	0.573	0.943
31	23 or	0.261	−1.618	1.393	0.490	−0.389	0.164
32	24 government	0.678	0.632	1.044	0.560	0.148	0.560
33	25 from	0.358	−1.624	2.187	0.420	−1.009	1.572
34	26 but	0.552	0.439	0.249	0.448	−0.395	0.585
35	27 I	1.181	1.594	0.769	0.602	0.254	0.570
36	28 on	0.387	−0.322	0.247	0.462	0.141	0.709
37	29 states	0.407	−0.113	0.419	0.280	−0.577	0.883
38	30 we	0.562	0.576	1.564	0.294	−0.558	0.430

that Lee has a better claim to the authorship of our second batch of his letters than either Smith or Sidney? (The Sidney papers were chosen as a fairer
specimen of Yates's usual style than the selection that includes his "Plan of
Union.") Columns A and B show the thirty most common words in descending order of their frequency in the main database. Column C shows their
mean frequencies, all represented as percentages of that set; column D shows
the corresponding standard deviations. Columns E and F show the scores
for our test-piece, "Lee2," and the z-scores based on them. Columns G and
H, columns J and K, and columns M and N treat our three candidates, Lee1,
Smith, and Sidney, in exactly the same fashion. The absolute differences
shown in columns I, L, and O show how far each of the candidates differs
from Lee2 for each of the thirty words. At the head of these three columns,
the thirty differences are summed up and reduced to their mean differences.
The entries in I4, L4, and O4 are the mean differences between Lee2 and
Lee1, Smith, and Sidney, respectively. At 0.679, Lee1's mean difference, or
"delta score," is much lower than those for Smith or Sidney. A delta score can
thus be defined as "the mean of the absolute differences between the z-scores
for a set of word-variables in a given text-group and the z-scores for the same
set of word-variables in a target text." The use of z-scores makes it possible
to obtain cognate figures for all the words in a hierarchy when the original
frequencies fall away sharply from top to bottom.[9] The object is to treat all of
these words as markers of potentially equal power in highlighting the differences between one style and another.

A procedure that could not satisfy this simple trial would not be worth
pursuing. But the delta procedure comes into its own when it demonstrates
that Lee2, for example, is less different from Lee1 than from any other of
our twenty-five authorial sets. Table 4 shows the outcome when an open,
multiauthor version of the procedure is used to test Lee2, Smith2, and Yates
on the full list of 250 variables, the most common words of our main set.

In Table 4, the delta scores are accompanied by "delta z-scores" derived
from the full set of twenty-five delta scores for our main authors. Not only
does Lee2 differ less from Lee1 than from any of the other twenty-four,
but the delta z-score of −2.825 shows what a potent difference it is. In the
second set, Smith1 leads the field and scores strongly, as he should. In the

---

9. An outline of the calculation and use of z-scores can be found in introductory
manuals of statistics, but readers in need of such help may be best served by the
lucid account in Anthony Kenny, *The Computation of Style* (Oxford: Pergamon, 1982),
57–58.

TABLE 4. Delta Rankings of Twenty-five Authors for Three Control Specimens

	Lee2 250 words			Smith2 250 words			Yates 250 words		
		delta	delta Z		delta	delta Z		delta	delta Z
1	**LEE1**	0.865	−2.825	**SMITH1**	0.869	−2.114	Hamilton	1.054	−2.106
2	Centinel	0.965	−1.802	Grayson	0.894	−1.858	Wilson	1.081	−1.658
3	PA Minority	1.038	−1.057	Monroe	0.936	−1.441	Madison	1.098	−1.360
4	Madison	1.050	−0.930	DeWitt	0.953	−1.280	Agrippa	1.100	−1.339
5	Sherman	1.063	−0.802	**LEE1**	0.977	−1.042	**SIDNEY**	1.133	−0.772
6	ImpExam	1.076	−0.669	Cassius	1.026	−0.555	Cincinnatus	1.138	−0.686
7	Monroe	1.106	−0.367	Centinel	1.028	−0.529	Centinel	1.142	−0.618
8	Agrippa	1.113	−0.289	Sherman	1.037	−0.444	Landholder	1.146	−0.551
9	**SIDNEY**	1.116	−0.255	**SIDNEY**	1.061	−0.205	DeWitt	1.160	−0.320
10	Old Whig	1.122	−0.200	ImpExam	1.080	−0.019	ImpExam	1.162	−0.282
11	Cincinnatus	1.128	−0.135	Madison	1.080	−0.012	Monroe	1.170	−0.156
12	Cassius	1.148	0.066	Cincinnatus	1.086	0.045	**LEE1**	1.176	−0.052
13	Landholder	1.153	0.118	Pinckney	1.095	0.135	PA Minority	1.179	−0.003
14	Cato	1.157	0.163	Hamilton	1.097	0.154	Martin	1.182	0.047
15	DemFed	1.173	0.322	Old Whig	1.097	0.158	MD Farmer	1.189	0.159
16	DeWitt	1.177	0.361	Agrippa	1.119	0.374	Webster	1.207	0.465
17	Hamilton	1.177	0.365	Wilson	1.120	0.387	Pinckney	1.208	0.487
18	**SMITH1**	1.181	0.402	Cato	1.128	0.460	Cato	1.214	0.587
19	Wilson	1.186	0.453	Landholder	1.139	0.578	Old Whig	1.220	0.692
20	Pinckney	1.235	0.958	Jay	1.167	0.855	Grayson	1.222	0.731
21	Grayson	1.238	0.985	Martin	1.173	0.915	Jay	1.239	1.008
22	Jay	1.245	1.058	PA Minority	1.174	0.918	DemFed	1.250	1.199
23	MD Farmer	1.268	1.294	MD Farmer	1.203	1.205	Cassius	1.260	1.356
24	Webster	1.270	1.315	Webster	1.218	1.356	**SMITH1**	1.264	1.431
25	Martin	1.285	1.473	DemFed	1.279	1.960	Sherman	1.282	1.741
x	Lee2	0.000	xxx	Lee2	1.060	−0.214	Lee2	1.255	1.280
x	Smith2	1.060	−0.834	Smith2	0.000	xxx	Smith2	1.248	1.153
x	YatesP+L	1.255	1.164	YatesP+L	1.248	1.652	YatesP+L	0.000	xxx

Note: Analysis based on the 250 most common words of the main set of texts.

third set, the weak scores and low ranking for Sidney are further evidence of a sharp difference from Yates's letters and his "Plan of Union."

Table 4 completes the set of delta tests. It shows much closer affinities between Smith1 and the four dubia than between either Sidney or Lee1 and any of the four. The especially low ranking of Sidney for Brutus and of Lee1 for Federal Farmer is at least as important as the fact that Smith surpasses them both so easily. It will be seen that he leads the field for Plebeian and Brutus, runs a close second to Madison for Federal Farmer, and lies seventh for the little set comprising the papers of Lucius and Federal Republican. Madison, an inconceivable candidate, figures prominently in all four tests. This is a useful reminder that stylistic affinities often transcend ideological oppositions. Meanwhile, as can be seen across the foot of the page, the four dubia can be used in corroborative tests of each other's claims. They cannot be ranked, like the main twenty-five, because they do not participate in the establishment of the mean scores for the set or for the corresponding standard deviations. But when they are measured against those means, they serve as a valuable control group. The close affinities between Brutus, Plebeian, and Federal Farmer corroborate the affinities each shows for Smith1 and offset the fact that Madison slightly outranks Smith in the main results for Federal Farmer. By the same token, the low ranking of Smith1 for Lucius and Federal Republican is offset by the striking affinities between this last-named set and both Brutus and Plebeian.

Much the same results hold good when the length of the word list is altered. Brutus and the Plebeian stand firm with Smith throughout. Federal Farmer fluctuates between Smith and Madison. Lucius and Federal Republican behave as before, never quite approaching Smith but maintaining a strong resemblance to Brutus and Plebeian. The delta test, in short, stands along with the other tests employed. They all discountenance the claim that Robert Yates and Richard Henry Lee should be regarded as likely authors of the papers by Brutus and Federal Farmer, respectively. On the other side of the case, the likelihood that Melancton Smith wrote the three main dubia is upheld.

The evidence of mutual affinity, touched on above, needs to be set beside the form of evidence in which each specimen is tested on its individual merits. Cluster analysis is appropriate for this purpose because it offers rather a harsh test of the questions to be considered and also because the "family trees" in which the results are displayed speak so plainly for themselves.[10]

10. Cluster analysis compares the members of a set of specimens, each with every other, on the basis of their relative scores on a given set of variables. (In the present

Figure 1 represents the outcome of a cluster analysis in which our main twenty-nine specimens are compared with each other on the basis of the list of the one hundred most common words. It should be studied from the base upward, taking account of the way the clusters form and the rate at which they form. The authors are identified along the horizontal base of the figure. The true affinities are not between entries that merely stand beside each other before separating, like Webster and Cato, but between those that form unions, like Hamilton and Madison. The closest affinities of all are between the pairs that unite soonest, like Hamilton and Madison, Smith and Plebeian, and—on a point raised much earlier—Centinel and Pennsylvania Minority. We should spare a glance for the support given by Figure 1 to the belief that Samuel Bryan was both Centinel and a contributor to the report of the dissenting minority from his state. But the most prominent feature of Figure 1 is its linking of Smith with the four dubia in a position well apart from Lee and remote from Sidney.

Figure 2 differs from its predecessor in several important ways. It extends the word list to the 250 most common words of the main set. It includes both Lee1 and Lee2, Smith1 and Smith2, and Yates's "Plan of Union" and his more political letters as well as the papers he published as "Sidney." And, using all the longest and therefore most amenable of our texts by other authors, it takes each of them in two halves. The object is to test

---

case, the specimens are texts, the variables are a range of words, and the scores are standardized word counts.) For each specimen in turn, its differences from every other are calculated and then squared to eliminate the negatives. The sum of these squared differences is extracted. The two specimens showing the smallest such difference are then united. The next smallest such difference either unites two other specimens or adds a third member to the first pair. The next smallest difference is introduced in the same way, and the process continues until all specimens have been embraced.

The outcome is then plotted in a *dendrogram*, an inverted tree structure. As Figure 2 shows, the y-axis displays a progressive decrease in difference from 100 percent similarity down, and the specimens are arrayed on the x-axis. The twigs of the inverted tree show which specimens united first, as being least different from each other. These pairs and trios unite in branchlets, lesser branches, greater branches, and so on until all are united in one trunk, usually at a low or even negative level of resemblance. When specimens neighboring each other on the x-axis do not unite, their proximity to each other is usually a reflection of the configuration of other unions.

The statistical package used for the cluster analyses is MINITAB®. I follow David Holmes in the belief that, for such data as we are examining, Ward's linkages, squared Euclidean distances, and standardized variables yield the most accurate results. This pattern of preferences avoids any undue smoothing of data whose inherent roughness reflects the complexities of the language itself.

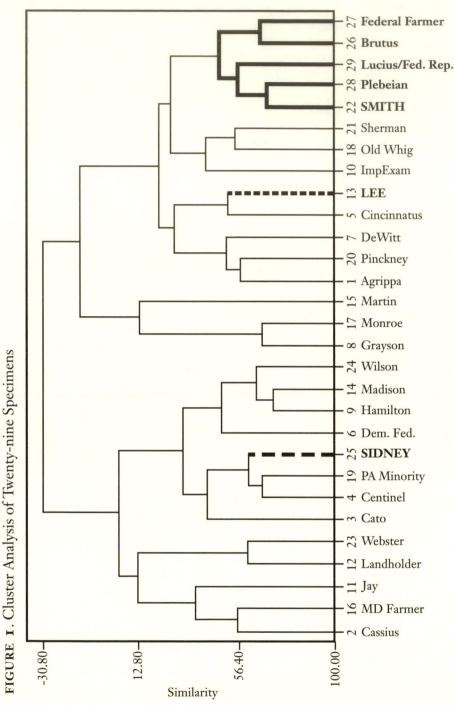

FIGURE 1. Cluster Analysis of Twenty-nine Specimens

27 Federal Farmer
26 Brutus
29 Lucius/Fed. Rep.
28 Plebeian
22 SMITH
21 Sherman
18 Old Whig
10 ImpExam
13 LEE
5 Cincinnatus
7 DeWitt
20 Pinckney
1 Agrippa
15 Martin
17 Monroe
8 Grayson
24 Wilson
14 Madison
9 Hamilton
6 Dem. Fed.
25 SIDNEY
19 PA Minority
4 Centinel
3 Cato
23 Webster
12 Landholder
11 Jay
16 MD Farmer
2 Cassius

-30.80   12.80   56.40   100.00

Similarity

Note: Analysis based on the 100 most common words in the main set of texts.

FIGURE 2. Cluster Analysis of Nineteen Authorial Pairs

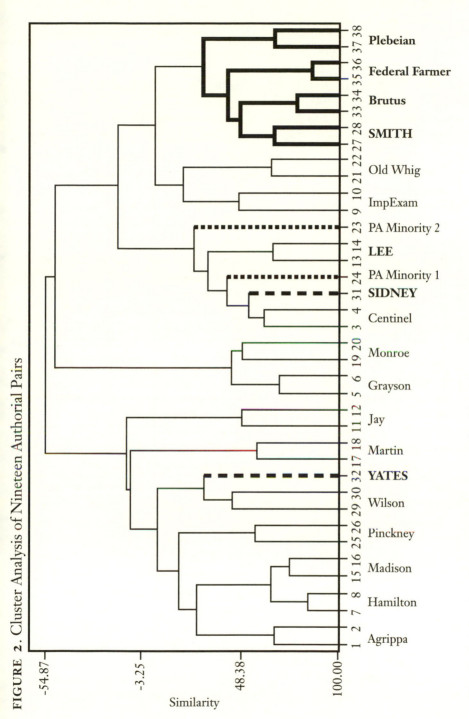

Note: Analysis based on the 250 most common words of the main set of texts.

417

whether the affinities observed so far are truly authorial in origin and not the product of some other, unrecognized determinant. If they are authorial, most of the halves should unite.

In the event, Figure 2 offers as clear a picture as anyone could wish. In seventeen cases out of nineteen, the two members of each authorial pair show a closer affinity for each other than for any of their rivals. The odds against a chance pattern of this kind are enormous. The union of the two Smith entries is especially striking because his two sets differ more from each other than most. Against this background, the exceptions are revealing. The two halves of Centinel make a pair, but the two halves of the "Pennsylvania Minority Report" stand a little apart from them and from each other. On the combined evidence of Figures 1 and 2, it seems likely that Bryan was indeed the author of part but not all of the "Minority Report." The fact that Sidney's papers continue to stand apart from Yates's other writings means that, for him alone of all these authors, it has not proved possible to establish a useful authorial signature.

Figure 2 would be even more potent if the two Yates entries behaved like Lee's, standing together but at a distance from Smith and the dubia. It should be noted, however, that the fact that *neither* of the Yates entries resembles Brutus has a strong bearing on one of the two principal questions of authorship at issue in this paper.

What conclusions can be drawn about the authorship of the four dubia? Smith's claim to the authorship of the Plebeian essay has never been contested. Except when the tests on the uncommon words became unreasonable, it has shown a consistent affinity for his other writings in every trial attempted in this inquiry. The case of the papers by Lucius and Federal Republican is less clear-cut. The analysis of comparatively uncommon words yielded strong results, but in the delta test, as illustrated in Table 4, Smith ranked a little outside the leading group. In the corroborative results at the foot of Table 4, it showed very strong affinities for Plebeian and for Brutus. And, again, in the cluster analysis of Figure 1, it stands with those same sets.

If the evidence of Smith's authorship of the papers by Brutus were less compelling, the fact that Robert Yates has proved so difficult to test would be a matter for concern. As it is, however, Brutus is consistently unlike either Sidney's papers or Yates's other writings. Brutus stands with the other dubia in its high incidence of Smith's uncommon words, and makes use of the most idiosyncratic of them. On all the common-words tests, the resemblance to Smith is strong and unfaltering. Unless the tests employed here are falling far short of their usual levels of reliability without showing any sign that something is amiss, they clearly favor the belief that Brutus was Melancton Smith.

All the tests employed upheld Smith's authorship of Federal Farmer's papers, while the claim for Richard Henry Lee found no support at all. The one point where Smith's claim falters is on the delta test for 250 words, where Smith ranks second after Madison. When the word list is reduced to 200 words and to 150 words, Smith's delta scores move up into first place. The pattern of evidence is consummated in Figure 2, where both Brutus and Federal Farmer lie even nearer than Plebeian to the two Smith entries.

An analogy with family resemblances sheds light on the little inconsistencies seen in the overall pattern of results. The members of a large group of siblings are likely to differ from each other in many ways. Their friends will often disagree about the resemblance of this one or that to most of the others and will see points of likeness that outsiders have not noticed. A detailed series of comparison between them and a large number of their fellows may well show that all of them—even the odd little one with freckles—are of common stock.

The relevance of the analogy to questions of authorial style rests on facts that are much better understood today than was possible before the advent of computers. Anyone who takes up a pen quickly displays a number of stylistic idiosyncrasies. Although they will often form statistically significant patterns, such idiosyncracies will not occur with mechanical regularity. Besides the adventitious irregularities of any human performance, there are the more powerful variations induced by a shift of subject, audience, or occasion, and even by the mere passage of time over a long career. Energetic pseudonymous writers may also achieve some measure of success in modifying their style from text to text. If Melancton Smith was, as this inquiry has led me to believe, the author of all four dubia as well as his convention speeches, the small stylistic differences we have observed should be expected. Far more worthy of remark is the unremitting fervor with which he pursued a high-minded but unsuccessful cause.

Appendix 2

APPENDIX 2. Dates of Appearance of the Federalist Papers, the *Federal Farmer,* and *Brutus*

Publius (Federalist Papers)	*Federal Farmer*	*Brutus*
	1 October 8, 1787	
	2 October 9, 1787	
	3 October 10, 1787	
	4 October 12, 1787	
	5 October 13, 1787	
		1 October 18, 1787
1 October 27, 1787		
2 October 31, 1787		
		2 November 1, 1787
3 November 3, 1787		
4 November 7, 1787		
5 November 10, 1787		
6 November 14, 1787		
		3 November 15, 1787
7 November 17, 1787		
8 November 20, 1787		
9 November 21, 1787		
10 November 22, 1787		
11 November 24, 1787		
12 November 27, 1787		
13 November 28, 1787		
		4 November 29, 1787
14 November 30, 1787		
15 December 1, 1787		
16 December 4, 1787		
17 December 5, 1787		
18 December 7, 1787		
19 December 8, 1787		

Publius (Federalist Papers)	*Federal Farmer*	*Brutus*
20 December 11, 1787		
21 December 12, 1787		
		5 December 13, 1787
22 December 14, 1787		
23 December 18, 1787		
24 December 19, 1787		
25 December 21, 1787		
26 December 22, 1787		
27 December 25, 1787	6 December 25, 1787	
28 December 26, 1787		
		6 December 27, 1787
30 December 28, 1787		
	7 December 31, 1787	
31 January 1, 1788		
32 January 2, 1788		
33 January 2, 1788		
	8 January 3, 1788	7 January 3, 1788
	9 January 4, 1788	
34 January 5, 1788		
35 January 5, 1788		
	10 January 7, 1788	
36 January 8, 1788		
29 January 9, 1788		
	11 January 10, 1788	8 January 10, 1788
37 January 11, 1788		
	12 January 12, 1788	
	13 January 14, 1788	
39 January 16, 1788		
	14 January 17, 1788	9 January 17, 1788
40 January 18, 1788	15 January 18, 1788	
41 January 19, 1788		
	16 January 20, 1788	
42 January 22, 1788		
43 January 23, 1788	17 January 23, 1788	
		10 January 24, 1788
44 January 25, 1788	18 January 25, 1788	
45 January 26, 1788		
46 January 29, 1788		

Publius (Federalist Papers)	*Federal Farmer*	*Brutus*
47 January 30, 1788		
		11 January 31, 1788
48 February 1, 1788		
49 February 2, 1788		
50 February 5, 1788		
51 February 6, 1788		
		12 February 7, 1788
52 February 8, 1788		
53 February 9, 1788		
54 February 12, 1788		
		12.2 February 14, 1788
56 February 16, 1788		
57 February 19, 1788		
58 February 20, 1788		
		13 February 21, 1788
59 February 22, 1788		
60 February 23, 1788		
61 February 26, 1788		
62 February 27, 1788		
		14 February 28, 1788
63 March 1, 1788		
64 March 5, 1788		
		14.2 March 6, 1788
65 March 7, 1788		
66 March 8, 1788		
67 March 11, 1788		
68 March 12, 1788		
69 March 14, 1788		
70 March 15, 1788		
71 March 18, 1788		
72 March 19, 1788		
		15 March 20, 1788
73 March 21, 1788		
74 March 25, 1788		
75 March 26, 1788		
76 April 1, 1788		
77 April 2, 1788		
		16 April 10, 1788

Publius (Federalist Papers)	*Federal Farmer*	*Brutus*
78 May 28, 1788		
79 May 28, 1788		
80 May 28, 1788		
81 May 28, 1788		
82 May 28, 1788		
83 May 28, 1788		
84 May 28, 1788		
85 May 28, 1788		

Bibliography

PRIMARY SOURCES

Brookheiser, Richard. *Alexander Hamilton, American.* New York: Free Press, 1999.

Brooks, Robin. "Melancton Smith: New York Anti-Federalist, 1744–1798." Ph.D. diss. University of Rochester, 1964.

De Pauw, Linda Grant. *The Eleventh Pillar: New York State and the Federal Constitution.* Ithaca, N.Y.: Cornell University Press, 1966.

Documentary History of the Ratification of the Constitution. 22 vols. to date. Edited by John P. Kaminski, Gaspare J. Saladino, Richard Leffler, Charles H. Schoenleber, and Margaret A. Hogan. Madison: Wisconsin Historical Society Press, 1976–.

Elliot, Jonathan, ed. *The Debates in the Several State Conventions on the Adoption of the Federal Constitution, as Recommended by the General Convention at Philadelphia in 1787.* Vol. 2. Philadelphia: J. B. Lippincott, 1863.

———. *The Debates in the Several Conventions on the Adoption of the Federal Constitution.* 5 vols. New York: Burt Franklin, 1888. Undated reprint.

———. *Debates on the Adoption of the Federal Constitution.* Vol. 2. Salem, N.H.: Ayer, 1987.

Schechter, Stephen L., ed. *The Reluctant Pillar: New York and the Adoption of the Federal Constitution.* Troy, N.Y.: Russell Sage College, 1985.

Storing, Herbert. *The Complete Anti-Federalist.* 7 vols. Chicago: University of Chicago Press, 1981.

Young, Alfred F. *The Democratic Republicans of New York: The Origins, 1763–1797.* Chapel Hill: University of North Carolina Press, 1967.

SECONDARY SOURCES

Adams, John, and Charles Francis Adams. *The Works of John Adams.* Boston: Little, Brown, 1851.

Beccaria, Cesare, Marchese di. *An Essay on Crimes and Punishments.* London: J. Almon, 1767.

Blackstone, William. *Commentaries on the Laws of England.* 4 vols. (1765) Chicago: University of Chicago Press, 1979.

Borden, Morton. *The Antifederalist Papers.* East Lansing: Michigan State University Press, 1965.

Cooke, Jacob E. *The Federalist.* Middletown, Conn.: Wesleyan University Press, 1961.

De Lolme, Jean Louis. *The Constitution of England.* Edited by David Lieberman. Indianapolis: Liberty Fund, 2007.

Farrand, Max, ed. *The Records of the Federal Convention of 1787.* 4 vols. New Haven: Yale University Press, 1966.

Hamilton, Alexander, John Jay, and James Madison. *The Federalist.* Edited by George W. Carey and James McClellan. Gideon edition. Indianapolis: Liberty Fund, 2001.

Lee, Richard Henry. *Memoir of the Life of Richard Henry Lee and His Correspondence with the Most Distinguished Men in America and Europe, Illustrative of Their Characters and of the Events of the American Revolution.* Philadelphia: H. C. Carey and I. Lea, 1825.

McGaughy, Joseph Kent. "The Authorship of *The Letters from the Federal Farmer,* Revisited." *New York History,* April 1989, 153–70.

Montesquieu, Charles de Secondat, baron de. *The Spirit of the Laws.* Translated by Thomas Nugent. New York: Hafner, 1949.

Webking, Robert H. "Melancton Smith and the *Letters from the Federal Farmer.*" *William and Mary Quarterly* 44 (July 1987): 510–28.

Wood, Gordon. "The Authorship of the *Letters from the Federal Farmer.*" *William and Mary Quarterly* 31 (April 1974): 299–308.

Index

abandoned property during wartime, free
use of, 3–11
abolitionism. *See* antislavery movement
absolute governments. *See* despotism
abuse of powers: by consolidated government, 30–32; in federal legislature,
22–23, 178, 196–97; unsecured powers
granted to federal government, 47–48
Acts, St. Paul before Agrippa in, 268
Adams, John: *A Defence of the American
Constitutions*, 50n35, 72n53, 73n54,
304n16, 368–69, 371–74; *Discourses on
Davila*, 368, 369n1, 371–75; on jury
trial by peers, 50; on natural aristocracy,
xxx–xxxi, 72n53, 371–76; Smith Circle
influenced by/opposed to, xxx–xxxi,
72n53, 304; vice presidential candidacy,
opposition to, 367–76, 393n2
Adams, Samuel, xiv
Additional Letters of a Federal Farmer,
xxviii–xxix
*Address and Reasons of Dissent of the Minor-
ity of the Convention of Pennsylvania*,
278n18, 399, 400–401, 413, 415, 416,
417, 418
*Address by a Plebeian to the People of the State
of New York. See Plebeian*
Address to the Citizens of Philadelphia
(Wilson), 138n99, 181n24
*Address to the People of the State of New York
on the Subject of the Constitution Agreed
upon at Philadelphia* (Jay), 285
ad valorem taxes, 215
advisory council to president, 329, 345,
348–49

Agrippa (Federalist writer), 399, 408, 413,
416, 417
Agrippa (Roman emperor), 268
alcohol, excise tax on, 207–8, 391–92
Alcoran (Quran), 223
Algerines, U.S. relationship with, 286
ambassadors and other foreign ministers,
supreme court jurisdiction over,
249–50
amendments to Constitution: adoption,
before vs. after, 59–61, 269–70, 274–81,
283–85; Anti-Federalist arguments
in favor of, 267–70; arms, on right to
bear, 344; assembly, on right of, 343,
347; bill of rights (*see* bill of rights); on
commerce, 328–29; on commissions,
writs, and processes in name of people
of United States, 329; conditions on
ratification, Smith's proposals for (*see*
speeches of Smith at New York ratifying
convention); on council to president,
329, 345, 348–49; on elections, 342,
344–45; on federal city, 330; federalist
arguments against, *Plebeian* presentation of, 270–74; *Federal Republican* on
abandonment of, 361–62; Federal
Republican Society formed for purposes
of, 377–81; on impeachment, 346;
on judicial rights, 342–43, 347; on
judiciary, 346–48; lack of Constitutional provision for, 51–52; Livingston,
Gilbert, letter to, 387; majority rules
regarding, 167; on military forces, 328,
344, 346, 347–48; New York committee,
proposals created by Smith for, 341–46;

427

Jefferson, Thomas, xii, xvi, 396
Jeffrey, William, xxii
Jews: ancient Israelites (*see* Bible); as
representatives, 104
Johnson, Seth, xxi
Jones, Samuel, 326, 333, 334, 339n2, 377n
Jones, Willie, 24n4
judicial review (appellate jurisdiction),
44–45, 46, 130, 136, 250–54
judicial rights: inadequacy of federal
provisions for, 182–83; proposed
amendments to Constitution regarding,
342–43, 347
judiciary: appellate jurisdiction, 44–45, 46,
130, 136, 250–54; *Brutus*'s interest in,
xxvii, xxxi, xxxii; conditional ratification
proposal, reasons for, 351; Congressional power to institute, 143–44; election
of, 263; grand jury, 143, 347; inferior,
superior, and special courts, 131; office
of U.S., exclusion of judges from, 346;
organization of, 127–36; pay of judges,
131–32, 259; proposed amendments
to Constitution regarding, 346–48;
removal from office, 234, 259–60;
Rutgers v. Waddington on judicial review
of statutory law, xxvii, xxxii, 3–11; Senate and, 266–67; separation of powers
not observed in organization of, 36, 44;
single judiciary system, problem of, 28;
Smith Circle's acceptance of need for,
xxx; state courts, adequacy of, 254–56;
in state governments, 67; unity of sentiment among opponents to Constitution
regarding power of, 277–78; Yates,
Abraham, Smith's solicitation of views
of, 332–34. *See also* jury trial; powers of
judiciary; supreme court
Junius, 79
jury trial: appellate jurisdiction and, 251–
53; in federal city, 166; in federal courts
for criminal but not civil cases, 130,
131, 133–36, 140–42; right to jury trial
of the vicinage, 27, 28, 43–44, 49–51,
65, 141–42, 286–87, 342–43, 347; state
requirements regarding, 67

Kaminsky, John P., 332n1
Kenny, Anthony, 412n9
Kings, second book of, Elisha's prediction
of Hazael's oppression of Israelites in,
197
Koran (Alcoran), 223

Lamb, John, xxi, 377n
land. *See* property
Landholder, 61n43, 399, 413, 416
Lansing, John: on amendments to
Constitution, 338, 377–78n; circular
letter to states on second Constitutional
Convention, committee to draft, 352n1;
on conditional ratification, 327, 349n;
Federal Republican Society and, 377n;
motion to debate bill of rights and
amendments, 341n; Yates's authorship
of *Brutus* and, xxiii, xxiv
large territories, problem of extended
government over, 27–29, 33, 156,
167–68, 174–79
law: Congressional power to pass any and
all laws, 200, 243–44; equity and law,
blending of powers over, 44, 136–37,
235–36, 246–47, 347; ex post facto laws,
49, 142, 183; fact and law, jurisdiction
as to, 132–36, 287, 347; judicial power
of interpretation of, 128–30, 236–39,
241–43; state laws, judgment as to validity of, 245–46. *See also* judiciary
Lawrence, Jonathan, 11
Lawrence, Nathaniel, 377n
Lee, Richard Henry: as author of *Federal
Farmer*, xiii, xiv–xvii, xxix, 397, 398, 419;
computerized analysis of known writings compared with *Brutus* and *Federal
Farmer*, 399–407, 410, 412–14, 416–19;
Constitutional Convention, failure to
attend, 24n5; personal attacks on,
61n43
legal fictions, 164, 245, 348
legislature: federal (*see* Congress); New
York state (*see* New York legislature)
*Letters from the Federal Farmer. See Federal
Farmer*

Webking, Robert, xvii–xx

Webster, Noah: in computerized analysis of Anti-Federalist writings, 399, 401, 413, 415, 416; *An Examination into the Leading Principles of the Federal Constitution* cited in *Brutus*, 209n, 224n70; review of *Federal Farmer* by, xvi

Welles, Sally (Sarah), 15n4

Western Territories: attachment to states, 51; British occupation of, 286; judicial proceedings in, 135, 142; Mississippi scheme, 331; Northwest Ordinance (1787), 135; sale of lands, 215, 271–72

Wiley, John, 11

Willett, Marinus, xxi, 377n, 393–94

Williams, John, 314n30

Wilson, James: *Address to the Citizens of Philadelphia*, 138n99, 181n24; on bill of rights, 48n31, 138n99; in computerized analysis of Anti-Federalist writings, 399, 413, 416, 417; on reservation of powers not expressly given, 181n24

Wolfius (Christian Wolff), 6

Wood, Gordon, xiv–xxvii

words, computerized analysis of. *See* computerized analysis of Anti-Federalist writings

writs, commissions, and processes in name of people of United States, 329

Wyoming Valley secession movement (Pennsylvania, 1787), 232n83

Yates, Abraham, xxii, xxvii, 332–35, 341n

Yates, Robert: as author of *Brutus*, xiii, xxi–xxv, xxix, 397, 398, 418; computerized analysis of known writings compared with *Brutus* and *Federal Farmer*, 399–405, 407–9, 412–18; on New York committee to debate bill of rights and amendments, 341n; "Plan of Union," 399, 400, 414, 415; *Sydney* (*Sidney*) papers, xxi, 399, 400, 403, 404, 405, 407, 411–16, 418

yellow fever, Smith's death from, xii

Young, Alfred, 357n, 367n, 383n2, 386nn2–3, 387n4, 389n5, 390n7, 396n6

Zuckert, Michael, 397

This book is set in Janson, an old-style serif typeface named for Dutch punch-cutter and printer Anton Janson. Research in the 1970s concluded that this face was actually the work of Hungarian punch-cutter Miklós (Nicholas) Kis, cut while he was an apprentice in Amsterdam about 1685. Janson shows a strong influence of the Dutch Baroque typefaces, and it replaced Caslon as the face of choice for fine bookmaking. A revival of the face was designed by Chauncey H. Griffith of the Linotype foundry in 1937. Janson's strong design and clear stroke contrast combine to create text that is both elegant and easy to read.

The display type, American Scribe, was modeled on the handwriting of Timothy Matlack, an early patriot who fought in the Revolution, sat as prosecutor at Benedict Arnold's court martial, and also penned copies of a number of documents for then-General George Washington. Brian Wilson of Three Islands Press adapted Matlack's compact but legible script for contemporary use.

This book is printed on paper that is acid-free and meets the requirements of the American National Standard for Permanence of Paper for Printed Library Materials, z39.48-1992. ∞